Jamaica in 1687

Jamaica in 1687

The Taylor Manuscript at the National Library of Jamaica

EDITED BY

David Buisseret

University of the West Indies Press
7A Gibraltar Hall Road Mona
Kingston 7 Jamaica
www.uwipress.com

The Mill Press
The Mill at Constant Spring
P.O. Box 167
Kingston 8 Jamaica

National Library of Jamaica
12 East Street
Kingston Jamaica

Paperback edition published 2010

Taylor, John.
Jamaica in 1687: the Taylor manuscript at the National Library of Jamaica /
edited by David Buisseret.

p. cm.

Includes bibliographical references.

ISBN: 978-976-640-236-5 (paper)

1. Taylor, John, 1664– – Manuscripts. 2. Jamaica – History – 17th century.
3. Jamaica – Description and travel. I. Buisseret, David. II. National Library of Jamaica.
III. Title.

F1870.T38 2010 917.292

Cover illustration: A map of the island of Jamaica, drawn in 1682 by William Hack, and dedicated by him to Captain Bartholomew Sharpe (3 feet 1 inch x 2 feet 3 inches). British Library, Additional Manuscripts 5414, 4.

Set in Adobe Garamond 11/14.5 x 27

Book and cover design by Robert Harris.

Printed in the United States of America.

Contents

Illustrations

Contents

Illustrations

Preface

Even by academic standards, this edition has taken a long time to reach publication. It was Anthony Gambrill who initiated the process, by paying for the Taylor manuscript's initial transcription by Elizabeth Pigou and Peter Smith; by that time, I had left my post at the University of the West Indies, but was able to revise the text over the course of several visits to Jamaica. These visits were generally subsidized by the Newberry Library, of Chicago, where I began working in 1980. For some time there were administrative problems, but these were overcome in large part thanks to the enthusiastic support first of Valerie Facey, and then of Linda Speth.

On technical questions, I seem to have been taking advice for many years. Some of my early informants are, alas, dead; I am thinking here of Bruce Barker, of Sir John Golding, of Professor Douglas Hall and of S.A.G. Taylor. For questions concerning the natural sciences, I have consulted Professors Ivan Goodbody, Ajai Mansingh and Girgis Sidrak, though I have no doubt not consulted them enough. Robert Barker of London has helped me to understand something of John Taylor's career in England, and Professor Jerome Handler has elucidated some points concerning slavery.

When I needed some concentrated time to work on the text, the Virginia Foundation for the Humanities gave me a fellowship to work at Charlottesville, where the Small Special Collections Library of the University of Virginia made available many seventeenth-century works for close comparison. In Virginia, my wife, Pat, helped a good deal with the passages concerning animals and plants; she also helped at the National Library of Jamaica, where we received every help from Eppie Edwards.

I was able to read a paper concerning the Taylor manuscript to a meeting of the Jamaican Historical Society, and derived useful information from its members; I have also greatly profited from the advice of James Robertson, who now teaches the course that I used to teach at the University of the West Indies between 1964 and 1980. In the final stages, I am much indebted to Vicki Via, postgraduate student at the University of Texas, Arlington, who in the course of her research in Jamaica made excellent images from the

Taylor manuscript for me; in this, she enjoyed the wholehearted help of Winsome Hudson and her staff at the National Library of Jamaica. Finally, in the editorial stages I have received more help than I could reasonably have expected from Shivaun Hearne.

To all my informants, and to any whom I may have forgotten, many thanks. I now hope, as Taylor did at the conclusion of his manuscript, that if those into whose hands the work may fall "shall find benefitt hereby, that then they will not think my houers in the collection ill spent"; I have certainly found them entertaining.

David Buisseret
Chicago, Illinois
Arlington, Texas

Figure 1 Portrait of John Taylor from the *Thesaurarium Mathematicae* (London, 1686).

Introduction

John Taylor's Life

Our author was born in 1664, the son of Richard Taylor, head of a family long established around Chale, in the Isle of Wight (off the south coast of England).[1] John Taylor was educated at home, and when he was seventeen had a special tutor for mathematics and other "knotty sciences", in which he wanted to specialize.[2] Following a year or so of this special tuition, Taylor claims that he "became master of those branches of the Mathematics springing from Arithmatick and Geometry: viz., Navigation, Surveying, Dialling, Architecture, Fortyfication, Gunnery". As we shall see, his mastery of some of these subjects was less than perfect.

In October 1683 he went to live on the mainland at Portsmouth, where he offered lessons in mathematics. This town was at the time being considerably developed as a naval base, and Taylor soon found pupils among the sons of the dockyard and naval officers. In April 1684, however, he fell ill and returned to the Isle of Wight in order to rest. Having recovered, he then went in October 1684 to London, where he again fell ill; "the phisittians advised him to shave his head, which was done, and he found great benefitt thereby". At London he pursued his mathematical studies, but then in June 1685 joined the royal army which was being raised to counter the Monmouth Rebellion in the West Country. As Taylor immodestly puts it, "he betook himself to His Majesty's service with all the resolution and bravery imaginable". He seems to have served as a cadet in "the Queen Dowager's Regiment of Horse".

1. Some information about the family may be found in the Isle of Wight County and Diocesan Record Office, Newport, Isle of Wight.

2. Much of what follows, including all quotations, comes from Taylor's manuscript.

Figure 2 Taylor's drawing of a soldier at the Battle of Sedgemoor, 1685, page 95. As the accompanying text explains, this is a "scytheman", whose "desperate weapon" was wielded by Monmouth's "tallest and lustiest men"; they were apparently very effective.

The royal army marched into the west of England and soon defeated Monmouth's scratch force at Sedgemoor, in spite of the devastation caused by Monmouth's "scythemen" (figure 2). Taylor survived the encounter, and came back to London with his regiment in July 1685. At the end of August, the "wars being over", and Taylor "weary of this wild kind of life", he left the army and resumed his study of mathematics, to which he now added chemistry. In December 1685 he returned to the Isle of Wight, but the following January was back in London, again studying chemistry. Soon afterwards he met and married his wife, and by June 1686 had finished the manuscript of his *Thesaurarium Mathematicae*, which was published that July and attracted favourable comment.[3]

Meanwhile his wife had become pregnant, and in August 1686 she left London, which did not agree with her, for the Isle of Wight. Taylor soon followed, but he became embroiled in a quarrel with his father-in-law. This became so serious that Taylor resolved to leave England in order to "seek his fortune abroad". He sold some of his property, set his wife and mother up with money as best he could, and went back to London. There he knew Jeremiah Arnold, of the "Royal Company of Merchants trading to Jamaica", and Arnold advised him that Jamaica was a promising destination.

He gave Taylor letters of introduction to the deputy governor, Hender Molesworth, and Sir Francis [?] Modyford. He also advised him to buy a stock of cloth for sale in Jamaica; this Taylor did, and invested as well in three convicts from Newgate prison. These three, Charles Gould, Ann Sharp and Susannah Caledon, had all been convicted for felony and were available for sale as indentured servants. Taylor paid fees of £6 to the Newgate jailor, and he agreed to pay £6 each for their transport to Jamaica on board the *Saint*

3. For this information, I am indebted to Robert Barker, once of Jamaica and now of London, England. See also E.G.R. Taylor, *The Mathematical Practitioners of Tudor and Stuart England* (Cambridge, 1954), 237–38.

George, then lying at London. His own cost for transport was £10; having paid this to the captain, on 17 October 1686 he saw to the loading of "his" convicts and his goods, and on 31 October the *Saint George* set sail for Jamaica.

It took the *Saint George* some time to clear the English Channel, and she was forced for some time to take shelter off the Isle of Wight. Eventually, though, the weather turned favourable, and they set sail for Madeira. This stage of the voyage was full of incident; at one stage Turkish pirates pursued the ship, and a little later it was discovered that many of the convicts had filed their irons off and were waiting their chance to take over the ship. Still, they arrived at Madeira on 29 November 1686, Taylor noting that he "was in perfect health, but remain'd extremly mellancholy". They stayed for a month at Madeira, loading stores and visiting parts of the island; they then set out across the Atlantic on 3 December 1686, making landfall on 25 December. The voyage had been fast, and was uneventful, except that at one stage the convicts broke into the liquor store, and became very drunk. By 29 December they were sailing past Santo Domingo, and on 1 January 1687 they arrived at Port Royal in Jamaica.

Taylor disembarked with the other passengers, and went to pay his respects to the governor in Spanish Town; then he returned to Port Royal, where he rented lodgings and saw to the sale of his servants. They fetched $145, leaving a positive balance of $45, but "not soe considerable profitt as he expected". Taylor now had to find a job – or, as he put it, to "prosecute his employ" – but on 18 January he fell gravely ill, and did not recover his strength until about the middle of April, some three months later. We cannot be sure what the illness was, but we do know that he had a high fever, that he was bled four times by the eminent Dr Trapham and that his recovery was helped by a dream. This illness consumed most of his slender capital, so when he was offered employment in Clarendon by Francis Blackmore he gladly accepted.

Blackmore and his wife lived near Withywood, where they owned "two brave plantations for sugar and indigo". Taylor was taken on as bookkeeper for Blackmore's and Thomas Sutton's estates, and was "mighty kindly used by that worthy gentelman and his good lady, whoe used him more like a son or a brother than as a stranger". On 18 April he "received his truncks of books etc. from Port Royall, which were brought to Witheywood by watter, and from thence to Mr. Blackmore's in his wain". It was at this time that Taylor began to compose his account of Jamaica, making it "his business to sirch and prie into the nature of all ye products of this island, and to collect their essence and natures".

Alas, these researches did not last for long, since early in May he again fell ill, this time with "the dry belley ache", and although he recovered after two weeks, doctors advised him to leave the island, as recurrences of the disease often led to paralysis. Taylor "therefore resolved to returne home to England, and to live there with his wife in that estate God had called him to". He said goodbye to the Blackmores, and took a sloop from Withywood Bay back to Port Royal, intending "at the first opportunity to return home to England". However, a curious chance intervened; meeting Captain Charles Talbot at Port Royal, the captain asked him if he would become ship's clerk for his ship, HMS *Falcon.*

Taylor agreed to this, and on 26 May went aboard the *Falcon,* where he "had a cabion provided for him in the stearage, and eat at the captaine's table. And he was somewhat weak and discontented, but seemed as cherfull as possible." Now began an entirely new phase in Taylor's life, as he cruised the Caribbean with Captain Talbot in search of pirates. It was a fortunate change for Taylor, who soon found himself "in much better health, and stronger than when he went on board, for the sea agreed with him much better than the shore".

HMS *Falcon* sailed on 23 July 1687 in search of pirates, returning to Port Royal on 4 September. Later that month she made a journey to Porto Bello; Captain Talbot died shortly after their return to Port Royal on 26 October 1687, and was succeeded by the lieutenant, Thomas Smith. In November they sailed for the Spanish wreck on the Ambrosian bank, off the north coast of Santo Domingo, where treasure was being recovered by divers; in returning from this voyage, in mid-December, they encountered the Spanish *flota,* or treasure-fleet, on its annual voyage to the New World. The arrival of the new governor, the Duke of Albemarle, was expected for much of the latter part of 1687, and he finally arrived late in December, to be met off Jamaica by HMS *Falcon.* His reception at Port Royal was a great festive occasion, amply described by Taylor in two different passages.

Albemarle had arrived on board HMS *Assistance,* and this vessel now replaced HMS *Falcon* as the Port Royal–based naval vessel. The *Falcon* spent the month of January, 1688, refitting at Port Royal, perhaps allowing Taylor more time to "range the woods and mountains, and observe all the curious products of this western island". On 19 February 1688 he records an earthquake at the harbour, and then three days later HMS *Falcon* set sail again for the Ambrosian bank; Albemarle was very anxious to claim his share of the plate that was being recovered from the Spanish wreck there. They spent some weeks with the divers, and then on 10 May 1688 set sail for England. This was an anxious time, for the reign of James II was being severely challenged; they must have been glad to learn from a passing vessel on 16 June that "England was in a peaceable posture". At the end of June they anchored in Plymouth harbour, and began the long process of paying off

the crew and decommissioning the vessel. On 18 August 1688 Taylor "made up the muster books", which are now preserved in the National Archives in London, paying the men for the period from 30 March 1685 to 25 March 1688. Then he went ashore at Deal, in Kent, whence he set out for London.

Leaving the capital on 8 September 1688, he returned to the Isle of Wight, where he met his wife and family and his "perfidious father-in-law". At this stage, pages 861–64 are missing from his manuscript, perhaps suggesting that he had made some unwise observations. At all events, he settled back into life on the island, and on 1 December "began the transcription of this work from the collection of our notes into this formidable volume". War with Holland had broken out early in October, and on 4 November a Dutch fleet was seen off the island. During December, William of Orange established his power, evicting James II and initiating a new phase in English political history. Meanwhile, Taylor laboured on, "in my now mellancholy retirement at home".

Presumably he largely finished his history in 1689, and did not long stay in the Isle of Wight. In 1696 he published an *Almanack,* and on the final page gives his address as being "my house near the market-place, Norwich", so he is likely to have lived there by then. He published another *Almanack* in 1701, but that is the last that we hear of him. What we already know of his life, all the same, shows it to have been an extraordinary one. To have spent some years in the West Indies, including some months in the Jamaican countryside, and then to have returned alive to England to write about it was a rare achievement in the seventeenth century. That is why the journal that he then composed bears close examination.

The Composition of Taylor's Manuscript

We can imagine Taylor well enough, sitting in his study in Chale on the Isle of Wight, pulling his ideas together. Presumably he had notes, made both when he was on the estate in Clarendon and during his shore visits while he was serving on HMS *Falcon.* We may be sure, too, that he had profited from conversations on board *Falcon* with shipmates such as Richard Bowes, who had some experience of Jamaica. He also must have had either originals or transcriptions of the various logs and muster-rolls that had passed through his hands, for he would otherwise not have been able to remember details such as the ships that passed into and out of Port Royal during his visits there or the names of quite obscure people whom he had met; these details are often accurate.

His work consists of three smallish leather-bound volumes, all paginated sequentially, from 1 to 854: volume one has 236 pages; volume two, 344 pages;

and volume three, 274 pages. Taylor wrote the page numbers in himself, and he sometimes made mistakes; thus there are a few omissions and duplications. It looks as though the manuscript was intended for publication, but it never reached that stage. It somehow entered the huge collection of Sir Thomas Phillipps,[4] celebrated nineteenth-century antiquarian, and was acquired by the National Library of Jamaica some forty years ago. Its various parts run as follows:

Volume I Taylor's History of His Life and Travels

Volume II Taylor's Present State of Jamaica

4. See "John Taylor's Life and Travels 1686–8", in *The Phillipps Manuscripts,* ed. A.N.L. Munby (London, 1968), no. 9251.

Although the manuscript gives an impression of homogeneity, being written in the same hand and apparently all at the same time, it in fact consists of three separate literary types. From page 1 to page 144, it is in diary form, describing Taylor's early life and adventures. At page 145 it takes on a new shape, that of the nautical log. From this point until the end of volume one at page 238, the narrative is in this specialized form, consisting essentially of an account of the progress of the *Saint George.* At page 239 begins volume two, and also a new stylistic form, in the section called the "Present State of Jamaica", which takes up the rest of the volume. This is the heart of the work, and is a comprehensive description of the island as Taylor knew it.

This literary form had a long history. There had been medieval accounts, such as that of Marco Polo, describing lands strange to Europeans, but the stylistic type to which Taylor's "Present State" immediately goes back is the descriptions of the New World composed by Spaniards in the early sixteenth century, in works by authors such as Gonzalo Fernández de Oviedo. In the later sixteenth century we find the first English examples of the genre, with the descriptions of the abortive Virginia colony, and then in the early seventeenth century there are abundant accounts of the area known as New England.[5]

The first English commentary on the Caribbean seems to be the one by Daniell Ellffryth of 1631,[6] followed by such well-known works as Richard Ligon's *A True and Exact History of the Island of Barbados,* published at London in 1657. The English seized Jamaica in 1655, and almost at once began composing short descriptions of it, which remained in manuscript, usually among the State Papers preserved at the Public Record Office (National Archives) and British Library in London;[7] some of these descriptions were eventually published in the first volume of the *Journals of the House of Assembly.*[8] In fact, so many attempts to describe new territories were being made at this time that in the proceedings of the Royal Society for 1666 "Mr. Boyle" actually set out the "General Heads for a Natural History of a Country", hoping no doubt to introduce some system into a rather chaotic situation.[9] Taylor conformed only in a general sense to Boyle's prescriptions.

5. See, for instance, John Smith, *A description of New England* (London, 1616); Frances Higginson, *New England's Plantation* (London, 1630).

6. *Daniell Ellffryth's Guide to the Caribbean, 1631,* ed. Stanley Pargellis and Ruth Lapham Butler (Chicago, 1945).

7. See, for instance, the numerous references in the *Calendar of State Papers, Colonial Series, America and West Indies,* referring to documents in the National Archives, and also British Library, Egerton MSS 2395, Harleian MSS 3361 and Additional MSS 11410.

8. *Journal of the House of Assembly* 1 (Jamaica, 1811).

9. For Boyle's "General Heads", see Charles Hutton, George Shaw and Richard Pearson, eds., *The Philosophical Transactions of the Royal Society* (London, 1809), 1: 63.1. This reference came to me through the kindness of Robert Bensen, of Hartwick College.

The first contemporary printed descriptions of Jamaica were published in the early 1670s. Both John Ogilby's section on Jamaica in his *America* and Richard Blome's *A description of the Island of Jamaica* were, however, quite short; mere summaries of the island's "situation", "commodities" and history. It was also in the early 1670s that the fashion began for publishing works entitled *The present State of. . .*; there were for instance works on France (1671), New England (1675), Carolina (1682) and England (1683) named in this way.[10]

There were no more printed works on Jamaica like those of Blome and Ogilby up to the time when Taylor began his work, though in fact Sir Hans Sloane was working there at the same period on what would become his great "Natural History", published in 1707 and 1725 as part of the two volumes of his *A Voyage to the Islands Madera . . . and Jamaica.* We may wonder, indeed, if the knowledge that Sloane had completed this work may have influenced Taylor against publishing his "Present State", for the manuscript shows every sign of having been carefully prepared for the printer, and it is hard to understand otherwise why it was not published at the time. Perhaps it was excessively royalist in tone, for the years after 1688.

Sloane has very little to say about the history or government of Jamaica, but his work on its natural history closely parallels Taylor's sections in the "Present State" running from page 334 to page 490. Sloane divides his description into eight categories: plants, trees, insects, animals, fishes, birds, serpents and stones, and these are also Taylor's groupings, though our author puts them in a different order and has eight subdivisions under "plants". Sloane's descriptions are also much drier and more professional than those of Taylor, who rarely mentions the Latin name for his subjects and frequently interjects his own ideas, along with more or less fantastic pieces of folklore.

After the first three main sections of his work – the diary, the nautical log and the "Present State", which together take us to page 598 – the rest of the manuscript consists of a further nautical log, describing the adventures of HMS *Falcon,* on which Taylor was serving and on which he eventually made his way back to England.

This Edition of the Manuscript

We have chosen to edit only the second half of volume one and the whole of volume two, covering pages 145 to 598 of the manuscript; this is roughly

10. Pinson de La Martinière, *The present state of France* (London, 1671); "A merchant of Boston", *The present state of New England* (London, 1675); "RF", *The present state of Carolina* (London, 1682); Edward Chamberlayne, *The present state of England* (London, 1683).

450 out of its 850 total pages. We have omitted the first half of volume one, because it deals with Taylor's origins and activities in England, which would chiefly be of interest to a biographer. We have also omitted volume three, pages 599 to 854, because this section of nautical log contains mostly information available from many other logs of the same kind.[11]

The manuscript was first transcribed by Elizabeth Pigou and Peter Smith, in the early 1980s, and has been revised for publication, over the years, by the present editor. We have tried faithfully to transcribe every letter in each word, a task rendered much easier once an electronic file had been compiled for the manuscript. We have, however, felt at liberty to introduce such punctuation and capitalization as was necessary to make the text comprehensible to a modern reader. Such a reader would do well to remember what Mark Twain once observed, and what Taylor fully shares: that he did not give a damn for a man who could only spell a word in one way.

The text has been annotated both for the meaning of words and for the significance of the discourse. Words with obscure meanings are followed by an asterisk and explained in the glossary. The notes have been composed with the average reader in mind, trying to answer the questions which might arise as that reader worked through the text. Original page numbers are indicated in parentheses, and all editorial comments and additions are contained between square brackets. "Not reproduced" means that an image appears in the manuscript, but is not copied for the edition; "lacking" means that Taylor dod not provide an image. In general, editorial comment is what might be called "minimalist"; we have tried to let the text speak for itself, without undue editorial intrusion.

The Language of Taylor's History

John Taylor used a remarkable range of words, beginning with the many quotations from the authors of classical Greek and Roman antiquity; here his favourites were Cicero, Horace, Ovid, Pliny and Plutarch, generally cited very appropriately. From them, too, he took those figures of classical mythology that described the passing days: Aeolus, Aurora, Phoebus and Pluto. His vocabulary also drew upon words common in medieval English, but growing archaic in his day: "fitch" for bean, "grundel" for a kind of fish, "palmer" for a worm, "pismire" for an ant, "pippen" for a kind of apple, "pompion" for a pumpkin, "sippet" for toast, and so forth.

More remarkably, he knew some Eastern terms such as "typhoon" and

11. Very many are preserved at the National Maritime Museum, Greenwich, England.

"scimitar", and clearly picked up many words from the cultures that surrounded the English bridgehead in the Spanish world. From the Spaniards he took terms such as "audiencia", "flota" and "tercio"; and from the North American Indians (presumably of the Carolinas) words such as "cawwough" (whose meaning I have been unable to elucidate), "hommeny", "wampum" and "wigwam", the latter sometimes used jocularly. The Caribbean peoples, presumably Tainos, gave him words such as "guava", "periaguer" and "zemis", as well as the proper noun "Haiti". From the Africans he took words such as "callalu", "baccara" and "tointa", while he also uses some apparently Jamaican constructs such as "mauger" and "picanniny". Occasionally he also uses words with a strangely modern feel, such as "operator" and "slack" (in the sense of "be not slack to do something").

As well as this wide range of words from a variety of cultures, Taylor also used contemporary English in an original way. Sometimes he would coin words such as "lignummetique" (woody) and "umbretique" (shady), and often he would coin pithy phrases, such as "many go from a tavern to a Tybourn", or "it is much easier to promise than to perform" or "counterfeited piety is double iniquity". Often, too, he would use irony, as when he speaks of the pirate Bartholomew Sharp's "merry boys" as they went on their destructive "military pilgrimage". This sort of jocularity is indeed a constant feature of his language. So water is "Adam's ale", a tasty supper is a "prickly dish" and West Indians are "Crebolians". Often he combines the jocular with the ironic. Thus, the Quakers are said to be ready to pledge the king's health: "nor will the quacks refuse to take a fee". A certain parson, addressing his congregation, is described as "preaching 'ore a lusty bowl of rum punch"; in general, Taylor makes the most of the comedic situations offered by alcohol, using a remarkably wide vocabulary.

Assessing the Contents of Taylor's History

John Taylor travelled to Jamaica in 1686 with all the prejudices and assumptions of an Englishman of his day. Thus he loses no opportunity for poking fun at women, and he was unable to think of Spaniards as being anything other than "base, treacherous and perfidious", only natural given their "proud, insulting disposition". He was, indeed, strangely ignorant about them, having very curious ideas about the career of Christopher Columbus and failing to realize, for instance, that the great navigator had once spent almost a year on the north coast of Jamaica. Taylor's more or less Spanish names for many of Jamaica's geographical features are also puzzling; some look as if they have been entirely made up, but others clearly resonate with later names. Perhaps the recent translation of Morales Padrón's *Spanish Jamaica* will lead to further studies in this neglected area.[12]

Taylor also had unfamiliar ideas about God and nature. He observed more than once that "God and nature make nothing in vain", and always assumed that everything that the Lord had made must have some utility for mankind. This led him to list a very large number of medical uses for the many creatures and plants that he describes; some uses seem fantastical, but others might still repay study. For Taylor, man and nature formed a unity, so that he came to have curiously modern ideas about the life lived in accordance with nature. By gluttony, for instance, man would abbreviate his days. For to eat excessively was to violate "the basic instinct of nature", which could for instance be seen in the way that a tree "feeds naturally". To drink excessively in the climate of Jamaica was even more foolish, as Taylor well understood.

In Taylor's world, spells and enchantment were omnipresent, particularly as they pertained to the former Spanish presence; this has been well brought out by James Robertson.[13] This belief in the magical seems to us curious, given Taylor's simultaneous insistence on his skill as a trained mathematician and surveyor; it was, however, commonplace in his day. He kept full, accurate and interesting logs of his voyages, and drew some reasonably accurate maps. But what are we to make of his assertion that by frequent strict observations, he had ascertained that the Blue Mountain was six miles high? Perhaps we should put this curious assertion down to a temporary lapse. After all, his calculation of the latitude of Port Royal was only about thirteen miles out, and he gives convincing explanations of Jamaican phenomena such as the diurnal variation of the wind.

In the past, his journal has been of most use for the description that it gives of pre-earthquake Port Royal. Historians and archaeologists have used this extensively, finding that on the whole it is an incomparably rich and accurate source. Perhaps, now, the publication here of his entire "state of Jamaica" will lead historians to pay attention to his description of other towns and other parts of the island, for these seem equally accurate and original. There is still much to be drawn, as well, from his description of the condition of the "English servants, Indians and Negro slaves",[14] as well as from his listing of the laws in force during the 1680s.[15] Perhaps, too, some specialists will be

12. Francisco Morales Padrón, *Spanish Jamaica*, trans. Patrick Bryan, Michael Gronow and Felix Oviedo Moral (Kingston, 2003).

13. See his "Rewriting the English Conquest of Jamaica in the Late Seventeenth Century", *English Historical Review* 117, no. 473 (2002): 813–39.

14. For a preliminary survey, see David Buisseret, "John Taylor's Ideas about Seventeenth-Century Jamaican Slavery", *Jamaican Historical Review* 21 (2001): 1–7.

15. See Vicki Crow Via, "A Comparison of the Colonial Laws of Jamaica under Governor Thomas Lynch, 1681–1684, with Those Enumerated in the John Taylor Manuscript of 1688", *Journal of Caribbean History* 39, no. 2 (2005): 236–48.

interested in his description of the coinage current in seventeenth-century Jamaica.[16]

Taylor is extremely judicious in his assessments of the relative virtues of European and West Indian products; there is, for him, none of the arguing about the debased nature of man and beast in the New World. Thus the oysters are better in Europe, but nothing there compares with the variety of Jamaican fish. Jamaican herbs, too, are to be prized for their rare physical properties, as is the island's fruit, much more varied than in Europe. On the other hand, "Europe is the lady Flora's garden, . . . and these western parts she hath withheld her favours from". So Taylor works through the various commodities, always offering a judicious assessment of each, and often explaining the prices that each would fetch for export at Port Royal.

His sections on animals, birds and fishes raise several questions. He is, of course, pre-Linnean, so that his categorizations are odd to our eyes: an iguana is a serpent because it lives in the sand, and a manatee is a fish because it lives in the sea. He does seem to give, though, a unique image of the fauna of Jamaica before the widespread establishment of the plantation system. Is it possible that he is correct in asserting that such creatures as Guinea dogs, anteaters, armadillos, flamingoes, macaws and electric eels once lived wild in the island? Many readers will assume that he is confusing Jamaica with other islands that he knew or had heard of. But we ought to notice that he, at least, was aware of this possible confusion, and took care always to explain what creatures did not live in Jamaica: such creatures as swans and rattlesnakes. Nor was he always as credulous as he sometimes seems; he took care, for instance, to remark that he did not believe what Pliny had to say about the ability of the remora to stop a ship, and asserts that "he made it his business to project and collect all things worthy [of] note".

Taylor wrote some years before the publication of Dr Hans Sloane's great work on the flora and fauna of Jamaica, and had no knowledge of Sloane's study. Yet it is curious how often his judgement coincides with that of the doctor, even though he always expresses himself in less learned language. Perhaps, in general assessment, we should think of Taylor as a sort of Hans-Sloane-in-the-street. He thus brought to his description of seventeenth-century Jamaica the eye of an amateur, but of an amateur who was not lacking some academic qualifications, and who had both a perceptive eye and the gift of turning some striking phrases.

16. For this study, it would be necessary to use John McCusker's *Money and Exchange in Europe and America, 1600–1715: A Handbook* (Chapel Hill, 1978).

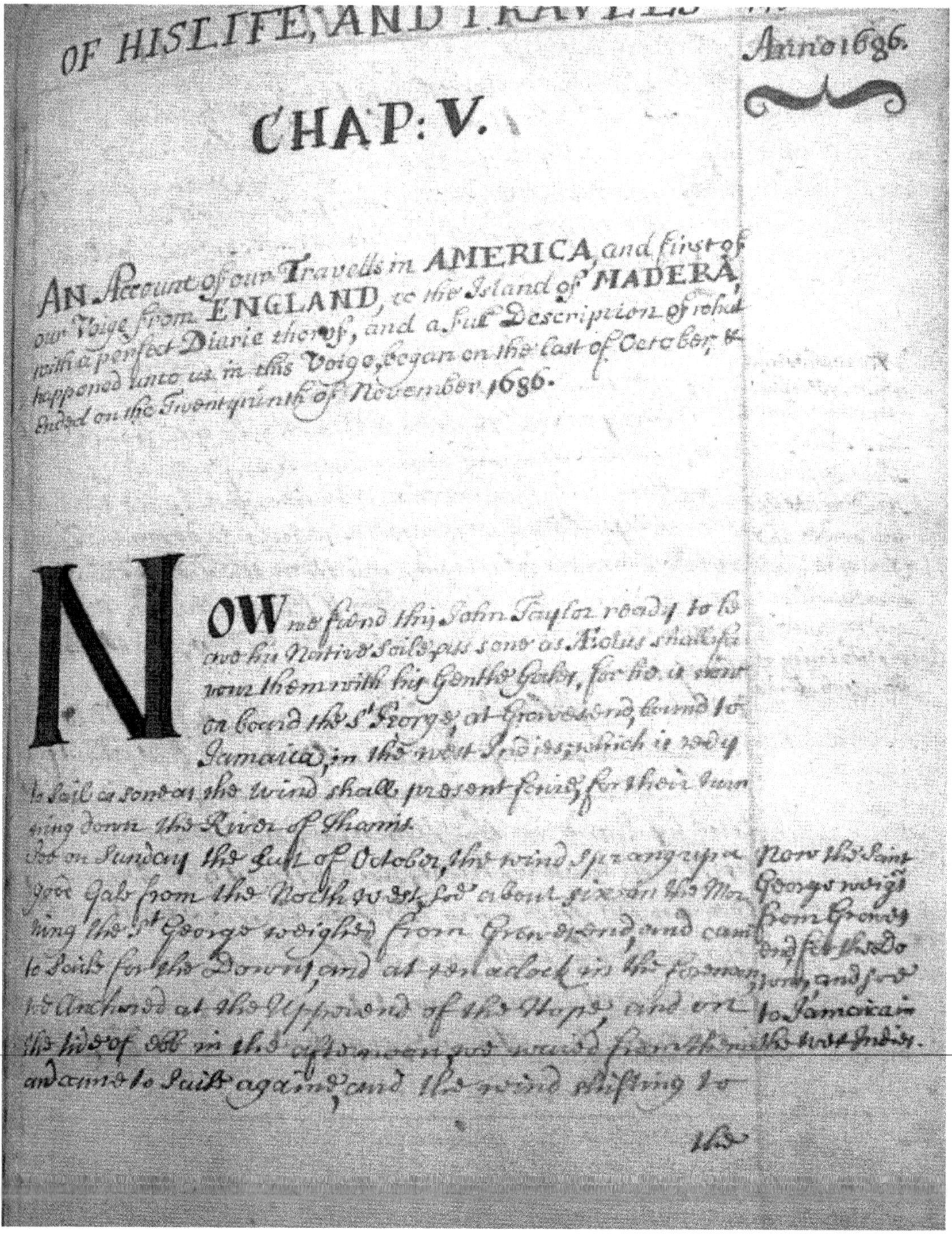

OF HIS LIFE, AND TRAVELS

Anno 1686.

CHAP: V.

AN Account of our Travells in AMERICA, and first of our Voige from ENGLAND, to the Island of MADERA, with a perfect Diarie thereof, and a full Description of what happened unto us in this Voige, began on the last of October, & ended on the Twentyninth of November 1686.

NOW we find thy John Taylor ready to leave his Native Soile, as soon as Aiolus shall favour them with his Gentle Gales, for he is sent on board the St George, at Gravesend, bound to Jamaica, in the west Indies, which is ready to sail as soon as the wind shall present faire, for their runing down the River of Thames.

So on Sunday the last of October, the wind sprang up a good Gale from the North West, so about six in the Morning the St George weighed from Gravesend, and came to Saile for the Downs, and at ten a clock in the forenoon we Anchored at the Upperend of the Hope, and on the tide of ebb in the afternoon we weighed from thence and came to Saile againe, and the wind shifting to

Now the Saint George weighs from Gravesend for the Downs, and so to Jamaica in the west Indies.

the

Figure 3 Page 145 of Taylor's manuscript.

Volume I

Taylor's History of His Life and Travels

Chapter V

(145) An account of our travells in America, and first of our voige from England, to the island of Madera, with a perfect diarie thereof, and a full description of what happened unto us in this voige, began on the last of October, and ended on the twentyninth of November 1686.

Now we fiend this John Taylor ready to leave his native soile, ass sone as Aeolus[1] shall favour them with his gentle gales, for he is now on board the *St. George,* at Gravesend, bound to Jamaica, in the West Indies,[2] which is redy to sail as sone as the wind shall present faire, for their turning down the river of Thamis.

Soe on Sunday the last of October, the wind sprang up a good gale from the northwest, soe about six in the morning the *St George* weighed from Gravesend, and cam to saile for the Downs, and at ten a'clock in the forenoon we anchored at the upper end of the Hope, and on the tide of ebb in the afternoon, we waied from thence and came to saile againe, and the wind shifting to (146) the east, we turned down midway betwixt the boith of Ouze, and Wollwich, and there came to anchor.[3] And on Moonday ye 1st of November 1686 the wind blew easterly, and about two in the morning we wayed* on the ebb, and turned down Oxenford, and Mr. Stone the pillot ran the ship ashore on the mudd, near the boith[4] in the midle of Lee. But the watter flowing, we sone got off, and turned down nine miles to the boith of the Ouz, and came to anchor in seaventeen fadom water. This day we had fair sunshine weather.

1. Aeolus, the wind god of Greek and Roman mythology.

2. The Customs records mention a *Saint George* as visiting Jamaica early in 1686; she was of 150 tons and then commanded by John Love. Public Record Office (henceforward National Archives), CO 142/13. It is possible that this was the same ship as our *Saint George,* whose voyage does not seem to be recorded in the Customs registers.

3. Figure 4 shows the kind of map that would have guided the *Saint George* from Gravesend to the Isle of Wight; it identifies many places mentioned in the text.

4. "Boith" may well be an early version of "buoy".

Figure 4 The Thames Estuary from *The English Pilot, The Fourth Book* (London, 1689). This is a chart of the kind that would have been used by the captain of the *Saint George* as he made his way down the River Thames from London (on the left) to Deal (lower right), where they set their pilot ashore.

Tuesday the 2nd the wind blew a good gale from the northeast, and the morning being close misty weather, we wayed not untill two in the afternoon, when the weather cleared up; then we wayed and turned down the river untill seaven at night, and then the tidd of ebb coming on we came to anchor in 11 fadom water, [illegible] of the midle bore from us south by east, and the boith of the Spitts bore from us south.

Wednsday the 3rd we had brave faire sunshine, fine weather and a good gale from the northeast; about four in the morning we wayed from thence on the tidd of ebb, and by eight in the morning the Nazeland bore from us northwest by west, and distant 9 miles, and by ten in the morning, the tidd being spent, we anchored to the eastward of the Longsand-head, in 15 fadom water. And about three a'clock in the afternoon we wayed from thence, and plied towards the channel (147), and by nine at night we came to anchor in ten fathom watter, the Northforland bearing from us south by west and distant two miles.

Thursday the 4th we had brave sunshine, faire weather, and a stiff gale from the northeast, soe at six in the morning we wayed, and by eight a'clock in the morning we arrived in the Downs, and set ashore Mr. Stone our pillot at Deal, and received on board from thence some hogs and fowles. Then we hoised in our boats, and made the best of our way for the Lizard, and at noon we were abrest of Dungeness. About six a'clock in the evening the wind increased, and it became fogy and rained hard, and about 11 at night we lay under a violent storm from the northeast, soe that we were forc't to scud under a foresaile and stand off onto the land, which by the dilligent plieing the lead[5] we were guided by.

Fryday the 5th the storm continued, rather blowing higher, but 'twas not so foggy, soe that at eight a'clock in the morning Selsey Island bore from us north, and distant nine miles. Soe we made the best of our way to have gone in at the east end of the Wight, to have anchor'd at Cowes, but when we were off south by west of the Culver clifts, and distant seaven miles, the wind drop't about at north and the storm increased on, and the fogg came exceding thick, soe that we were forc't to stand off to sea againe under a maine* and a fore course, and stood off and came in the channel, using our lead continually, and about 6 in the evening the wind chop't about north by west, a violent storm, and misty, so that about eight at night, thro' the badness of weather, we lost our foreyard and topmast, and were forc't to cut their shrouds,* soe that it all fell overbord and was lost in the sea. By this sad acident we had one man killed outright and another whose right thigh was broaken. About one (148) in the morning, by sounding we found ourselves to be nere the Nedles at ye southwest end of the Wight, and we fell in among som ships. But it being dark and misty, we knew not what they were, but by their speech we supposed them to be Dutch, as they proved to bee, soe we took what care the prepetuous* wind would admit us, to keep from running foul of them.

5. "Plying the lead" involved using a weight to check the depth of the water; this lead also had a concave base, which when smeared with tallow allowed the nature of the bottom to be gauged.

Saturday the 6th the storm was not soe high, but it rained hard, and continued foggy. About noon the wind blew moderatly from the west, and the weather cleared up, soe that then the Nedles bore from us north, and distant by estimation 7. And we saw about thirty sail standing in for Cowes, soe we stood in after them, and about three in the afternoon we came to anchor at Cowes in 9 fathom water.[6] Cowes Castle bore from us southwest, and Calshot Castle bore from us north and a half poynt west. Here we found at anchor 36 Dutch ships, six Swedes, ten English ships, two French ships, two Scots barques, and an Ierish pinck.* And about fouer a'clock this afternoon there were two men drowned, for as they in a small yaule were passing from the east to the west Cowes, their boat ran against the hawse* of a Dutch ship named the *Five Provinces,* and soe was overseet, and for all ye speedy assistance of many boats, it being a hollow sea* they were both drowned.[7] Most of these Dutch ships are bound for St. Heauls. Being thus by providence brought to his own native island, he remained exceding mallancholly, but resolved not to goe ashore to see his friends, nor to lett them know he was here, becaus their sorrow would but have agrived his, and their perswations he feared would have perswaided him from these his intended travels. Therfor he resolved to keep himself privat, tho' with noe small troble to himself.[8]

(149) Sunday the 7th the wind blew stifly from the west, and 'twas thick and foggy, rainy weather. We kept our convicts in irons* under the hatches, not suff'ring them to com above decks but two att once.

Moonday the 8th the wind blew moderately from the west, and 'twas brave fair sunshine weather, and this day we got up a new topmast and yard.*[9]

Tewesday the 9th the wind blew moderatly from the west, and fair weather. This day we imployed other seamen to help us in mending our riging, etc., soe that this day we compleated it, and bent new sails to yards and thereby repaired our damages sustained by the prepetuous* wind. Soe now we are redy to sail, as soon as the swift wing'd Aeolus shall befriend us with his gentel gales.

Wednsday the 10th the wind continued still at west, and the weather continued fair, and now this last night the convicts combin'd together to make their escape, and in the night they had some secret invention to cut off their irons, which was discover'd thus: one of them being let up to goe to ease himself in the head,* his irons (by an unwilling accident) fell off his

6. Figure 5 shows the approximate track of the *Saint George* to Cowes.

7. East and West Cowes face each other across the mouth of the Medina River, which can be turbulent. A "hollow" sea was one with deep troughs between the crests.

8. Taylor had grown up in the Isle of Wight, as he explains in the introduction.

9. The original topmast had been broken in the storm.

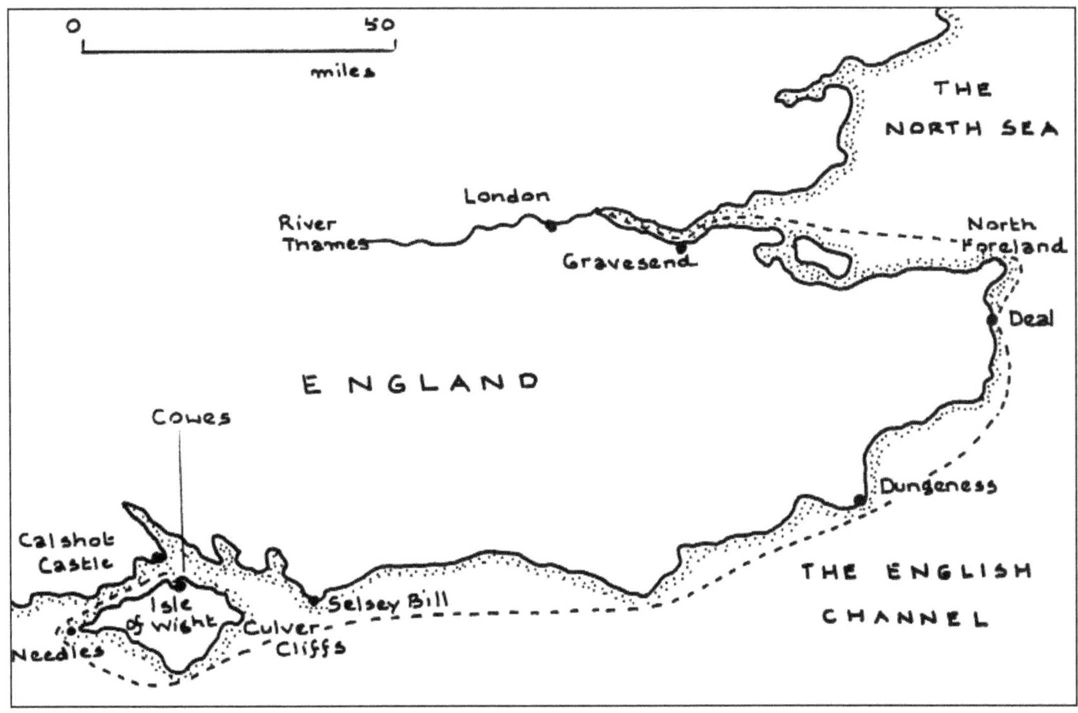

Figure 5 Track of the *Saint George* from London to the Isle of Wight.

legs, which being observed by some seamen on the deck, it was seen to be fill'd off. Upon which they were all called up two by two, and none of them had their irons on, but had fill'd them off. Upon which they were all put into new irons, and close handcuf't with irons, and all of them in the top chaine stapled down to the deck, and the hatches closely laid over them, and two centrys to watch them night and day. Then their cloths, beding and what else (150) could be thought on was dilligent sirch't, and yet nither saw, file, knife or any other thing wherwith they could thus cut off their irons could be found. Neither would they ever in the whole voige confess their dissigne, or with what they cut off their irons, but every day after, during the whole voige, they were stricktly sirch't. They were all fastened to the top chaine, except the five women, which had only irons on their leggs, and went at large, and one young man John Eldred (which was transported for fellony, not a servant, but taken care of by his father for his passage, and also after his comming into the country) which had irons only one his leggs, and confined to the great cabbien.

Thursday the 11th the wind sprung up a good gale from the north-north-east, soe about five in the morning we (and 57 saile more) wayed from Cowes and made the best of our way to get out of the Nedles. Thus this John Taylor hath now left his native country, his deare wife, tender relations, and what els was deare unto him, and remained very sad at these his parting privatly from them. Yet he had hopes to enjoye a happy return to his country, and a joyfull enjoyment of those which were deare to him, which were the only supports of his in his troubles. Soe about eight a'clock we were gott cleare of the Nedles,[10] and by noone most of the fleet was out of sight, for the Dutch fleet stered overe to the coast of France, soe that we had now with us but a small pinck* named the *Rose,* bound for Antiego in the West Indies. The pinck slow'd to keep us company; at six at night Portland bore from us north, distant 9 miles.

(151) Fryday the 12th we had fair weather, and a moderat gale from the east to the northeast. At 8 the Lizard bore north dist. 9 miles.

Saturday the 13th we had fair weather and a fresh gale from the east to the east-north-east. At nine last night we took our departure from the Lizard, in the latitude of 50° 00'; from whence we stered till this day noon was southwest, and distance run was 107 miles. By observation we found ourselves in the latitude of 48° 12'.[11]

Sunday the 14th we had fair weather, and the wind from the east to the northeast by east, and from yesterday noon to this day noon our course was southwest, and distance thereon sail'd 50 mils. This day the convicts were let out of irons, and had liberty to walk on deck, but were not suffered to com on the quarter deck,* cookrome or steerage. Now we found ourselves to be by observation in the latitude of 46° 55'. In the evening we espied two sailes which wee supposed to be Turck.[12] They gave us chace, soe with all expedition we put our ship in a defensive posture, all things being prepared redy to fight. We arm'd the convicts with small arms, and each man was quartered in proper places. We had on board, with the seventeen convicts, 65 men and two boys. Thus being redy, our captain with his men went to prayer, and then each man refresh't himself with a full cup of brandy punch, and were resolved to fight to the last man against those barbarians. The convicts seemed very caraigous,* and I believe would (if we had engaged) have fought stoutly. We took the *Rose* pinck on the towe by our streame cable* out at the gunroom port,* and Mr. Burns hir master with six men and two boys (all their company)

10. These are the great cliff-islands at the west end of the Isle of Wight.

11. Figure 8 reproduces a contemporary chart of the route from "the Lizard" to "Desartos". It is possible to plot the track only approximately, for Taylor gives no figures of longitude, which was at the time very difficult to ascertain.

12. The Turkish empire extended at this time along the whole coast of North Africa, and was the home of the "Barbary pirates" who were the scourge of "Christian" shipping. The arming of the convicts on the threatened ship is reminiscent of the occasional arming of slaves in Jamaica, as on the occasion of the French invasion of 1694. David Buisseret, "The French Invasion of Jamaica, 1694", *Jamaica Journal* 16, no. 3 (1983): 31–33.

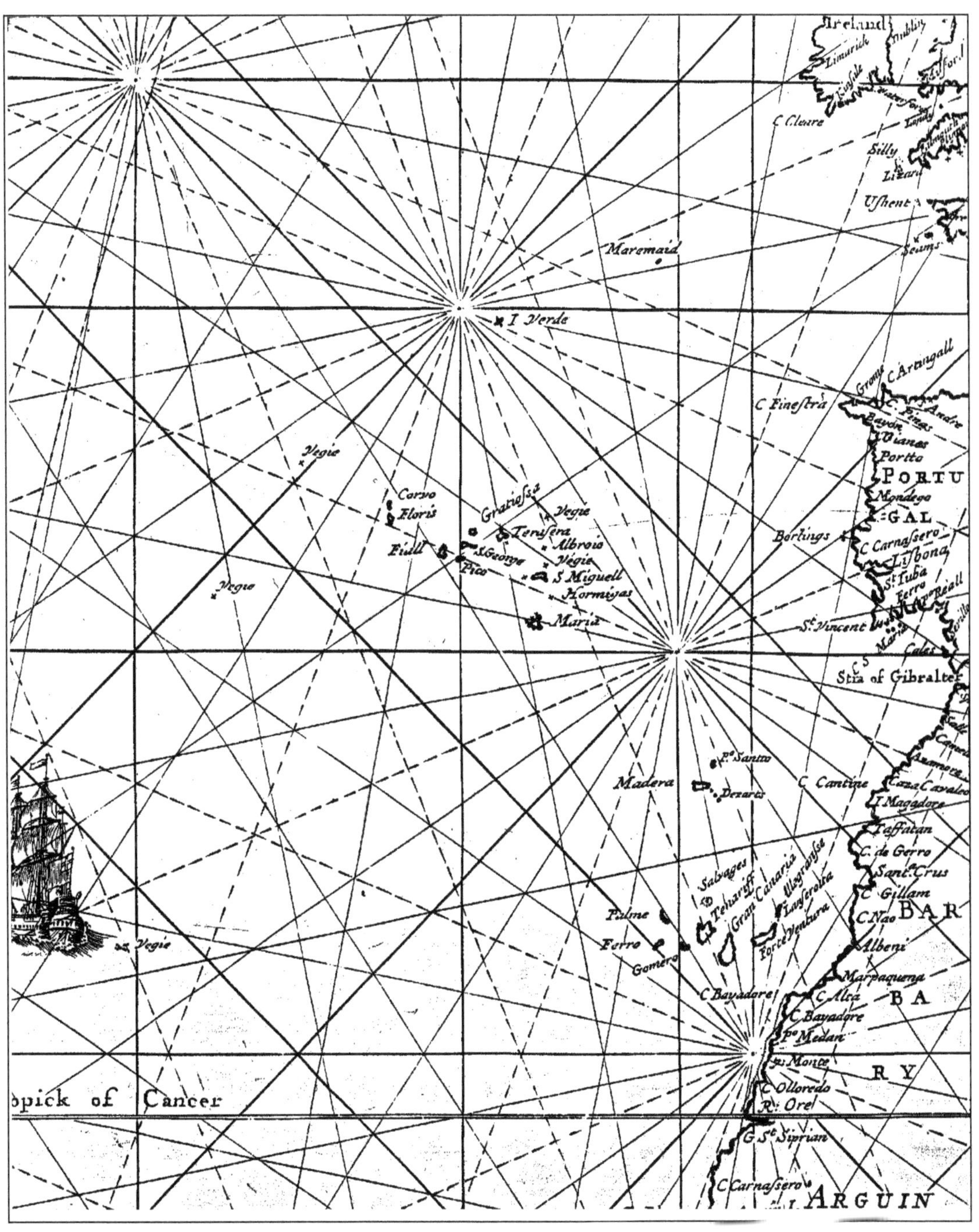

Figure 6 Part of the northeastern Atlantic Ocean, from *The English Pilot*. This chart shows the Atlantic Ocean from the Lizard (top right) to "Madera", where the *Saint George* put in before the transatlantic crossing.

came on board of us, where they thought themselves most secuer, for the pinck had noe guns, and therefore could have made but small resistance.

Moonday ye 15th by fouer a'clock in the morning we had lost sight of the two saile which the last night gave us chace, (152) soe that now the master of the *Rose* pinck went on bord and we quitted hir from tow. We had a fresh gale from the east-north-east, to the east-south-east. Our course was south-south-west, and our distance sail'd was 59 miles. By observation we found ourselves in the latitude of 44° 07'; in the evening we had som raine with thunder and lightning.

Tewesday the 16th we had fair weather, and a fresh gale from the east to the east-north-east. Our course was south-south-west, and our distance sail'd 54 miles, and by observation we were in the latitude of 43° 12'. At one in the afternoon we met with a French merchant's ship. This evening we lost sight of the *Rose* pinck.

Wednsday the 17th we had fair weather and a fresh gale from the northeast. Our course was south-south-west, and our latitude by observation was 40° 00', and our distance sail'd was 105 miles.

Thursday the 18th we had fair weather, with a gentel gale from the north-north-east to the south. Our course was south-south-west-1/2 west, our distance sail'd 45 miles, and by observation we found ourselves in the latitude of 39° 21'.

Friday the 19th we found fair weather and but litle wind, which blew from the southeast by east. Our course was south and distance sail'd was 15 miles. By observation we found ourselves in the latitude of 39° 05', and about six in the morning it fell calm, and soe continued.

Saturday the 20th we had faire weather, and an easy gale from the south-east by east. Our course was south 1/2 west, our distance sail'd was 36 miles, and by observation we found ourselves in the latitude of 38° 30'.

Sunday the 21st we had faire weather, and a brisk gale from the southeast to the east-south-east. Our cource was south-south-west, our distance sail'd was 115 miles, (153) and by observation we found ourselves in the latitude of 37° 19'.

Moonday the 22nd we had hazy, rainy weather, but a good gale from the east by south. Our course was south by west, and 1/2 westerly, our distance sail'd 132 miles, and by observation we were in the latitude of 35° 12'.

Tewesday the 23rd we had fair weather, and an easie gale from the south-east by east. Our course was south-south-west, our distance run was 39 miles, and by observation we were in the latitude of 34° 17'.

Wednsday the 24th we had showers of raine, and an easie gale from the east, with thunder, and much lightning. Our course was southwest, and our distance sailed 21 milles, and we found ourselves by observation in ye latitude of 34° 27'.

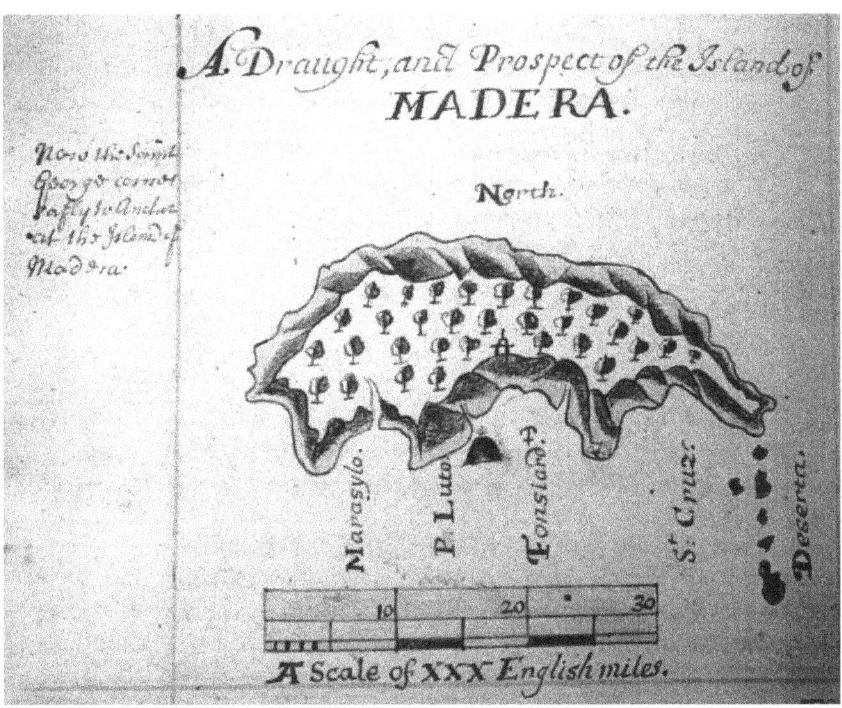

Figure 7 Taylor's "A Draught and Prospect of the Island of Madera", page 154. This little sketch offers a rough idea of the shape of Madeira, with its harbour at Funchal ("Fonsiard"). The scale is fairly accurate.

Thursday the 25th we enjoyed brave fair weather, and a stiff gale from the south. Our course was southwest by west, our distance run was 12 miles (by reason of a leak which we lay by to repaire). Our latitude by observation was 34° 25'; at night we had raine.

Friday the 26th we had fair weather, and a good gale from the south by west, to the east. Our course was southwest by south 30° 15' southerly, distance sail'd 48 miles and our latitude by observation was 32° 36'.

Saturday the 27th we had fair weather, and a fresh gale from the east by south to the northwest by north. Our course was south 23° 00' westerly; distance run was 60 miles.

Sunday the 28th we had fair weather, and a fresh gale from the north to the west by north. Our course was west 15° 00' southerly, our distance sail'd was 72 miles, our latitude by observation was 32° 20'.

(154) Moonday the 29th we had fair weather, and litle wind variable on all points. At fouer in the morning the southermost of the Desartos[13] bore east by south and distant 6 miles. At noon we came to anchor near Fonsiard in the Island of Madera, in 3 fathom water.[14] The castle on the rock bore north-

13. The Islas Desertas lie just to the southeast of the island of Madeira; "Fonsiard" is Funchal.

14. Figure 7 shows Taylor's map of Madeira; there is a description of the island in T. Bentley Duncan's *Atlantic Islands* (Chicago, 1972).

north-west 1/2 northerly from us, and the easternmost castle bore from us northeast. Thus by God's Divine Providence this John Taylor is safly arived to ye Island of Madera, whoe all the term of the voige was in perfect health, but remain'd extremly mellancholy.

(155) The island of Madera is one of the wester islands of the third part of the world called Africa, being in the latitude of [blank], and longitude of [blank]. The length of this island is forty miles, and the breadth is eighteen miles. On the northside is all invironed with rocky cheves and hills, and soe westward untill you come to the Bay of Marasylo, ther is noe convenient place to anchor. And soe all round from the northside to the eastward untill you've gott within the Desarts into the Bay of Sancta Cruze, their is noe anchorage, it being all high rocky cheves to seaward. Now on the south side of this are three commodis bays, as Marasylo, Fonsiard, and St. Cruze, but Fonsiard is the cheif place of trade, soe that ships trading hither seldom anchor elsewhere. Here is built a fine small town, and in this bay are two small rivers (which run some way up in the island) of fresh water. That to the eastward is called Rio Fonsiardo, and that to the westward is caled Rio Luto.

Oposit to the mouth of this river, about two mill off in the bay to the westward lies a small, high rocky island, about one mile round. On the top of this rock is built a strong castle of stone with about 20 copper pieces of ordnance.* This castle is of good defence to ye bay and town, and is called Forta de la Luto. Also on the top of the hill opposit to the bay is built another strong castle of stone, haveing two batteries, one of eighteen, and the other of twelve peices of ordnance; this castle covers the whole bay. Also on the easternmost part of the bay towards Sancta Cruze is another strong castle built of stone, haveing sixten peices of ordnance mounted thereon; this flanks Fonsiard to ye westward and St. Cruz to the eastward and this bay of Fonsiard is rocky, haveing from 3 to 8, 13 etc. fadom water. The town hath in it two churches, one monastry, and about 500 houses (156). The Bay of Marisylo is about six miles broad and fouer mils deep; 'tis rock foul ground, haveing from 3 to 5, and soe to 11 fadom water. Here is a river of fresh water, which empties itself into this bay, called Ryo Marasylo. Here are som few vintage houses, and one church.

The Bay of St. Cruz to the eastward is about eleven mils broad and five mils deep. Here you have from 2, to 5 and 9 fathom water. All along the shore are built vintage houses, and in the codd* of the bay is a small town of about 100 houses and a monastry. Towards the east end of this bay and island lie five small rocky island, extending themselves from that point, about 12 milles to the southerward, called the Desartos. These islands are soe rocky that they are neither planted nor inhabited by any, and have deep chanels betwixt them, soe that thro' their dangerous rocks which lie in them, makes the passages soe difficult, that few ships venter betwixt them. Also, about a mile to the westward of the second of these islands lies another small rock island, soe that the number of the Desertos are six small rocky islands. Now when the island of Madera bears from you southwest, and distant 15 miles, it appears thus [figure omitted].

This island of Madera is inhabited by the Portugusse, and is very frutfull (157) in good frute, as lemons, orange, pomegranets etc. and yeild aboundance of grapes, and good wines of diverse sorts both red and white, is made here yearly, and transported in aboundance to diverse places of the English setlements in the West Indies. For above twenty saile of ships is loaded yearly from here to supply not only Jamaica, by which you may judge of the great plenty which is made here yearly. Their wine is their only commodity, and keeps longer and better than any other wine whatsoever caryed to the West Indies. As for corn, or flesh, this island afords in no great plenty. But they are supply with corn etc. from other parts soe that this populus island lives at ease and plenty.

About thirty-five miles to ye eastward of Madera lieth the island of Porta Sancto, the westermost point whereof at "A" lies due east from the point "A" of Santa Cruz, on the island of Madera. This island of Porta Sancto is not now neither planted nor inhabited, but thereon the inhabitants of Madera keep some horses and other catle. This island hath bin often setled by the Portuguise, but the Turck coming thither did often plunder them and cary them away prisoners, soe they found it not worth setling. This island bearing from you south, and distant 21 miles, it appeareth then thus [plate omitted].

(158) Now we must hereunto annext a nauticall table callculated according to the work of a voige from England to Madera, which will make the whole work plain and obvious att one view [figure 8].

(159) Now to returne to our discourse againe, you must understand that as soon as we were come to anchor at Madera, and had securly moored the ship, then all the convicts were comitted to irons again, and put under hatches, and two centinals set to watch them night and day soe long as we should continue here. About two a'clock in the afternoon our captain went ashore, in order to dispatch his buisiness there with the merchant with whome he was concerned. And we went on shore with him, to see the country, and about six in the evening we return'd on board.

Tuesday the 30th, and last, the wind blew moderatly from the west by north, and west by south; we had faire sunshine weather in the morning. We began to put on shore those commodoties assigned to some merchants here residing, and about six in the eavening wee had deliver'd all our goodes that belonged to merchants on this island and made preparation to stowe everything which we were to receive on bord the next day. This day in the

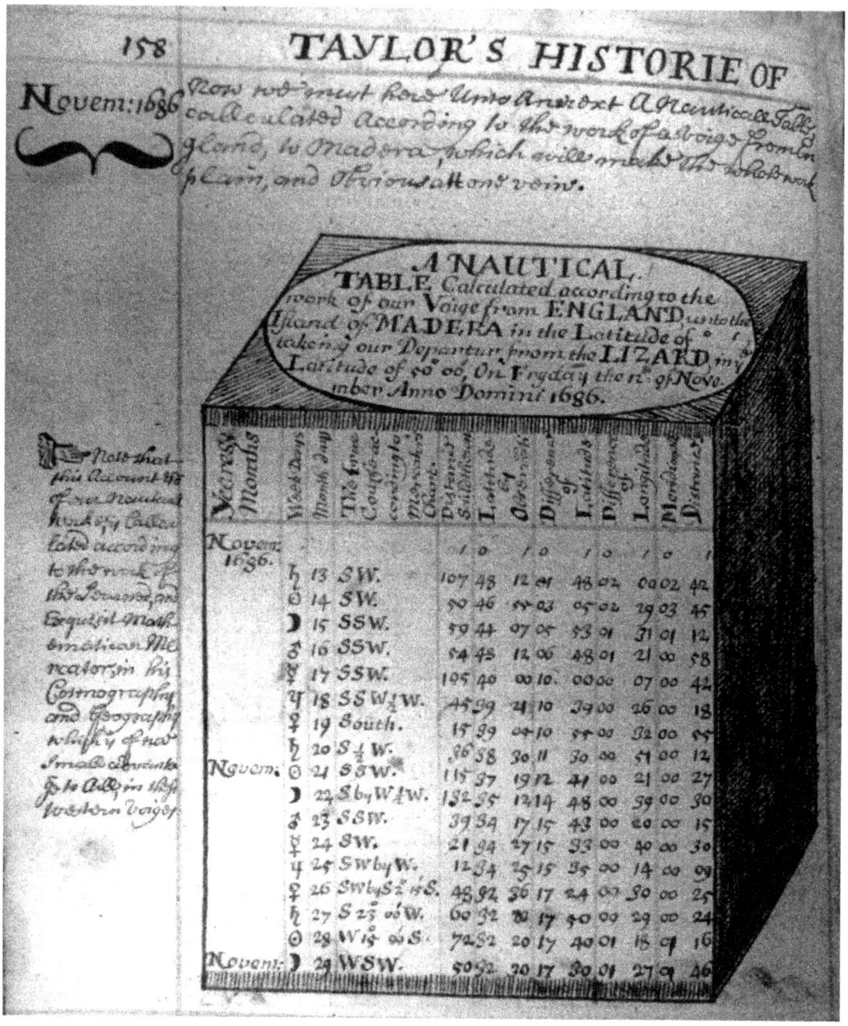

Figure 8 Taylor's "Nautical Table" of the journey from England to Madeira, page 158. It is curious that Taylor gives this "table" the actual appearance of a sort of table, with each day's readings duly noted.

morning I went on shore, and remain'd there untill ye eavening, and this morning there sail'd from hence two catches* that were laden with wine; the one was bound for New England, and the other for Jamaica. Soe that now here remained only us, two Dutch flyboats,* and one Dutch pinck. This day the inhabitants on shore inform'd me that on Saturday last there came a Turck laner [?] full of men, which for all the castles firing at them were so desperat to take and carry away out of the road one Dutch pinck and one English pinck, with those men which were on board of them. This night we have had some showers of rain.

difficult, that few ships venter betwixt them. Also, about a mile to the westward of the second of these islands lies another small rock island, soe that the number of the Desertos are six small rocky islands. Now when the island of Madera bears from you southwest, and distant 15 miles, it appears thus [figure omitted].

This island of Madera is inhabited by the Portugusse, and is very frutfull (157) in good frute, as lemons, orange, pomegranets etc. and yeild aboundance of grapes, and good wines of diverse sorts both red and white, is made here yearly, and transported in aboundance to diverse places of the English setlements in the West Indies. For above twenty saile of ships is loaded yearly from here to supply not only Jamaica, by which you may judge of the great plenty which is made here yearly. Their wine is their only commodity, and keeps longer and better than any other wine whatsoever caryed to the West Indies. As for corn, or flesh, this island afords in no great plenty. But they are supply with corn etc. from other parts soe that this populus island lives at ease and plenty.

About thirty-five miles to ye eastward of Madera lieth the island of Porta Sancto, the westermost point whereof at "A" lies due east from the point "A" of Santa Cruz, on the island of Madera. This island of Porta Sancto is not now neither planted nor inhabited, but thereon the inhabitants of Madera keep some horses and other catle. This island hath bin often setled by the Portuguise, but the Turck coming thither did often plunder them and cary them away prisoners, soe they found it not worth setling. This island bearing from you south, and distant 21 miles, it appeareth then thus [plate omitted].

(158) Now we must hereunto annext a nauticall table callculated according to the work of a voige from England to Madera, which will make the whole work plain and obvious att one view [figure 8].

(159) Now to returne to our discourse againe, you must understand that as soon as we were come to anchor at Madera, and had securly moored the ship, then all the convicts were comitted to irons again, and put under hatches, and two centinals set to watch them night and day soe long as we should continue here. About two a'clock in the afternoon our captain went ashore, in order to dispatch his buisiness there with the merchant with whome he was concerned. And we went on shore with him, to see the country, and about six in the evening we return'd on board.

Tuesday the 30th, and last, the wind blew moderatly from the west by north, and west by south; we had faire sunshine weather in the morning. We began to put on shore those commodoties assigned to some merchants here residing, and about six in the eavening wee had deliver'd all our goodes that belonged to merchants on this island and made preparation to stowe everything which we were to receive on bord the next day. This day in the

158 TAYLOR'S HISTORIE OF

Novem:1686 Now we must here Unto Annext a Nautical Table calculated according to the work of a Voige from England, to Madera, which will make the whole work plain, and obvious att one view.

A NAUTICAL TABLE Calculated according to the work of our Voige from ENGLAND, unto the Island of MADERA in the Latitude of ° ' taking our Departure from the LIZARD, in ye Latitude of 50° 06', On Fryday the 12th of November Anno Domini 1686.

Note that this Account is a nautical work, Calculated according to the work of the Learned, and Exquisit Mathematician Mercator, in his Cosmography and Geography, which is of no small advantage to all in these western Voiges.

Yeeres & Months	Week Days	Month Days	The true Course according to Mercators Chart	Distance Sailled	Latitude	Difference of Latitude	Difference of Longitude	Meridional Distance
Novem: 1686.					° '	° '	° '	°
	♄	13	SW.	107 48	12 41	48 02	00 02	42
	☉	14	SW.	50 46	55 03	05 02	29 03	45
	☽	15	SSW.	59 44	07 05	53 01	31 01	12
	♂	16	SSW.	54 45	12 06	48 01	21 00	58
	☿	17	SSW.	105 40	00 10	00 00	07 00	42
	♃	18	SSW½W.	45 39	21 10	39 00	26 00	18
	♀	19	South.	15 39	04 10	54 00	32 00	55
	♄	20	S½W.	86 38	30 11	30 00	51 00	12
Novem:	☉	21	SSW.	115 37	19 12	41 00	21 00	27
	☽	22	S by W¼W.	132 35	12 14	48 00	59 00	30
	♂	23	SSW.	39 34	17 15	43 00	20 00	15
	☿	24	SW.	21 34	27 15	33 00	40 00	30
	♃	25	SW by W.	12 34	25 15	35 00	14 00	09
	♀	26	SW by S 2° 15' S.	48 32	36 17	24 00	50 00	25
	♄	27	S 23° 00' W.	60 32	30 17	50 00	29 00	24
	☉	28	W 15° 00' S.	72 32	20 17	40 01	15 01	16
Novem:	☽	29	WSW.	50 32	30 17	30 01	27 01	46

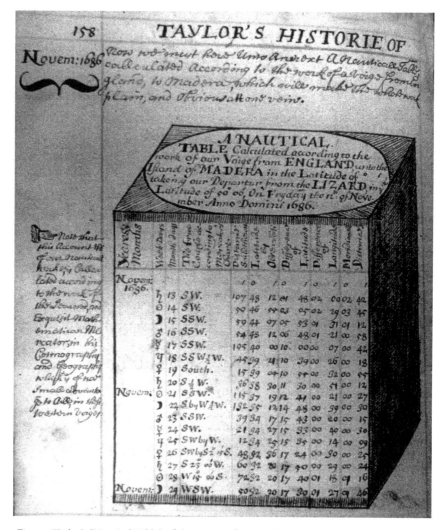

Figure 8 Taylor's "Nautical Table" of the journey from England to Madeira, page 158. It is curious that Taylor gives this "table" the actual appearance of a sort of table, with each day's readings duly noted.

morning I went on shore, and remain'd there untill ye eavening, and this morning there sail'd from hence two catches* that were laden with wine; the one was bound for New England, and the other for Jamaica. Soe that now here remained only us, two Dutch flyboats,* and one Dutch pinck. This day the inhabitants on shore inform'd me that on Saturday last there came a Turck laner [?] full of men, which for all the castles fiering at them were so desperat to take and carry away out of the road one Dutch pinck and one English pinck, with those men which were on board of them. This night we have had some showers of rain.

(160) On Wednsday, being the first of December, we had faire weather and a fresh gale from the west to the north by east. This day I went again ashore, and went some mills up into the island to see the vinyards, etc. with a gentleman of mine acquantance and English marchant here, and this day we received on board 15 tunns* of red Madera wine. In the eavening I took my leve of this gentleman; I came on board bringing with me a quarter cask of white Madera wine, which I had bought for my sea store.

Thursday the 2nd, this day we had fair weather and a moderat gale from the west. And we received on bord fifteen tuns of wine more, which was all we where here to take in, the which being stowed, we losed our foretopsail and haled* home the sheate to give notice of our saileing on the morrow if ye wind proved faire. Thus thro' the providence of Divine Mercy we leave this John Taylor, now in perfect helth, tho' still sad and discontented, redy to saile for Jamaica in the West Indies, and thus conclude this chapter of our life & travels.

Chapter VI

(161) Of our voige from the island of Madera unto the island of Jamaica in the West Indies, with a perfect diary therof, and a full description of what happened unto us in the term of the voige, began on Fryday the third of December, and ended on the third of January 1687.

On Fryday being the third of December Anno 1686, early in the morning, befor that Phoebus[1] with his golden beams had throly chas't away the dark shades of the sable night, and bespangled the earth with his refulgent raies did Eolus favoure us with his gentel gales from the northwest by north to the north-north-west. Soe that at 5 this morning the *St. Gorge* fiered a gun in order to way, and by six in the morning we came to saile. And about two in the afternoon we took our departure from Punta Luto, which then bore from us south and distant ten miles, and steared southwest by south.

(162) Saturday the 4th we had thick cloudy weather, and the wind blew hard from the northeast. Since we took our departure from Punta Luto our course hath binn southwest by south, and our distance run hath bin 145 miles, and by observation we found ourselves in the latitude of 29° 07'. At night we had som squalls of rain.

Sunday the 5th we had fair weather and a fresh gale from the northeast. Our course was southwest, and our distance sailed thereon was 135 miles, and our latitude by observation was 27° 41'.

Moonday the 6th we had faire weather, and the wind sprung a good gale from northeast, and soe to the northeast by north. Our course was southwest, and distance sail'd theron was 126 miles, and our latitude observation was 26° by 15'.

Tewesday the 7th we had cloudy weather, with squalls of rain and a fresh gale from the northeast by north to ye northeast. Our course was southwest, and distance sail'd thereon 180 miles, and our latitude by observation 24° 06'. Now the convicts were let out of irons.

1. Phoebus was the sun god of Greek mythology.

Wednesday the 8th we had squalie, rainny weather, and a hard gale from the northeast to the northeast by east. At one this morning we crost the Tropick of Cancer. Our course was southwest, and 02° 00' westerly, and distance sailed thereon was 186 miles, and our latitude by observation was 22° 16'. Under the Tropick (and soe under the Tropic of Capricorn), are a sort of a [junte?] bird, called a tropick bird. These birds as they soare aloft on the wing seme to be of a milkwhit culler, about the bigness of a sea mew, and historians say they have but one feather in their taile. Whether that be soe or noe, I can't tell, but here in the morning we saw abundance of them, flying about the ship, very high. These birds are never found noewhere but under the Tropicks, and about thirty miles to ye northward and southward thereof, for when we were now past 30° from the Tropicks we saw noe more of them (163). What I wonder at most concerning them is, whether or not they hover in the air at night, or where they rest, and breed, on the watter, for think I have seen them under the Tropick of Cancer, when there was no known land for them to rest on in above 870 miles.[2] Therfor, I conceive that as they feed on fish, soe they rest their wearyed bodys on the surface of that element which their prey lives in, and perhaps breeds on it also.[3] Suer I am that these birds far distant from land must either rest in the aire on their wing, or else repose themselves on the water. For suer I am that for all thir swiftness they are not in a night's time able to obtain those land thus distant from them. They are footed like a duck, and in the aire appeare thus: [figure 9].

Figure 9 Taylor's drawing of a "Tropic bird", page 163. Taylor began, clearly, with the intention of making many drawings. But he may soon have realized that to give birds a distinct appearance required more artistic skill than he possessed.

2. The Tropic of Cancer is the area at which the vertical midday sun reaches its greatest distance north of the equator, and the Tropic of Capricorn is the area at which the sun reaches its greatest distance south of the equator.

3. "Mew" was an archaic word for a gull; Taylor is correct in thinking that these birds sometimes rest, floating on the water.

Thursday the 9th we had cloudy weather with raine, and a stiff gale from the northeast by north, to the northeast by east. Our course was west by south 1/2 southerly, our distance sail'd theron was 174 miles, and by observation we found ourselves to be in the latitude of 21° 40'.

(164) Friday the 10th we had fair weather, and a moderat gale from ye northeast unto the north-north-east. Our course was southwest by south 1/2 southerly, our distance sail'd theron was 183 miles, and our latitude by observation was 20° 36'.

The last night the convicts by some invention goot thro' the bulkhead of the lazareta,[4] and stole from thence 46 bottles of clarret, and one Cheshire cheese and som other things which they had in their bedding etc. (which the last day was not sirch't as formerly). But they sone became drunck with the wine, soe that three of them got up in the foretop, carying a bottle of wine up with them, and there sang and made merry, and one of them, his name was William Hicks, formerly curat at Stanes near London, but now for fellony condemned to die, and was caryed in a cart with a halter about his neck to Tibourn,* and their thro' the King's clemancy had a reprive, which was procured by Father Peters the King's confessor.[5] For this father coming to Newgat* to him after his condemnation perswaided him from the Protistant religion (or rather from noe religon) to be a Roman Catholick, by which means he obtained the benefitt of transportation.

This [blank] Hide being drunck in the top, soe that he thought himself now the nighest heaven that ever he should be, and then threw a botle overbord, which being observed by the seamen, and Captain Johns[6] acquainted therwith, the convicts' roome was sirch't, where they found most of them drunck, and the empty botles, and found the place where they had gott into the lazareta. Soe fouerteen of them were again fastened to the top chaine, and stapled down on the deck of the forecastle, there to induer the weather and to be well heat by the burning sun, for they had nothing over them. As for the other three, one was confin'd to the great cabbin as befor (165), and the other two haveing behaved themselves allways civilly had their liberty to walk at large. Their names were William Clerk a foolish gentleman, convicted for stricking a woman dead by the unhappy thro' of a glass bottle; the other's name was Thomas Lucon, formerly a cadet in the Lord of Oxford's regiment, who was convicted as an adherent to robery commited nere Kingsington, and therefor transported. These two haveing allways behaved

4. A lazarreto was originally a place for lepers, but the term was also used for a place between decks on a ship, used as a storehouse.

5. Father Edward Petre was a Jesuit who enjoyed the confidence of King James II.

6. Taylor here called the captain "Johns", but elsewhere he also calls him "Jeans" and "James".

themselves sivill had their liberty to join the rest, for the first two men they had their liberty also. The convicts being thus secuered, we removed all the goods out of the lazareta and stored it in the hold for further security.

Saturday the 11th we had fair weather, and a moderat gale from the east-north-east and east by north. Our course was west by south, 1/2 southerly, our distance sail'd theron was 153 mils and our latitude by observation was 19° 51'.

Sunday the 12th we had fair weather and a fresh gale from the northeast unto the east by north. Our course was west by south, our distance sail'd theron was 129 miles, and by observation we found ourselves in the latitude of 19° 31'.

Moonday the 13th we had fair weather and a fresh gale from east-north-east to the northeast. Our course was east by south 1/4 southerly, our distance sail'd theron was 145 miles, our latitude by observation was 19° 10'.

Tewesday the 14th we enjoyed fair weather, and a moderat gale from the east-north-east to the east. Our course was west-south-west, our distance sail'd theron was 138 miles, and our latitude by observation was 18° 15'.

Wednsday the 15th we had faire weather, and a good gale from the east-north-east to the east. Our course was west-southwest, our distance sail'd theron was 138 miles, and our latitude by observation was 17° 24'.

(166) Thursday the 16th we had fair weather, and a moderat gale from the east-north-east unto the southeast. Our course was west by south, and our distance sail'd theron 126 miles, and our latitude by observation was 16° 14'.

Fryday the 17th we had fair weather all day, but squalls of rain at night. We had a good gale from the east by north unto the southeast. Our course was west by south, our distance sail'd theron was 126 miles, and our latitude by observation was 16° 35'. This day the convicts had their day's allowance of bread and other provitions deliver'd ofto them at noon, becaus some of them otherwise would have ben starved. For now haveing won away one the others cloths, they began to play for the victualls,* soe that some had two or three men's allowance and those that lost it like to starve. And soe this course was taken to prevent this disorder. Also this day all the convicts except the nave Popish priest [blank] Hide,[7] and an Irish ladd called Teig were sett at liberty from their irons. But those two remained soe resolut and disorderly, that they were stapled down to the deck in the darke lazareta, to see if this sable retierment would mitigate their stubourn and resolut spirits.

Saturday the 18th we had a good gale from the east-north-east and fair weather. Our course was west, and distance sail'd theron was 123 miles; our latitude by observation was 16° 20'. In the evening 'twas a easie gale.

7. This seems to be William Hicks, as above.

(167) Sunday the 19th we had squals of rain and the wind blew hard from the east by south unto the south. Our course was west 02° 00' northerly; our distance sail'd theron was 93 miles, and our latitude by observation was 16° 23'.

Moonday the 20th we had fair weather, and a good gale from the southeast to the east. Our course was west 02° 30' southerly, our distance sail'd theron was 78 mils, our latitude by observation was 16° 51'.

Tewesday the 21st we had fair weather and a moderat gale from the east to the east by south. Our course was west 03° 15' southerly; our distance sail'd theron was 111 miles, and our latitude by observation was 16° 21'. This afternoon we met the ship *Victoria* of New England, which came from Maryland, and was bound to Barbados, and that day had bin in the latitude of 16° 40' and he now by his work was distant from the Desiada[8] 520 miles at this day noon.

Wensday the 22d we had fair weather, and a fresh gale from the east by south to the east. Our course was west 02° 00' northerly, our distance sail'd theron was 219 miles, and our latitud by observation was 16° 21 minutes.

Thursday the 23d we had fair weather, and a good gale from the east to the southeast. Our course was west 07° 00' northerly, our distance sail'd theron was 93 miles, our latitude by observation was 16° 34' (168). About one in the afternoon we spoke with the *Swan* pinck of Bristol,[9] bound for Antego, and had bin from Milford in five weeks and two days.

Fryday the 24th we enjoyed a good faire weather, and a brisk gale from the east by south to the east. Our course was west by south, our distance sail'd thereon was 108 miles, and our latitude by observation was 16° 11'.

Saturday the 25th we had fair weather, and a good gale from the east by south. At six in the morning we mad the island of Desrada, lieing in the latitude of 16° 20'. This island bore from us north-north, and distant 40 miles, and then appeared thus, as the figure presents: [figure omitted]. This island of Desrada is one of the Caribe Islands of about 30 mils round. 'Tis now inhabited by none, for the French have of late twice tried to setle it, but the Indians have come from the other islands in their canoes and cut them of, soe that 'tis now neither inhabited nor planted. Nither is their any catle theron but som few gotes, soe that their resort none thither saveing the wandering Indians which sometimes visit it. Our course since yesterday noone to today at noon hath bin west by north 1/2 northerly, and our

8. This is La Désirade, lying just to the east of Guadeloupe; see figure 10 for the route of the *Saint George* through the Caribbean Sea. Many of the islands quoted by Taylor may be identified on this map. It was common practice for captains to verify their position by hailing other vessels, newly come from land.

9. The *Swan* was bound for Antigua and had come from what is now Milford Haven.

Figure 10 Map of part of the West Indies, from *The English Pilot.* Here we see the general map of the West Indies, showing the island of "Desseada", where the *Saint George* entered the Caribbean Sea, and then the successive islands: Montserrat, Puerto Rico, Hispaniola (Haiti) and so forth.

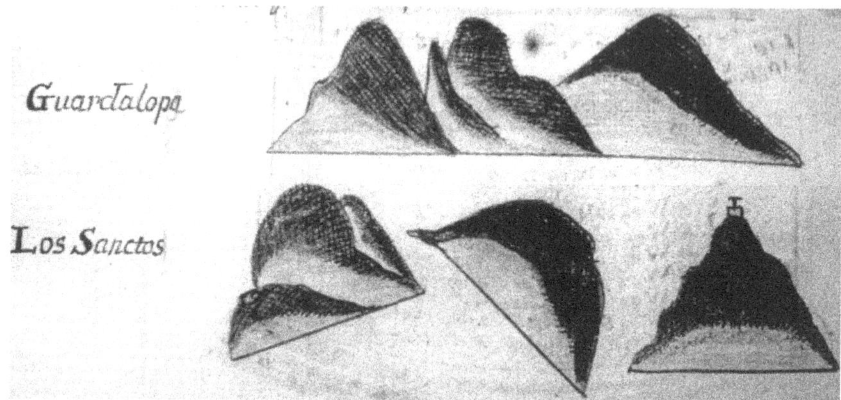

Figure 11 Taylor's "profile" of Guadeloupe and the Saints, page 170. Seventeenth-century sailors made much use of "profiles" or "landfalls", which were attempts to identify islands by showing what their appearance was from the sea.

distance sail'd since then hath bin 111 miles, and our latitude by observation was 10° 17'. Thus haveing obtained a sight of this known land, it will be necessary hereunto to annex a nauticall table callculated according to the work of the voige [figure omitted].

(170) Now to proceed on our discourse. This being the day of Our Saviour's nativity, we happylie again enjoyed sight of land and we had brave, fair, warm weather, full as hot now as 'tis in England in the midst of summer. Thus we continued on our course, sailing allong thro' these Caribe islands, soe that at noon the island Guardalope bore from us north and distant 9 miles. This is a high rockie island, not verey woody, and is not planted nor inhabited by any, only the native Indians. This island when it is posnated [?] as aforesaid, appeareth thus: [figure 11].

About one in the afternoon we were abrest of the Sanctus Islands. They are three high, barren rockey islands, not woody. They are not inhabited nor planted, but sometimes the Indians resort from those of the Caribe islands, which they inhabite, thither. One the top of one of these islands is a hermit's house. These are barren and very high islands, and when they beare north and distant six miles, they all appeare thus: [figure 11].

(171) Now we had sight of Mountserrat, which bore from us northeast and distant by estimation 18 mills. This island is a high rock island, inhabited by English and French, and appeareth thus: [figure omitted].[10] About three a'clock we had sight of the island of Antego. It then bore from us south, distant about twenty mils. This island is a commodious island, and planted and inhabited by the English, and then appeared thus: [figure omitted].

10. Taylor is here probably thinking of the island of St Kitts, shared at this time by the England and French.

Sunday the 26th we had fair weather, and a good gale from the east-south-east. Our course was west 04° 00' northerly, our distance sailed was 120 miles; our latitude by observation was 16° 40'. At noon we made Insula Sancta Cruze, distant 50 mils, and bore from us northeast by north, and appeared as the figur "C" [figure omitted]. And also we made Sabia, bearing from us north east by north, and distant 45 mills, and appeared as the figure at "H" [figure omitted].

(172) Moonday the 27th we had some showers of rain, and a moderat gale from the east by south to the northeast. Our course was west 0° 00' northerly, our distance sail'd theron was 124 miles, and our latitude by observation was 17° 13'.

Tewesday the 28th we had fair warm weather, and a good gale from the east by south to the northeast. Our course was west by north, our distance sail'd was 138. This day we observed not as haveing sight of known land. At eight this morning the west end of Porto Rico bore from us northeast, distant 21 miles, which then appeareth thus: [figure omitted].

Wensday the 29th we had some showers of rain, and a fresh gale from the east to the northeast by north. Our course was west 1° 00' northerly, and distance sail'd theron was 166 miles. At six last night we made the island Savona at the east end of Hyspaniola. It bore from us north, and distant 18 miles; 'tis verey low (172) land. And at eight we were to the westward of the city of Sancto Domingo (the metropholis of the island of Hispaniola), from whence toward Cape Alta Vela are fouer great hills tending with low points to the east and west. At noon the westermost highland bore north-north-west, and distant by estemation 21 mils, and lies to the westward of Santo Domingo 60 miles. And from this land runs away a low point, south west, to Cape Alta Vela, distant 30 mils. At 2 a'clock in the afternoon the island Beate bore from us southwest by south, tis very low land, an island about 12 mills round, all which I should have given you the draughts* and prospects of. But because when we come to describe the island of Hispaniola and islands adjacent we shall fully describe it (in page [blank]),[11] we therefore for brevity sake omitt it here. Now also the island Cape Alta Vela bore from us north, and distant 9 mills. 'Tis a high round rock, or rather hillock of red sand, wheron nothing growes, about a mile round at ye base, and now appeared thus: [figure omitted]. It lies in the latitude of 17° 20'.

Thursday the 30th we had faire weather, and a fresh gale from the east-north-east, to the east. Our course was west 04° 00' southerly, and our distance sail'd was 154 miles. At 6 a'clock in the morning Illa Vacus (or Cow Island), bore from us north, and distant north 15 miles. This island is verey

---

11. The description of Hispaniola is found on pages 59–65 of this present edition.

(174) low land, being in the latitude of 17° 18', and to ye westward of Cape Alta Vela 108 miles, and appear'd to us now thus: [figure omitted].

Fryday the last we had fair weather, and a moderate gale from the east to the north-north-east. Our course was west 10° 00' northerly, and our distance sail'd was 104 mils. At 8 in the morning we spoke with two sloops* which belonged to Jamaica, and were bound to windward. And at noon, Cape Tiberon (or Sharck) bore from us northeast by east, and distant 36 miles, At six in the eavening it rained verey hard. Thus this yeare is finished, and we leave this John Taylor in good health, and still mellancholy, whoe to devert himself made it his buisiness to keepe a nauticall account of the ship's way, and to draw according to perspective optique all the prospects of all notable headlands etc. Thus we end this year 1686.

January 1687

Saturday being New Year's Day we had brave fine weather, and a good gale from the east to the southwest by south. At noon we espied the northeast part of Jamaica (175), which bore from us west, distant by estimation 112 miles. Our course was south, and distance sail'd 26 miles.

Sunday the second we had much rain, and a small gale from the south to the southeast. At six last night Yallows[12] on the southside of Jamaica bore from us west 1/2 southerly, distant 45 miles. At 2 in the afternoon we came to anchor six miles off of Porta Royalla Point, to the eastward. At six this morning we spook with ye *Faulcon.*[13]

Monday the 3d we had a fine day, and a good gale from [blank]. About ten a'clock in the morning we wayed, and about noon we came to anchor in Port Royall harbour, in 11 fathom water. And here we found 56 sale of merchant men, and about 70 sloops of the island. Being thus come to anchor, the convicts were all let out of irons, and our pinnace* prepared to goe ashore. This day we had a new moon about 55 minutes past five in the eavening in the meridian [blank], but according to the meridian of this place, the new moon happned twenty minutes past noon, for here is 5 hr 30 min meridianall difference. Thus the ship *St George* of London is saff arrived at hir desired port, and we leave this John Taylor in good health, and making preparation to goe ashore, and thus we conclude this sixth chapter of the history of our live and travells.

12. This landfall was named after the Spanish *hato de ayala.*

13. HMS *Falcon,* a frigate, had operated off the coast of Scotland in the summer of 1685, as Taylor explains in the early pages of this history. Eventually, as we shall see, he spent many months on board her; see figure 16.

Chapter VII

(176) Of our liveing at Jamaica in the West Indies, with a full account of our life, and of all remarkable passages which happened unto us there, from the third of January untill the twenty-sixth of May ensuing, in Anno Christi 1687.

Haveing in the former chapter given an account of our arrivall at the island of Jamaica, one of the Peruvianian[1] islands of America, now under the royall scepter of His Majestie of Great Britain, James the Second, and inhabited and planted by the English, and governed by his Grace Christopher, Duke of Albermarle, and his Deputie the right worshipfull Hender Molesworth Esquire, we now come to give an account of our sucess there.

Now you must understand that about two a'clock in the afternoon on Moonday the third of January 1687, this John Taylor went on shore with Captain Janes, and some gentlemen of the place, which were come on boarde to wellcome (177) Captain Janes to the port. And being come one shore he went to dinner allong with some other gentlemen of Captain Janes' acquaintance, at an ordinary* at ye "George"[2] on Port Royall at Mrs Mann's,[3] where, haveing dined, Captain Jeans with his securities for his true tradeing at the Port (according to an Acct of the Island in that case made and provided)[4] went to Santa Jago de La Veiga to perform the accustomed dutie to the goyernour there residing, which was the Right Worshipfull Hender Molsworth Esquire, then Deputy Governor under his elected Grace the Duke of Albermarle.[5]

---

1. This strange word probably derives from the time when the name Peru was applied to the whole of South America.

2. This tavern was described in 1682 as "fronting to the old market place". See Michael Pawson and David Buisseret, *Port Royal, Jamaica* (Oxford, 1975; rev. ed., Kingston, 2000), 232.

3. Perhaps the wife of John Man, the surveyor-general. Ibid., 116.

4. This act governing trade in Jamaica is summarized under Taylor's list "of the laws and customs of Jamaica", p. 285.

5. The governor resided at what is now Spanish Town; the arrival of Albemarle was imminently expected.

Soe this John Taylor accompanyed them thither, in order to pay his respects to the Governour and deliver his letters of recomendation to him directed from the Right Worshipfull Sir Thomas Duck, Knight, and Mr. Jerimiah Arnold Esquire,[6] both members of the Merchants' Royall Company tradeing hither from London.

Soe they went in a wherry* from Port Royall to Passage Fort, and from there in a hackney coach* they went to Sainta Jago de La Viega, where about four a'clock they arived and had admitance forthwith to the Governour. And Captain Joans haveing dispatch't his buisiness, this John Taylor presented his letters to the Governour, which he did him the honour forthwith to read, and calling him into a privat rome said to him to this effect, (178) "Sir, these two worthy gentlemen by whome to me you are recomended are my worthy and much respected friends, and for their sakes assuer yourself that I will allways studie to serve you in anything I can. Therefore be at noe times slack to acquaint me with what you desire, and if it laies within my spheare, I will soon assist you therin. And sir, according to those cappacities, which by these worthy gentelmen you are recomended, you need not feare within a reasonable time but to meet with encouragement in some measure corresponding your merits. In the meantime assuer yourself that I will recomend you to ye gentry of this island, remain your friend and assist you in anything I can. Therefore in order to your employ, 'tis my advice for you to sell at Port Royall, it being the most commodious place for proffit and advantage on this island".

Here he ended, and after John Taylor had returned him suitable thancks to his extream sivility, he took his leave of the Governour, and with Captain Joans and the other gentlemen returned in the coach back to Passage Fort, and from thence in a wherry they went on bord the *St. George,* where they laie all night. But ye two gentlemen which were with us went in the wherry-bote ashor at Port Royall.

On Tewesday the fourerth of January, the ship *St. George* sail'd to the wharff over against *La Vera Cruze,* Alley, and began to unload, and this day John Taylor gott him a privat lodging at one (179) Thomas Tilbays[7] a merchant on Porta Royall, and gott his cloaths, books, and all his goods on shore to his lodging, where he lay all night. But his servants remain'd on bord with the other convicts untill ye day of sale (which according to an acct of the island is not to be untill the end of ten days after their arrivall there, that soe the planters may have notice thereof and soe supply themselves with such servants

6. These figures are hard to identify, though one of the Royal Africa Company merchants was Thomas Ducke. See K.G. Davies, *The Royal Africa Company* (London, 1957), 67.

7. This might be Thomas Tilley. See Pawson and Buisseret, *Port Royal,* 229.

as they want),[8] which would be on Wednsday the 12th of January ensueing. Haveing thus provided himself with a lodging, and gott his goods on shore, he intended on the morrow to goe and pay his respects unto the worshipfull Sir Francis Modyford, Knight, in order to deliver him his letter of recommendation from Mr. Thomas Boon, Esquire, of London, a merchant of the Royall Company, and now he remain'd ashore in health. But the hott weather occationed him to have an intolerable pain in the head, for it was extream hott and drie weather and had bin soe for about a month, soe that the country fear'd a drought, because that in the last and this month yt used to have seasonable ráines, which now failing was the occation of their feare.

On Wednsday the fifth Sir Francis Mudiford came to Porta Royalla, soe that thereby John Taylor's journey was saved. So he went to Mr. Cransborough's at the "Rose and Crown"[9] on Porta Royall, where he delivered him his letter from merchant Boon, and hee after the perusal thereof gave him good encouragment, promising him to doe what lay in his power for him.

(180) Soe after he had return'd him thancks for his curtisie and acceptance he took his leave of him, and return'd to his lodging. Now he remain'd at Porta Royall untill Friday the seaventh, on which day Captain Beachman, in the *Rose* ship of London, came to anchor in Porta Royall harbour.[10] And on Saturday the eight of January, the ship *Dove* of Boston, in New England, arived here to anchor. And on Sunday the ninth instant, the *Faulcon* friget return'd in from cruseing and came here to anchor.[11] This week we have had verey hott, drie weather, with much thunder and lightning.

Now this John Taylor remaines at Port Royall, makeing preparation for his imploy. And on Tewesday the eleventh a sloop belonging to Mr. Thomas King, of Port Royall, was seized by the King's Naval Officer here residing, to whit Captain Charles Talbot commander of the *Faulcon,* and Captain Willson,[12] for that the said sloop, contrary to a late acct of the country, had

8. This act is also summarized under Taylor's list "of the laws and customs of Jamaica", p. 285. It is not clear whom Taylor means by "Sir Francis Modyford"; "Thomas Boon" may be George Boun, an assistant of the Royal Africa Company. See Davies, *The Royal Africa Company,* 378.

9. This tavern cannot now, alas, be identified.

10. The Customs records show that Captain Francis Beauchamp brought the *Rose* of London into Port Royal on 10 January 1687. His cargo included twenty passengers, wine, flour and dry goods. National Archives, CO 142/13, fo. 22; see figure 12.

11. The logs of the *Falcon* have survived and show that she indeed came into Port Royal harbour in January 1687. National Archives, Adm 51/345.

12. Trading with the Spaniards was contrary to the Navigation Acts, which were enforced at Port Royal by the naval officer, Reginald Wilson. He was also responsible for compiling the Customs returns, which allow us to know which ships entered and left the harbour. See William Claypole and David Buisseret, "Trade Patterns in Early English Jamaica", *Jamaican Historical Review* 5 (1972): 1–19.

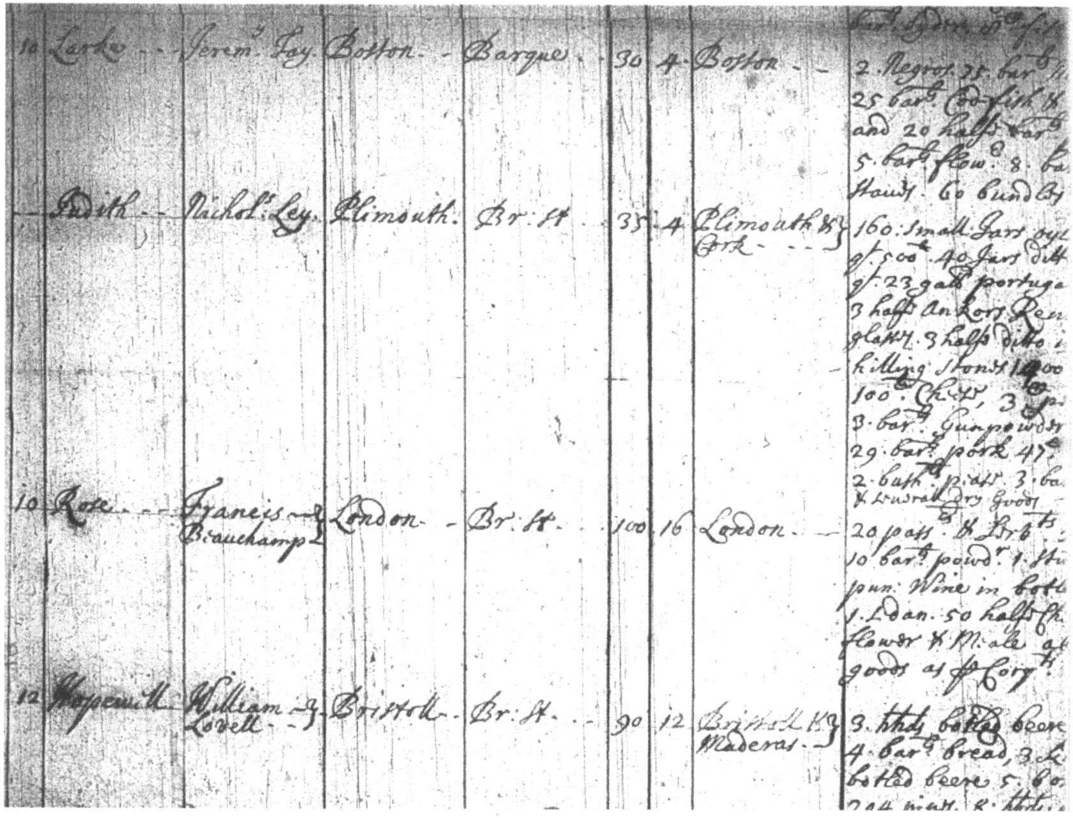

10	Larke	Jerem. Fay	Boston	Barque	30	4	Boston	2 Negros 35 bar[illegible] 25 bar. Codfish & and 20 halfe bar. 5 bar. flour 8 [illegible] Staves 60 bundles
	Judith	Nichol. Ley	Plimouth	Br: It	35	4	Plimouth & Cork	160 small Jars oyl [illegible] 40 Jars ditto [illegible] 23 galls [illegible] 3 halfe ankers [illegible] 3 halfe ditto [illegible] 100 [illegible] 3 bar. Gunpowder 29 bar. pork [illegible]
10	Rose	Francis Beauchamp	London	Br: It	100	16	London	20 potts [illegible] 10 bar. powd. [illegible] Wine in bottles [illegible] 50 halfe [illegible] flower & Meale [illegible] goods as [illegible]
12	Hopewell	William Lovell	Bristoll	Br: It	90	12	Bristoll & Maderas	3 hhds bottled beere 4 bar. bread, 3 [illegible] botled beere 5 [illegible]

Figure 12 Part of the registers of the Naval Officer at Port Royal, to show the entry concerning Francis Beauchamp (National Archives, CO 142/13, fo. 22). These registers were kept in accordance with the Navigation Acts, to ensure that all vessels followed the rules concerning ownership by English shippers.

bin a-trading with the Spaniards, the which being proved, the said sloop was forfeited and seized unto His Majestie's use.

Wednsday the twelfth of January, being the tenth day after our arrivall here, and the day of sale of the convicts and servants, Captain Joans about 10 a'clock in the morning hoisted up his ensigne,* and fiered a gun according to the custom, to give notice therof. Soe now this John Taylor went on board, and had the opportunity to dispose of his three servants. He sold his man servant, Charles Gold, for sixty dollars, to Mr. William Pott, the marsharall at Port Royall, and he sold Ann Sharp to Mr. More, a merchant in Port Royall for 45 dollars, and his other servant Susanah Carseldon he sold to Mr. Colson vintner at Withywood for 40 dollars.[13] Soe that his three servants yeilded him 145 dollars, that is £36–05s–00d according to ye custome of the island. His

13. None of these three purchasers can be identified.

servants being thus sold, (181) he payed Captain Joans 72 dollars or 18 pounds for their passage.

Soe that all his goods being on shore, his servants sold, [and] their passage discharged, he had a generall discharge from Captain Joans and soe he went ashore. Now after he had paid Captain Joans the 72 dollars, he found he had remaining 73 dollars or £18–5s–od pounds, soe that by these servants, computing their fees and other charges, he got clear 45 dollars or £9–15–00 sterling, which was not soe considerable profitt as he expected. Also by this time he had disposed of all his other goods, and he found after all his expenses were discharged, he had bye him about 225½ dollars, which according to the custom of the island was £56–07–06, but in sterling was but £48–17–04. Soe he found by profit on his goods, and exchange of mony, full twenty pounds sterling he had gained by this voige. This day Captain Joans disposed of all his convicts, and last night one of them whose name was Lancelot Lucon[14] fell overboard and was drown'd. And this day Captain Joans haled of from the wharf, haveing unloded etc. his ship. Thus we leave this John Taylor indeferent in health, ashore at his lodging, whoe now haveing completed his maritime affaier, resolved in the beginning of the next week to prosecute his imploy, soe that this week we have had nothing else worthy note. Only on Saturday the 15th, the ship *Phillip and Martha* came here to anchor from the Bay of Campechay loaden with logwood.[15] All this week we have had verey hot, dry weather, with much thunder and lightning and strong sea, and land breezes.

Now to proceed on our discourse, you must know that on Monday the 17th of January this John Taylor went from Port Royall to Sainta Jago de la Viega about some buissiness of his employ, intending to return ye next Wedensday, being 19th instant. But it soe pleased the Divine power (182) of Heaven to afflict him with a tedious fitt of sickness. For on Tewesday, the 18th of January, he was seized with a vidious quotidan feaver, which encreased violently on him, soe that he was constrained to remaine at St. Jago de la Vega, and lodged at one Mr. Bond's there, at ye signe of the "Crowne".[16] Being thus seized, and the feaver encreasing, Dr. Trapham was sent for to him, whoe ingeniously did what he could for him, soe that he was let bloud fower times, and underwent emeticks, vicicelors etc., but nothing prevailed to

14. This must be the unfortunate young man formerly identified as Thomas Lucon.

15. In fact, the *Philip and Martha,* Captain Jeremiah Conway, a Jamaican sloop of sixteen tons carrying logwood, was entered in the Customs records on 25 February 1687. National Archives, CO 142/13, fo. 13.

16. It has so far proved impossible to identify this tavern, in spite of recent intensive research at Spanish Town.

abate the malignatie of the destemper, soe that Dr. Trapham and Dr. Rose[17] gave it as their opinion that he would die of this destemper, the which continued violently on him untill the end of this January, with noe signe of ammendment nor hopes of recovery, soe that he was reduced to perfect weakness. Howe're the phisition used all means convenient, if possible he might recover his health again.

Thus we conclude this month, and leave this John Taylor being verey weeak at St. Jago, tho' still it plesed God to give him his sences patiently to bear this afflictions, hoopeing that God would yet restor him to health, and lengthen out his days, that he might happily return to his dear relations, and end his dayes in peace in his native country, which he much desiered.

Now we intend in this our history to keep a constant account of the time, as near as possible. Therefore 'twill be necessary here to note, that on Moonday the third, about 55 minutes past 5 a'clock at night, the moon assumed to himself an increasing light, and on Moonday the 10th, at 24 minutes past noon, the moon was at hir first quarter. On Tuesday the 18th, at 27 minutes past 1 afternoon received his full borrowed light, and on Wednesday ye 28th, past one in the afternoon, the moon was deprived of half his borow'd glory, in the latitude of London. But if you would have the exact variation of the lunatary light, according (183) to ye latitude of Port Royall, on ye island of Jamaica, you must know their is 5 houers and 30 minuts meridianall difference[18] betwixt it and ye meridian of the famous city of London, according to which the new moon happen'd here on Monday the third, 20 minutes past noon, in the meridian of Port Royall. The which being prescribed, we conclud this remarck of our time in this month of January, Anno Christi 1687. All this month here was noe rain.

February 1687

To return to our discourse again. Wheras in the end of the last month we left this John Taylor verey sick and weak, soe in the beginning of this month we find him, whoe soe remained without any signe of amendment, untill Thursday the 10th of February, on which day thro' divine mercy his fever began to abate, soe that now, contrary to all expectations, their was hopes of

17. Thomas Trapham was a leading doctor at Jamaica at this time, and the author of *A Discourse of the State of Health in the Island of Jamaica* (London, 1679), which Taylor occasionally cites. I learn from Dr James Robertson that "Dr Rose" is presumably Hans Sloane's future father-in-law. These family connections are unravelled in the introduction to D. Crossley and R. Saville, eds., *The Fuller Letters 1728–1733: Guns, Slaves and Finance* (Sussex, 1991).

18. The difference is about 77 degrees, which is a little over five hours.

his recovery, and on Tewesday the 15th his fitts missed him, and on the 17th being Thursday he satt up, while his beed was made, which before he had never done since Tewesday the 25th January last. And soe he satt up daily, and remained exceding mallancholy and weak untill the end of this month, and was not able to walk the length of his chamber without the assistance of one to support him. In this his sickness, towards the later end of this month, he was verey pencive and sorowfull, conceiveing in his mind that God laid this heavey judgement on him, because he put not his trust in God's Divine Providence, in reference to his support and well being in England, and to punish him thus for this his rash leaveing of wife and relations.

This lay heavey upon his spirit, and was a sore trouble unto him, soe that he was much dejected, and soe remained untill Sunday the 27th, at which (184) time he received much comfort from the saying of the learned Saint Austen, which then came fresh in his memory, which was this: "Unde autem timor, quia judex venturus est? Nunquid injustus? Nunquid malo volus? Nunquid invidus? El nihil horum. Quis ergo venturus est? Quare no gaudes? Quis venturus est judicare te, nisi qui venit judicari propter te?" i.e., "And why art thou afraid (saith S. Austen) that he should come as a Judge? Why, is he an unjust Judge? Is he a malitious Judge? Is he envious and spightfull? Noe, not at all, and whoe then shall come to judge thee? Why dost though not rather joy therat? That he who shall be thy judge is he who in time past came himself to be judged for thee". And again in another place saith St. Austen: "Perversum est, et nescit utrum venum, quem diligis, timeri ne veniat; orare veniat regnum tuum, et timere ne exaudiaris. Optas ut veniat, quem times ne veniat: corrige te, ut non ores contra te." "This is" (wieth St. Austin), "perverse dealing, and far from sincerity, to feare his comming whom thou saith thou used to pray that his kingdom come, and yet to fear that thou should not be heard. Doest thou desier his comeing, whom thou fearest least he should come? Why then amend thyself, lest thou prayest against thyself".[19]

These words of that ancient Father, with some pretious promises in the holy scripture, comforted and revived his dejected spirits, soe that he was fully perswaded that God in his due time would remove this affliction from him. Whereupon he rested contented under his misery, resolving to trust in God's mercy, which was able to give all thing for his own glory sake. Thus he rested fully satisfied therein, being assisted therto by the saying of the learned Tertullian, which then (185) came fresh into his memory, which is thus: "Proinde a quo petam ut accipiam? Apud quem quaeram ut inveniam? Ad que pulsabo ut aperiatur mihi quis habet petentiare, nisi cujus omnia, cujus sum etiam ipse qui petavit"; ie., "Therefore of whom shall I ask, that I may

19. It has so far proved impossible to find this saying in the works of St Augustine.

receive? At whom shall look, that I may fiend? At whom shall I knock, that it may be opened unto me? Who hath to give to him that asketh, but he whose are all things, whos also I am?" These words of Tertullian added much comfort to him.[20] Thus wee leave him sick and weak in an unknown country, and among strangers whoe were extreamly sivill to him. Many worthy gentlemen of the island came daylie to visit him, and his worthy friends Dr. Trapham and Dr. Rose used all dilligence for his recovery.

Now to proceed in our prescribed method of this our history, 'twill be necessary to observe that on Wednsday the 2nd of this month, 23 minuts past 6 in the eavening, the moon began to borrow its wonted light from the golden raies of the sun. On Tewesday the 8th, at 28 minuts past 11 at night, the terrean body of the moon was half illuminated by ye generous sun. On Thursday the 17th, at 27 minuts past 7 in the morning, the moon received his full borrowed light, and on Saturday the 20th, two minutes past two in the morning, the terrean body of the moon was deprived of half hir borrowed glory. In the meridian of London also know that Shrow Sunday[21] hapned on the sixth of this month. All this month nowe we have had noe raine, but much thunder, lightning, and strong bress of wind, soe that the planters begin to want for provitions, and greatly feare a dearth. And thus we conclude this month of February.

March 1687

To procede on our discourse in a genuine method, you must know that (186) this John Taylor remained verey week untill the 20th of March, not being able to walk abrod, nor to walk without a staff to help support his feble body, which by this sickness was worn away to a semeing skeliton. Yet nevertheless he remain'd cheerfull and contented under this affliction, in hopes of a recovery to his perfect health again. Now on Thursday the 24th at night, he had a most remarckable dreame, which we have thought fitt here to insert, which was thus.

He dreamed he was in an unknown place, walking, which to his knowledge in all his travels he never saw, and entering in at a gate he continued walking, as it were up a step hill. But being weary, he look't back, but the gate was vanish't, soe that he saw noe sight thereof, nor nothing like the place which he before saw. But on his right hand was now a huge, highe stone wall, and on his left, a craggy, rocky, steep cleave.* And the passage

20. The words are found in Tertullian, *Adversus Marcionem*, book 4, ed. Ernest Evans (Oxford, 1972).

21. Shrove Sunday, Monday and Tuesday precede Ash Wednesday.

wheron he stood, betwixt the wall and the cleave, was verey narrow, soe that he was much troubled, fearing he should fall over the deep cleave. Soe he thought to returned back towards the place where the gate was, takeing great care for fear of falling. For the passage was scatter'd with broken stones and rubish which sem'd to him to be left by workmen, at the building of the wall, which seemd newly finished; therfor he fear'd stumbling at those scater'd stones. But being come down to the place where the gate was, he found nothing but a high rock joyning to the wall and extending itself to ye edge of the cleave. Being much trobled to thinck how he should get out of this dismall place, he looked about to find a way out, but could fiend none. At last he espied a hole thro' the rock, where the gate was, thro' the which he attempted to gett out, first with his head foremost, then with his feet, but all in vain, for he could not get thro' the hole in the rock, Whilst he was thus striveing, he heard (187) a voice behind the hole in the rock spak and say: "Had it not bin for this strong wall, many would be undon forever". Then the voies stop't, and after some sillence the gate againe appeared, and the rock vanished, and there came in at the gate a lusty, fatt, portly gentelman (by his semeing garb), whoe took him by the hand, and leading him out thro' the gate bid him be carfull for the futur. Upon which this John Taylor awoake, and was much much trobled therat, but at last conceiving it a signe of his deliverance from his present greivious sickness, he was much comforted therby in hopes of deliverance.

Thus it pleased God to give him an answer to his prayers, and a signe of deliverance, for this day he was much better than ever he had binn in all his sickness, and soe grew better and better, unto the end of March, but was not strong enough to walk abroad, for as yet he remain'd very week. Thus his case stood untill ye end of March 1687.

Now must we deragate* from our discourse, and tell you the remarkeable occurances which happened in our native country in this month, the which since our return home from the West Indies we have gather'd from the notes of a learned and worthy friend of mine, in the prosecution of which you must understand that His Majesty of Great Britain, James the Second, was pleased for the true contentment of his desenting Protestant subjects to put forth an order of conncil, for to grant all liberty of concience in the worship of God. Thus in his declaration which came forth, he declared to heartily desire to unite all his subjects in a bond of peace and love that soe all persicutions might be layed asid. This His Majestie's declaration for liberty of concience came forth on Fryday the 25th of March, and was to begine on Easterday being the 27th of this instant, (188) March Anno Christi 1687. This His Majestie's gratious declaration for liberty of concience and tolleration being come forth, the desenting Protestants of most parts of Great Britain made their humble address of thancks to His Majestie for this new liberty.

And because I may never forgeet my native island, I shall here insert their addresse, which was thus as followeth, according to ye originall coppy:

The humble address of the desenting Protestants of the Isle of Wight, unto his Sacred Majesty of Great Britain, James the second:[22]

> We Your Majestie's humble devoted subjects durst not adventured to have presented our addresse, loaden with thanckfullness to your royall hands, for your most gratious declaration for liberty to us, in the service of God, had not your seren acceptance of others, and a deeper sence of our duty, given birth therto. 'Tis not, dread soveraigne, dissembling flattery, which is but guilded hypocrasie, but the reall sentyments of loyall verety, which has moved us to soar soe high, being perswaided the omission of what we now humbly perform, would be noe less enjurous to your Sacred Majesty (to whom under God we enjoy our liberty), than it can be offencive thus to presume to offer up our sacrifice of thanckfullness to your sacred self. Your Majesty have to your eternall honour rightly attributed to ye great God (whose deputie you are) the sole monarchy 'ore the consciens, concurring therin with many noble Princes before, which divine oracle you have fully and freely proclaimed (189) to the constant judgement of your royall mind, and by your gratious acct evidenced the same, wherof we reap the benifitt. Now the God of Princes recompence your royall favour, bless your seren majesty with long days of government, uninterrupted health, felicity in all your royall relations, guide your great councill and afaires, and at last crown you with everlasting joy in Heaven and eternall glory and honour on earth, which is the prayer of your faithfull and loyall subjects. May it please Your Majesty. the hearts of your loyall subjects are like Rebecca's wombe[23] in which loyallty and gratitude strives for the preeminance, but we prefer loyalty in the first place, and in the second we present gratitude for Your Majestie's gratious declaration, under the sunshine of this Your Majestie's gratious tolleration and protection. May we live to the glory of God, and a faithful obedience to your sacred Majesty, to whom we wish perpetuall felicity.

On Moonday the 28th of this instant, March, Anno 1687, at Hereford, hapened a violent storme about three a'clock in the afternone, continueing untill about six a'clock.[24] It threw down the steple of the church and other buildings, killed about 13 persons, and hurt many others. At six it began to thunder and lighten dreadfully, with hailestones as bigg as eggs, after which followed an earthquacke, and about 9 a'clock at night appeared a great light as at noonday, out of which appeared two arms and two hands. In the right hand was a drawn sword, and in the left a cupp of blood. Also in the aire

22. Perhaps *The Humble Address of the Presbyterians . . .* (London, 1687).

23. Jacob and Esau, contending brothers, came from the womb of Rebecca, Genesis 25:22.

24. England is periodically visited by severe storms; it was probably mentioned in an almanac.

there appeard a cornfield reddy to be mown, and a sith lieing by itt (190). And a voice was heard to cry, "Wo, Wo, Wo, to these inhabitants, for he cometh which shall come, and you shall see him". At which the people were much afrighten'd and made a great outcry. And many women for fear fell in travel, amongst which was one Mrs. Mary Palmer, which then was dellivered of three children, which had all teeth, and spoke.[25] The first said, "The days appointed that none shall stand". The second said, "Where shall be liveing to burey the dead?" And the third said, "Where shall be bread for the hungary?" And then, they all died. The mother being in a destracted maner sone expier'd after them. This sadd catastrophy is of a certain truth, soe known 'ore all that county, and the whole British nation.[26] Also at the same day it rained abundance of wheat in the city of Salsbury, and county of Wiltshire, which thousands of people are eye witnesses too. Also the divile appear'd to the prisoners in Dorchester Jayle.[27]

Now before we conclude this month, you must note that in the meridian of London, the moon began to assume its borrowed light from the refulgent raies of the glorius Phebus on Thursday the 3rd, 3 minutes past 4 a'clock in the afternoon. On Thursday the 10th, at 49 minutes past 8 at night, the moon was half illuminated. On Fryday the 18th, at 17 minutes past midnight the terrene body of the moon received its full borrowed lusture, and on Saturday the 26th, at 47 minutes past 10 before noon, the moon was deprived of half hir borrowed glory. All this month we have had here very hott weather, with much tunder and lightning, and small bries.* Only about the middle of the month, we had som few showers of rain, which signified nothing to prevent the drought feared. Soe that all things began to get very deare, and plantation provition begines to faille, and English provitions to be now verey deare.[28] Thus ends March.

April 1687

(191) Returning to our discourse againe, wheras towards the late end of the last month John Taylor's fitts left him, and he began to gather strenght, soe now on Sunday, the 3d of this month, it pleased God to enable him to walk abrod. Soe that he went to St. Paul's Church in Sainta Jago de la Vega, and

25. Mary Palmer's history probably also comes from an almanac.

26. This is a relatively early use of the adjective "British", for although James I had become "King of Great Britain" in 1604, the geographical entity did not correctly exist until the Union of 1707.

27. This too sounds like an extract from an almanac.

28. "English" provisions, which had to cross the Atlantic Ocean, would indeed become dear if the local provisions such as corn and yam became scarce.

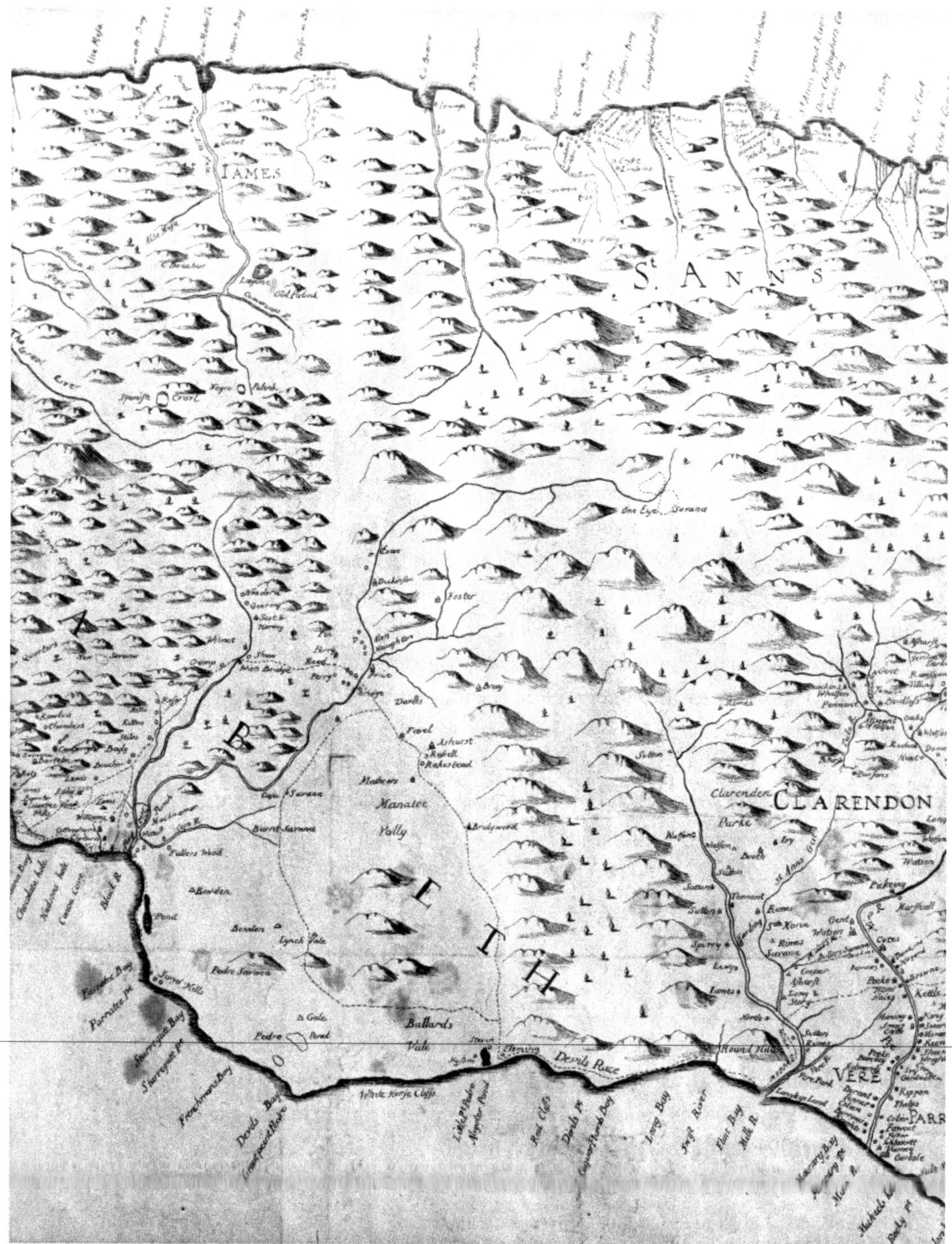

Figure 13 Detail from *A New and Exact Map of Jamaica* by Bochart and Knollis (London, 1684). On the bottom right of this image may be seen the Rio Minho to the right and the Milk River to the left. "Sutton" and "Rimes", where Taylor was employed, may be seen near the mouth of the Milk River.

heard Dr. Bennet preach, in which sermon he received much comfort.[29] Thus being become indeferent,*[30] on Thursday the 7th he paid all his debts, which he had incur'd in this his sickness to his phisitions, nurse, landlord, and other expences, which on the whole amounted to 32 pounds 12s 06d. Soe that thro' this expence he had left but 16 pounds 04s 10d sterling. Now on Fryday a worthy gentelman, one that had come to vissit him in this his sickness, came to town. His name was Francis Blackmor, a very loyall and worthy gentleman.[31] This gentleman and his lady coming to town, as you have head, perswaid this John Taylor to settle in there quarters, and goe down with them to their house, and take it for his home, untill such time as he had regained his strenght and setled himself. This kind profer of this worthy gentelman was by him kindly received and embrac't, so that on Moonday the 11th he went down with them in their coach to their house at Rimsbery in the presinct of Clarindon near Carlisle Bay (or Witheywood).[32] This Francis Blackmore Esquire was a verey wealthy gentleman, haveing two brave plantations for sugar and indigo, and about 250 Negro slaves.

This John Taylor being thus gon down into Clarindon, as you 'ave (192) heard, he was mighty kindly used by that worthy gentelman and his good lady, whoe used him more like a son or a brother than a stranger. For they provided all things for him, that soe he might recover his strenght again. Thus God in his Divine Mercey stir'd up this worthy gentleman, who was altogether a stranger to him, to be a semeing father by his kindness, and a reall friend by his assistance both by help and councill. Soe that now his dream was fullfil'd, for that gentelman which then lead him out of that gate did represent, and was the perfect idea, of this worthy gent who thus caryed him to his house, and took this tender care over him.

To proceed, being indeferent on the 18th of this instant Aprill, he received his truncks of books etc. from Port Royall, which were brought to Witheywood by watter,[33] and from thence to Mr. Blackmore's in his wain.* Thus John Taylor's strenght daylie encreased, and he made it his business to

29. Mr Bennett was listed as rector of the church at Yallahs in 1682. *Calendar of State Papers, America and West Indies, 1681–85* (London, 1898), 79. Perhaps he had come to preach at Spanish Town, though surely in the church of St James.

30. This term probably means that he was neither ill nor particularly well.

31. This is probably Francis Blackmore, member of the council, whose family came from Somerset in England; he died in 1697 and is buried in Spanish Town Cathedral. See Philip Wright, *Monumental Inscriptions of Jamaica* (London, 1966), 112.

32. Rhymesbury is about five miles west-south-west of May Pen, but it does not seem possible to identify the estate upon which Taylor would now spend some time. The little town of Carlisle, or Withywood, lay about ten miles south-east of Rhymesbury, at the mouth of the Rio Minho. See figure 13.

33. The roads were often difficult, so that heavy goods frequently moved on coastal sloops.

sirch and prie into the nature of all ye products of this island, and to collect their essence and natures. And by the latter end of this month, he became indefrent, and had an employ percured for him by this worthy gentleman (Mr. Francis Blackmore Esquire), worth no less than 150 pounds yearly. The employ was to look to his, and Thomas Sutton Esquire,[34] their Negro slaves, all their affaires, and accounts in their plantations. And he was to have resided at Mr. Blackmore's, whoe would have (beside his yearly salary) diet'd him at his own table, given him the keeping of a horse, and a Negro slave to wait on him. Thus God, thro' his divine mercey, deliver'd this John Taylor from his tedious sickness, restored his health, raised up friends for him in a strange country, and setled him in a good beinge.

(193) Thus we have given you the true state and condition of this John Taylor duering the whole term of this instant Aprill, the which we shall here conclude, after we have taken notice that on Saturday the 2nd at 8 minutes past 2 on the morning, the moon began to assume new encreasing light (in the meridian of the famous city of London). On Saturday the 9th, at 25 minutes past 2 in the afternoon, the moon was half illuminated by Phebus's golden raies. On Sunday, the 17th day at 18 minutes past 3 in the afternoon, the moon shin'd in its full borrowed glorey, and Sunday the 24th, at 2 minutes past 4 a'clock in the afternoon the *terrena luna** was deprived of half hir borrowed glory, in the meridian of London. But its variation of chang, in the meridian of Jamaica, must be calculated according to the merridianall difference of these two places. All this month we have had exceding hott, dry weather, with much thunder and lightning towards eavening, but noe raine to refresh the burned earth, and thus endes Aprill.

Maie 1687

Continueing on our discourse, you know that at the later end of Aprill last, we left this John Taylor at Mr. Blackmore's in Clarindon on Jamaica. Soe in the begining of this month there we fined him, indeferent, and intending the next week to begin on his aforesaid employ. But the divine power of Heaven thought fitt again to afflict him, for on Moonday the second of this instant May, he was violently seized with destemper called *illiace passio,* but by the inhabitants and phisitians there the dry belly achh, which increased soe violently on him that untill the 10th he lay as on a rack of torture, and (194)

34. Thomas Sutton died in 1710, and is buried in St Peter's Church, Alley. Wright, *Monumental Inscriptions*, 149. He had a series of estates along the Milk River in western Clarendon, not far from "Rimes", which is probably Taylor's Rhymesbury (figure 13). In 1690 "Sutton's" was the site of a major slave uprising. See Michael Craton, *Testing the Chains* (Ithaca/London, 1982), 76–77.

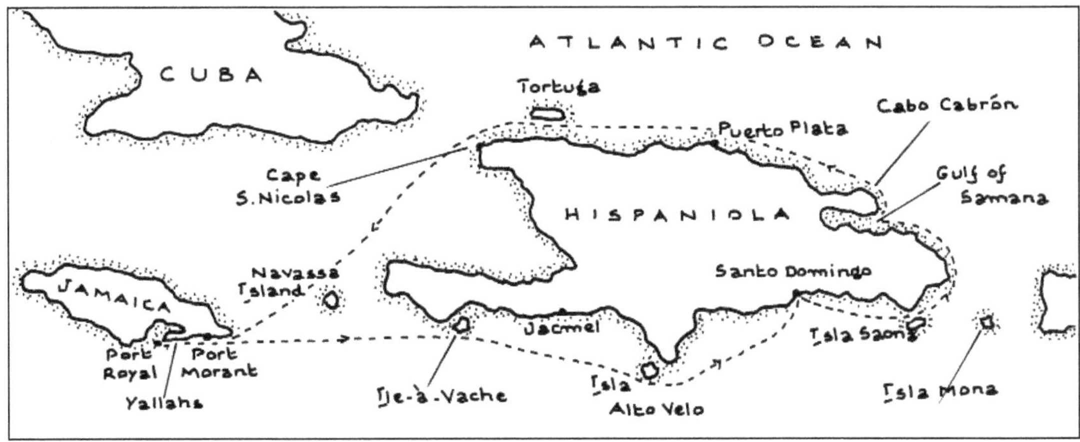

Figure 14 Map of the journey of HMS *Falcon,* May 1687–July 1687.

extream missery. Soe that one Dr. Sperry[35] was sent for to him, which applied thing sutable to the distemper,* which about the 15th of this month removed it. Now this physitian advissed him, that if this destemper seized him soe again (the mallignity was soe violent in this hott countrey), that it would endanger the loss of the use of his limbes, as it did to all whome it seized a second time. Some it had deprived for ever and others having bin seized therewith remain'd lame for two or three years and then but in part recover'd them, tho' never more (whilst they remain'd here) their perfect strenght. This was Whitsunday, to wit the 15th day.

John Taylor being again recovered remained exceding mallancholly, to thinck of his hard fate, thincking it the hand of God, to thus aflicte him for his wrash leveing his wife etc., and concidering in his late dream, he was fearfull least God should again thus aflict him, and he be deprived of his limbes, and soe be made therby uncapable of accting for his maintinance, should become misserable. He therefore resolved to returne home to England, and to live there with his wife in that estate God had called him to. Being resolved to return home, on Wednsday the 18th of May he took his leave of Mr. Blackmore & his much respected friends, and having his goods convey'd down to Witheywood Bay, he went the same day in a sloop from thence to Port Royall.

35. In his *Discourse of the State of Health in the Island of Jamaica,* Dr Trapham devotes a whole chapter to the "Dry Belly Ach", which he describes as "A dreadful Distemper". In fact, it seems to have been lead poisoning, brought on by drinking rum distilled in leaden pipes. See Carl Bridenbaugh and Roberta Bridenbaugh, *No Peace beyond the Line: The English in the Caribbean 1624–1690* (New York, 1972), 193–94. Dr Francis Sperry was noted as practising at Port Royal in 1673. Pawson and Buisseret, *Port Royal,* 224.

Being come to Port Royall, he went to lodg at Port Royall, resolveing at the first opportunity to return home to England. But soe it happened that being in company one day with the worthy gentelman Major Beckford, Governour of Charles Fort,[36] to whom (by the aforesaid friend of his Mr. Francis Blackmoor Esquire) he was recommend, the said (195) gentleman promised him to procure him his passag home in the *Faulcon* friget, which at the comeing of the Duke (which was daily expected) was to returne to England.[37] Soe Major Beckford recommend this John Taylor to Captain Charles Talbot, commander of the *Faulcon,* whoe on Saturday the 21st sent for this John Taylor, and after some discourse he order'd him to come on board, as soon as he had heer dispatch't his business, and promised him that he should act as his clearke, receive wages accordingly, and would diet at his table, and have all things commodious for his quallity, and further that he would doe him any kindness he could.[38] Thus John Taylor return'd him thancks and the worthy gentleman which procured this, and made preparation for his going on board. Thus God again assisted him.

But before we conclude, we shall take notice that ye moon began to assume hir new encreasing light on Sunday the first, at 40 minutes past noon. On Moonday the 9th the moon was possessed of half hir borrowed glory at 55 minutes past 7 in the morning. On Tewesday ye 17th the moon appear'd in hir full glory, att 4 minutes past 2 in the morning, and on Moonday ye 23rd the *terrena luna** was deprived of half hir borrowed lusture at 12 minutes past 6 at night. And on Moonday the 30th, the moon lost hir borrow glory, and at 54 minutes past midnight she began to encrease hir borrowed light, for then ye new moon happened in the meridian of London. And at Jamaica as is before shewed how to be knowledgeable of things being prescribed, we conclud this seventh chapter of the history of our life and travels.

36. This is probably Peter Beckford, Port Royal merchant and founder of a large Jamaican dynasty.

37. The Duke of Albemarle, the new governor, had fallen ill in England and did not arrive until Monday 19 December 1687, as Taylor describes below pp. 300–305.

38. In the introduction, Taylor mentions Captain Charles Talbot as having commanded HMS *Falcon* in Scotland during the summer of 1685.

Chapter VIII

(196) Of our goeing on board His Majesty's Ship Faulcon, with an account of the overthrow of the notorious pyrat Banister[1] *by Captain Charles Tolbot in the Faulcon, with an account of all notable passages which hapned to us, from the twenty-sixth of May, untill ye thirteenth of July following in Anno Domini 1687.*

Seeing in the former chapter we gave you an account of John Taylor, his resolutions of goeing on board His Majestie's Ship *Faulcon,* now at anchor in Port Royall harbour, under the comand of that worthy gentelman and valiant captain, Captain Charles Tolbot, we now come to procede on our discourse, in order to which you must understand that, on Thursday the twenty-sixth of May 1687, this John Taylor sent his books etc., and went himself on board the said ship, and was there entertain'd as cleark and was extreamly siviley entertained by that worthy Captain Tolbot and other officers. Soe he had a cabion provided for him in the stearage,* (197) and eat at the captaine's table. And he was somewhat weak and discontented, but seemed as cherfull as possible.

Now that we in this chapter may proceed in a due method, you must now know that on Fryday the 27th of this instant May, came in Captain Bartholomew from London in the ship *Mary,*[2] and also there came in a small ship from Dublin in Ireland, with a katch* which came from thence loaden with provitions, but were rob'd by ye notorious pyrat Banister in the *Golden Fleece* nere ye east end of Hyspaniola, takeing from the ship hir main mast and what else he pleased. And from the catch he took away hir whole cargo of beef, flower, and other Irish provitions.[3] This day we had hot, dry weather, with thunder and lightning.

---

1. For an account of the exploits of Joseph Bannister, see Pawson and Buisseret, *Port Royal,* 69–73.

2. In fact, the ketch *Mary* came in from Boston on 17 May 1687. CO 142/13, fo. 26.

3. Having escaped from captivity in Port Royal in January 1685, Bannister had since then been cruising off the east end of Jamaica. But he was captured in January 1687, and the engagement which Taylor is about to describe, accurately it would seem, in fact took place in June 1686, before Taylor joined the *Falcon.*

Saturday ye 28th we had verry hott weather, with much lightning and verey strong sea breezes.

Sunday the 29th we had orders from the Deputie Governor of Jamaica, Hender Molsworth Esquire, to prepare with all expedition to goe look for this pyrat Banister. This day the weather was as yesterday.

Moonday the 30th we were employed in geting on board a month's provition from the store house, and in takeing in watter, which was brought us by the Port Royall cannoas which were prest for expedition;[4] ye weather hot and dry.

Tewesday the last of May, in procecution of our orders, about five a'clocke in the morning we wayed, and the *Drake* with us (commanded by Captain Edward Spragg)[5] came to saile. And about eight, the breze being spent, we anchor'd to the eastward of Gun Key in 15 fadom water, and the *Drack* anchor'd by us. This day since we come to anchor we had wett squallie weather; thus endeth May.

June 1687

(198) On the first of June, being Wednsday, we waied with the *Drake,* and came to saile plieing to windward, to look for Banister.[6] At six in the afternoon Yallows Point bore from us east-north-east. This day we had faire hot weather with thunder.

Thursday ye second we had fair weather, and a moderat gale from the east to ye northeast. At six this evening Porta Morant bore from us northeast by east, and distant 9 miles.

Fryday the 3rd we had faire weather, and a moderat gale from the east-north-east to ye east by south.

Saturday the 4th we had faire, hot weather, and a moderat gale from the east by south, unto the east by north. At 10 this morning the east end of Jamaica bore from us southwest, and distant 21 miles.

Sunday the 5th we had fair weather, and a moderat gale from the east by north. Our course was by the logg, east 14° 00' southerly and our distance sailed was 16 miles. At six a'clock the island Navasa bore from us east-north-east, distant 15 miles and appeared thus: [landfall not reproduced]. This Navasa is a little low sandy island, whereon growes but little wood. 'Tis about

4. These "Port Royall cannoas" were used to fetch drinking water from the Rock, near present-day Rockfort; such vessels could be "pressed" into involuntary service just as seamen could be.

5. This cruise is described in Pawson and Buisseret, *Port Royal,* 72–73.

6. The various place-names and the rough track of the *Falcon* are identified on the accompanying map, figure 14.

two mills round, and exceding full of guaanas, the which we shall describe hereafter, when we come to treat of the products of Jamaica in America in page the [blank].

(199) Moonday the sixth we had faire weather, and a moderat gale from east-north-east to ye southeast by east. In the evening we had som raine. We mett Captain Doegood in the *Concord*.[7]

Tewesday ye 7th we had fair weather, and a moderat gale from ye southeast to ye east-north-east. At noon the east end of the Navasa bore from us south by east 2° 00' southerly, distant six miles. We found the curant here now to set strongly to the westward. At six in the eavening we made the wester cape of Hyspaniola called Tiberon, which then bore from us southeast by east, distant 12 miles. Now being to the northward of the Navasa, we found noe curant.

Wednsday the 8th we had fair weather, and a little wind variable on all points. At nine at night we came to anchor near Cape Tiberon in 28 fathom water.

Thursday the 9th we had a fair weather, and a good gale from the east-north-east. In the morning we wayed and came to saile, and at noon we came to anchor in a bay about 6 miles to the eastward of Cape Tiberon in 9 fathom watter, and our boats went ashore for watter.

Fryday the 10th we had fair weather, and a moderat gale from the east-north-east. At six this morning we wayed and came to saile, haveing goot on board some wood and water. At six at night Cape Tiberon bore from us northeast, distant 15 miles.

Saturday the 11th we had faire weather, and a moderat gale from the east by south to the northeast. At six in the eavening Cape Tiberon bore west by north, distant 21 miles.

(200) Sunday the 12th we had some raine, and a fresh gale from the east by north, to the southeast by east. At noon, Illha Vacus (or Cow Island) bore from us east by north, distant 15 miles, and at 7 in the evening, the tabular land of Hispaniola bore from us north distant 14 mills. This day John Taylor arived to the age of twenty-three years.

Moonday the 13th we had much raine, and a moderat gale from the us east to the southeast. In the morning we spook with the ship *Swallow* of Bristol, which came from Ireland, and was bound to Port Royall.[8] At six at night the west end of Illha Vacus bore from us north, distant 15 miles.

Tewesday the 14th we had misty wett weather but a moderat gale from

7. Captain Robert Doegood commanded the *Concord*, a large ship registered in London which left Port Royal for England the following October. National Archives, CO 142/13, fo. 118.

8. It does not seem possible to identify this ship.

the southeast to the southeast by east. At six at night Cabo Jaquemelo bore from us north by west, distant 21 miles.

Wednsday the 15th we had in the morning faire weather and a moderat gale from the southeast to ye east by north. At noone it became hazzy soe that we could not see land, but at six in the eavening 'twas cleare soe that St. Brigeh (on Hispaniola) bore southeast by east, distant 18 miles. This day 30 minutes past ten before noon the moon was at full.

Thursday the 16th we had fair weather, and a godd gale from the east by south to ye south by east. At six at night Illha Altavela (or high saile) bore east by south distant 12 miles.

Fryday the 17th we had fair weather and a fresh gale from the east to the east-south-east. At 8 this morning Illha Altavela bore from us northwest distant 11 miles.

Saturday the 18th we had fair weather and a strong gale from the east by north to ye east-south-east. At 10 in the morning the wind blew soe hard that it brought our main topmast by the board; (201) it broak in three peices. Soe we lay bie to repaire, and by six in the eavening, we had got up a new toppmast, and repaired all the damage, and then we began to make the best of our way, plieing to windward. Now Illha Altavela bore from us northwest by north, distant 9 miles.

Sunday the 19th we had fair weather, and a moderat gale from the east; at noon Altavela bore from us northwest, distant 21 miles.

Moonday the 20th we had fair weather and a good gale from the northeast by east to the east. At noon Illha Altavela bore from us northwest, distant 24 miles.

Tewesday the 21st we had fair weather and an easy gale from the east-south-east to the east-north-east. At noon Illha Altavela bore from us northeast by north, distant 21 miles. This day, 52 minutes past midnight ye moon was at first quarter.

Wednsday the 22nd we had fair weather, with an easy gale from the east by south to the northeast by east. Att 9 a'clock this morning we and the *Drack* came to anchor in Bahu Cavelero, on the south side of Hispaniola, in 24 fadom watter, with the easter low point (called the Salt Ponds) bereing from south by east and the two humocks, called the Vergin's Papps, bore from us north by east and we lay about a mile from the shore. Our boats went ashore to cut down wood and fill water in the afternoon.

Thursday the 23rd we had rainy weather, and a moderate gale from the east by south, and this day we got on board nine tunns of watter, and som wood. At six in the eavening we and the *Drack* wayed, and stod to windward to look for [blank] Banister according to our orders.

(202) Fryday the 24th we had some raine, and a moderat gale from the east

to the northeast. At noon the west point of S. Domingo bore from us north by east distant 24 miles, this being the feastday of Saint John the Baptiste.[9]

Saturday the 15th we had fair weather all day, but some raine at night; the wind blew from the northeast. At noon, Santa Domingo bore northeast by north from us, distant 12 miles, and about two a'clock, we with the *Drake* came to anchor there, in 7 fadom. The extream point of the citie to seaward bore from northwest by north, and the round tower on the east side the havena* on the point to seaward bore from us north-north-east distant one mile. Being com there to anchor, we saw a great many horsemen riding down to the shore, and they put out their flagg* on the round tower. We salutes them with 21 guns; they from the forts returns us as many again for thanck.

Soe the pinace being hoisted out and man'd, Lieut. Tho. Smith went to shore to have heard tidings of Banister. Being come to the shore, he was mett by the governor of the city, and about 100 horsemen; soe the governor would grant us noe produce, nor let us come on shore, but talk't to the lieut. in the barge, which they would not suffer to come within a boat's lenght of their wharfe. Soe jelously fearfull are these treacherous and prefidious Spaniards that they are afraid of their very friends least he should be as treacherous as they are base and servile spirited.[11] Thus the lieutenant after some discours with the governor of this city return'd on board.

Now this being the cheife citty both for largness, strenght, and (203) wealth on the island of Hispaniola we will here give you a true description thereof, with an accurrat mapp, or draught of the same, as it appear'd to us when we now lay there at anchor, which is thus as here followeth: [figure 15].

(204) This city of Santa Domingo is the metropolis of Hispaniola. It hath a commodious haven and a good depth of water, soe that ships can saile in or out full loaden, for you 'ave at least three fadom of water. The ships here hale close to the shore as at Bellens-Gate* and unloade.[12] 'Tis a city extreamly rich of a large extent. In it are many fair buildings, as their great cathedrall (as "a"), the Audienci or Governour's House (as "b"),the Placa Major (or market place) (as "c"). St. James Monastry (as "d"); also toward the westward point of the city next the sea is built a strong lunalary fort of twelve pieces of ordnance, bult to cleare the town if taken by latharone* or others. This city

9. The day 24 June is indeed the feast of St John the Baptist.

10. The journal kept by Lieutenant Thomas Smith is preserved at the National Archives, Adm 51/345.

11. Considering the activities of the English in the Caribbean, which had recently included the seizure of Jamaica, the cautious behaviour of the Spaniards is entirely understandable.

12. Billingsgate, in London, lay handily alongside the river Thames.

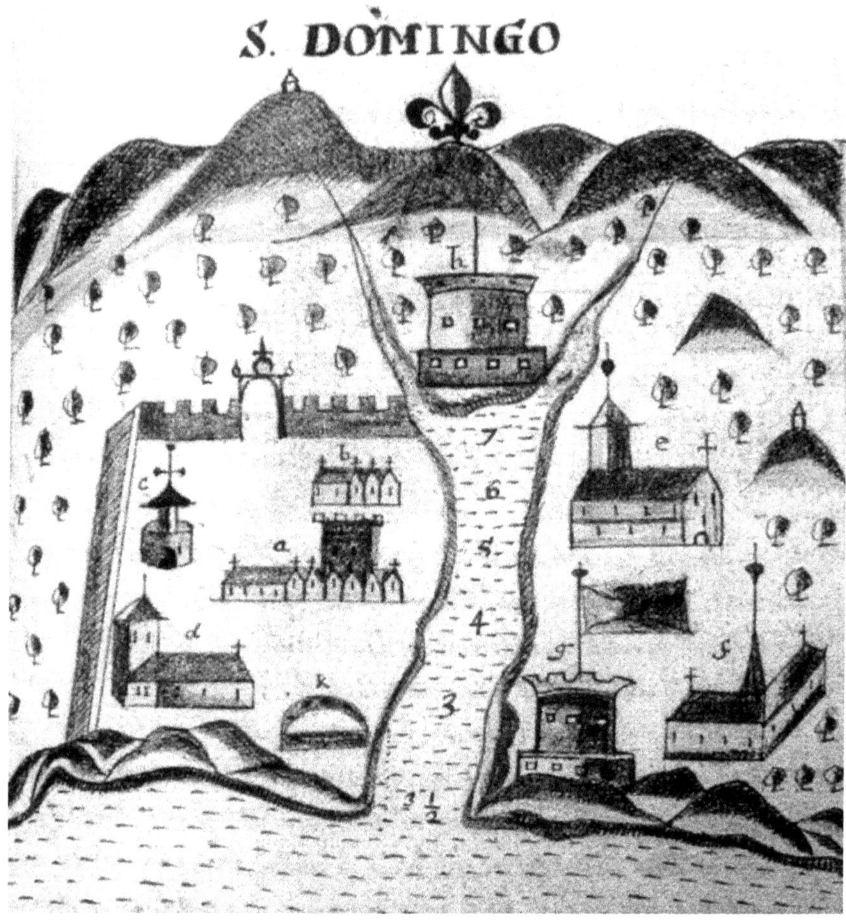

Figure 15 Taylor's plan of Santo Domingo, page 203.

is also wall'd round and hath 170 cannons round the walls. It hath but on gate we could descern which is at the north end therof.

In fine 'tis full of houses, well-peopled and exceeding rich in gold and silver and is the magazine* of Hispaniola.[13] Without the city 'tis verey wood to ye mountaines, on the top of which is a lookout where they keep constant watch. At the upper end of the harbour is a strong fort built of stone with three battery of 30 cannons mounted; on the east sid of the harbour is abundance of houses built by the watter-side, with a well-built church called S. Pedro's (as "e") and a verey large monastry called Nostra Seniora de Rosana, (as "f"), and at ye exterior point to seaward is built a strong round fort of three batterys haveing 30 brass guns mounted thereon, (as "g"). This is called Fota Royalla, and that (as "h") at the uper end of the haven is called Fort Havanna. 'Tis

13. Figure 15 gives a good idea of this city; see also the numerous plans in Fernando Chueca Goitia and Leopoldo Torres Balbés, *Planos de ciudades iberoamericanas y filipinas existentes en el Archivo de Indias,* 2 vols. (Madrid, 1981).

said here are in the city and on this side 5000 houses. Thus we have described the city of St. Domingo in ye (205) latitud of 18 degrees north latitude. Also on this side the haven on a high round hill is another lookout where they keep watch night and day. In this city are about 50 soldiers of old Spaine and about 100 hors, which keeps guard at day, and rides the patroule at night, and this much for Santa Domingo.

To proceed on our discourse againe, we being denighed to com ashor as you have heard, we therefor about 10 at night, when the wind sprung up a good gale from the north-north-east, the *Faulcon* and the *Drack* way'd from Santa Domingo, and plied to windward.

Sunday the 26th, we had rainy weather and a moderat gale from the east by south. At noon the west point of Illha St. Catalina bore from us northeast distant 9 miles, and at six at night the east end of Mona bore from us northeast by east distant 12 miles; this is also caled Savona.[14]

Moonday the 27th we had bad rainy, squally weather, with a strong gale from the east by south to the east by north. This day at noon 'twas soe hazy we could not see the land.

Tewesday the 28th we had faire weather and a moderat gale from the east to ye northeast, distant 21 miles we were from Savona at 8 in the morning, which then bore from us east by north. At noon it bore northwest by north, distant 6 miles.

Tewesday [*sic*] the 29th, at 29 minutes past one afternoon, the moon began to renew itself in the meridian of London. This day we had fair weather and a good gale from the northeast to the east by south; at six this morning Mona bore south by west, distant twelve miles.

Wednsday [*sic*] the last, we had fair weather and a good gale from the (206) southeast by south. At noon we came to anchor with the *Drake* in the Gulph of Samana, in 15 fadom water. Culow Island then bore from us south-east, and the Cape east. Being at anchor we espyed two boats under a small island, distant from us 2 miles, and they espying us made ye best of their way to an island 5 miles distant from us 5 miles. Haveing sight of these boates, the *Drake*'s pinais and ours were man'd and sent to discover what they were. About fore in the afternoon, the boats return'd, and informed us that at the bottom of that bay, in the gulfe, Banister was, and another small ship with them, and they were on the careen,[15] and further that they had pitch there tents on the island, and had hal'd their guns ashore and fortified themselves with two baterys, the one of six, and the other of ten gunns.

14. Saona is an island distinct from Mona, and about fifty miles to the west of it.

15. To "careen" a vessel was to tip it sharply, first on one side and then on the other, in order to work on the hull, often damaged by worms.

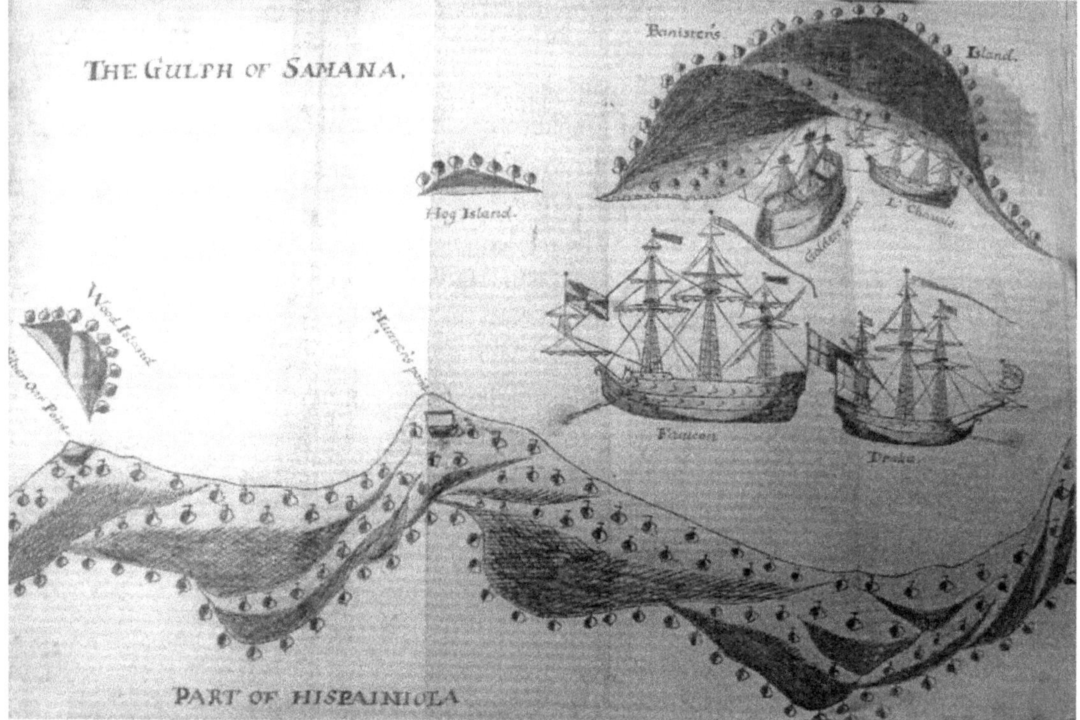

Figure 16 Taylor's drawing of "The Gulph of Samana" with Bannister's and the naval ships, page 208. HMS *Falcon* and *Drake* are here seen in the foreground, with Bannister's two ships trapped in the bay behind them.

Now that we may make all plaine, we have annex't hereto a map and prospect of the island, bay, ships and all other things here necessary to be known [figure 16].

Being enform'd thereof, the *Faulcon* and *Drake* wayed about three a'clock, all things being put in a fighting posture and in less than half an houer we came to anchor within musket-shott of Banister. They immediately fier'd at us (without shewing any ensigne) from their batteries, and with their gunns shott very furiously, and wounded one of our men. Being come to anchor in 5 fadom watter, we with all expedition bent out our best bower,[16] and brought our broadside to bear on them and fier'd with our uper and (207) lower fire of ordnance and our small shot on the quarter deck with good success, soe that we shattered the bowes of the *Fleece* all to pieces, and utterly distroyed his great ship *Fleece* and soon beat them from their cannon, which they plied violently against us, with little damage.

Yet they being beat from their small ordnance, did nevertheless with greatest resolution imaginable continue firing with their small arms against us

16. To "bend the best bower" was to use a powerful cable, an anchor carried in the bows of a ship.

ded and shelterd by the thick woods) untill such time as the
ad cover'd the earth with hir silent vaile; then seased they from their obstinat resistance, and all was silent. In this conflict we had three men kill'd outright, and two wounded; what number of Banister's wer slain, we could not learn. Thus night being come, we clens'd the ship and prepair'd all things in redyness to fight the morrow morning. And thus we end this month of June, leaving this John Taylor in much better helath than when ashore on Jamaica, tho' he stil remained very mallancholy.

July 1687

Thursday [*sic*] the first of July, in the morning before that Aurora had fully withdrawn the sable curtain of night and illuminated this western world with hir (208) refullgent raies, did this obstinat pyratt sound a levet* with his trumpets, and fiered fouer cannons and severall volies of shott at us, with little hirt, not wounding one man. Then the *Faulcon* brought hir starbourd side to bear on them, and soon return'd them satisfaction from the mouth of their cannon, upon which they forsook their batteries, and betook themselves to their small arms, for this our broadside of double and catridge did them much damage, yet still they continued fiering at us graduallie six musquets at a time from the woods about the middle of the island, thereby to withdraw us from distroying their battery (which was built of stones and old trees) with our cannon. Soe we kept all day long fiering at the *Fleece,* and theirby reducet hir to such condition that 'twas imposible for hir evermore to swim. For oftentimes we plac't 20 shots of our lower fier in hir bowes and quarter, soe that we saw both planck and timbers fly from hir. But as for the *L'Chavale* the French privater she goot in soe near to the shore that we did hir but little damage.[17]

In fine we demolish't their batries, and fire their ships all to peices. Yet they continued fiering at us with their musquets, and we at them with our cannon, as long as light would admit. This night we had continuall rain with the wind at north and northeast. Now haveing little wind we wayed our best bower and (with the *Drake*) warp'd off in the night, 'till we were out of their shot, (for we could lie (209) here noe longer, because we had verey litle powder and shoot left). But now the wind encreaseing we came to anchor about two cables' lenght to the westward of Cabbadg Island in 75 fadom water near Hog Island.[18]

17. Taylor's plate shows how this smaller ship lay almost out of range.
18. These islands may be seen on Taylor's plan, figure 15.

Saturday the 2d we had aboundance of rain, thunder and lightning, with the wind at east, soe that we could not turn out of the Gulph of Samana at break of day. Banister fiered severall great and small shot, but hurt us not, soe we kept warping* out untill we goot about two miles from the island; then we came to anchor about noon in 15 fadorn water. Now we espied three boats, the one a large English pinnace roaeing with nine oars, the other a man-of-war cannoa or periaguer* which might carry 20 oars, and the other a small cannoa which we supposed they had binn to fetch water.

Sunday the third we had abundance of rain, thunder and lightning, tho' the sun shin'd for the most part, with ye wind at east, and northeast by east. This morning we heard a great noise from Banister's island, and saw a great smoak, which continued about half an houre. I suppose they blow'd up somwhat and fired their great ship. This day we continued warping out, and by sounding we found very uncertain ground, from 14, 9,7 to 5 fadom water. Then have you the clearest ground, or part of the bay, haveing a fine gray oozy sand, intermix't with small stoons, and shels. This day we continued warping out.

Moonday the 4th we had much rain, thunder and lightning (210), and the wind blew strongly from the east, soe that we could not geet out; yet we continued warping out.

Tewesday the 5th we had much rain, thunder, and lightning, and ye wind at east, soe that we could not plie out of the gulph, yet we continued warping out.

Wednsday, the sixth we had fair weather for the most part and a good gale from the east-southeast. About 5 this morning the *Faulcon* and *Drake* wayed, and we came to saile, and by noon, we were abrest of Cabbadge and Curlou Island, where by sounding we found very uncertaine ground. At the first cast we had 7 fadom, then 9, then 11, then 17, and the next noe ground at 50 fadom, (about a mile to the eastward of Curleue Island). Then the next cast 17 fadom, then 6½ fadom with rocky ground. Also we found a sandbank mixt with scater'd rock, lieing from Curlue Island southwest by west, distant 5 miles, wheron is seaven fadom water. About 5 a'clock in the eavening we were got cleare of the gulph, and at six Cape Caberoon (or gote) bore from us north by west, distant 9 miles, and appear'd thus: [landfall not reproduced].

Thursday the 7th we had fair weather, and a good gale from the north to the east-south-east. At noon Cape Francisco bore from us south-south-east, and distant 18 miles. Here we found a very strong currant setting to the northwest. Our course was west-south-west and distant sailed 51 miles. Now (211) Cape Sainta Francisco appear'd thus: [landfall not reproduced]. This day at 51 minutes past 4 in the afternoon the moon was at hir full quarter. At six in the eavening, Porta Plata Hill bore from us south-south-east, distant 15 miles from us, and appear'd thus: [landfall not reproduced].

Fryday the 8th we had fair weather, and a good topsail gale from the east. Our course was west by north, and distance sail'd was 147 miles. At six in the eavening, Cabo Sainta Nicholas bore southeast distant from us 15 miles, and appear'd thus: [landfall not reproduced].

Saturday the 9th we had fair weather, and a fresh gale from the east-north-east to the south. At 10 this morning Cabo Tiberoon bore south by east, distant 24 miles, and appeared not high, soe that from Cabo S. Nichola to Cabo S. Maria our course was southwest.

Sunday the 10th we had fair weather, and but little wind, and that variable. And from 8 last night till this day noon was flat calme. And at six in the morning, Navasa bore east by south, (212) distant 12 miles. And at six in the eavening the east end of Jamaica bore from us northwest, distant 9 miles and appeared thus: [landfall not reproduced].

Moonday the 11th we had fair weather, and good gale from the east-north-east to ye north by east. About noon we came to anchor with the *Drake,* neare Porta Royall. Point Cagada bore from us north-north-west distant 3 miles.

Tewesday the 12th we had fair weather and a strong sea breez from the southeast, and about 10 a'clock in the morning the *Faulcon* and *Drake* wayed, and about 11 we came to anchor in Port Royall Harbour, in 9 fadom water. Thus thro' God's Divine Mercy we return'd safe to anchor at our Point, with victory, and good success. And thus we leave this John Taylor on board the *Faulcon,* in much better health, and stronger than when he went on board, for the sea agreed with him much better than the shore. And thus we conclud this eight chapter of the history of our life and travels.

Chapter IX

(213) Of all notable actions which hapned to us, from the thirteenth of July 1687 untill the fouerth of September following, with a full account, and a perfect diarie, of the proceedings of His Majestie's ship in hir second voige to look for Banister and othere pyrats.

Proceding forward on our discource, wheras on Tewesday the 12th of July past His Majestie's ships the *Faulcon* and the *Drake* came in to anchor at Port Royall, soe now you must understand that on Wednsday the 13th, we had here at anchor very hott, dry weather, with much thunder and lightning. This morning our Captain Charles Tolbot and Captain Spragg went to Sainta Jago de la Vega, to pay their respects to the Governour, and accquaint him with her success against [blank] Banister, and to know his pleasur further. This day our Pursser* Mr. Plumber was put ashore sick and John Stride on of the late wounded men was put ashore also there for his more speedy (214) cure.[1] This day came in here a katch and a pinck from New England, [and] a small ship from Irland belonging to Captain Swimmer.[2] Also this day there sail'd from here Captain Laycock and Captain Bennet, both bound for London.[3] And also there sailed from hence two sloops, bound to cruze off of Cathagen, therby to met with a sloope which the Spaniards had latly taken from Mr. Jennings. In the eavening our Captain Talbot returned on board, having orders from the Governour with all expedition to fitt out to sea, to look again for Banister and other pyrats, and Captain Sprag had the like orders.

1. Taylor's account of the engagement, spuriously inserted in the year 1687, remains convincing to the end; HMS *Falcon* did indeed lose ten men in the course of the engagement, according to the *Calendar of State Papers, Domestic Series*: James II, vol. II, art. 961. Jonathan Plummer, purser, died on 23 July, and Jonathan Stride on 30 July. National Archives, Adm 33/132, 106 and 109.

2. This ship is not to be found in the Naval Officer's registers.

3. Captains Richard Laycock and Edward Barrett, of the *Hunter* and the *Susannah,* left Port Royal on 4 July 1687. National Archives, CO 142/13, fo. 117. See figure 17.

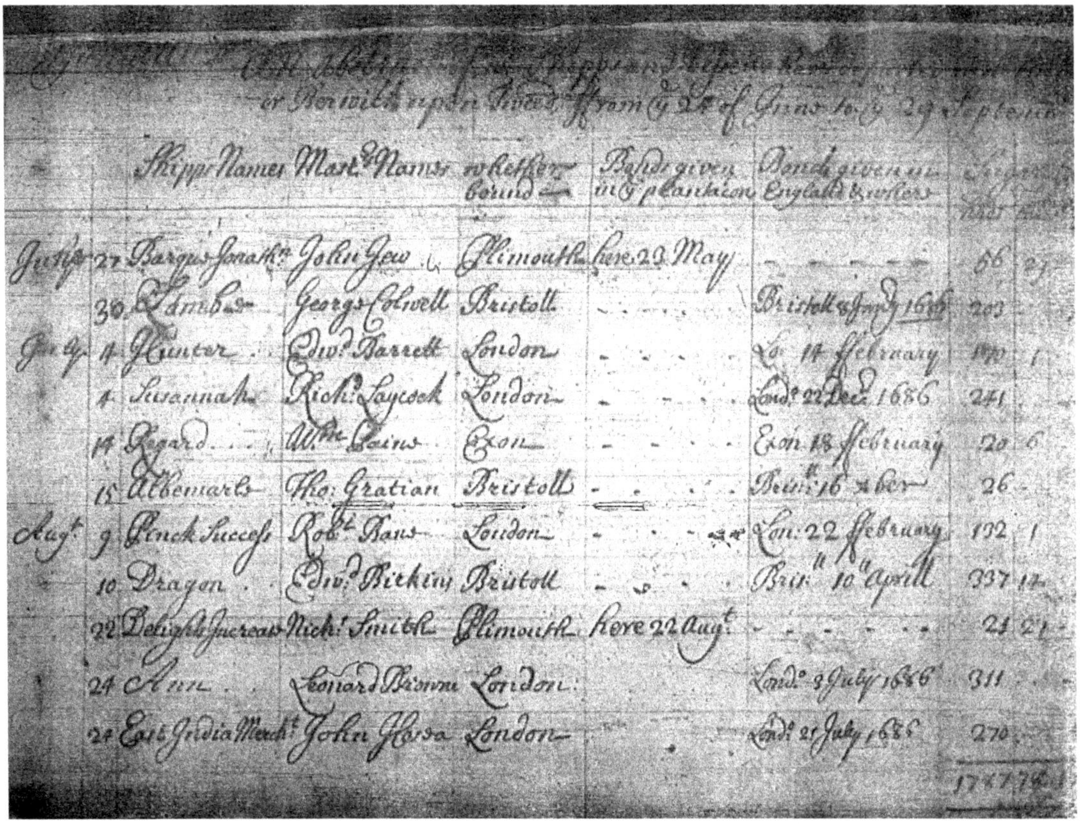

		Shipps Names	Mast. Names	whether bound	Bonds given in ye plantation	Bonds given in England & where		
June	27	Barque Jonathan	John Jew	Plimouth	here 29 May		56	2[illegible]
	30	[illegible]	George Colwell	Bristoll		Bristoll [illegible] 1686	203	
July	4	Hunter	Edw. Barrett	London		Lo. 14 ffebruary	170	1
	4	Susannah	Rich. Laycock	London		Lond. 22 Dec. 1686	241	
	14	Reward	Wm. [illegible]	Exon		Exon 18 ffebruary	20	6
	15	Albemarle	Tho: Gratian	Bristoll		Bris. 16 xber	26	
Aug.	9	Pinck Success	Robt. [illegible]	London		Lon: 22 ffebruary	132	1
	10	Dragon	Edw. Pitkin	Bristoll		Bris. 10 Aprill	337	1[illegible]
	22	Delights Increase	Nich. Smith	Plimouth	here 22 Augt.		21	21
	24	Ann	Leonard Browne	London		Lond. 3 July 1686	311	
	24	East India Merchant	John [illegible]	London		Lond. 21 July 1686	270	
							1787 [illegible]	

Figure 17 Part of the registers of the Naval Officer at Port Royal, to show the entries concerning captains Laycock and Barrett (National Archives, CO 142/13, fo. 117).

On Thursday the 14th we had hot dry weather, with thunder and lightning. This day we hal'd down the *Faulcon* and clean'd hir sides, putting on a pair of botter topps.[4] And this day at 24 minutes past six in the afternoon, the moon was at full in the meridian of London.

Fryday the 15th, we had the same weather as yesterday, with strong sea and land breezes; this day our boats went to the Rock for watter.[5]

Saturday the 16th, we had the same weather still; this day our boats goe to the Rock for water.

Sunday the 17th, we had still hot dry weather. Today our boats came from the Rock with water.

Moonday the 18th we had hot weather, with thunder and lightning; this day the *Drake* with a small sloope sail'd hence bound to the Gulph of

4. This curious phrase defies comprehension.
5. "Rock" refers to Rockfort, where there was a particularly pure source of water, much used by the ships at Port Royal.

Samana. And this day our boats were imployed in bringing on bord wood from the store house.[6]

Tewesday the 19th, we had the same hott weather, etc., and this day our boats were imployed in bring on board from the store house our (215) provition of bread, beef, porke, flower, oyle, oatmeall, pease, rum and sugar, suffitient for two months.

Wednsday the 20th, we had still hott, dry weather, etc.; this day we goot on board our amunition, and gunners', carpenters', and boatswains'* stores, and now we are redy to saile, in compliance to our late orders received from the Governour.

Thursday the 21st, about fouer in the morning the *Faulcon* wayed from Port Royall, bound to windward to looke for [blank] Banister and other pyrats. But about 8 a'clock the sea breez coming strongly, we came to anchor in 9 fadom water, without the town, 'ore against Plumb Point.[7] This day 12 minutes past 8 before noon, the moon as at hir last quarter in the meridian of London.

Fryday the 22d, about 8 in the morning, we wayed and came to saile, but about nine it fell flat calm (and soe remain'd all day) by which means we came to anchor again in 8 fadom water.

Saturday the 23d we had fair weather, and a stiff gale from the east by north. About 5 a'clock in the morning we way'd and came to saile, plieing to windward.

Sunday the 24th we had fair weather, and a moderat gale from the east by south, to the east by north.

Moonday the 25th, wee had fair weather and a fresh gale from the west by south, to the northeast by east. At six this morning the east end of Jamaica bore from us west-north-west, distant 18 miles.

Tewesday the 26th, we had fair weather, and a fresh gale from the east-north-east to the east by south, and now we found the currant to be strongly to the eastward.

Wednsday the 27th we had fair weather, and a moderat gale from the east-north-east to the south-east by east. About six in the (216) morning, we espied a saile bearing down to us, but haveing made us he clap't on a wind soe that we gave chase after hime. And about 10 a'clock we fiered a gun to leeward, to make him bear down to us, which he refused. So we continued the chase

6. This was the storehouse under the control of the resident Naval Officer and prominent Port Royal resident, Reginald Wilson. Pawson and Buisseret, *Port Royal,* 63–64.

7. The *Falcon* had used the early morning land breeze to get out of Port Royal harbour, but was then halted at Plumb Point when the normal diurnal sea breeze came up. *Falcon's* track during the cruise is plotted on the accompanying map, figure 18.

still geting way on him. About one in the afternoon we fier'd another gun at him, and then he laid by for us, and hoised out his pinnace, and soe did we, and Lieutenant Thomas Smith went on board him and brought from on borde with him the Captain, and an Englishman, and they were examined by Captain Talbot. Soe we found it to be the *La Maria,* a French privatere, which belonged to Porta Guavas,[8] and had 16 gunns, and one hundred men on board. Soe the Captaine and the Englishman being examin'd, they return'd on board their own ship, in their cannoa, and ster'd away for Porta Guavas. This day at noon the island Navasa bore from us south by east, distant 15 miles.

Thursday the 28th we had fair weather all day, but a very wett night, the wind but litle and variable till 11 a'clock, then sprang up a good gale from the northwest. At noon Cabo Tiboroon (or Cape Shark) bore from us southeast, distant 13 miles, and at six in the eavening it bore east by north, and distant 4 miles. Now it began to raine verey hard.

Fryday the 29th we had fair weather, and a good gale from the southwest. About 10 this morning the *Faulcon* came to anchor in the bay of Tibberoon in 9 fadom water, about one mile from the shore. At 8 at night we wayed from hence, and came to saile, plieing to windward (4 mins past 4 in the morn).

(217) Saturday the 30th we had fair weather all day, and a good gale from the southeast, but we had little wind at night. At 8 this morning Cabo Tiberoon bore from us north and ½ easterly. At noon it grew hazzy; wee could not see land. At 6 in the eavening 'twas cleare, and the west end of Illha Vacus bore from us northeast distant 12 miles.

Sunday the last of July, we had fair weather, and a good gale from the southeast. We plied to windward, and at noon Cabo Boao bore from us north, distant 18 miles. Then we espied a saile, and giveing hir chase we found hir to be the *Mary* of New England, bound to Jamaica.[9] And thus ends July.

August 1687

On Moonday the first of August we had fair weather and a mooderat gale from the east-north-east; we continued plieing to windward. About 8 at night Illha Hacken bore from us north-north-east distant 9 miles, and now we stood off, the wind blowing from the east by south.

Tewesday the 2nd, we had fair weather, and a moderat gale east by south. At six at night Zambay's west point bore from us north distant six miles.

8. This is probably Petit Goave, just to the west of Port-au-Prince, Haiti.

9. The *Mary* of Boston, Captain Edward Henfeild, with a cargo of wood and fish, arrived at Port Royal on 19 August 1687. National Archives, CO 142/13, fo. 31.

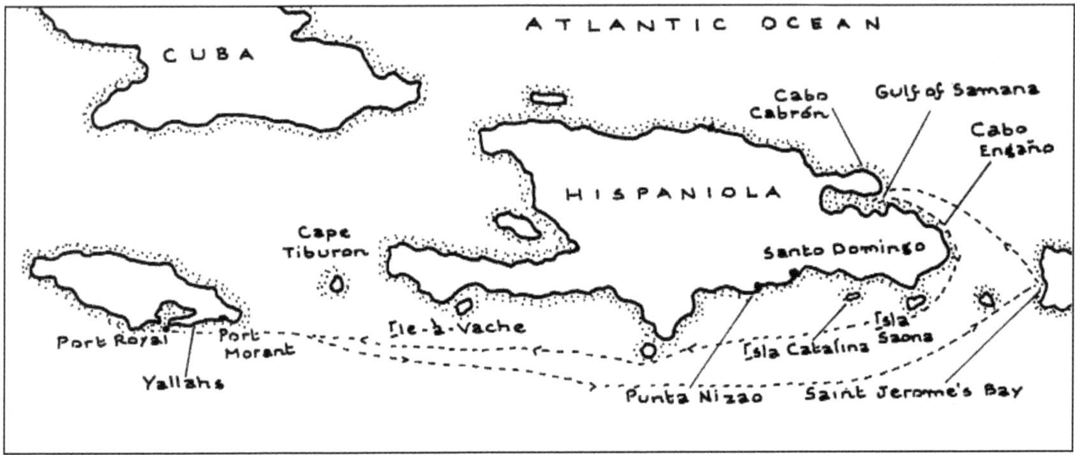

Figure 18 Map of the journey of HMS *Falcon,* August 1687.

Wednesday the third, we had fair weather and a moderat gale from the east-south-east. At noon Illha Altavela bore from us east by north, distant 21 miles. We espied a saile and gave chase, but when we came near we found her a sloop plieing to Leeward, we supposed to Jamaica, soe we gave [up] our chase and plied to windward (218) againe.

Thursday the 4th we had squally weather, and a stiff gale from the northeast. At noon Illha Altavela bore from us north by east, distant 21 miles. At night we had squally, tempestuous weather. We stood off E. south-east, with two reeffs in our topsailes.

Fryday the 5th we had wet, squally weather, and a stiff gale from the northeast. At six in the morning Illha Altavela bore northwest by north, distant 21 miles. All night we had squally weather, with gustes of wind.

Saturday the sixth we had wet, squally weather, with gusts of wind from the north-north-east. At six this morning Vaia Hocda, (which is 45 miles from the east end of Altavela) bore from us northwest, distant 12 miles. At ten at night the weather grew worse, soe we tack't and stood off southeast, then southeast by east, and then southeast and then east by south. This day, att 18 minutes past 6 in the morning, the moon was at hir first quarter in the meridian of London.

Sunday the 7th we had fair weather, and a moderat gale all day from northeast. But at night the wind was variable, blowing from the east-north-east, then east by north, and then east by northeast. At noon the west point of Cavalero Bay, called Ocoa, bore from us north 45°. Now we stood into the shore till six in the eavening, and then stood off againe.

Moonday the 8th we had dark, hazzy weather all day, soe that we cold not see land, with raine, and a stiff gale from the east by north. Towards 8 it cleared up and then the wester part of Sainta Domingo, called Punta Nisao, bore from us north, and distant 18 miles.

(219) Tewesday the 9th we continued plieing to windward, haveing fair weather, and a moderat gale from the east-north-east, with some thunder, and lightning. At 8 at night Illha Catalina bore from us east, 20 miles.

Wednsday the 10th we had fair weather, and a moderat gale from the east by north; at noon the west part of Illha Catalina bore from us north, distant 15 miles. We still plied to windward with an easi gale at night.

Thursday the 11th we had fair weather, and a moderat gale from the east-south-east. At 10 in the morning the midle of Hibano bore from us north, distant 12 miles; we still plied to windward. Now this Hibano is a good sandy bay, and is seen, and lies 23 [miles] to ye east-ward of Catalina Illha. Nowe note that from Punta Nisao, the wester point of Santa Domingo, to Point Dorado, or the east most part of ye island of Hispaniola I found by my often geometricall observations to be but 115 miles (tho' sailers, and others falsly make it 150 miles).[10] Thus from Punta Cysaida to Illha Catalina is 65; from Catalina to Punta Hibano is 23 miles, from thence to Punta Dorado (or Dolphin) is 27. Also I observed that from the wester part of Illha Savona to the southwest point of Catalina was 24 miles.

Fryday the 12th we had fair weather, and a moderate gale from the north-east by north. At noon Punta Dorada bore from us northeast, distant 18 miles, yet we could not weather it. Then we tack't about and stear'd east-south-east. About six we continued on our course stearing northwest by west.

Saturday the 13th we had fair weather, and a moderat gale from the east, to the east by north. At noon it proved callm and then Illha Zeachy bore from us northeast, distant 12 miles and appeared thus: [landfall not reproduced]. (220) And this day at 11 minutes past 8 in the morning, the moon was at full in the meridian of London.

Sunday the 14th, we had faire weather, but untill 10 a'clock in the morning we lay becalm'd, but then the wind sprung up at northeast and vered to the northwest. At noon Illha Zeachy bore from us northwest by north, distant six miles. At eight at night the *Faulcon* came to anchor, under the west end of Saint John's, or Porta Rico,[11] in 13 fadom water, with a designe to anchor on the morrow in St. Jerom's bay, and water their. Here we rod at anchor all night and 'twas callm. This day John Taylor was seized with a plurasie,* and remain'd ill after his being let blood for it, soe that he kept his cabien.

10. On this occasion, Taylor's figure seems very accurate.

11. Puerto Rico had indeed been known for many years as San Juan, which is now the name of the capital city.

Moonday the 15th, we had fair weather and a moderat gale from the northeast. At 5 in the morning we wayed and prepared to goe into St. Jerom's Bay to water, it being a fine cleare sandy bay, haveing three rivers of puere fresh water which emptieth themselves into this bay. About 10 a'clock in the morning we came here to anchor in 13 fadom water, close to the north land within half a mile to the shore. Now the north point forming this bay (as "a") bore from us northwest, distant ½ mile. The southermost point forming the bay bore from us south and Illha Zeachy bore from us west-north-west. And now being come here to anchor, our boats went ashore for water. Now that we may make all plaine we now present you with a draught therof in the next pages [figure 19] (221)

[This bay] is about 4 miles deep and hath good anchorage all towards the norther shore which you must keep abord. For to the southward of the bay we found all flats and a reif of rocks from the souther point to seaward about 4 miles, and hath but three fadom water thereon. At the entrance into this bay by the norther shore you have 15 fadom water, then 13, 12 and 11 fadoms, then toward the easter shore on river you have a sand banck cleare from rock wherein is 6 and 5 fadom water. Being off of the banck you have noewhere less than 9 fadoms unles on a small sandbank which lies about a mile from the north river wheron is 7 fadom watter. Att this bay the Spanish fleet stop to water when they come from Spain, and disperse themselves each to his respective port; see the mapp therof.[12]

Tewesday the 16th we had fair weather and a moderat gale from the northeast. This day our boat went ashore for wood and watter. And now you must know that John Taylor being indeferent went on shore and took a true draught and prospect of the said bay, rivers and all places notable appertaining therto which we have present you with in the next page.

Wednsday the 17th we had fair weather and the wind moderat from the north. Our boat went ashore and about 10 a'clock we had sight of three saile coming round the south point, upon which we losed our fore topsailes and fiered a gun to call our boats abord. About noon we were under saile and about one we spoak with them. They were Spaniards come from Spain and bound down to Leeward. (222) Saint Jeromo's Bay on Porta Rico, or Saint John's Island is in all respects according to this following chyrographicall[13] draught thereof [figure 19].

(223) Thursday the 18th we had fair weather and a good gale from the

12. Taylor did not in fact provide a map of the track of the *flota* or annual treasure-fleet, which sometimes put in to Puerto Rico on its way to Veracruz.

13. The accepted spelling would be "chorographical", describing a map that was neither small-scale ("geographical") nor large-scale ("topographical"), but somewhere in between.

Figure 19 Taylor's map of Saint Jerome's Bay, page 222.

northeast to the east, and east-south-east. Our course was west-north-west, our distance sail'd 48 miles. At six in the eavening Cape Samana (or Sugar Loaf Hill) bore from us west by north, and distant 21 miles, and appeared thus as at "A", etc.: [figure 20].

Fryday the 19th we had fair weather and but litle wind from the northeast to the east, and soe to the east-south-east. At noon Cabo Caboroon bore from us west by northwest, distant 18 miles and appeared thus [landfall omitted]: our course since yesterday hath been north-west by west and our distance sailed 36 miles. And now we being nigh the Cape (bound into ye Gulph) and ther being but litle wind we lay to all night. This day at 56 minutes past 2 in the afternoon the moon was at hir last quarter in the meridian of London.

Saturday the 20th at dailight we bore in for the Gulph of Samana, haveing the wind moderat from the southeast, and at one in the afternoon we came to anchor there in (224) 15 fadom water neare the east kay, called by us Cabbadge Island, by reason their grows a great many cabbadg trees thereon. Now before we proceed further in our diary, we will here give you a true description of the Gulph of Samana, with an hydrographicall chart therof, as far as from the Cape Caberoon, to a part thereof called by us Low Point, which is as follows; therefore to illustrate it, we have here added a map of the said Gulph of Samana, or Sainta Rasel, as at first cal'd by the Spaniards.[14]

A description of the Gulph of Samana, part of Hispainiola

This Gulph of Samana was at first called by the Spaniards Sainta Rassell, and is formed at the entrance or mouth by two capes, the one called Cabo Samana (or St. Rasel) extending itself northeast to seaward, the extrem point of which at sea appears conicall and high, and is therefore by some caled Sugar Loaf Hill. To the westward the mouth of this gulph is bounded by Cabo Caberoon, (or Cape Goate) which extendeth itself to seaward towards Scott's Bay, north-north-west. These two capes form the mouth of the Gulph. They beare east by north, and west by south from each other and are distant asunder about 40 miles. 'Tis not truly known how far this Gulph extends itself into the country, because here are many fllats soe that 'tis thought noe vessels have bin up in its salenas.* Howere' it reach about 50 miles up (225) into the country as farr as the city called Samana, and Sainta Cruz built on the southeast side of the Gulph is plainly evident, which places are inhabited by the Spaniards. Now some say that this Gulph windeth itself about up the countrey, with some ten miles of the city S. Domingo and others say it emptieth itself out by the mouth of Scott's River into Scott's Bay, and soe maketh an island of that part, which I doo not at all believe, but this the prefidious Spaniard tell us.[15]

On this southeast side of this Gulph there are these bays, salenas, lagoons, and rivers, as high as Sainta Cruz: (viz) Salena Grande, Bahu de Orange, Lagoone Le Grande, Rio de Lorke, Rio de Manatee, and Bahu Santa Cruz. Here is caught aboundance of good fish, as manatee, tortoise, Jew fish, mullets, etc.; this sides is inhabited by the Spaniards, is verey woody, and yeilds muche brave fruites as oranges, lemmons, mammes, sappodillas etc. 'Tis verey full of wild beves,* horss, hogs and goates, which are here at most times fatt, because they have good food and plenty of grass and frutes to feed on. Now on this side of the Gulph, as fare as Sainta Cruze all upwards, 'tis a good, sandy, cleare [word obliterated], with verey few flatts or rocks, and all along within a quarter of a mile of the shore, there is noe less than three fadom watter, and from thence to 5, 7, 10, 15, 20, 30 and 50 fadom watter, a midchannell, and sometimes noe ground att 100 fadom.

14. Taylor may be thinking here of Cap Rafael. In the following section, he gives English names to the capes and islands, without regard to their existing names.

15. Taylor's idea of the geography of the Gulf of Samana is very approximate; it neither leads into Scott's Bay (Bahia Escocesa) nor does it come within forty miles of Santo Domingo.

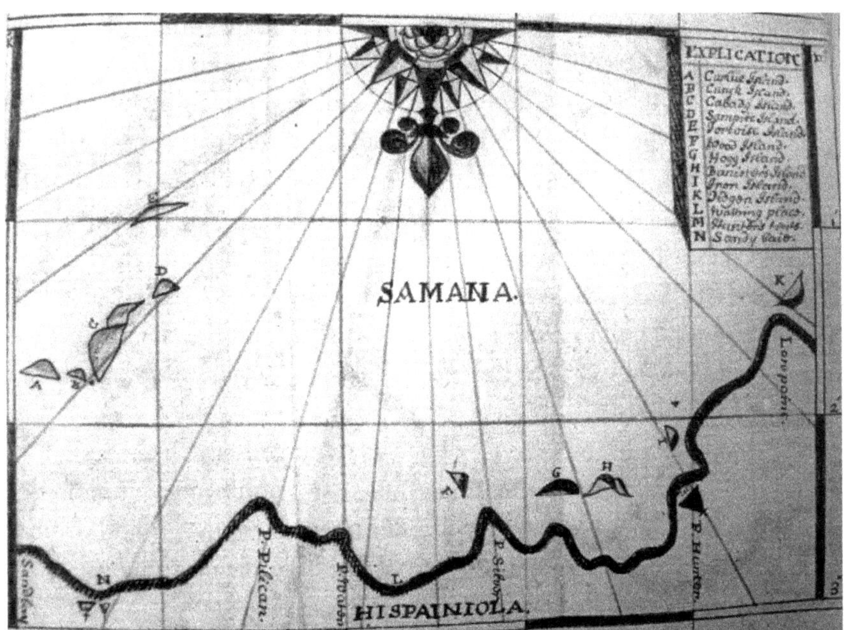

Figure 20 Taylor's map of Samana Bay, page 207.

On this side there are noe island or kays of note. As for the two towns, to witt, Samana and Sainta Cruze, they are mean places of noe strength, and inhabited by the Spaniards. And you must note that from the city Sainta Cruze, over to the low point the Gulph is 8 miles broad, rocky and shol'd, tho' in the midle of the Gulph 'tis 40 fadoms deep. Now come we to describe the northwest side of this Gulph of Samana, and that we may make all plaine we will begine with Cabo Caborone, or Cape Goat. Now you must understand that being within a mile of the midland of the Cape, and it bearing due west from you, (226) the first point of land you shall then see is Maingrove Point, which then bears from you south-west by south, distant 5 miles. And here you have noe ground at 50 fadom watter all along within two miles of the shore.

Now where Maingrove Poynt bears from you due west, and distant from you half a mile, then have you 22 fadom water, and then it opens to your veiw another point of land called Rock Point (see the mapp), then bearing from you southwest by west, and distant from you three milles. Here are three great rocks which stand up high out of the watter (as you see in the mapp). But as yet you can see but two of 'em plain, by reason of the point. Now you must stere south-south-west, untill you are abrest of this rock point, and you shall have 17 fadom watter all along on that course.

Being come abrest with Rock Point, there have you but 9 and 9½ fadom watter, about two miles from the shore, for here runs out a sand-banck mixt with whit scattered corall rocks, which lie off from Point Rock south-east by south about three mills. This banck or reife is above a mile broad. Now have you sight of Cabbadge Island, and of Curlu Island, and of Sandbay Point. Now being abrest of Rock Point and distant one mille, Curlue and Cabadge Island then seme united in one, and bears from you west-south-west 05° 40' southerly. And Sandbay Point bears west by south 05° 30' southerly, and is distant three miles, and Curlu Island thereabout. Now you must stere in a midchannell betwixt Sandbay Point and Curlue Island, and you will find all along verey rocky, foule ground, and will have 15, 16, 16½ and 17 fadom watter. Now you will have sight of Cunck Island, Sampire Island, Tortoise Island, and Pidgion Island, and of Point Pillican, bearing west by south and 1½ mile distant from Sandbay Point.

Now being come abrest of Curlue Island you will have 9 and 11 fadom watter; (227) then must you continue your course untill you come abrest of Cabbadge Island, and here you will find foule, uncertaine ground, from 9 to 11, and 17 fadom water. Being abrest of Cabbage Island, you must steare southwest by west, untill you bring Sampier Island to beare from you southeast, and distant 3/4 of a mile. There have you 15 fadom and good, clean anchoring ground. Thus we have given you directions how to saile into this gulph on the northwester side. Now come we to describe the gulph.

Now know that at the entrance of this gulph, you have noe ground at 50 fadom water, untill you come to Maingrove Point. There have you 22, 25 and 29 fadom water. When you are abrest of the midle of Maingrove Bay, and Curlu Island bears from you southwest by west distant 5 mills, you have then a sand-banck, mixt with scater'd rock, whereon is but 7 fadom water. Now being abrest of Rock Point, you have but 9 fadom and a half, and soe for the other depths from the entrance into this gulph on this northwest side; see the mapp, which will make all plaine, without a tedious rehersall thereof here.

Now to discribe the islands here first before we treat of ye main, you must know they are in number ten, we shall begin with them, as Curlu Island, Cunck Island, Cabadg Island, Turtle Island, Sampier Island, Wood Island, Hog Island, Banister's Island, and Pidgeon Island. Now first, Curlu Island is a small island full of woods about a half a mill (228) round. Heron breed abundance of whit curlues, and other birds, soe that it seems so thick of birds and nestes, that it resembles bees at a hive. And we call it Curlu Island from those birds which breed theron. And when it bears from you north, then those islands shew themselves thus: [landfall not reproduced] From Curlu Island to Cunck Island is about 100 paces. This island is a high rock on which grows woods, wherein abundance of birds breed. Betwixt these islands is from 3 to 5 foot water, here an abundance of cunck is to be got, soe that you may load a bote with them in a little time.

From Cunck Island to Cabadg Island is about 50 paces. Here have you 6,

9 and 11 foot water. This Cabadg Island is about two mills round, with a sanday, deep bay to the southward. On this island is aboundance of good cedars, olives, and other choice trees. 'Tis full of pidgeons, curlus, and other birds but here are noe beast theron. Here is a swamp, and fresh watter, and abundance of cabadg trees (from whence it takes its name). Here are some guanas, and abundance of soildiers;[16] here are mullets and other such good fish to be caught. Also on the easter part is steep cleaves, and nature has made a great cave to run in under the shore of this island. Sometimes tortoses are caught (229) here. Tortoise Island (or Turtle Island) is a low, sandy island, almost levell with the water, about half a mile broad, whereon grows nothing but a litle sampier.* And here we found noe liveing things, but some few lizards on this island. At the season the hauksbill turtoise comes and layes their eggs (from whence it receives its name). This island lies distant from Cabadg Island about 1/2 a mill. Here you have from 2 to 6 fadom water betwixt them, and now Sampire Island is a small, high, rocky place, about 100 paces round, and about 20 paces from Cabadge Island, betwixt which at ye most you hav but 13 foot watter, rocky and uncertain. On this island grows abundance of brave sampier and nothing else but a few scrubed bushes.

Wood Island is a small, high island, wheron grows abundance of brave cedars and other timber. It lies about 50 paces from Silver Oar Point; at noe time there is not above 3 foot watter betwixt them. Here are found good crawfish. This island is about half a mile round, and appear thus as you see in page 208. Hog Island is a low, small sandy island whereon grows some few trees. Here we found two hogs which Banister had left and therefore we call it Hog Island. It appears as in page 208.

Banister's Island lie about 1/4 of a mile from Hog Island. 'Tis a high, woody, steep island, about 3/4 of a mile round, and a brave place to creane* a ship at, for heare you have 7 fadom close to the shore. This island is extreamly thick of woods and appears as in the figure in page 208. It lies 1/3 of a mile from ye shore.

(230) Iron Isle is a small, high island, about 200 paces round, and 1/3 of a mile distant from Banister's Island, and soe called becaus we found iron hidd thereon. This island is very woody and appear as (h) in the figure [not reproduced] and hath by it two rocks. Pidgeon Island is a small, low woody island, opposite to Low Point, about a 1/2 mile round. And hereon we found multitudes of pidgeons, and parrats. This island appears as the figure (k) thus: [figure not reproduced].

Thus we have discribed the islands thus farr up in the gulph. But to make all plain, veiwe the map of the gulph, which will make everything plaine, as

---

16. Meaning here soldier crabs.

the depth of watter, rocks, sand banck etc. This part of the gulph is stor'd with plenty of excelent fish, such as baracodas, mullets, Jew fish, etc, and the main* is exceding frutfull, very woody, and extreamly full of wild hogg, but here is not soe plenty of beevs, as on the other side. This side of the gulph from Low Point to Cabo Cabaroon is not planted nor inhabited by the Spaniard. We found none here but some six French hunters, which hunt in these woods, and have a hutt near ye waterside where they trade with sloops, etc, which come in here to wood and water.[17] Thus we have given you a full and plaine description of this Gulph, the lick noewhere else extant, which we took noe small paines to collect and describe.

(231) Now to proceed on our discourse again, wheras on Saturday the 20th of August last, about one a'clock the *Faulcon* came to anchor in the Gulph of Samana, you must understand that being here we found the old weather, for we had much thunder, lightning, and raine. About three, haveing securly anchor'd our ships, our boats were sent to view Banister's Island, where we found the hulck of the *Fleece,* Banister's ship, which after our departur from him on the 4th of July last past, he had set on fier, and burnt hir down to the watter to the gun deck. Here we found where they had sunck 22 of their guns, and put a bow on them. Also here we found some iron, rigging and some barels of Irish beef, which they had left behind them. Soe we found they fitted the *La Chavale,* and went away with hir, carying with them their best riging [and] provitions, and burning the other sails and riging, and soe quited this place to them soe fatall.[18] We saw severall places like graves, where we suppose they buried their dead.

Sunday the 21st we had rain, thunder, and lightning, yet the sun shin'd all day. At night it rain'd excecively. This day the wind blew from the east by north. This day we got up 8 of their guns, and brought them on board.

Moonday the 22nd the weather and wind as yesterday. This day our boat was employ'd in waying of the guns, and we gott 7 more of them on board.

(232) Tewesday the 23rd we had still wett weather, and a moderat gale from the north-east. This day we gott up all Banister's guns, which he had sunck in 2 fadom by the island, and this day we goot on board thus we found 22 of Bannister's guns, 7 more of Bannister's gunns which were by him hidd, the which we goot on board, and put them amidship in the hould. And this day our men rangeing in the woods on Bannister's Island found 20 barells of Irish beef, and 15 of flower, which they had left hid.[19] Also some of the men goeing

17. This was a common phrase in Taylor's day when ships put in to replenish their supplies.

18. Taylor's account agrees here with that in the *Calendar of State Papers (America and West Indies) 1685–88,* entry 839 of 31 August 1686.

19. It is impossible to know, now, how long these barrels might have remained useful in the tropics.

ashore on Iron Island, found a small katch anchor, and some other ironwork hid there; also we found two live hogs, on Hog Island, ye which Banister for hast had left there.

Wednsday the 24th we had still wett weather etc., and the wind blew moderatly from the southeast. This day our boats were imployed in geting on board wood and som water, for we stay'd here in expectation to spak with som of Banister's men, which the French hunters informed us to be in the woods, and that they would bring us to the spech of them soe that they would inform us further.

Thursday the 25th we had much rain, with thunder and lightning, and the wind blew moderatly from the southeast. Our boats went ashore for wood and watter.

Fryday the 26th we had the old, wett weather etc. still, and the wind blew moderately from the east. This day our boats went (233) ashore for wood and watter. And this day we caught a great many mullets and other brave fish with our saine* which we hal'd on the bay at the south side of Cabadge Island. Also we goot abundance of young white curlues out of the nest from Curlue Island, of which it is as thick as a beehive seameth with bees. Soe that here we had good fish, fowls and fresh hog plenty; which we could bie a good side of a lustie fatt, wild boare, for a quart of brandy of the French hunters, which would daylie supply us therewith.

Saturday the 27th we had brave, faire sunshine weather all day and night, with little thunder and lightning, with a good gale from the east, to the east-north-east. This day we intended to have sailed from hence, but that their came in a small French sloop, with 20 men in it, from Porta Gunivas, under pretentions to hunt for hog and beves, but we supposed rather to fetch away Banister's men which were lurcking in the woods, and to carry away those things which he had left hidd. Therefor we stayed here to see and observe their motions. This day at 59 minutes past 7 at night the moon becam new in ye meridian of London.

Sunday the 28th we had brave fair weather in the morning, and a good gale from the east. About 4 in the morning the *Faulcon* wayed from Samana, and we came to saile bound to Port Royall in Jamaica, and by 8 at night we turn'd it out of the Gulph and were goot cleare of the Cape, for then Cabo Cabaroon bore from us north by west, distant 9 miles, and appeareth as in page the 210. We stood off untill (234) 12 at night stering north-north-east.

Moonday ye 29th, we had faire weather, and a moderat gale from the east to the east by north; we stood off untill 2 this morning, stering north-north-east; then we plied to windward. At 4 in the morning Ponta Engano (or Point Sword) on the east end of Hispaniola bore from us southwest distant 15 miles and appeared thus: [landfall not reproduced].

Tewesday the 30th we had faire weather and a moderat gale from the east to the north. By noon we weather'd Punta Engano; it then bore from northwest by west, distant 9 miles. We now stear'd south intending to goe to Sainta Domingo, to look for the *Drake*. At six in the eavening, the east end of Illha Savona bore from us north-north-west, distant 9 miles. We now sterrid west; towards night the wind blew hard from the south.

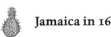

Wednsday ye last, we had faire weather, and a stiff gale from the south to the southeast. In the night, the wind had thrust us off of S. Domingo, which at 4 in the morning bore from us north distant 21 miles. Soe we stood down Bahu Cardeto, but not finding the *Drake* there, we made the best of our way (235) to Jamaica. Now at noon Cabo Zephrigia (which is ye easter part of Los Caveleros) bore from us north by west, distant 4 miles. And at six at night, Cabo Vel Illha Altavela bore from us west-south-west, and distant from us by estimation 15.

Thus here we conclude this month of August, and leave this John Taylor not well (tho' beter than when ashore), being troubled with a flux* and he remained verey mallancholly and reserv'd, altho' Captain Talbot was extemely kind to him, and he wanted for nothing that these parts would aford to supportt or refresh his spirits. Howevere he bore up as well as he could, and made it his buisines to project and collect all things worthy note in this his voige which you are here presented with.

September 1687

On Thursday the first we had wet squally weather and an easy gale from the east-north-east unto the southeast. At noon Illha Altavela bore from us north, distant 24 miles. At six in the eavening the highlands caled Yaquimo or Iaquemell bore from us north, distant from the shore 12 miles . 'Tis high tabular land and easily known.

Fryday the 2nd, we had fair weather, for the most part, with some few showers, and a moderat gale from the northeast, and east-south-east. At noon Ilha Vacus bore from us north-north-west, distant 6 miles; we had a eastward curant.

(236) Saturday the 3rd we had fair weather, and a good gale from the east-north-east to ye east. Our course was southwest, and our distance sail'd from yesterday noon to this day noon was 176 miles. At noon we made the east end of Jamaica bearing from us west, distant by estimation 31 miles. At two a'clock we came up with the *Rose* pinck, which had bin at Madera, and was now bound to Jamaica.[20] At six at night the east end of Jamaica bore from us

20. It does not seem possible to identify this little ship.

northwest, distant 12 miles, and appear'd like the figure in page 212, therefore see the prospect.

Sunday the fouerth we had fair weather, and a good gale from the east-south-east. At 4 a'clock in the afternoon the *Faulcon* arived safe to anchor in Port Royall Harbour on Jamaica, in 9 fadom watter. Here we found ye *Pedro* at anchor, near Gun Kay.[21] Now the church bore from us east, and Charles Fort S.E., Gun Kay then bearing south-southeast. Now we found our Purser Mr. Henry Plumber and John Strid both dead and buried; these we left here the one sick, and the other wounded, when we went out on this voige.[22] Thus thro' Divine Providence, the *Faulcon* arived in safety to hir port, and we leave this John Taylor now in indeferent health, and thus we conclude this ninth chapter of the history of our life and travels, and shall now fall in hand with the second part of this our history, in which you shall find a full and perfect description of the island of Jamaica in America.

21. This ship, too, defies recognition.

22. See note 1 above (p. 52).

Volume II

Taylor's Present State of Jamaica

Chapter I

(239) Of the discovery of America by Don Christopher and of that part therof now called Jamaica, with the manner of the Spaniards' setling theron, with the most memorable transsactions, till taken from them by the English, Anno Christi 1655.

Don Christophe Columbus, the famious discoverour of America, or the newfound western world, decended of honourable extraction, by birth an Italian, (240) for he was born at the city Nerni, in Genoa, in the year 1447.[1] His parents took great care in his education, for he was sent to Rome and their by equisite tutors instructed in all the liberall sciences, and being a youth of a pregnant fancy, he well improved his time, gratefully answering his cultivators' labour and his parents' expence, and being arived to manhood he was taken from thence and sent away in the Christian army, to the holy war, where he behaved himself with that courage, valour and humility, that he got the applause and love, both of his superiours and inferiours.

These wars being ended he was employed in the king of Portugall's service at sea, in which he took much delight and accrued to himself noe small honour, but when the King his master called home his fleet from sea, this aspiering soule betook himself to his studies again, but more particular he buisied himself in the mathematicks, and ruminating on the spheares of the world; and considering in his mind how much of the vast tract of the earth was yet undiscover'd, and how honourable the discovery of those occult parts would be to the discoverour, and advantageous to the world; and he being also peious, as well as valiant, he thought it his dutie to attempt the same, were it only for the sake of its undoubted inhabitants, which were undeniablie ignorant of a true God, and Christianity.[2]

1. The most reliable tradition has him born at Genoa in 1451. Taylor's account of his education is a fantasy.

2. Taylor correctly observes that Columbus was exceptionally well-read, as may be judged from his *Biblioteca Colombiana,* still preserved at Seville.

Thus piously and honourablely prompt forward (by more than an ordinary power), he adresed himself to the king of Portingall his (241) master, discloseing to him his whole intentions and designes. The which the king of Portugall haveing with his councill considered, and debated on, he promised him assistance with shipps, and what else was necessary for such an expedition. But 'tis much easier to promise than to perform. What 'ere it was, somewhat changed the mind of the king soe that he neglected to doe what he had promised. Don Columbus haveing waited a whole yeare at court and fiending his proffers and services slighted, he was much troubled therat, but nevertheless desembled the matter as well as he could, resolveing not yet to stopp from his designe, but to reveall it to some more potent prince, which better knew how to use the same.

Whilst he was proposeing the same to himself, he was seized with sickness; therefore he dispatch his brother Don Philip to the court of England, to proffer his service to his renowned majesty of England then Henry VII, but as the fates would have it, the ship wherein Don Philip was embarqued was seized on the sea by pyrats in their voige towards England, and careyed away he and his company prisoners.[3] Don Columbus not knowing anything thereof, waited with the greatest impatience imaginable; and hearing nothing from his brother he therefore thought that his brother's proffers were slighted by king Henry, as they had bin before by the king of Portugall. Being much trobled at this surmise, he did what he could to compose his dissatisfied spirits and yet further resolved on a third attempt which was this.

(242) Don Columbus therupon redresses himself to Phillip, the king of Spain, whoe after mature deliberation with his councile on these honourable proposalls, promised him imediate assistance which ships and all other things convenient for shuch an expedition. Upon which the king of Spaine forthwith fitted him out with two stout ships, with men, victualls, and amunition sutable to such a voige. Thus the Genoese Don Christopher Columbus, haveing prepared all things for this his voige, set saile with his company on the 14th of February, anno 1492 from Castile, bound on this most honourable discovery of the new western world.[4]

Now the brave Columbus is at sea, where both winds and weather seem to smile on (and arrogantly strive to furthere) this noble atempt of his

---

3. Taylor seems here to be telling the story of his 1476 trip to England, during which the Genoese fleet in which Christopher Columbus was travelling was attacked by French pirates; Columbus lost all his trade goods and narrowly escaped capture by swimming ashore and making his way to Lisbon.

4. Taylor's story is here rather approximate. It was to Ferdinand and Isabella, the "Catholic Kings" of Spain that he addressed himself, and the three little ships set out early in August 1492 from Palos.

generous soule. But haveing sailed sixty days before an eastern wind, and not espieing any land, the Spaniards not being used to such long voiges began to mutinie, declaring they would not saile the ships any further but would return. Don Columbus being not a little troubled and supprized hereat, knew not well what to doe to allay this unexpected broile,* but at last thro many fair words, and oblidgeing promises, he prevailed soe farr with them, as to continue on their voige three daies longer, which being expired if then they had not sight of land, he promised them to return back. For this warry Italian haveing observed the clouds to arise from the horizon of a more clearer, and brighter colour, than hitherto they had don, was well assuer'd they drew nigh some land.

(243) And so accordingley it proved, for haveing continued on their course som two daies more, towards the eavening they espied fire, an evident token of some adjacent countrey. On the third day in the morning they espied land, and bore down to itt. Now the before dissatisfied Spaniards began to rejoice, and be well contented, and praise the worthy conduct of their noble captaine.

Soe they came soon to anchor, and went ashore (as historian tell us neare Sainta Domingo),[5] where they found a most uberous* island in its butifull verdure, full of well-proportioned inhabitants. This island was by the natives in their Indian language called Hatie, but Don Columbus in honour to the king of Spaine his master named it Hispainiola.[6]

The Spaniards haveing taried here some few days, and haveing taken some Indians prisoners as trophys of this famous exploite to cary home to Spaine, and haveing suffitiently refresh't themselves with those rarityes which they found here, they hoised saile and stod allonge shore to the westward, intending to saile round this island, and soe return home to Spaine. Now cruseing round the west end, they espied Cuba, which haveing taken a view off, they returned towards Spaine, to carry the happy news of this his discovery to King Philip, his master, where being safe arived with his two ships he was received with all possible honour due to such a brave discovery. And the next spring there was orders given by the King for the (244) fitting out a fleet of about twenty saile of the best ships of Spain, well victuall, armed and man'd, to prosecute this discovery, and setle the parts allredy found.[7]

For now the young cavaleres or tyros* of Spain, as well as the more grave or ancient heroes, were bent to try their valour and fortune with this noble

5. In fact, somewhere in the Bahama islands, probably on San Salvador.

6. It is interesting that Taylor knew the indigenous name "Haiti".

7. Columbus did indeed return with two ships, to Ferdinand and Isabella; the new fleet consisted of seventeen ships.

Don Collumbus, in the conquest and setling of this newfound western world, soe that in a short time the fleet was soon fitted with stout captains, able seamen, and valiant soldiers, besid which there were many persons of honour which accompanied him in this his intended second navigation to America.

Being thus fitted, the fleet putt to sea in the begining of March anno 1493, and meting with prosperous winds and good weather, in a short time they arived at Hispainiola,[8] and in his passage thither, he discovered many of the Caribe island, Saint Christopher's being the first land that they now made, and soe called after his name. Being safely arived to Hyspainiola, the whole fleet came to anchor in Cavolero Bay, where they landed about 1200 soildiers, whoe metting with litle resistance from the natives march up into the countrey, took many prisoners, and killed many thousands of Indians, untill these blody thirsty Spaniards with slaughter were glutt with blood. Also many of the natives were babtized, and converted to the Christian religion; the residue for sheltor fleed to the mountaines, which were by (245) the industrious cruelty of the Spaniards soon destroyed. Soe that in a short time the cruile Spaniards became masters thereof, leaving the island to lament its lost of above 100,000 of her native inhabitants.

Don Columbus haveing left suffitient strenght on Hispaniola, and some ships to cruse round the same and yeild them succors on occation, he with the rest of his fleet wayed from thence, and bore down to the westward, in order of a further discovery, and in two days time they discovered the island now called Jamaica but by Columbus then named Ilha Sainta Jacobi,[9] where being come to anchor with his fleet, at the place now called Old Harbour, but by them called Porta Dogua, he landed and found the inhabitants such as on Hispaniola without apparell, of well proportion and featured of a cleare complexion, and kind behaviour, but soe ignorant that they thought the Spanish horsemen to have bin but one creature, and imortall. But that doubt continued not long, for haveing taken one of them prisoner, they put him under water untill he was dead; and then they found them to be mortal lick themselves.[10]

They record the time by a confused knowledg of the moon's revolution; they acknowledged a deitie, and worshiped divelish spirrits, which they called Zema, in memory of which they kept images made of cotton wool, which

8. The fleet set out on 25 September 1493, but it did indeed enjoy a swift passage, arriving at Dominica on 3 November 1493.

9. Columbus arrived at Jamaica early in May 1494; it is not clear why Taylor thought that he gave the island this Spanish name.

10. This story of the Spaniard, drowned in order to check on his mortality, comes from Theodor de Bry, *Americae* (Frankfurt, 1596); see figure 21.

Figure 21 Theodor de Bry, Indians with the Spaniard (*Americae,* part VI [Frankfurt, 1596]) (by courtesy of the Newberry Library, Chicago). This engraving of three episodes distinct in time shows a Spaniard being thrown into the river, then pulled out after he had drowned and, finally, being shown to a ruler, as proof that Spaniards were not immortal.

they had in great veneration supposing the spirrits of Zema or their gods were there, nor durst they offend them, which if they did the divile would come and distroy their children, for such was the subtilty of that lieing disceaver, that to blind them, he caused those puppets to move, and make a noise, (246) by which means they were afrightned into their idolatrie.[11] However, they were of good morall principalls, being just in their promises, and punctuall to their word, and very kind in their entertainment, incouraged thereto by a certaine conceived opinion, that whoe 'ere live well and die in the deffence of their countrey shall after death goe to a certain place of bliss beyound the mountaines, and there be forever happy.

11. Taylor had become aware of the nature of *zemis.*

Soe naturall is the knowledg of the soule's immortallity, and of some *ubi** for its future reception, that we find some track thereof in the most barbarouse and occult nations. Soe farr were they sencible, that whilst the Spanish fathers, whoe under pretence of instructing them in the knowledg of God and Christianity rob'd them of their gould, that then would they say to them, holding up a piece of gold in their hands, "Behold! this is your God, O barbarous Spaniards, for whilst you tell us of a future being, you robb us of our lives and wealth which is not becoming as you call yourselves piouse Christians", by which you may gather of their witty accuity that they were not ignorant in morall intelects; thus we have given you a description of those native Indians.

Now to proceed; Don Columbus haveing landed here found it a pleasant soile, and the Spaniards soon become masters thereof, useing the like barbarous cruilties which they had done to the natives on Hispainiola, for som they killed with their arrows, swords (247) lances etc; others they flea'd* alive to make them confess where they had hid their treasure, others were torn to pieces by dogs, to make them confess and to be a terrour to others; and those pore wretches which were fleed to the caves, woods, and mountaines for shelter were by these bloody monsters of men hunted, and found out by doges, and hundreds of them burnt togeather in the caves, in the which they were privatly hid. By which means they were soon expiated* and but few left alive, for the Spaniards themselves report that they kil'd above 60,000 of the natives on this island of Jamaica,[12] and those Indian women which they had spared were soe incensed against those cruill Spaniards that they would distroy the fruite of their woomb as soon as borun, that soe they might not live to serve soe cruill a nation as those Spaniards were.

Now Don Columbus and his soldiers haveing distroyed the natives and being sole masters of the place, and haveing stay'd their as long as they thought fitt, they wayed and came to sea and bore away for Cuba, where when Don Columbus had landed about 1600 soldiers and left some ships to cruse there, and to attend the army, he then bore away from Cuba to Hispainiola, where he allso left what shiping and men he could possibly spare, and with the residue sailed for Spain, where they safely arived and in a short time after this brave Columbus died, and was with all imaginable funurall pomp and state buried in the great church at Sevill, (248) Anno Christi 1493, and in the fortie-sixth year of his age, being much lament by

12. "Expiated" is an archaic word for "extinguished". Taylor's figure of sixty thousand is not far from some modern estimates, though most scholars now believe that most damage was done by exposure to European diseases.

all, for indeed, in him Spain was depriveed of that ornament, which all the world envied her enjoyment of.[13]

Now the next spring, ships were sent from Spain with fresh succors to those of Hispaniola, and Cuba, and to setle Jamaica and other new found places, as well as to prosecute the discovery further. Also ships were fitted out by the Portaguise, English and French and sent hither to discover other lands not yet found; now the Spaniards againe arived at Jamaica, and began to setle at Porta Dogua (now called Old Harbour),[14] wher they began to build houses and setle plantations of corn, fruits and coco, and now daylie new settlers and new inhabitants flocking hither appare from Spain, soe that this land in a few years began to wakes* strong, and increase in its plantations, etc., the King of Spain takeing great care of this island, for he sent hither some noble man of Spain every third yeare to govern this place, and sildiers to defend itt, and soe then the other governour went home to Spain and the newcome governour received his authority to whom they yeilded all due obedience, paying to the King his annuall tribute.[15]

Now the island being come to some matuerity, the Spaniards began to build a large city in a spatious savana or Indian cornfeild, about 12 miles from Porta Dogua, (249) which city they called Sainte Jago de la Vega (i.e. Saint James of the Plane). This city was built in the form of a quadrangle, the streets being about fouer miles long and the city nigh as broad; here they built a large church, dedicated to Saint Paul, and a large monastry called Nostra Segniora de Rosaria;[16] also they built at Cagada Harbour at the pass, a small fort (now called Passage Fort) to defend that pass, for now by reason of this town of Saint Jago de la Vega, ships from Spain began to resort to this harbour, but their cheife port was at Porta Dogua, or Old Harbour. Thus the Spaniards extended theire settlements in the most comodious places on the south side from east to the westward, towards Punta Negrill.

Whilst the Spaniards were thus setling the southside, the Portaguise were doing the like on the northside hereof, for they built a very large town their

---

13. It is curious that Taylor knew nothing of the third and fourth voyages of Columbus, in the latter of which he spent a year marooned in Jamaica. He died on 20 May 1506 and was buried at first in Spain, then in the West Indies and then, in 1899, perhaps in the cathedral at Seville.

14. It is not clear where Taylor gets the name Porta Dogua for what must be Puerto Esquivel, on Old Harbour Bay, though this is the second time that he has referred to it. In fact, the Spaniards settled first on the north side, at Sevilla la Nueva (by St Ann's Bay).

15. In fact, the island developed very slowly, because it had become a hereditary possession of the Columbus family, and the Spanish kings showed little interest in it, particularly after the landing in Mexico in 1519.

16. Taylor's description of the founding of Spanish Town, following the recommendations of the various versions of the Laws of the Indies, is quite accurate, though he exaggerates its size and seems to mistake the names both of the church and of the monastery.

dedicat to Saint Ann, which they called the town of Saint Ann's, in which town they built a verey larg church, dedicat to Saint Peter, and a spatious monastry, called Nostra Segniora de Anna. About this town, and soe extending towards the east and west on this northside, they had many good plantations and setlements, for they proceeded industriously, successfully, and increased yearly in strenght.[17]

But about the yeare 1600, wars breaking forth betwixt the kings of Portugale and Spain, the Spanish inhabitants of Jamaica now thought it time to expell their Portaguise neibours from off this (250) island, wherupon the Spaniard with *animia animus* consent[18] rose in arms against them, and after many skirmishes, the Spaniards being two to one with them, drove the Portaguise out of their towns and possetions, soe that the Portaguise agreed (thō' sore against their wills) to leave this island, and the residue which were left of them were sent home in some ships of Spain to Lisbon with what little of their wealth which the Spaniards would suffer them to carry away with them off this place.[19]

The Spaniards now being quit of there feares and of their enemeys, and haveing all the island to themselves, began to build the town and monastry of Saint Mary's[20] and setle in those partes of the island, and by this time their plantations and setlements were come to considerable maturitie producing plenty of corn, fruite and othere provitions. And the island yeilding them plenty of excelent beef, hog, goat, fowles and fish of sundrie sortes in great abundance, and being supply'd from Spain with strong and delitious viands* and sumptious apparell, and having Negro slaves brought them from Africa to doe their labour in the fields, and fiending here gold and silver in abundance, which they diged out of the bowels of the earth with little trouble, they now being at ease and quiet became above measure arrogant, proud, and lazie, soe that they neglected their plantations and setlements, leaving it for the most part to the management of their Negro slaves, (251) themselves takeing their fill of pleasure on the bed of luxury, sloath and idleness, for they were not used to such plentyfull liveing in old Spain.[21]

---

17. Taylor confuses a Portuguese presence at St Ann's Bay with the work carried out there by the Spaniards between 1508 and 1534. But he is probably correct in claiming that there were Portuguese on the north side in this area, to judge by the names to be found in the plat-surveys at the National Library.

18. That is, with one accord.

19. This is a garbled account of the Portuguese revolt of 1640 against Spain, though it is not clear that it had any repercussions on Jamaica.

20. Presumably Port Maria.

21. This is a rather whimsical account of Spanish Jamaica, where little precious metal was found. But it does catch something of the atmosphere of the island as an agreeable backwater in the Spanish empire.

Soe that now they all thought themselves as great as Ceaser; for naturally you shall find all Spaniards of a proud, insulting disposition when they are masters; but being subdued, you shall fiend them of a base, cowardly evil spirit. In fine let them be either masters or servants, they will never faile to be detrious at their naturall accomplishment of stealing, for they are in generall most notorious theives at all times and places where opportunitie presents, which is soe well known to the whol world that themselves can't assume impudence enough to denigh.

Thus we leave Jamaica one of the Peruvianian isles in America, as then in its present state when inhabited by the prefidious Spaniards, and governed by the Marqueness Segniora Margareta Perez de Gusman, an ancient lady of Spain, Anno Christi 1655.[22]

22. The governor in 1655 was Juan Ramirez de Orellana. But Taylor may have heard something about Teresa de Guzman, who was indeed the widow of the governor Pedro Caballero. See Frank Cundall and Joseph Pietersz, *Jamaica under the Spaniards* (Kingston, 1919), 43–48.

Chapter II

(252) Of the takeing of Jamaica by the English, and of the great lost which they sustained at their attempt on Hispainiola; also how the Spaniards attempted to have retaken Jamaica, but were defeated. With a description of the English, their settlinge, planting, building and fortifying of the same. With an account of the many notables victories since obtained by the English against the Spaniards in America, as also a full account of all noteable transsactions under its severall governours, from its first setling by the English until this present government under His Grace Christopher Duke of Albemarle.

Section I

Of the takeing of Jamaica by the English, and of the great lost which they sustained at their atempt on Hispainiola.

The sacred hunger of gold is that which spurs men on to the most disparat attempts which can be proposed or imagined: what is (253) that which makes monarchs disagree, but ambition, and avarice. This gold was the bait which stir'd up Oliver that fell tyrant with the greatest secrecie and silence imaginable to fit out a fleet of stout ships, well victualled, man'd, and rigg'd for a long voyage. None knew his intent or whither he would send them; such was always his polocy.[1]

The fleet being ready to put to sea, he gave the command of them to three of his creatures, (viz) Collonel Venables was admirall in the *Switzer,* Collonel Godson vice admirall in the *Torrent,* and Collonel Dawleigh was reer admirall in the *Portland,*[2] and the fleet consisted of twenty-five sail of men-of-war, as the *Switzer, Torrent, Portland, Glouster, Lawrell, Lion, Boar, Massamose, Cardiff, Tallamoro, Indian, Coronation, Mathias, Gift, Selbey, Grant, Holland Arms,* etc., with other small ships, which were loaden with provition and to

1. The purpose of Oliver Cromwell's Western Design has never been clear; see, for instance, S.A.G. Taylor, *The Western Design* (Kingston, 1965), 2–6, and Frank Strong, "The Causes of Cromwell's West Indian Expedition", *American Historical Review* 4, no. 2 (1899): 228–45.

2. These three leaders were Robert Venables, William Goodson and Edward D'Oyley; see C.H. Firth, ed., *The Narrative of General Venables* (London, 1900).

attend the fleet, soe that the fleet concisted of about forty sail,[3] in which was full 20,000 soldiers[4] and seamen with victualls, stores, arms, ammunition, etc. accordingly for a whole year's voyage.

Thus the fleet being redey set sail from the Downs bound to the West Indies against the Spaniards there, on the second of February Anno Christi 1655,[5] haveing orders to touch at Barbados, St. Christopher's, Nevis, and those windward islands inhabited by the English; and to take in from these islands what men they could spare, then to bare down to Hispaniola and take it from the Spaniards.[6]

The fleet meting with prosperous winds and good weather soon (254) arrived at those windward islands, and having received from thence what men they could spare, to the number of about 2,200 men, the fleet then with all expedition bore down to Hispaniola, where they safely arrived on the 20th of April in Cavalero Bay, about 30 miles to the westward of Saint Domingo, where they came to anchor. Now the fleet being come to anchor, the General called forthwith a council of war, and demanded of their captains what were their sentiments, either to land all the soldiers at once near Sainta Domingo, or to land them there, and so march up to the town. The captains unanimously affirmed it was their oppinion to be the best way, and most saffest, to land the army as near as possible to the city of Sainta Domingo, by which means they might with ease supprize and take the city of Sainta Domingo with the lost of verey few men; by which means being masters of their cheife strenght and head, they might then with the more ease subdue the body and conquer the island. And that wheras if they should land the army at any considerable distance from the city, that then what with long and tedious marches in that hot country, thro the burning sand and wild woods; and by the great advantages the enemy then would have to lie in ambuscados, and so on all opportunities be a great detriment to the army in their march, which could not be without great danger and lost of many (255), if not to the destruction of the whole army.

These with many othere weightier arguments they used to persuaid the Generall from the later, and encourage him in the former; however he harkened not unto them, but landed the army there on the low point of

3. Taylor counts eighteen men-of-war, and most of these were correctly identified except for some malapropisms (*Switzer* = *Swiftsure, Torrent* = *Torrington, Massamore* = *Marston Moor,* and *Coronation* = *Convertine*). See the list giving "the dispersal of the fleet", 1656, National Archives, 1/32, fo. 194; and also John F. Battick, ed., "Richard Rooth's Sea Journal of the Western Design", *Jamaica Journal* 5, no. 4 (1971): 3–22.

4. This number seems high; there were slightly fewer than ten thousand soldiers.

5. Late in December 1654; see Firth, *Narrative of General Venables,* 144–45.

6. This is a fair summary of the orders given to Venables. See ibid., 111–15.

land to the eastward of Cavalero Bay called Zephrisia, where he landed 15,000 men, and made proclamation at the head of the army that none under pain of death should take anything from the Spaniards to the value of a dollar.[7]

Thus the army being landed sett forwards on their march, thro thick and unknown woods, where the Spaniard lieing in ambuscade cut them of at unawars on all advantages in a most miserable manner, so that what with the heat of the weather, what for want of rest and watter the army became faint and dejected, so that the enemy had all possible advantages on them, issuing out from their lurcking places, and kill them with their launces at pleasure. And then they could easily retreat where the English, being unacquainted, durst not follow, soe that in their march thro the thick woods and burning sands, what with those that died with thirst and wearynesse, and those which were kill'd by the Spaniards, the number of the dead was no less in their two daie's march than 2,560 men.

But the army at last thro many difficulties arrived at (256) Sainta Domingo. Venables sent in a trumpeter and demanded the city, upon which they put abrode a white flag and desired a parly might be had, so the governor whose name was then Don Francisco de Algondony[8] came to ye audiencia,* and Venables the English generall was admited thither in order to the parly, the English army being drawn up within pistol shott of the walls of the city. And notwithstanding the many difficulties they had waded thro to get thither, yet nevertheless they were as fierce as lions to have fallen on, and would without doubt have soon taken the citie with the lost of but a few men, for the city was then of no considerable strength.

The parly being ended, and Venables returned from the audiencia, the treacherous Spaniards at once discharged a whole volley of great and small shott against the English, which being so nigh at hand and unexpected made miserable havock and slaughter amongst them, putting them into a great disorder; however they soon rallied again, and with the greatest bravery imaginable were falling on to storm the city, when that the treacherous Venables caused a retreat to be sounded. So the army were forc't to march back again without effecting anything save the losing of their lives. The Spaniard at all opportunities and advantages fell on them from out their ambuscados, and cutting them off with ease, so that they report to this day they killed the English until they weary of killing them.[9]

---

7. The army landed on 14 April and not 20 April. But Taylor's account up to the council at Santo Domingo is accurate; see the documents printed ibid., 127–36.

8. It is impossible to know where Taylor found this name.

9. Taylor's story of the parley and of Spanish treachery seems generally invented.

The English army at last being arrived nere their ships (257) to Punta Zepripria, after their muster there they found that they had lost 7,700 men, besides 385 which they had wounded, the most part of which soon after died.[10] Thus in great haste they were ship't on board, and the fleet stood too and fro along shore, none knowing Venables's intentions. But he was generally hated by all his captains, and had the general curse of all men for this unheard-of treachery. Some say that he was hired by the Spaniards with vast sums of gold to be thus base, and others say that this hapened by the hypocrasie of his wife, by whom he was swai'd and ruled, for she satt with him in his councils of war.

Now because Venables could not for shame return home without affecting anything, he called a councill of war and concluded to bear down to Jamaica, according to which they arrived there on the eight of May 1655 in Cagada Harbour, where having had a consultation they forthwith landed at Passage Fort on the 10th of May anno 1655 with about 6000 men, where they mett with but little resistance, for the Spaniards sone quitted the ffort and retreated in the woods towards Sainta Jago de la Vega. In the rode the Spaniards had made several entrenchments to obstruct their passage in thir march towards that town. Then on the tenth of May, 1655, was Jamaica taken possesion of by the English in the name of Oliver then Pretector of England, with the lost but of seaven men killed, [and] a few wounded; here the army staied this night.[11]

On the morrow morning there came down a trumpeter with (258) a white flag from the Marqueness, then governor of the island, whose name was Segniora Margareta Perez de Gusman, with a message to the Generall which was to this effect, that on condition the Generall with his army would forthwith quitt the island, she would forthwith pay as much redey money or plate as should discharge and pay the whole fleet evere since it had been out of England, and for allowance of time untill they might competently return; further that she would give to every officer, soldier, and seaman (belongin to the fleet) to each as much mony or plate, as his pay would amount unto in two years' service, according to that station they respectively acted in. By now this you may plainly percieve that the island was vastly rich at that time.[12]

But this proffer was by Venables refused, and the messenger [?] departs with an answer accordingly to the Governess, and the army now set forward in their march toward the town, meeting with some few skirmishes, and were

---

10. This figure of nearly eight thousand men is clearly much too high.

11. This paragraph is accurate, down to dates and numbers; the information must have remained firmly in the minds of Taylor's informants.

12. This offer seems to be imaginary; moreover, the island was far from rich. A summary of the terms may be found in Taylor, *The Western Design*, 60–66.

three daies before they arrived thither, tho' with the lost of a very few men. And being arrived there, they took that town of Sainta Jago de la Vega without any opposition, for the inhabitants had withdrawn themselves out of the town into the woods and mountains, with their wives, children, and cheifest riches, flieing from the northside o'er to Cuba and other parts as fast as they could. And such treasure which they could not carry with them, it they buried in the bowels of the earth, and in caves, and as still is reported (259) by many, that they performed spells over it, so that it lies still undiscovered, being inchanted by magicque art, which inchantments are not yet broken; thus with ease the English became masters of that island.

But although the inhabitants for the most part fleed off the island, yet there remained many of the Spaniards behind, lurcking in severall bodys in the woods. Which being discovered, the English army was divided into severall bodys and sent out after them; they kill'd many of those Spaniards, took many prisoners, and forc't the rest off the island.

Also there was out in the woods about 800 Negros, Spanish slaves, out in a body, which through persuation came in and submitted themselves to the English, many of which were made free, and had land aloted them,[13] but those of them which were not made free soon revolted again, and were at last by the English cut off and distroyed, and thus the island was solely enjoyed by the English, the Spaniards and Negros being subdued.

Now Generall Venables having seen things in this posture made what hast he could to wood and water his fleet and return home for England, and gave the government of the island to Colonel Dawghleigh, whom he left President, and to guard and assist the island, he left fifteen sail of men of war to remaine there as the *Torrent, Laurell, Lion, Bear, Massamor, Indian, Gift, Coronation,* etc., with severall other small vessels; the (260) charg of this fleet he comited to Colonell Godson, whom he left admirall thereof.

The generall Venables having put things in this order, he with the residue of the fleet towards the later end of August wayed from Jamaica,[14] and made the best of his way for England, where he arrived with shame and dishonour for his treacherous bussnes towards the English on Hispaniola, and was never imployed any more in the service, but was slighted and scorned by all men of worth and repute.

Now the Protector forthwith sent supplies from England to Jamaica, with provitions and other necessities, with many more new inhabitants, which

13. Here Taylor is thinking of the capitulation of Juan de Bolas, described in S.A.G. Taylor and David Buisseret, "Juan de Bolas and His Pelinco", *Caribbean Quarterly* 24, nos. 1–2 (1978): 1–7.

14. In fact, it was on HMS *Marston Moor* that Venables sailed back to England on 4 July 1655; this retreat led to his disgrace.

resorted thither both from England and Ireland, as also many resorted from Barbadoes, Nevis and other of the windward islands to Jamaica, so that it began to populate. For about the later end of November there arrived from England the *Maremaid, Church, Hope, Saint Paul, Welcom,* etc., men of war, with severall other merchant ships which arrived here with provitions and passengers which come hither to inhabit.[15] Thus the island began to setle and increase amain* in those hir new inhabitants, which dispersed themselves unto the severall parts of the island; some betook themselves to setling of land and planting of tobacco, sugar, corn, cotton, coco, indigo, etc.; others made it their bussines to settle pens and crawles of beves and hogs; others betook (261) themselves to hunting of the sturdy bore and wild bulls, which here the woods abounded with, some to building, and what else was profitable; thus the island began to populat and setle.[16]

Section II

How the Spaniards attempted to have retaken Jamaica, but were notabley repulsed, with the maner of the English, their manner of setling, building, planting, and fortifieing of the island.

To proceed in a genuine method, you must understand that towards the later end of November, 1656, the Spaniards attempted to have retaken Jamaica from the English. For 2,500 Spaniards came over from Cuba, and landed at Rio Nova on the north side of the island, wher they built a fort, and had fortified themselves there with ordnance and strong batteries; this fort they had built on a small hill nigh the said river. Also they built houses there, and waited daily for other succors from Cuba, and also Spain; thus these Spaniards lay here full four months 'ere they were discovered.

These Spaniards being discovered, Colonell Dawleigh with about 1,500 men with all expedition went against them, and in two ships they were conveyed thither, where being landed, they fell to storming of the fort, in the (262) passage to which they met with much difficulty, for the Spaniards fired furiously at them, and there was much fell'd wood and trees. Nevertheless they stoutly stormed the fort, and after about three hours' contest they became masters of the fort and routed the Spaniards and

15. Taylor is thinking of the fleet commanded by Robert Sedgwick, which arrived on 1 October 1655. Taylor, *The Western Design*, 90.

16. Taylor is describing the way in which the various regiments of the invading army were settled along the south coast of the island, from what is now St Thomas westwards to what is now St Elizabeth.

demolish't their works, killing many of them. For the Spaniards fought desperatly to the last, and takeing many of them prisoners the rest made their escape into the woods, and so made their escape off to Cuba as well as they could.[17] The Spaniard being thus routed it hapned that on the morrow their came in here a vessel from Cuba, loaden with wine and provitions for those Spaniard, who not knowing anything of their defeat came heare boldly to anchor, and was immediately taken by the English, who made themselves toperingly merry with the good wine and other liquors that they found in her.

Thus the English haveing beat off the Spaniards, and being fred of them, each man returned home to his respective employ, and new inhabitants coming hither dayly the island began to populat and setle amain and to proceed forward in their planting, etc., for here they had good store of beves, and hog in great plenty, of tame Spanish catel feeding in the savanas or large planes, besides multitudes of them wild in the woods, which they could kill with ease. But at (263) last with their often fiering at them, the tame cattel in the savanas became wild, and betook themselves wild to the woods and mountains, so that they were hard to become at, for you must know that when the Spaniards kill their tame beves which feed in the savanas, they struck them with their launces, and never to shoot at them with guns, so that now the cattle were afrighten'd with the fir and the noise thereof, and so becom wild.[18]

By this means the price of fleash was much increased in such sort that many eat young horse flesh, for beef was now sold there for two royalls* a pound, for although the island was full of cattel, yet their was no catching them but by hunting, which if they soe caught in the mountains, they preserved by takeing out all the bones, and then drieing it in the sun after they had put a small quantity of salt thereon; this they called jerk't beef, or hog, soe that those which betook themselves to hunting got considerable profitt thereby.[19] Also all provitions, and everything which was brought out of England hither, as flower, bred, brandy, win, clouth, etc. was here sold most excessive dear, soe that a gallon of brandy was heare sold sometime for five dollars, but generally for fouer dollars a gallon. Yet still the island began to populat and increase wonderfully in its setlements and plantations, which now thrive and produce frute (264), so that now in some plantations they

17. Taylor is thinking here of the two Spanish expeditions; one arrived towards the end of July 1657, and was defeated that October near Ocho Rios; the other landed in May 1658 at Rio Nuevo, set up a fort there, and was dislodged from it in a fierce little battle the following June. See Taylor, *The Western Design*, 146–80.

18. This mismanagement of the abundant cattle led to the conclusion that the army had "starved in a cookshop"; see Taylor, *The Western Design*, 71.

19. For a fuller description of this process, see below, p. 135.

began to make sugar and rumm, which was a great help and supply to the islands.

And now seeing ships cheifly resorted from England to Cagada Harbour, the English therefor began to build houses and to take up land on Punta Cagada, (which befor was a dispised place and therefore soe call'd by the Spaniards,) and to make wharfs as at Belengsgate,* and build storehouses theron, which place soe built the English named Port Royall, which hath 'ere since increaced in well-built brick houses, a church, and five forts, soe that now there are noe less than 500 well-built houses in formidable streats.[20]

But when it pleased God to disperse England's cloud and bless us with the benign aspect of our happy and good monarch, Charles the Second of ever blessed memory, whose heart and eyes were allwaies open to doe good to all his dominions, he was pleased to take into his princly consideration his late inhabited island of Jamaica, for the which he took what possible care he could for the speedy increasing of its strength, saftie, peace and wealth.[21] In order to which he sent thither an honarable and loyall governour, the right worshipfull Coll. Sir Thomas Minns Knight, which made it his buissinies by all possible means to advance the growth of the island in safty, peace and wealth. For first he built Charles Fort and began to fortifie Port Royall, and put the island into a due military possture, by ordering the inhabitants of (265) all parts of the island into a due order of melitia, haveing thereby form'd severall reigments of the inhabitants into proportionable bands, both of hors and foot, the whole then amounting to 1,200 horse and 4,500 foot. Thus this honourable Governour proceed to build up and establish the strengh of this late setled Jamaica.[22]

Now he proceed yet further, that soe he might establish its peace and saftie within itsself, for he brought the island into a *lex methodica,** for he constituted a councile and assembly of twelve men, of the best credit and reput, which were at all times to seet in councile with him on all spetiall consultations, himself being their head, and represent lord chanceler, and they the twelve judges; these he ordain'd. Also he constitute a court of grand judicature, to be held fouer times a year at St. Jago de la Vega, wherin all civile causes in the lawe were desided, as they are at the King's Bench barr at

20. For this emergence of Port Royal, see Pawson and Buisseret, *Port Royal,* 7–22.

21. With "England's cloud" dispersed, and the Commonwealth over, Charles II in 1660 had to decide whether or not to retain Jamaica, which had been seized in the days of Cromwell.

22. Taylor here describes the measures adopted by D'Oyley's successor, Lord Windsor. See Frank Cundall, *Governors of Jamaica in the Seventeenth Century* (London, 1936), p. 10–15. However, he gives Windsor a name like that of Christopher Myngs, a notable admiral/freebooter of the time in Jamaica. For a survey of these developments, see "A brief survey of Jamaica [1600]", British Library, Harleian MSS 336, fo. 38.

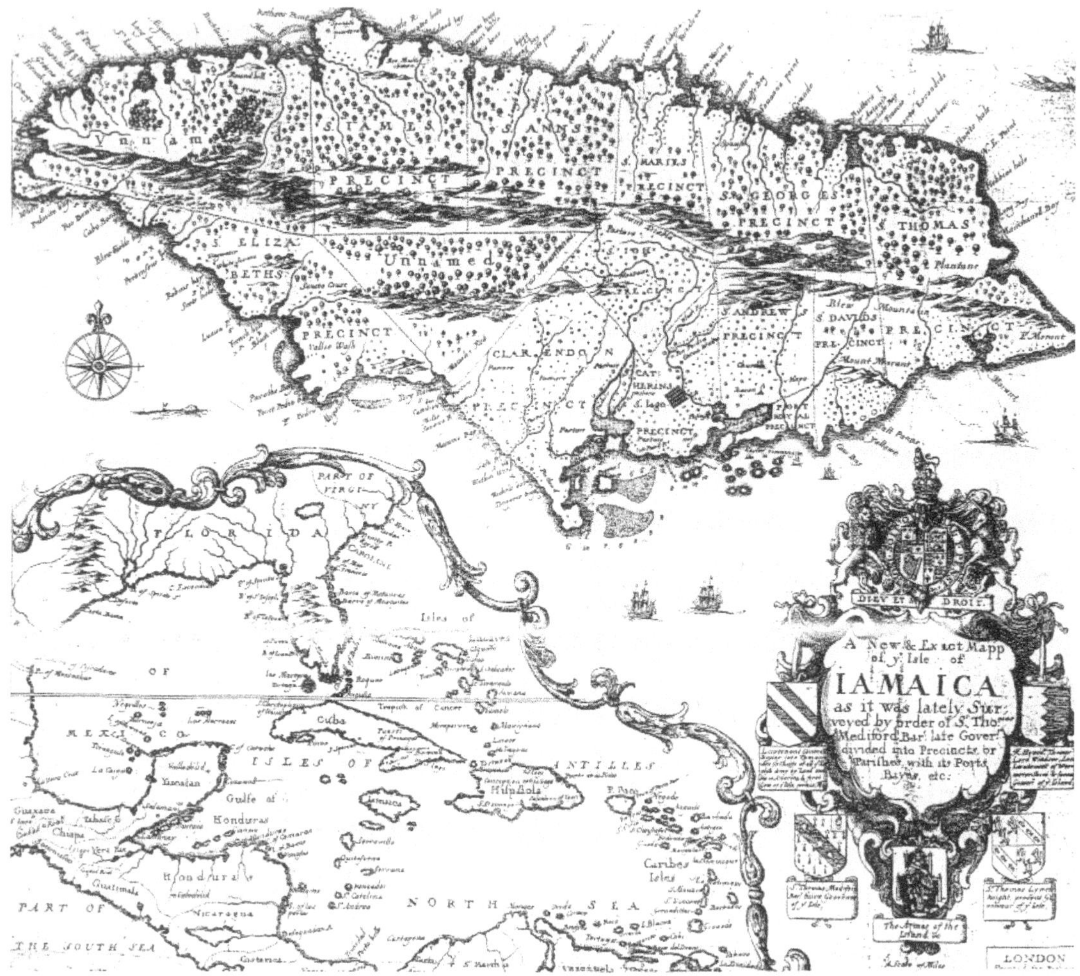

Figure 22 Richard Blome, *A new and exact mapp of ye isle of Jamaica* (London, 1671), from his *New survey of Jamaica.* This early map shows the division into precincts; it also shows, at the foot of the elaborate cartouche, a curious version of "the armes of the Island".

Westminister. Overe this court he instituted a Cheife Justice, and another to acct as the king's Aturney Generall. Now the first Thursday in everey month all causes depending on Chancery were ordered to be tried before the Governour (at the audiencia at St. Jago de la Vega), he acting as Lord Chancillor.[23]

Further, this worthy knight divided the island into severall persincts, and in each ordained petit courts, to be held fouer times yearly as our quarter sesions are in England, wherin all petit* causes were to be dissided by the

23. On these policies see A.P. Thornton, *West-India Policy under the Restoration* (Oxford, 1956), 39–66. It is curious that Taylor uses the Spanish word *audiencia,* meaning the high court or the building in which the court sat.

(266) respective judge, justices of peace and juriours for that persinct,[24] for there were justice of the peace now constituted in each persinct. Thus the island being putt into a *lex methodica,* the governour, which represented the King's person in Parliment, the councile of assemblie which represent the body of the House of Lords in Parliment, and the justices of the persincts which represented the House of Commons, assembled together unto the audience or court house at Sainta Jago de la Vega, where in a due and regular method they satt in concile, by which body thus assembled there were many good and holsom* lawes ordained and recorded and authorized by their joint consent, under the broad seal of the island, for the more suer, quiet and peaceable government of the inhabitants of the said island. This councile or grand assembly was to seet as often as the governour or succeding governours should thinck fitt to assemble them.

Thus this prudent Governour proceed to establish and build up the strenght, peace, and quiet government of this island; now that he might also advance its groath and wealth, and thereby reduce it to a more florishing state, he by a patten* from His Majestie of Great Britain obtained and setled here a factory of the Royall Affrican Company of Merchants, which brought Negro slaves hither, as they had done before to Barbados, etc.,[25] by which means the plantations improved (267) appase, and their commodities of sugar, indigo, cotton etc. began to be plenty, which drawed merchants and shiping thither daylie, both from England and Ireland, loaden with bread, flower, brandy, wine, cloath, and all other nessessarys and vendable marchandizes, and were loaden home with sugar, indigo, ginger, cotton, logwood, fustick,* and other American commodities.

By which means the industrious planter lived in great peace, ease and plenty, soe that the island began to grow exceeding rich. But that which cheifly advanced its wealth was the vast sums of money and plate brought in hither by the English privateers, which by their great courage and unheard-of attempts they took daily from the Spaniards.[26] And here we shall give you an account of the most noble attempts the English hath made with good success against the most eminent places of strenght that the Spaniards cann glory in, which they posses in America.

---

24. "Precinct" was a late-medieval term, originally ecclesiastical, to describe an administrative area. In contemporary English terms, it was larger than a hundred, but smaller than a county. Figure 22 shows how Jamaica was divided into these precincts.

25. At the time when Taylor was writing, Barbados remained the West Indian island to which most African people were being brought by the Royal Africa Company. See Davies, *The Royal Africa Company.*

26. For a recent summary of these activities, see Pawson and Buisseret, *Port Royal,* 25–44.

Section III

An account of the many notable victories obtained by the English against the Spaniards in America since their takeing of Jamaica, and first a description of the takeing of the city Panama by Sir Henry Morgan Knight, anno 1670.[27]

Omitting the discourse of privaters which resorted to Jamaica (268) at the first setling of the island, compossed of Dutch, French, and the least part of them English, which brought thither abundance of wealth, we shall here begin with the account of the notable expedition of Sir Henry Morgan Knight, in his takeing of the city Panama, in the province of Castella del Oro, in America.

Sir Henry Morgan Knight, on the 14th of August 1670, haveing a commission from Sir Thomas Mudiford then governour of Jamaica, put to sea with eleven saile of ships and 600 men. And on the second of September with his fleet he arived at Illha Vacus,[28] which was the place appointed for the fleet to meet att. On the sixth of September, Vice Admirall Collier was dispatch with six saile to take prisoners for inteligence, and victualls for the fleet, from off ye coast of the main, haveing with him 350 men. On the last of September one of those ships return'd to Illha Vacus commanded by Captain Morris, haveing taken a Spanish ship commanded by Emanuel de Rivera, which hade latly [illegible] and burnt on the coast of Jamaica. On the seaventh of October, the fleet reseived some small damage by a storm, the which they soon repaired, and this being the place appointed for their generall rendevouze, other ships came to them, soe that by the later end of October there was seaven saile of English more added to the fleet.

Now on the eight of November Vice-Admiral Collier returns with his fleet to Illha Vacus, and brought with him provition and prisoner which he had taken on the main for inteligence. These prisoners enform'd Sir Henry Morgan (269) that the President of Panama, Donn Juan Perez de Guzman, had of late granted out comisions to take and distroy all English shipps, and that they with all expedition were armeing against the English, and prepareing to put to sea.

Admirall Morgan being advertized hereof forthwith called a councill of warr, consisting of thirty-seaven commanders, who unanimously gave it as

27. Morgan received his commission from Modyford in July 1670; that same month the English had made peace with Spain by the second Treaty of Madrid. For an account of the Panama raid, see Sandra M. Petrovich, *Henry Morgan's Raid on Panama: Geopolitics and Colonial Ramifications, 1669–1674* (New York, 2001).

28. This is Taylor's dog-Latin name for the Ile-à-Vache, an island off the southwest coast of what is now Haiti, and was then Santo Domingo.

their oppinion that it would be most advantageous and safe for the English trading to Jamaica, etc. forthwith for them to make the best of their way towards Panama, and seize that city first because that the President therof was raiseing open hostility maratime against the English, to the great annoyance of our merchants' ships etc. and trading in those parts. Which proceedings of the president of Panama they were well assuered of, not only from the oathes of the Spanish prisoners, but also by the originall commisions themselves, which were their in council produced. This papably appearing by plaine proof, the Admirall and his council agreed forthwith to dirict their course towards Panama.

Soe on the eight of December 1670, Sir Henry Morgan with his fleet wayed from Illha Vacus on the southside of Hispaniola and bore away for Illha Providence (or the isle of Providence),[29] wher the fleet safe arived on the 15th of December instant, and made themselves masters of those two islands with little resistance (270), and being masters of the islands they used the inhabitant verey civilie and kindly, not plunder them att all, by which means some of those inhabitants profered the English to be their guides in their march towards the city of Panama.

Sir Henry Morgan haveing thus taken the islands of Providence, soe then the Admirall haveing call'd a councile of warr forthwith dispatch away Captaine Bradly, with three ships and 470 men, with some of the inhabitants of Providence which voluntary took up arms as guides in the English's service, to take the citie of Chagre.[30] Soe Captaine Bradly left the fleet, and on ye 27th of December 1670 he landed his men within fouer miles of the castle, and soe silently in the night they made their approach towards it, where being arived they stoutly began to storm the same, and the Spaniards as bravely resisted in the most desperat maner imaginable, but providence soe order'd it that a guard's house built of wood, which stood on the walls being by accident set on fier, it blowed up, and made a large breach in the wall. By which means the English entered with the greatest bravery imaginable, and the enemy as stoutly resisted to the last man; neither would they receive quartar, soe that the English kill'd them all to the number of 360 men. On the English's side were kill'd in this action a captain and a lieutenant, with twenty-eight others, and their were 96 of them wounded; (271) amongst ye which was the brave Captain Bradley, who in two days after died of his wounds.

The English thus being masters of Chagre, and Sir Henry Morgan being advertised therof, he forthwith and his fleet sail'd from Providence, and on the second of January 1671 he with his fleet arived thither. And goeing up

29. Isla de Providencia, about 130 miles off the coast of Nicaragua.

30. This city lay on the river Chagres, whose valley gave access to the road to Panama.

the harbour they ran fouer of their ships aground, which were there lost, but not one man drowned; the Admiral's ship was one of them. Thus fiending the river to be shoul'd and dangerous, they therfore fitted out 7 of their ships of least draught of water, with men, arms, etc. proportionable, leaving the rest of the fleet behind in Rio Chagre, and left Captain Norris with 300 men to guard them, and ye castle. In the meantime the Spaniards were not idle, for they in the passage towards Panama, betwixt Chagre and Venta Cruz, had intrench't themselves, and made six severall bateries and brestworks of retreat.

Now on the ninth of January 1671, Sir Henry Morgan with those seaven saile wayed from Chagre, and made the best of their way up the river, to atend those which march't up land by the side of the river. Upon the aproach of the English the Spaniards basely quited their first entrenchment, and set it on fire (as afterwards they did all the other), without strickeing one stroake.

But now the river would admit of a passage for the fleet no further, for they found it verey shoul'd and dangerous. Wherfor Admiral Morgan left the fleet here (272) under the care of Captain Delander, and 200 men to guard the same. Then Sir Henry Morgan with the rest landed and began their march towards Panama, marching thro' wild and thick woods for twenty-fouer miles, where their was noe path but what their pionners* cut before them. Thus they bravely continued their march, untill they arived at Venta Cruz, which was a narrow and dangerous pass, the which was defended by a strong body of the Spaniards to obstruct their passage towards Panama. But Captain Rodgers who comanded the forloarn hope[31] sone routed the Spaniards, which basly betook themselves to their hells, and ran away like lusty fellows, and thus the English became masters of the pass. In this acction the English had only three men slightly wounded, but what the enemy lost was they could not never learne.

Thus the army continued on their march untill they arived at a village called Venta Cruz on the river Chagre, which place also the Spaniards had basely quited, and sett on fier. This is a fine vilage and the place wher the Spaniards embarque all their goods, plate etc. which they send from Panama to Spain. The English being arived hither they were now greiviously put to a strait for want of food, for here they could gett but very litle, and they were also extremely galed in their march by the Spaniards' ambuscados, for the English still drove the Spaniards for above three miles before them, the way being soe narrow that the English could march (273) but three men abrest,

31. A "forlorn hope" was in military parlance a body of men assigned to some dangerous task, like leading the whole army. The phrase, which came from the Dutch, has passed into modern usage.

the way being verey deep and steep, by reason of which the enemy had great advantage to interupt and hinder their march.

However, the English stoutly continued on their march till they were gott clear of this dangerous passage, and safely arived on a larg savana or statly plain, with the lost but of three men kil'd and seaven wounded; here they'd the desired sight of the South Sea.[32] On this savana they found a great heard of cattle, soe there they haulted, killing what of them they thought fitt, and refreshed themselves with food and rest without any opposition from the enemy.

Now on the seaventeenth of January 1671, the English began to march again towards Panama and the eavening they had sight of the enemy, which was drawn up in batalia* 2,100 foot and 600 horse. But it being late, the English encamp't themselves that night without being allaramed by ye enemey. On the morrow morning as soon as Phebus with his golden raies had chac't away the sable night, and had iluminat these southwestern parts of the world, then there might you have here seen this truly expert soldier Sir Henry Morgan at the head of the English, which then wer drawn up in order of bataile in a formidable tertia.[33] The vauntguard conteyning 300 men were lead and commanded by Collonel Prince and (274) Major Morris; the main body containing 600 men was led by Sir Henry Morgan and Collonel Collier, and the rearguard conteyning 300 men was led by Collonel Beldry Morgan. In this order the English were drawn up and began to march towards ye enemey. In the meanwhile the Spaniards had drawn up themselves in a place of great advantage, soe that the English were forc't to wheel to the left to gaine a hill hard by, which they haveing obtained, by this policie of Sir Henry Morgan the enemy was forc't to fight the English at noe small disadvantage, by reason they had not rome enough to whele their main body, for that there lay a bogg in their reer before which they drue up to entrap the English.

Now the trumpets on boath sids began to sound their martiall blast, and Don Francisco de Hare who commanded the Spanish calverey gave the first onseet, rideing furiously on full speed towards vauntguard of the English, which by reason they had noe pikes to defend them from the horse, they doubled their ranks to the right, and closed their files to the right and left inward, by which they bravely maintained their ground against the horse, killing many of them and Don Francisco de Hare amongst the rest. Thus the Spanish horse proveing unsuccessful whel'd off to the right and the Spanish infantry began to advance.

(275) Whilst that the Spanish infantry was thus marching against the

32. Now known as the Pacific Ocean.

33. This odd word is clearly from the Spanish *tercio,* a division of infantry.

English in their front, Lo! the Spaniards were also practizeing a cunning stratagem in their rear. For when the Spanish infantry engaged the English in the front, then did they indeavour to force in above 2,000 oxen into their reare, to disorder them. But they let them allone quietly till they came nigh at hand, then they one a suddain fir'd at their drivers, and loudly ratled their drums, which soe afrighted the oxen (which were not accustomed to such kind of musicke) that they turn'd head upon their drivers, and soe were soon forc't back with ease, which otherwise would have proved of dangerous consequence. This stratagem proveing unsuccesful, and the Spanish infantry being received by the main body of the English with a brave voly, soe that scarce a shot flew in vaine, and then with ye left winge fell on them with that vigor, soe that they were sone defeated, and bettook themselves to flight in a great consternation. Happy was he which could first get into the city Panama,[34] where they had 200 fresh men, all the streets being barocaded, and they had place theire 32 brass peices of ordnance to flanck the streets [and] allso to flanck the gates and passage towards the city. They had built two forts, on the one of which was mounted six, and on the other, eight brass peices of ordnance.

But after all this great preparation, at the approach (276) of the English towards the gates of the Panama the president caused the city to be fier'd, and the cheife fort to be blown up, which was don in such hast that 40 of his soldiers were blown up with the blast, and the city being built of timber 'twas all soon consumed to ashes, except the audiencia, the convent of Mercedes San Joseph, with the suburbs of Melambo, and Pierde Vidas.[35]

The English haveing thus routed the Spanish foot in the feild, with all expedition they followed them into the city, which was all on flames, where they met with but small resistance, which was from a body of the Spaniards gathered together in ye plaza major,* which only discharged some few ordnance and small shot at them, killing 3 and wounding five, and then quited the place and betook themselves to their hels after their companions. Soe that by two a'clock in the afternoon the English had quiet posestion of the city, which was all in smoake and flames and was notwithstanding their utmost endevour burnt down, all except the audiencia etc. and about 300 houses in the suburbs of Melambo, the which with great care was preserved. In this honourable and desperat accion Sir Henry Morgan had but six men kill'd and ten wounded, but of the Spaniards about 460 were found slaine, 900 taken prisoners.

(277) Thus by the prudent conduct of the right worshipfull Sir Henry

34. This is the city of Old Panamá, some five miles west of present-day Panama City.
35. See Petrovich, *Henry Morgan's Raid.*

Morgan, and by the undaunt'd valour of the English, was the strong and potent city of Panama taken, and by its own treacherous inhabitants fier'd and burnt to ashes, and its butie consumed, which befor was the glory of Castella del Oro and the greatest mart for silver and gold in the whole world. For in it were wont to be treasur'd up all the plate and gold brought from the mines of Potozi and Peru, with pretious stones and jewels of inestimable value. And it also received all the goods and merchandize brought from Old Spain in the king's great fleet (which is first landed at Porto Bello and Venta Cruz, and brought to this city on horses and mules), and deliver'd to galloons of the grand Flota or plat fleet all the plate and gold brought from the mines of Potozi and Peru. In fine, 'twas a magazien of wealth, and Spain's great treasurey.[36]

In this acction did this worthy knight soe order all afairs that never man behaved himself with more braverie, valour, and resolution to accomplish what he had undertaken, shewed more soldierlike conduct, nor took more care to prevent disorder and irregularitie amongst his men (not only by his own example, but also by strick martiall order) than he did. For being master of the city he took care of the women and childrend, causing them all to be brought to one place, and a strong guard to be set over them, to protect (278) them from the violence and rudeness which should be offer'd unto them, soe that none durst afront them, under pain of severe punishment.

Thus the English being sole masters of Panama remain'd there for the space of a whole month, makeing daily inroades for above fifty miles into the province of Castella del Oro, all round the city about the countrey, meting with small resistance. Soe that in that time they got aboundance of plat and other riches, and took full 3,560 prissoners, of all sorts and qualities, to whome they gave good quarter and sivile entertainment.

Now on the 14th of February 1671, Sir Henry Morgan with the English quitted Panama, and cary'd their prisoners as well as their plunder allong with them, and directed their course towards Venta Cruz, which is fifteen miles distant from Panama. The English being arrived in safty at Venta Cruze they then stayed ten days to refresh themselves, but cheifly to give time for the Spaniards to ransom their wives and children, with the Spanish fathers, which the English then had taken prisoners here. After they had stayed the limited time, and the Spaniards had ransomed all of note and quallity, they set the other Spanish women and children, which remain'd unransom'd, at libirtie, but kept all their Indian and Negro slaves, which they had taken from the Spaniards, as part of the plunder to be divided amongst the English.

36. This summary of the importance of Panama is in general accurate; it was indeed the port of transshipment for treasure from Peru.

Soe on the 24th day of February 1671, the English marched from (279) Venta Cruze forwards towards their ships which they had left in the Chagre River, under the care of Captain Norris and Captain Delander. Where Sir Henry Morgan and the English being arived, they found all in safty, where after they had divided the plunder amongst the soldiers and seamen, they were all ship't on board, and made preperation to return to Jamaica, where they all safely arived in a short time. By this acction Admirall Morgan and the English got much honour, and the next yeare, when Admirall Morgan went home to England, His Majesty of Great Britain was pleased to confer on him the honour of knighthood, for this good service which he had don.[37]

In this expedition the English gott noe less than 60,000 pounds sterling, which was accounted noe considerable bootie if you consider the vast wealth of Panama; the reason why they here found noe more wealth was because that the Spaniards had notice of their approach two months before they came there, in which time they had convey'd away most of their trasure to Lima or Cyndada des les Reines in Peru. For they had sent thither a ship of 700 tuns, loaden with gold and pretious stones, and another of three hundred tunns, loaden with gold. For the Spaniards, hearing of the aproach of the English, were in a great consternation; the president of Panama sent forces everywhere to obstruct the passag of the English towards the city. Also at Panama they (280) caried the image of the Imaculat Conception dalie in open procession about the city, attended by monks of the church of Saint Francisco, and by the nuns of ye lady Rosario des Santa Domingo, and the convent Mercedes San Joseph; nay the president himself, Don Juan Perez de Guzman, was now afrighted into such devotion, that he presented to the image of the Imaculat Conseption, and to the saints and patrons, all his jewels and reliques which he had obtained in his pilgrimage to the Holy Land. Also he offer'd an image of the Blesed Virgin Mary, a diomond ring to the value of 40,000 dollars, invoacking hir aid.

Thus we have here given you a full description of the English, their desperat attempt against the Spaniards, their takeing their chife of Panama, by which means the Spaniards were forc't to sue for a peace to His Majesty of Great Britain. For in the later end of Aprill 1671, there was a peace concluded on at Madrid, betwixt his excelency Sir William Godolphin Knight, embasador for His Majesty of Great Britain at the court of Spain, and the Conde de Penaeranda, betwixt the English and Spaniards in the West Indies.[38] And in the begining of July following Sir Thomas Linch then

37. The circumstances of this knighthood are explained in W. Adolphe Roberts, *Sir Henry Morgan, Buccaneer and Governor* (New York, 1933), 201–3.

38. The treaty of Madrid had in fact been signed in July 1670, long before Morgan's raid; it was ratified in August 1671.

Figure 23 A Description of the South Sea and Coasts of America (London, *c.*1684). This simple little map shows Bartholomew Sharp's outward journey, up the west coast of South America, and then his return to Barbados ("Sharp's reditus").

receiving the government of Jamaica, forthwith on the 10th of the said month dispatch away Collonel William Beston in the *Assistance* friget, to the city of Cathagen with orders there to congratulat the peace, and demand of (281) the governour all English prisoners.[39] Soe after Collonel Beston had dispatch his buissiness with the governour of Cathagen, he safly arived to Jamaica, bring with him 38 Englishmen which had binn prisoners there. And thus we have finished our discription of the takeing of the city Panama by the English, by which means Jamaica was much inrich't, and now we shall fall in hand to give you an account of the adventurs of Captain Bartholomew Sharp, in the south seas of the America.

Section IV

Of the adventures of Captain Bartholomew Sharp against the Spaniards in the south sea of America.[40]

Captain Bartholomew Sharp and about 300 merry boys more of Jamaica went from thence privatly arm'd, in a small ship from the northside of the island, to Darien, on the main of America, where being arived they enter'd themselves into the emperour of Darien's service, dividing themself into two companys tho' they were to acct jointly together; 150 men were putt under the comand of Captain Coxen, and 150 under the comand of Captain Sharp. These two captaines received comisions from the emperour of Darien to fight against the Spaniards. For you must know that this Indian emperour hath continuall warry against the Spaniards. This emperor was of a tall lusty stature, araied in a lose mantle of puer (282) gold, and his son the king of the Golden Cape Indians was arraied in a whit cotten vest fring'd about the neck; his belt (wherin hung a good semeter*) was curiously made of tigers' teeth, on his head was a kind of bonnet or hat made of puer gold, and in his nose hunge a jewel of gold made in the form of collop shell,[41] which is the fashion amongst those Indians. This emperour of Darien and the Indian king with about 200 of their subjects joyn'd themselves to the English in order to march with them up the river of Darien against the Spaniards.[42]

---

39. The activity of HMS *Assistance* was carefully noted by William Beeston in the "1671 Journal of William Beeston in the *Assistance*", British Library Add. Mss. 12424.

40. The classic account of Sharp's exploits may be found in John Esquemeling's *The Buccaneers of America,* ed. W.S. Stallybrass (New York, 1987). Plans of many of the places mentioned may be found in Derek Howse and Norman Thrower, eds., *A Buccaneer's Atlas: Basil Ringrose's South Sea Waggoner* (Berkeley, 1992).

41. This probably refers not to the archaic word "collop", but to the scallop shell.

42. The "emperor of Darien" clearly exists as a cover for piracy.

Thus the English with the Indians haveing prepared cannoas for the passage up the river, they secuer'd their ships in an obscure place for the Indians to guard till their return back. Soe on the fifth of Aprill 1680, they began their march up the river, and thro' weary marches, and difficult passages in canoas, they made towards Panama, and on the 15th they took the fort of Sainta Maria and the town, in which they found not much treasure, because the Spaniards som few days before had removed their dust gold from thence. Here the Indian emperour and's subjects return'd back.

Soe on the 16th of Aprill Captain Sharp and Captain Coxen with the English left Sainta Maria, and continued their march up the river of Darien in their canoas, where on the 20th they mett with three Spanish barques (283). Soe they assailed them, and by their valour soon becam masters of two of them, but the other ran from them. This good success put life and courage into the English, which in this their passage had indured much wearyness, hunger, and want of provition; here they found good wins and other provitions. Thus being masters of two stout barques, they ship't themselves therin and quited some of their canoas.

The English still made the best of their way up the river of Darien, and on the 16th of Aprill 1680 they took another stout barque of Spain, in which they found 60,000 dollars and some other plate. This barque they also man'd, sending away all their prisoners which they had taken in these three barques in one of their canoas, after which the English went to Illha Tobago to refresh themselves.

On the thirtenth of May they left Tobago and put to sea, and in a short time they arived at Quibible, where landing thro' their rash boldness they were beat on by the Spaniards, haveing seaven of their men kill'd, and they were forc't to retreat to their ships. Soe they put to sea again and on the 20th of May 1680, they took another Spanish vessel loaden with monteg de porko[43] and maize. Now there fell some difference betwixt Captain Coxen and Captain Sharp, soe that they divided their plunder, and soe Captain Coxen with 100 men left Captain Sharp, whoe with two hundred of ye English (284) still continued on their voige resolving still to fight under the emperour of Darien's commistion. Thus Captain Sharp with his company bore away to find out a convenient place to caren their ships att.

Thus when Captaine Sharp had caren'd and fitted his ships, they on the 25th of July 1680 set sail to the southward, and on the 25th of August following they came up with a Spanish ship which they stoutly boarded and took. It proved to be a small Spanish man of warr fitted out of Wyake commanded by Don Thomas de Algondony on purpose to take Captain

43. This is one of Taylor's curious invented words, referring to hog-lard.

Sharp. Now the English being masters of hir, they took out the prisoners, hir mainmast, and what else they found of worth in hir, which being don they sunck hir in the sea, and then the English continued plieing to the southward.

On the fouerth of September 1680, Captain Sharp and his company took another Spanish vessel, which was bound for Lima or Cindada des les Rynes, in which they found a considerable booty of plat, the which with her main mast and what was else of value they took out of hir, and then turn'd hir adrift, and again they continued plieing to the southward untill the 26th of October following, at which time they were like to be starved for want of water, they being come to the allowance of a pint of water for a man a day, soe that water was worth with them 30 dollars a pint, to such which would spare his allowance. But Providence soe order'd (285) it that on the 25th of October they made land and came to anchor at Cabo Helve, where they went ashore in their canoas, and found some few Indian wigwams, and a small Spanish village. And here they took 20 Indian prisoners, and forthwith they wooded and water'd their ships.

Now by those Indians which they had taken they were enformed that there was nigh at hand a sugar worke. Soe they went up to it, and found the people all gon, soe they loaded themselves down with sugar, wine, pork and other things which they their found, and soe safly return'd on board. Now on the morrow there came down to La Helve some Spaniards with a whit flag, desiering them not to spoile the sugar worke and they would give them a hundred beves, or hoggs, within three days. Soe Captain Sharp stai'de here in expectation of their promise, but the perfidious Spaniards insted of bringing down the beves, they brought down 300 Spanish horsmen, the which by the English were beaten and put to flight.

Now Captain Sharp and his company haveing wood'd and water'd their ships and refresh't themselves here, they on the fifth of November 1680 wayed from La Helve, and stood to sea, plieing to the westward, and on the third of December following they arived nere the city Coquimbo, where in the night they landed 85 men befor the city, whoe meeting (286) with the Spanish patroule consisting of 150 horse Captain Sharp with 85 men, which he led, made head against them, giveing them orders to fier but five at a time untill the other 50 men were come upp. Soe with the greatest bravery imaginable Captain Sharp fell on the patroule, and killed 26 of them (for scarce a shot flew in vain) and put the rest to flight, Captain Sharp haveing but one man slightly wounded. By this time the other 50 English were com up, and soe they began to march towards the city, passing thro' many difficulties. For they followed the patroule which made their way over ditches and swamps, that therby the city might have time to carry away their most valuable treasure.

But the English being arived at the city soon became masters therof without scarse any resistance. Here they feasted themselves with variety of good flesh, frutes, and wine, which is here made in great plenty. Also here they found store of European frutes as apples, pears, apricoes etc. This city of Coquimbo lies in 29° 50' south latitude; it stands on a small riseing ground, 'tis built in the form of a quadrangle, being full a mile square, and in it are nine churches. Its cheif commodities is copper and gold dust.[44] Now on the fifth of December instant Captain Sharp had a parly with the governour of this city, who was Don Ferdinando Cindagondony, who (287) agreed to ransom that city for 95,000 dollars. But the disceitfull Spaniard, instead of performeing his promise, sent an Indian which swimed off in the dead of the night, and had brought off fier balls which he had fixed to the ship, and soe satt hir afier. But this being by the English presently perceived, they sone extinguished the fier, and took the Indian. Now this not takeing effect, the governour caused the sluces to be open'd, and soe lay'd the water into the town about anckle deep. Captain Sharp was exasperated with this prefidious dealing of the Spaniards, and therupon fier'd the city, and return'd on board with his plunder. And haveing turn'd these Spanish prisoners which he had before taken ashore here, the English on the seaventh of December wayed from hence, standing to ye westward.

Soe on the 25th of December 1680 Captain Sharp with his company safely arived at the island of Juan Fernando, where they came to anchor to fitt and repaire their ship.[45] On this island they found plenty of good provition of flesh and fruites, which stood them in noe small stead. Now whilst they lay here afitting of their ships, there was a mutinie raised amongst ye men, which was like to prove of dangerous consequence, but was at last appeased thro' the persuation of some amongst them, more prudent than the rest, soe that all was well again. And by the 12th of January Anno (288) 1681, when that morning their boats espied three ships, upon which with all expedition Captain Sharp made to sea, and these three saile gave hir chase, but the admirall sailing better than the other two, soe that she was about six miles distant from them. Upon which Captain Sharp tac't about, resolveing to board him, altho' he had 12 peices of ordnance, and the English none. The Spaniard perceiveing this, tac't and bore down for his companions, soe then Captain Sharp plied to westward and by night he had lost sight of them.

Now on the 27th of January 1681, Captain Sharp set some of his men

44. On Coquimbo see Esquemeling, *The Buccaneers of America*, 271–73, 390–91; on the latter pages there is a plan of Coquimbo Bay.

45. On the island of Juan Fernandez see ibid., 393–402; this passage includes two landfall-views and a map.

ashore on the coast of Arica,[46] to take prisoners for inteligence, whoe haveing taken som Indian prissoner, they inform'd the English of the strenght and situation of the city Aryca. Soe then Captain Sharp made the best of his way thither, and towards the morning Captain Sharp landed nigh the city, with 95 men who comming before the city soon put too flight above 200 Spaniards, which stood to oppose them and followed them into their brestwork, alltho' the Spaniards furiously discharged their cannon on them from the fort. Nevertheless the English briskly ataquet the brestwork, and after a sharp encounter the Spaniards yeilded and began to cry for quarter, which the English granted (289) to these Spaniards.

But the other brestwork still continued fiering at the English, which they resolutely storm'd and took, puting all to the sword, for they were a sort of mulatos, which never give quarter to any, therfore they were thus dealt with. The English thus haveing taken the brestwork soon became masters of ye city, where being called alltogether in the Plaza Major they found they had more prissoners than men of their own. Soe the English forthwith secuer'd their prisoners, and march to storm the fort, puerly for the sake of the guns, for here they might have had as much coined dollars and plate and gold as they had bin able to have born away quietly without further resistance, the place was soe vastly rich. But they want guns to defend their ship, which being obtained they could also comand this wealth too.

Thus the English approach't to storm the fort, which made stout resistance against them, killing many of their men. Also the militia coming down upon them, they were forc't to desist, and with noe small danger and lost they fought their way to their boats, haveing 28 kil'd, 17 wounded, and their chirurgeon* taken prisoner. Thus by this attempt for the desier of the ordnance, they lost all that vast booty which they might have obtained with ease, and bin freed from the great lost which they now sustain'd by this desperat atempt.

This city of Aryca lies in 18° 29' of (290) south latitude, is built in a vally by a river, and is a city of a larg extent. In it are five churches and it hath a verey good and comodious harbour, and the inhabitants are of a good complection and stature. In fine, 'tis a vast, rich city, it being the treasury of the mines of Potozy.[47] Near to this city is a mountaine out of which the Spaniards dig salt in lumps of two or three hundredweight.* Captain Sharp being thus frustrated of his disigne here, and have lost soe many of his men, was much troubled therat, and on the last of January he wayed from Aryca, and plied to the westward allong shore.

46. For a plan and description of Arica, see ibid., 410–11.

47. The silver mine at Potosí was indeed legendary for its wealth.

Now on the 13th of March 1681, Captain Sharp with his company safely arived at Gwasko, where after they had goot on board wood and water, with some fresh provitions, and had refresh't themselves, on the 15th of March they wayed from thence and continued plieing westerly, and on the 27th following they arived at Helo, which lies in 17° 49' south latitude and is a very plesant and plentyfull place. Here Captain Sharp with the English went ashore to refresh themselves, and to take prisoners for inteligence. And here they stayed untill the last of this instant March, at which time they wayed from Helo, and plied to the westward, meting with fair weather.

But nowabouts happen'd another broile, for forty-five of Captain Sharp's men now refused to fight in the emperour's service, but resolved to leave Captaine Sharp. Whereupon they (291) had their shares deliver'd them, and were put on board the rest of the ships, and on the 17th of Aprill 1681 they quit'd Captain Sharp and the emperour of Darien's service. Soe that Captain Sharp had now left but 117 of his company, the rest being gon and dead. These men leaveing their captain put him to noe small trouble, and was a great weakening to the emperour's service. However, he continued his resolution to fight still under the emperour's commistion, and so plied to the westward, meting with good weather. And on the eight of May 1681, Captain Sharp and his company came safe to anchor in the Gulph of Nicora, wher they took some Indians prisoners, by whom they were [informed] of two barks which were up in that gulph, the which they tooke and found in them a considerable booty. Here they stayed to caren and fitt their ship, and gett on board what provitions they could, the which haveing compleated on the 29th of that instant May, Captain Sharp wayed from hence and stod to ye westward.

On the 10th of July 1681, Captain Sharp took a Spanish ship loaden with coco and som plate, the which after they had taken out of hir, and took out hir mainmast and riging, they turn'd hir adrift with those Spaniards which they found in hir and then plied again to the westward haveing good weather.

On the 23rd of July 1681, Captain Sharp took another Spanish (292) ship loaden with brandy, wine, oyle and frute. Also she had in her hould 670 piggs* of metall which the English supposed to be tinn, and therfore they tok in but two of them, only to make bullets withall, but when they came to Antigo they found their mistake for that it was silver. For they there sold about one third of one of those piggs (which they had left unmilted) for 75 pounds sterling. Thus the English haveing taken this prize forthwith took out of hir all hir brandy, wine, oyle and fruite, and soe quited hir leaving that vast treasure in hir which amounted to noe less than 150,750 pounds. And thus thro' ignorance did they lose this vast treasury which they were sole masters of.

Now Captain Sharp and his company haveing obtain'd good provitions and liquors, were resolved to return home with what Providence had bestowed upon them. Soe in procecution of which they stood to sea, meting with many storms and bad weather, untill they came into 50° 37' south latitude to an island which they called the Duke of York's Island, where they stayed to refresh themselves with fish, fowles, and some good fruites which they here found. For now they were grat disharten'd of ever getting thro' the straights of Magellanica, and resolved to seek some other passage further south.

(293) Therefore on the thirteenth of November 1681, Captain Sharp way'd from the Duke of York's Island, and made what saile they could in order to their finding out a passage further south, still meteing with cold, sharp, windy weather. Thus they continued on their course till towards the later end of November, at which time provitions began to be verey short with them, being almost spent. Soe that they killed one hog, which was all they had left, and a spanell dog which they bought of one of their quartermaster for 40 dollars, on Christmas Day for their dinner. And now they had noe sort of flesh either fresh or salt left them but lived all togeather on hommeny,[48] or boil'd maize and oyl. But yet they had good liquors indeferent plenty amongst them still.

Thus Captain Sharp continued on his course untill the 28th of January 1682, on which day they happily made the island of Barbados, and meeting with the *Richmond*'s pinnace whom Captain Sharp invited on board, being desierous to know how affairs stood since their maratime pilgrimage. But they would not come on board, but made the best of their way into the island. Upon which Captain Sharp being afraide least he should be taken by the *Richmond* friget, forthwith bore up his helm, and stood away for Antego, where on the last day of this instant January they arived in safty, and forthwith shared (294) their plunder which amounted to 26,560 pounds.[49] As for their ship, 'twas given to six of them, which had gamed away the most part of their mony. These forthwith put again to sea with hir, and the rest shifted for themselves as well as they could. Some went home to England, others went to New England, but the most part of them went to Jamaica where they lavishly spent their wealth to the inriching of that island.[50] Thus we have finished the description of the exploits of that valiant soldier and seaman, Captain Bartholomew Sharp, in his adventures against the Spaniards in the south seas of America.

48. Hominy is coarsely ground maize.

49. This encounter with HMS *Richmond* is described in Esquemeling, *The Buccaneers of America,* 473.

50. Some pirates, such as Sir Henry Morgan, did indeed spend some of their loot in establishing estates in Jamaica. See Pawson and Buisseret, *Port Royal,* 39.

We might hereunto annex the takeing of the city of Vera Cruz, with eight ships, and not above 1,000 men, commanded by Captain Van Horn, which exploit was proformed in May 1683, wherin they goot noe less than 800,000 dollars besides aboundance of plate, gold and jewles, and brought away with them from thence 1,230 Negro, Indian and malato prisoners which were worth, and by them sold, for noe less than 14,500 pounds.[51] But because the major part of Van Horn's men were Dutch and French, they haveing only with them 100 English, commanded by Jacob Hall a Bermodian, in a small vessel of eight gunns, and one [blank] Spru which went away from Jamaica in a small sloop, and soe enter'd himself under Van Horn's service, and also becaus but a few of them return'd to Jamaica to spend their wealth, by reason (295) that privateres were ther soe narrowly look't after there, for all which reasons we have here omited a large description of this exploit, and so we shall conclude this fouerth section of the second chapter of our present state of Jamaica.

Section V

Of the care that hath allways bin taken by His Majesty of Great Britanie for the suppressing and distroying of pyrats in America.

His Majesty of Great Britain, whose eye and heart were ever open to doe good to all his subjects, was gratiously pleased to take into his princly consideration the great damage which the bucaniers and other pyratts did dayly doe not only to Spaniards, but also to his own subject setled in America. And seeing that many of those bucaniers were of his own subjects, whoe under pretence of lawfull comissions which they had given them from the governers of His Majesty's plantations there, did dayly in those parts not only plunder the Spaniards contrary to the late peace but did also rob both English and Irish ships tradeing in those part, which was noe other but notorious piracey, therfore that he might redress such greivences, he first stricktly comanded all his lieutenants in those parts not to grant out any (296) more such commissions, under pain of His Majesty's high displeasure, but forthwith, within the space of three months, to call in all such commitions which they had already granted. And that also such which refused to come in within the said limeted time should forthwith be proclaimed pyrats and rebells to His Majesty, and be proceded against accordingly. Further His Majesty gave

51. For the sack of Vera Cruz in 1683 by Nicholas van Hoorn, Michel de Grammont and Laurens de Graaf, see David Marley, *The Sack of Veracruz: The Great Pirate Raid of 1683* (Ontario, 1993).

order to all the captains of his frigets which he sent to those his American domminions, to be att all times redy to seek out, take and distroye all piratts whatsoever that they had notice of in those parts.

In compliance to these His Majestie's orders, Captain Charles Carlisle, comander of His Majestie's Ship the *Francis,* by order from Sir William Stapleton governour of Nieves, burnt the ship called the *La Trampuse* comanded by that notorious pirrat Hamline, which plundered all nations on the coast of Guinea, haveing burnt 17 ships after he had drown'd their men and rob'd them of their treasure, eleven of which wer English.[52] Besides, he had rob'd above twenty more he had let goe with their ships. This notorious pirrat being on the carrean in Saint Thomas's Road, one of the Virgin Islands, was there found out and burnt by Captain Charles Carlisle on the 20th of August 1683.

On the ninth of Aprill 1686, Captain Banister, commander of the *Fleece* (a stout merchant's ship of thirty-six (297) gunns and about 160 men, which he had got privatly aboard from off Port Royall) in the night cut his cables and ran out of the harbour of Port Royall in Jamaica, and being at sea he became a pirat and plunder'd not only the Spaniards, but merchant ships tradeing to Jamaica also.[53] For on the 26th of May 1687, their came in a ship and a katch from Dublin in Ireland, which made complaint upon oath to the Governour of Jamaica, that they being off of the east end of Hispaniola in order to this passage hithere, were both of them their seized and rob'd by Banister, whoe took from the ship hir mainmast, and what else he thought fitt, and from the katch hir whole cargoe of Irish provitions of beef, flower, bread, etc.

Upon this complaint Captain Charles Talbot in His Majesty's Ship *Faulcon,* and Captain Spragg in His Majesty's Ship the *Drake,* by orders from the Governoure of Jamaica then Hender Molesworth Esquire, forthwith put to sea in order to look for Banister, and on the last of June 1687 they found Banister in the Gulph of Samana on Hispaniola with ye *La Chaval,* a small French privatere, in his company, both which were then comming off of the carren. Now they haveing hal'd ashore their guns on the island, and fortyfied themselves, they obstinatly fier at His Majestie's (298) frigets without shewing any colours. And soe they continued for two days together with all boldness imaginable, in which time the *Faulcon* and *Drake* continued fiering at Banister's ship with their cannons, by which means they tore hir all to pieces,

52. For an account of the capture of the *Trompeuse,* see the *Calendar of State Papers, America and West Indies, 1681–1685,* no. 1188.

53. Taylor here repeats his misdated but essentially accurate account of the misdeeds of Bannister, carrying it on to the pirate's death in January 1687.

and uterly stopped hir forever putting to sea again. But they could not come to burn hir because of Banister's baterys on the shore, and his men on the island whoe were shelter'd with the woods, and kept fiering with their musquet continually at them, by which means such an atempt would have binn exceding dangerous, for Banister was extreamly resolute. Here the two frigets stay'd as long as they had any amunition left, and then they (haveing uterly distroy'd Banister's ships) way'd from hence and bore away for Jamaica.

Now the ffrigots being departed, Banister with all expedition sett his ship on fire, sunck his guns in the watter, and put what of his goods, provitions etc. he possible could on board the French privatere and hid the rest of it in the woods on Banister's Island in the Gulph of Samana, which being don he imediatly put to sea with those few Englishmen which he had left, for the major part of his men now deserted him, soe that he was forc't to be rul'd by ye comander of the French privater. Not long after they had bin at sea, they came up with a Spanish (299) barque and took hir, which being taken the commander of the French privater gave to Banister, and forthwith put him and his men aboard with what arms, provition, amunition etc. they would spare him, and soe bad him adiue, leaveing him to shift for himself as well as he could.

Thus Banister haveing another vessle bore away for the Musceto Islands, ther to refresh himself and to ease his dejected spirits for some time. Fore you may easily conceive his troble was great, to be thus brought into soe mean a condition. Being there arived he went ashore and with the wonted sivility of those Indians he was received and entertained. But now another sad and fatall accident befell him, fore whilst he and six of his company where ashore asleep in their tent, the rest of his men ran away with his barke, soe that now he had no other help or relieve but what he received from these pore loveing Indians.

Thus here we leave Banister liveing in a miserable condition, and come to tell you that after the frigots were ariv'd to Jamaica and had gott on bord provitions, they were forthwith sent to sea again, by the Governour's orders. Soe the *Drake* sail'd from Jamaica on the 18th of July 1687, with a sloope to keep hir company, and were both bound to look for Banister. And in the 21st following (300), the *Faulcon* also sail'd from thence, with the same orders. Now the *Drake* cominge into the Gulph of Samana, and findeing he had burnt his ship, and gon away in the French privater, Captaine Spragg with the sloop forthwith stood to sea to look for him. Meanwhile Captain Tolbot arived in the Gulph of Samana, and after he had gott up Banister's guns, and what else they found worth anything which he had left behind him, and soe left Samana and made the best of their way to cary newes to the Governour in what condition things stood with Banister.

Now the *Drake* had not bin long at sea, but that she spoak with a sloop which had tutch* at the Muscetos. This sloop informed Captain Spragg where Banister was and of his fatall chance. Soe Captain Spragg with the sloope made the best of their way towards the Muscetos Islands, where being arived the Indians soon inform'd them where Banister was, whom they soon apprehend. He was in disguise a-roasting a plantaine, in a pore Indian wigwam. In his takeing they met with little resistance, for only one of his miserable companions fier one musquet at Captain Sprag, which slightly wounded one of his men. Thus this miserable Banister was taken and with him three Englishmen and two boys, the which I belive were now reducet to such misserable condition that they were weary of their lives.

(301) Now Captain Sprag haveing taken Banister and his men, he with the sloop imedatly wayed from thence and made the best of their way towards Jamaica. Now you must understand that the Governour's orders was thus, that when Banister was taken he and his men should be kept alive untill such time as they were brought in sight of Port Royall, and then they should be hung up at the yeard-arms untill they were dead, and in that posture they were to hang untill the ffrigot was come to anchor in Port Royall harbour, and then be cut down and buried in the sea. Soe Captain Sprag being arived within sight of Port Royall on the 15th of September forthwith hanged up Captain Banister and his three men by their neeks at the main and foreyard arms. But the two boys which were servants to Banister were not put to death, but were set at liberty at Jamaica. But now they for formality sake were brought in hanging by their armholes, at the mizonpeek* in that posture. The *Drake* came to anchor in Port Royall harbour, and Banister and the three others being dead they were cut down, and cary'd off to sea, and hove overboard neer Gun Kay, by Port Royall.[54] Thus wee have given you a full account of the overthrow of the misserable Banister, who not long befor was a welthy captain of good repute in Jamaica, and might have lived long and happy had not he turned pyrat.

(302) On the later end of December Anno 1687, Captain Bear, a man of good repute and an ancient trader to Jamaica, in the *Golden Fleece,* a ship of about 400 tunns and 30 guns, went away privatly from Neives, and joyn'd himself to Spaniards, and is now turned pyrat in the Gulph of Florida, where he lurcketh to surprize the English in their homeward-bound passage.[55] On the 15th of January 1688, he met with three saile of English as Captain Napman and two others, and rob'd them, takeing out of them what he

54. This was the common fate of pirates, a miserable end.
55. It does not seem possible to identify this Captain Bear.

thought fitt, and then let two of them goe.[56] But he carry'd away with him a ship of about 200 tuns, called the *Little Henry*, commanded by Captain Morris, which was loaden from Jamaica with sugar and bound home to London. This ship he keep with him two months, and then haveing rob'd hir set hir at liberty.

In the begining of May 1688 we here at Jamaica that this pyrat Bear hath lost his ship, and that he is building of him another, near the Havan on the coast of Cuba, for he is shelter'd and supported by the base, treacherous and perfidious Spaniard. Thus we have given you an account of the continuall care that His Majestie of Great Britain hath allways taken to suppress and distroy all English and other pyrats in those parts, that soe English merchants might quietly trade with safty to His Majestie's dominions in America. Allso in this chapter we have also fully sett (303) forth and discribed all noteworthy transsactions and occurances, which have happened at Jamaica since its first setling by the English from time to time under its severall governours, 'till now 'tis under the government of His Grace Christopher, duke of Albemarle, which being compleated, wee shall now conclude this second chapter of our present state of Jamaica.

56. This is no doubt Joseph Knapman of the *Loyall Merchant*; see Pawson and Buisseret, *Port Royal*, 95–96.

Chapter III

(304) Of the situation of Jamaica as to its latitude and longitude, lenght of days and nights; of its temprature of aire, heat, cold, wind, rain, tunder, lightning, earthquacks, tides and other occurrances.

The island of Jamaica is situated in the latitude of 17° 20' and in the longitude of 304° 15', and its cheif place of trade called Port Royall is situated in the latitude of 17° 44'.[1] In this clime the days and nights all the yeare round are allmost of an equall lenght, the longest day being but thirteen houres and eight minutes long, and the shortest day enjoyeth the light of the glorious Phaebus full ten houres and fifty-two minuits above hir horizon, soe that there is not at noe times full three houers difference betwixt the lenght of the days, or nights, in the latitude of Jamaica.

(305) This island is moderatly temperat, the whether being seldom hotter than 'tis in July in England, and in the heat of the weather her is but little difference all the year round, which is when the north brezes come, for the wind blowing off the land in the morning strongly till towards ten a'cclock fans and colds the earth, and the sea brezes coming in about noon refresheth the place, by which means 'tis thus temperat.[2] The hottest part of the day is betwixt nine in the morning untill one in the afternoon, for till then the breezes blow not strong. Before and after the said space of time, the brezes by there gentill blast make the weather moderat all day.

The nights are as cold as they are in England in the begining of Aprill, if not colder. For there falls great dues,* and the land brezes blow very strong for the most part, that I have found it soe cold there from midnight untill past two a'clock in the morning, that I have often shoak with cold, which coldness proceeds from the grose dewes and densitie of the aire. The northside of this island is much more agreable to newcomers from England than the southside, for 'tis much more colder being continuall faned by the breezes, refresh't by the cold streams and gentel murmur of many delightfull rivers, and is allways

1. The actual latitude is 17 degrees, 56 minutes, about thirteen miles different.
2. This is a good description of "diurnal variation".

Figure 24 Detail from Taylor's map of Jamaica, page 329. It will be noticed that Taylor carefully inserts the same place-names as those that he cites in his text.

in its butifull verdure whereas the southside is often schorch't by the burning raies of Phaebus. Yet notwithstanding 'tis not half soe well setled and planted or inhabited as the southside, by reason of many runaway Negros, which lie there lurcking in the woods and mountains, and have of late done much mischife there.[3]

Here in time of the norths* the nights are verey cold, soe that I have heard the planters affirm that in the morning before (306) the sun ariseth, they have often seen a kind of a white hoar frost on the leaves and grass; the which I should not have beleived, had I not in time of the norths found it there as cold as ever I did in England in the later end of March. Those dues and densities which soe cause it are vereie prejudiciall to the health of every man, but much more so to newcommers, untill such time as they are habituated to the place.

The winds which commonly blow here is an easterly wind, blowing from the sea, and therefore called the sea breez, which here begineth to blow commonly about noon, and soe increases till towards the seting of the sun. And then it begins to abate; by teen at night 'tis flat calme, the sea brez being quite spent, and about midnigh the wind begins to blow strongly from off the land, and therfore called the land breeze which increaseth till towards eight, and then it abateth soe that by nine or ten the breze is quit spent, and 'tis commonly flat calm till about one in ye afternoon.

And here 'tis strange to conceive the nature of the land breze, for it blowes at one and the same time from every part of heaven off the land. For being at the east end of Jamaica you shall find the wind to blow off the land due west; being at P. Negrill you shall find the wind to blow directly from the east. When you are on the southside of this island, then shall you find the land breze to be noe other than a strong north gale of wind, and soe the wind blows directly of the land from all points of heaven during the time of the strenght of those land brezes. To define the true reason and philosophicall cause therof, it is noe small difficulty, it being verey intrinsique* and obscure, but in my oppinion 'tis most apt and reasonable to conceive, that the (306) wind in time of the seabreze are gather'd together and confined above those clouds which continuall hang below the tops of the mountaines, which during the time of the sea breez is forced from all parts thither. But when the seabreez is spent and the wind which befor was forc't into the confin'd reigon of ye grosse clouds, finds herself freed from the forceing blast of the eastern winds, then with more than a common violence doth the wind force its way thro' those clouds, and by their hasty rushing forth out of their confined reigon, it breaks its way thro' and soe flies furiously out on all

3. It is true that the north side was inhospitable to planters until the Maroon Treaties of 1739 and 1740.

points, like as when water falleth on a stone from alloft, it dasheth itself theron, and flows all round, and extendeth itself like the refullgen raies of Phaebus.

And altho' this may strongly affect some, yet thousands are still liveing which have visited those western parts of the world, have bin *oculi festes*[4] therto and will confirm the same. For the great Jehovah which created everything is able to command anything, to perform its faccultie in that manner he in his divine wisdom shall thinck fitt, which the heathens themselves did generally beleive, and did often in their writings sollomly acknowledg it to be an undeniable truth, wittnes Ovid in these words:[5]

> Tum Freta diffudit, rapidisque tumescere ventis
> Iussit et ambitie; circundare littora terrae.

In those western parts of the world, the wind most commonly towards the later end of November begins to blow strongly from the north, day and night without scarse any intermission at all. And these northern gales commonly continue untill the later end of December, by reason of which the sea (308) runs verey high and turbulent all round the island.

On the 15th of December in Anno Christi 1683, the norths were then soe violent that most of the ships and other vessels that were then at anchor in Port Royall harbour brook lose from their anchors and fell foule with one another, and beat their sides against the wharfs; nay such was the prepetuity of the blust'ring winds and turbulant seas, that Port Royall was in danger to be lost, for the sea broak in upon the Point, and overeflowed it by Morgan's Line. And seeing the Point lies verey low, and that ye surfface above the rock is only a losse sand, the sea by its breaking in made severall channels quite thro' it to the harbour and much damnified the eddiffices and buildings towards the seaside by washing and spoyling their foundations. Soe that the inhabitants, what with their fears and doubts to thinck what now to be the end of this sad catastrophy, were soe afrigtned that many of the more timerous sort left their houses, caring with them their children and cheif movables, to St. Jago de la Vega and to Ligourney. But after the norths were over, they repaired breaches and strenghtened the weak places towards the seaside.[6]

But in March 1684 there came such violent south winds that by its intermissive blowing raised the sea to that height, that it overflowed the Point

4. That is, eye-witnesses.

5. This phrase comes from the *Metamorphoses* of Ovid. The translation by Frank Justus Miller (2 vols. [Cambridge, Mass., 1977], book 1, lines 36–37) is as follows: "Then he bade the waters to spread abroad, to rise in waves beneath the rushing winds, and fling themselves round the shores of the encircled earth."

6. Taylor correctly assessed the vulnerability of the spit, where a town had been established in 1655 with little consideration of the danger.

in some places. For such was its violence that it oversett some houses on Port Royall, and made a chanel quit thro' the Point from the south sea to the harbour, soe deep and large that ferry boats rowed to and fro therein, by which the Point was in great danger of being lost and the inhabitants in much fear, soe that they to prevent a further danger deserted the Point in abundance. For sure (309) it is had the wind continued but a small time longer, it would have bin fattal to Port Royall. But the Divine Omnipotent haveing shewed the lewed inhabitants what they deserv'd and what he was able to inflict, mittigated justice with mercey, soe that the wind ceased, and by degrees the moveing sea became quiet. Soe that with much cost and labour the breaches which ye sea had made were repaired, and the whole banck against the seaside was strenght'ned with guacum piles[7] and stones, and a sand banck cast high over it. Never since hath their bin any strong norths, or souths, nor any considerable damage by ye sea bin aggitated. By this you may conceive, 'tis truly difficult to comprehend the true philosophicall reason of the strange accidents of the wind in those western parts, and of its prodigious and strange effects, which it hath often produced.

But notwithstanding this island is much more serean and happy than the Windward Islands, called the Caribe Islands, inhabited by the English etc., which at a certaine time of the yeare are much damnified by tempestious hirocladons[8] or hurricans, which Barbadoes, Neives, Antego, Saint Christopher etc. yearly fells, to their great anoyance and prejeduce to those ship then there at anchor, many of which are by those huricanes cast away. For when they preceive those huricanes comming, they they cut their cables and stand to sea, it being the place of their greatest safety. However, many of them are there by the violence of the weather bore under water.

For in August 1684 the ship royall called the *Francis,* comanded by Captain Charles Carlisle, was in the huricane lost att Barbadose, and never heard of, where she was cast ashore. 'Tis beleived that the storm run hir under water, and soe she sanck (310) down right. And I heard a gentelman of good repute often afirm that he being then in a merchant's ship at Barbados, cut and went out to sea with the *Francis,* and that being at sea the *Francis* was about one hundred paces ahead of them when the violence of the hurrican fell, and that then it grew soe dark that they could not see hir, and he beleves that then she sunck, and run underwater, for she was never heard of afterward.[9]

7. Piles made of *guaicum* or lignum vitae.

8. The word "hirocladon" for a hurricane seems unique to Taylor.

9. On 14 May 1684, Sir William Stapleton wrote to the Lords of Trade and Plantations from Nevis: "I conclude that [Captain Carlisle] was lost in the storm that struck Barbados – a thousand pities, a brave hopeful young man." *Calendar of State Papers, America and West Indies, 1681–1685,* no. 1681.

Now this strange hurricans never of late hath reached soe far as Jamaica, for 'tis observed there hath binn none there this sixty-seaven years; for the last that was hap'ned in August 1622, which was thirty-three years befor the English had possestion thereof, as hath since bin reported by the Spaniards to have then done much mischeife, by overseting houses, distroying fruites, tree, etc. To define the true cause of the hirocladons 'tis alltogether impossible, but I conceive it to be of the generation of ecnephias, it being an exhalation first inclosed in the grosse clouds, and then it break forth mixt with a presterick flame,[10] and by a violent motion becoms a kind of typhon, for it falleth with a strong and powerfull whirling; and being reveribated into aire, forces all things before itt and soe becometh a hirocladon, hurrican, or perfect storm.[11] These are accompany with much rain, soe that (311) you would thinck heavens were desolveing itself into a second deluge. Also now the thunder roars soe that the orbs seem to crack assunder, and the distroying lightning breaks forth, mixt with the distroying thunderbolts, which rents the stronge mountains, distroys building, buries ships in the sea, and in fine 'tis soe teribley miserable, that 'tis alltogether impossible to find out a hierologliphick to sett forth those groaning and devasting missery which attend it.

For they are not like other storms, who remain in the horizon untill the powerful Phaebus hath exhail'd them back, but this continues untill such time as its atoms[12] have adhered to moist bodys. Some are of the opinion that ye origonall cause of these storms proceeds from the melting of snow in ye northern and remote countrys, which ariseth out of the earth after 'tis moistened with much snow, and being exhail'd and confin'd above the cloudes, becomes an ecnephias, and by its firce breaking forth a perfect typhon. Befor these huricans happen their are many evident signes of its aproach, as the dimness of the stars in the night, the paleness of the sun, the unaccustumed echoes or resounding of the woods, and the watter in spring changeth its collour and looketh laccid;[13] (312) all which are suer tokens of an approaching huricane, which being observed all ships prepare to putt to sea.

In this island of Jamaica, and in all other places which lie betwixt the equinoctiall* and tropick of cancer, they 'ave the sun passing by their zenith

10. A prester was a scorching whirlwind. *Oxford English Dictionary* (hereafter cited as *OED*). It is not clear what Taylor meant by "ecnephias".

11. Taylor is here groping towards an understanding of the formation of hurricanes, though he could not guess that they were generated many miles to the east of the West Indies. It is curious that he knows the word "typhoon", which had come from the Chinese and was new in his day.

12. The word "atom", meaning a very small particle, began to be commonly used in the seventeenth century. *OED*.

13. This word seems to mean reddish, from the same lac-root as lacquer and shellac.

twice a yeare, and 'ave one summer and two winters, and hath three shadows. For when the sun is in the equinox, to wit on the 10th of March, ther at noon they have noe shadow, but when the sun is in the northern signes, they have a southern shadow. And when the sun is in the southern signes then 'ave they a northern shadow. When the sun is in Cancer which is our sumer, then is their winter, and their second winter is when the sun is in Capricorn, which is also our winter, their sumer being whilst the sun is passing thro' the celestiall Aquarus, Pices, Aries, and Taurus, which this yeare begineth on the 9th day of January 1689, and endeth on the ninth of May following. Now their first winter begineth when the sun entereth into Gemini, and is at hight when the sun is in the last degre of Cancer. Then it begins to grow hoter and soe increaseth till ye sun is enter'd into the first degre of Libria (and then it begins to grow colder and colder), which is on the 13th of September 1689, and ther begineth their second winter which endeth on the 9th day of January 1690.[14]

And then begineth their summer in this island of Jamaica, the Phillipin and Molluca islands, Guinea, Mexico, and all other parts of the univers lieing betwixt the equinoctiall and tropick of Cancer, tho' indeed in the heat of the weather there is little difference all the yeare round, neither are the woods ever deprived of their butiful verdure, as they (313) are at winter in England.

Now in this island of Jamaica the rains happn not as in the Europian countreys, but commonly happen in January and June, and sometimes continueth raining for a whole twenty days or more together; by which means ye rivers are fil'd, and the earth becomes fitt for planting. And those raines the inhabitants call the seasons, for then they plant corn, sugar canes, indigo, etc. Now in time of those raines there is great plenty of wild fowle as duck, teal, widgeon, etc. found on this island of Jamaica, for hither then they resort in great plenty, and are sold in the markets at a reasonable rate.

But of late there hath happ'ned many droughts at Jamaica, which hath binn of noe small detriment to the painfull planter. For from the later end of December 1686 untill the later end of August 1687, there fell but little rain at Jamaica, but was continuall hot, burnning, scorching weather, with small brezes for the most part, soe that the plantations fail'd to yeild incouragement to the painfull planter, for its plants was schorch't up. And those statly savanas which befor was far greener than European medows, were now burnt up and looked like new fallowed ground.* By which means the planters sustained great lost in their heards of catell, for the starved cadavars lay everywhere stincking in the savanahs and woods, and by the brooks' sides where they went to quench their burning thirst, where haveing

14. Taylor seems largely mistaken in this zodiacal account of Jamaica's seasons.

to allay their heat overfill'd their starved panches[15] with water, they soe fell down, and there died in abundance.

By this drought the island was much impoverished, for such which in seasonable weather could make a thousand pounds annually from (314) off their plantations, could now not make enough to find them plantation provitions, for that they had neither potatos, yamms, maize, pease or casava bread, for all was distroyed by the drought. Soe that they were forc't to maintain their Negro slaves with English and Irish provitions, which they now bought of the merchants on Port Royall at a verey dear rate, to the great detriment of the inhabitants, espetially to those of the southside which was allmost transform'd to atoms, according to the poet alluding to droughts:[16]

Behould the heavens above lick burnning brass!
The earth's as iron, flowers, trees, hearbs and grass,
Have lost there fragrant green; are turned yallow.
The brook are dri, the panting cattel bellow.
The fatt and flowering plaines are schorch't and burnt
And trees their fruites are into atoms turn'd.
The clefty earth, hir craveing mouth setts 'ope,
Unto the empty clouds as 'twere in hope
Of some refreshing showers which might allay
Hir fierry thirst, but they soon fly away
Not yeilding unto hir the least releife
Therefore she languish's and pinnes with griefe
Man walks lick dried-up statues. Birds they fall
From towering wing. Beast pinne, die in the stall;
The aire which heretofore was well perfum'd
With pleasant smells, and to itself assum'd
A sacred odour; but now stincketh more
Of roten cadavers, than heretofore
The poisinous stinch of black Caribian's den,
The fume wherof distroy'd birds, beast and men.
But when the showers return'd then joy did spring
All creatures did rejoice, the birds they sing,
(315) The face of nature smiels, the feilds adorn
Themselves with rich embroderies of corn,
The flowers their charming butie doth present
Unto the captive'd eyes; and for their scent
The sweet Arabian gums cannot compare
which thus perfume the circumambient aire.
Thus are the frowns and smiles of mighty Jove
Sent down on man, pore mortall from above!

15. By "panches", could Taylor mean pouches?
16. I have not been able to discover the author of this powerful poem.

Thunder and lightning is here verey frequent, soe that commonly it thunders and lightens every day towards eavening from different quarters, but it seldom or never of late hath done any considerable damage either to trees, plants or fruites. Only the two last years to witt in 1686 and 1687, the piemento trees in some places have bin blasted by lightning. On this island, I could never heare of any, that ever there at any time saw any appearance of those fiery meteors which retaines the name of Ignis-fatui,[17] which is soe frequent seen and tallk of in England (by the name of Jack with his candle, will of the wisp, etc), which is rather an appearance of fier than reall fier, and is nothing but a certain viscious substance, reflecting light, and that most commonly in the darckest night. 'Tis evaporated out of a moorish fatt mier* ground, and flie most by fenns, where they are generated, and by reason of a flux of aire they follow those that fly from them, and flies from those which follow them.[18] Neither on this island could I ever hear of any, that have bin troubled with that fiery meteor called *flamma lambentes* or the hagg, which are (316) discovered in horsses' mains, men's hair and such licke, and is a vapour reflecting light, composed of some fatt matter.[19]

I have read a story of a certain Carmelite, that as often as he put his head into his coule,* a faint flame issued out.[20] But in this island of Jamaica are commonly seen those fiery meteors, which hang in the aire which are called fiery dragons, dracks, etc., which is nothing but a certain weak kind of lightning, which falleth without noise, and by the aire receives its form, and the slowness of its falling demonstrates a great mixture of watery exhalations in it. The nature of those meteors is the same with corruscations, which is the sudain kindling of an oylei vapour, which varies its shape, according to the combustable matter which 'tis composed of.

This island, as well as other parts of America, is subject to earthquack, the which of late years have not bin so frequent as formerly, neither hath it don any considerable dammage. About the begining of March 1686 there was a certain astroleger (as he pretended), which reported at Port Royall that by reason of an earthquack and other badd weather, (which should happen within a few months) the Point should be swallowed up in the sea. This vaine foretelling was by many observed, and many for fear removed themselves from off the Point. But the predicted time being come, their hap'ned noe

17. *Ignis fatuus,* or phosphorescent light that sometimes seems to hover above marshy ground. *OED.*

18. Some of Taylor's explanations of natural phenomena are remarkably convoluted.

19. "Hag" was in the seventeenth century said to be a kind of light that appeared at night on horses' manes and men's hair. *OED.*

20. Carmelites are an order of friars, sometimes known as "White Friars". Taylor refers to a Carmelite monk, who put his head into his hood.

such earthquack as was foretold, but however there chanc't to fall much rain, wind, thunder, and lightning, and soe it past off.[21]

On Sunday the 19th of February 1688 there happened at Porta Royall a strong earthquack which continued for about the (317) space of three minutes. The inhabitants were much afright'ned thereby, for it threw down three housses, and shatter'd the tiles off most houses, and did much damage to glass windows, and to glasses, and earthenware in shops; nay 'twas soe violent that the ships were tossed therwith as they lay there in the harbour, and some small vessels which anchor'd near the wharff broke lose, altho' at the same time 'twas flat calm, for it began about 10 a'clock in the morning, when the breezes were spent.

I was an eyewittness to the truth hereof, being then in His Majestie's Ship the *Faulcon,* which was then at anchor in Port Royall harbour, and lay about a mile and half from the shore, and saw and felt the same in hir, for she was tosed violently therewith. But thro' Divine Mercy 'twas sone over, and noebody destroyed thereby, nor noe considerable damage as other places have suffer'd by earthquak. Witness the late dredfull earthquak at Malligo, which threw down many strong and statly structuers, distroyed many of the inhabitants by its sudain fall, and burri'd them in its ruines, which was so lately done that 'tis yet still fresh in memory to all Europe.[22]

Indeed, 'tis one of the scourges of the Almighty to punish man for sinn, and is demonstrable, was there occasion to prove fier and water in the caverns and pitts of the earth, from whence earthquakes are generated. For seeing from a subterraneous humid body vapours are raised, espetially by subterraneous fire, as they increase become condens'd, and by continuall increasing with new water as they there meet with, become to great for the cave they are inclosed in, which for want of passage causeth (318) the earth in that place to shake and tremble, till either it breaks the ground for passage, or sincks itself by its force into the rocks.[23]

Their are many signs of earthquacks before they come, as black streacks under the sun, the springs and fountaines trobled and unholsome, a strange calmnes of the aire, and birds forebear to warble forth their pleasant notes, all which are apparant signes of an approaching earthquake. But this island is freed from the slaverey which the major part of the American islands groan under the burden of, namely those strange typhons, or huricanes, which yearely oppress the Windward Islands as Barbadas, Antego, St. Christopher, Neives etc., but hath never reach't so far as Jamaica since 'twas inhabited by

21. As these passages show, the disastrous earthquake of 1692 was not altogether unexpected.
22. This was indeed the site of a disastrous earthquake in 1688.
23. Taylor's idea about the cause of earthquakes seems close to the mark.

the English. Soe terible are those typhons, or huricanes, that in time therof the inhabitants of Antego etc. are forc't to fly to the hills for shelter, the which sometimes are thrown down therby.

I have heard this story creditablely reported by severall gentlemen of Barbados, that about some ten years agoe, there was a couple of gentlemen whose plantations joyn'd to each other and both were situated on the side of a hill. Now 'twas extream dry weather, soe that plantation provitions were scarse, and the gentleman whose plantation was lowermost at the foot of the hill was but a new setler, and therfore he had noe plantation provitions to maintain his slaves. Therfore he desired his neibour which lived above him to sell him some potato (of which he had in aboundance). But he out of pure malice would sparr him none, swearing that if one of his potatos would save his life (319) he would not soe much as spare him a lefe of one of them.

But it soe fell out that same night following there happned a greivous hurrican, and an earthquake, which soe shook that hill that the ground whereon the potatos grew was thrown down, and by the rains forc'd and wash't down into the other gentelman's plantation. Soe that he who denighed to assist his neibour had not one potato left, for they were all standing on the gentelman's ground, which he swore he would not spare a leafe of one of them, and now he was forc't to be beholding to him for his own potatos. In this appears the just hand of God against the malitious spight of that planter, whoe deniged his neiboure a small curtisie which would have don him a considerable kindness, and himself no harm at all, but have bin rather a profitt.

The seas in those western parts of the world are obsarved seldom or never to ebb, nor flow above a foot. But here are verey strong currants, which sometime by a full moon seteth strongly to the eastward, and sometimes the same moon make a westward currant, the reason of which the best of pillots and marinners using those parts are not able to discribe, and indeed we need not wonder to see men at a stand herein in the defineing the secreet of nature's work, when Aristortle himself, that great and eagle-eyed philosopher, and reader of the works of nature, was confounded herein, which put a finall period to his future contemplations. However, 'twas with great admiration observed that on the 13th of January 1688, as the tide ebbed at Port Royall in Jamaica above 5 foot, none there liveing evere remembred it to have ebb'd soe far before. Thus we have finished this chapter, and have delivered all its paragraphs in as concise a method as possible.

Chapter IV

(320) Of Jamaica, its towns, parishes, ports, harbours, capes, bays, rivers, mountaines, savanas, islands, kays, setlements, mines, etc., with a description of sundry inchanted places, creditably reported by the inhabitants of the island, where 'tis thought the Spanish treasure lieth hidd, with an accounte of what hunters and others have seen and reported in refference therto.[1]

According to a due and genuine method proceeding on in the description of Jamaica, as now in its presen state, 'twill be truly requisit in this place to give a description of its towns etc., in order to a due procecution of which, know, that the towns found in this island are first:[2] Saint Jago de la Vega, Port Royall, Ligurney, Passage Fort, Old Harbour, Carlisle Town, or Withywood; these are all the towns and places of note, which here in this place we shall not largly discribe, because we intend to treat of them more at large elsewhere.

This island of Jamaica is verey mountainous and woody and is full 170 miles longe, and about 70 miles broad[3] and is by the English divided into these parishes, or presincts (viz): Saint Katherin's, St. Dorothy's, St. Ann's, St. Mary's, Clarindon, Vere, etc.

The cheif ports of Jamaica are these (viz) Port Royall, Port (321) Dogua, Emyas, Portland, Pedro, Allaparsonia, Negrill, Ebasere, Comoma, Saint Lacsi, Beseropunta, Porta de Besero, Maribone Maltaboon, Fora Cabasa, Tutiloise, Porta S. Antonio, Candido, Ianta, Windward Point, Porta Morant, Yallowe's Point, Plumb Point, and Punta Cagada. These are the cheife ports, and capes, or headlands, belonging to Jamaica.[4]

1. For an interpretation of Taylor's references to "enchanted places", see Robertson, "Re-writing the English Conquest", 813–39.

2. Taylor goes on to cite six of them; "Liguaney", roughly where the National Library of Jamaica now is, must have been very small.

3. Taylor's figures are a little high.

4. Some of Taylor's ports and capes (Port Royal, Portland, Pedro, Negril, Lucea, Port Antonio, Windward Point, Port Morant, Yallahs Point, Plumb Point and Cagway Point) are entirely recognizable, and logically listed. But the names of many others are now lost, or are so mangled as to be unrecognizable. They would repay study: Candido, for instance, may be Puerto Escondido, the Spanish name for Holland Bay; Fora Cabasa may be Oracabessa; and Port Dogua is surely related to Doggeri Bay.

The cheife harbours of Jamaica are these (viz) Port Royal Harbour, Old Harbour, or Spanish Harbour, Founts, Lainuna, Sivila, Palmero, Alestro, Old North Harbour, Saint Ann's and Morrant Harbour.[5]

The cheife bays of Jamaica are these (viz) Carlisle, or Withywood Bay, Maccare, Oristan, Bleufeildbay, Montago, Medilla, Maiguana, Guiagoe, Lamaena, Fishers Bay, Yallowes Bay, Bull Bay, and Cow Bay.[6]

The cheife rivers of Jamaica are these (viz), Ligourney River, Rock River, Saint Jago River, Old Harbour River, Drie River, Milke River, Rio Morant, Rio Coquibano, Black River, Rio Limor, Rio de Taure, Hommora, Ebneras, Rio Nova, Rio Grande, etc. These are all the rivers of note, all which are well stored with variety of good fish.[7]

This island of Jamaica is as it were a perefect mountain from whence it takes its name of Jamaica.[8] 'Tis a verey mountinous island, and woody, but above all there run a ridge [of] exceeding steep mountans quite thro' the island, from the east to ye west, whose top are allways seen far above the clouds, which continually hang below the tops of those mountains. These montain by my often strick observations I have found to be somwhat more than six mile high, from their horizontall base, or surfface of the watter.[9] And they are divided into fouer parts (viz) Morant Mountains, Blew Mountains, Olimpus, and Monta Diable, (322) all which mountains are soe very high, soe full of thick woods, soe cold and sharp aire is the aire there, bessid 'tis thought it rains continually theron, by which means they are seldom frequented by travalers, inhabited by hermits, or visited by hunters, altho' those mountains are well stored with beeves, hogs, picaries,* raccons, etc.

From these mountains the rivers fall and take their begining here, being very steep and violent, soe that these mountaines are allmost inaccesible. The island is indeed very full of mountains, not one half of the land being either plane or plantable, altho' there are by the laborious industry of some thrifty planters some most fruitfull, large and plesant plantations on the sids of the mountains nere their verey topps, as at Ligurney where they 'ave run their plantations up some miles on the sides of those mountaines.[10] Also there

5. Again, Founts, Lainuna, Palmero and Alestro cannot be identified even though Taylor confidently marks them on his map (figure 24).

6. Most of these bays are identifiable, if garbled: Medilla, for instance, is surely Mellilla, at Port Maria. But from there eastwards and southwards the names become very difficult: Maiguana, Guragoe, Lamaena and Fishers Bay.

7. The arrangement of these rivers does not seem as logical as that of the ports, harbours and bays. As before, there are some unidentifiable names: Rio Coquibano, Rio Limor, Rio de Taure, Hommora and Ebneras.

8. It is now often said that the name means "land of wood and water".

9. This is one of Taylor's grosser exaggerations, and hard to explain in the light of his supposed mathematical skill.

10. Taylor must be thinking here of Red Hills, Constant Spring and Hope.

are some raged paths over those mountains in the most low places, from the north to the southside, but verey troblesome to be passed either for hors or man,[11] for that their are noe inns to refresh the weary travelours, only at Capil Rod Mother capps,[12] who setts open hir cellar, where all travelers may allay thire thirst, and freely tiple on adam's alle with free cost. These paths are but seldom frequented, for such which have occation to goe from the northside to Port Royall, or from thence to the northside, commonly goe by water in sloops, which trade round the island and resort to those parts.[13]

Now let us descend from those steep and cragy mountains and fix our eyes on the statly plaines, plesant savanas of old the Indians' corn fields,[14] which you shall view in its (323) continuall butifull verdure, lick our Europian medows adorn'd with flowers in there prepetuall gaity etc., and perfum'd with the fatt jecimons,* and other plesant smells. On these savanas you shall find great heards of cattel mutually sporting themselves in these full fod pasturs, where you shall find the strong and sturdy bull, the swift and nimble Spanish horse, the harmles lamb, the furious bore, and the lacivious goat, all feeding and mutually sporting together in great abundance.

These savanas or plains are now used for pasturage, and soe was befor by the Spaniards, but they were the cornfeilds where the native Indians planted their maize, casava etc. Some of these savanas or plains are of a large extent, containing noe less than 5,000 acres of land, full as good pasture in seasonable times as our Europian medows are. These savanas are not allowed to be taken up or planted by any, but are common pastures for the adjacent inhabiteres.[15] And the cheife savanas of Jamaica are these (viz) Morant Savana, Yallows Savana, Ligourney Savana, Saint Jago Savana, St. Katherin's Savana (or Cit. Butler's), Saint Dorothy's Savana, where St. Dorothy's church stands, Ketle Savana (in Clarindon), Milke Savana, Lime Savana, Old Woman's Savana, Blewfeild Savana, Savana Liamor, Saint Ann's Savana, and Savana Ociero Dispinosa etc.[16]

Now let us cast our eyes from off those statly plains, and fix them on those litle kays, or small adjacent island, which lie all round Jamaica. Nigh the shore are the Jamaica islands, being in number about 41 (324) and are as followeth

---

11. S.A.G. Taylor describes this trail in *The Western Design,* 40.

12. "Mother capps" means in the open air. Taylor means that there are no lodgings at all, and only water to drink.

13. It will be remembered that this is how Taylor himself went from Port Royal to Clarendon.

14. This seems to have been an English misconception; see Taylor, *The Western Design,* p. 209.

15. On this early common land, see W.A. Claypole, "The Settlement of the Liguanea Plain between 1655 and 1673", *Jamaican Historical Review* 10 (1973): 13–14.

16. Of these, only Savana Liamor and Savana Ociero Dispinosa cannot be identified; Edward Slaney's map of 1678 is particularly helpful for savannahs. See figure 25.

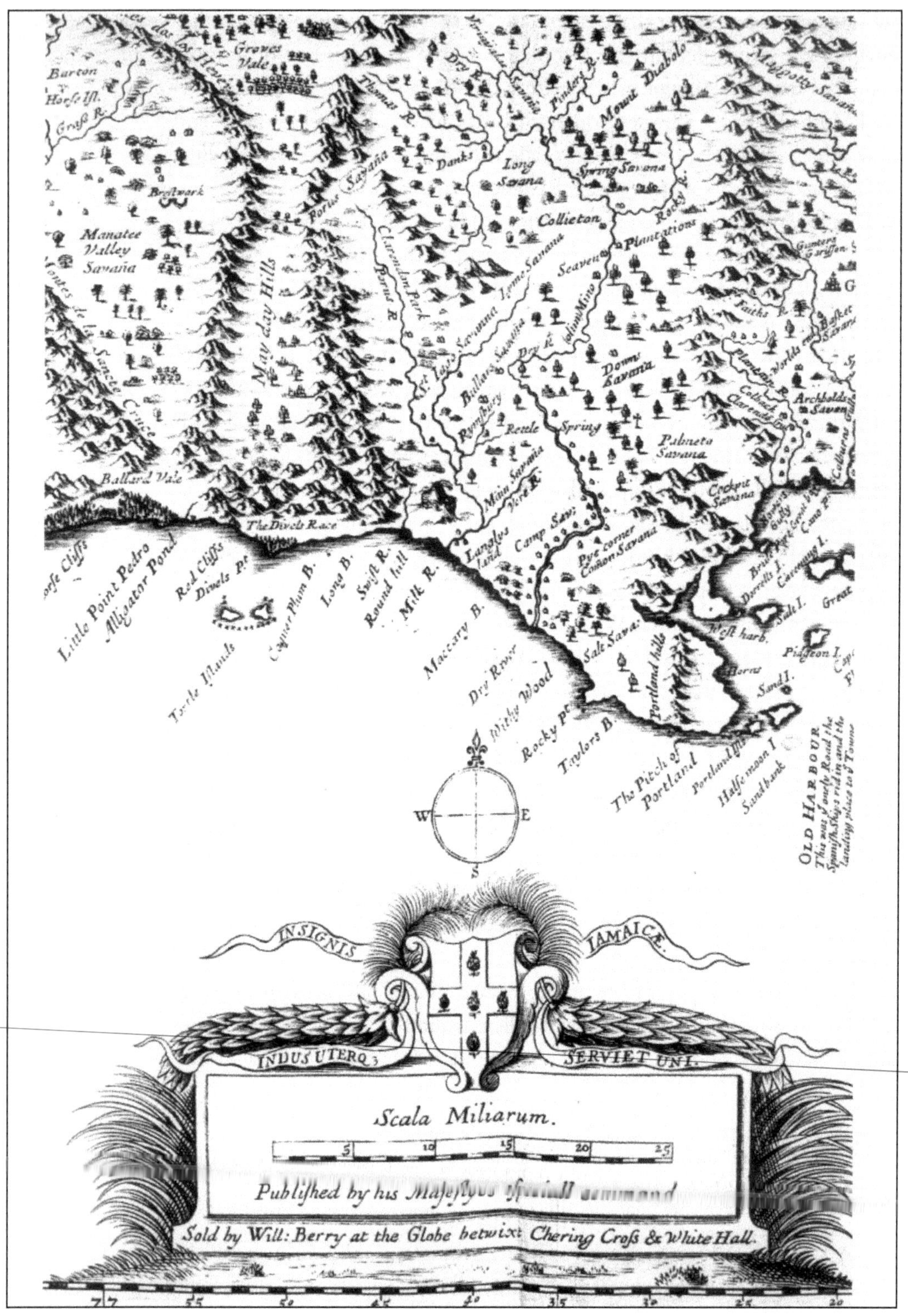

Figure 25 Detail from Edward Slaney, *Tabula Jamaicae Insulae* (London, 1678). This detail shows how abundant the areas called "savannahs" were in Jamaica at this time.

thus: first Sweatman's Island is a small island latly cutt off from the northward exterior point of Punta Cagada, within the harbour of Port Royall, whereon is now a cut river, thro' which boats pass to Ligurney, etc. On ye island Mr. Sweatman hath builded a well-built brick hous and planted a garden. In the next place we must consider Cagada Kays or islands, which are in number eleven. These are small kays, which lies allmost level with the water, on somme of which grows some scrubed maingrove busshes. They lay about two miles from Port Royall, and are posuated as you see in the mapp, haveing deep watter betwixt most of them. Three of the biggest of them are called thus: "B" is Gun Kay, "C" Drunken Kay, and that which lies to the westward of Port Royall is called Saltpond Kay, wheron they dig limestones. In the next place we must concider Dogua Kays, which are fouer small islands almost levell in the water, whereon grows nothing but sampier, and lies about three miles from the shore, to ye eastward of the eastermost point of Dogua Harbour. About a mile west of these kays is another small island about a mill about lieing indeferent high above the water, and is very rocky and woody. Now the next island of note is Green Island, which lies opposit to Old Harbour, about three mils from the shore, and is full three mills long, and two miles brood. 'Tis a high rocky woody island, full of willd hoggs, and on it breads aboundance of doves and pidgeons. This island belongs to Major Reeves.[17]

Two miles to the southward of this island lies another low woody island, about a mill round called Hog Island, becaus thereon are keept aboundance of wild hogs. This island also belongs to Major Reves. The next island is Pigeon Island, which lies (325) about three miles to the southward of Hogg Island.[18] 'Tis a high rocky, woody island, wheron breed multitudes of doves and pidgeons, soe that the trees at there breeding times are loaden with nest and young ones, as our groves are in England with rooks in their breeding times, soe that people resort hither at the seasons to catch them. This island is about two miles long, and one mile broad.

Next to this island lies Portland Kays which are eight small rock islands; one of these island lies about a mile from the shore, and 4 [miles] west by north from Green Island. 'Tis a small sandy island, wheron grow some scrubed maingrove busshes. Next to this kay lies two small islands within two mills of Portland shore, being west-south-west, southerly from Pidgeon

---

17. This is probably Thomas Ryves, member of the horse regiment in 1680 (National Archives, CO 1/45, fo. 59) and correspondent of Thomas Blathwayt. See Kenneth Ingram, *Manuscripts Relating to Commonwealth Caribbean Countries in United States and Canadian Repositories* (Barbados, 1975), 305.

18. Pigeon Island lies in Portland Bight; Taylor's Hog Island is probably modern Goat Island.

Island, distant about five mils. These are two small low kays wheron grow som maingrove busshes. Next to this kay are five more small islands lieing east-north-east from Portland Point, the eastermost being distant from Portland shore above seaven miles. These are low rocky islands, wheron grows but little wood, about which is a shoul'd sand, mix't with scater'd corall rocks; none of these islands are plantable. Now com we to Oristan Kays which are two small islands lieing about two mils from the shore. They are low and of a wet sand, wheron grow maingrove bushes; round these island lies a flat sandbanck, as you see in the mapp.[19]

Next come we to Ebosere Kays, which are three small, low, rocky islands, wheron grows noe woods. These islands lie about a mill from the shor, and about a mile distant from each other, as you see in the mapp. Betwixt these islands you have noe less than three fadoms water. Now we come to Kay Bessero which is a small island, wheron (326) grows some maingrove bushes. This island lies about a quarter of a mile off of Punta Besero. Next to this lies Montago Kay, or Butter Island; 'tis an island about two miles long, and a mile broad. It lies of a tolerable hight out of the water; 'tis not verey rock, but is all overgrown with woods. This island would prove fertill if planted, for 'tis of a good soile, and lies about a mile from the shore of Montago Point.[20]

Now come we to Porta de Besero kays, which are fouere small, low, sandy islands, wheron grow some maingrove bushes. These islands lie in the cod of Porta Besero bay, in all respects as you see in the mapp. In the next place we come to Guiago Kay, which is a small, sandy, low island wheron grows nothing but sampier, and it lies about half a mile off from Punta Guiago. Then come we next to Kay Anthonia, which is a small, low island covered with maingrove bushes. This island lies about to the northward of Porta Sainta Anthonya, distant one mile.[21] Now come we to Kay Candido, which is just such another island as Kay Antonia, and lies about a mile to the northward of Lo Candido. Lastly we come to Morant Island, which is a small, low, bare, sandy kay, lieing nere the easter point at the entrance into Morant Havan.[22] Thus have we given a full description of all the kays and islands which are adjacent and belonge to Jamaica, soe that you may perceive all plain and obvious, if you peruse our mapp of Jamaica in America.

Now we might here give you a description of the principall plantations and setlements on this island, and a catalong of the planters' names of cheife note and quality (327) which are those to windward. Collonel Holliard at Morant, Smith Kelley Esquire at Yallows, Mr. Watterhouse, Collonl Ballard,

19. Oristan is the Spanish name for Bluefields; it is not clear to which cays Taylor refers.
20. Taylor seems to be thinking of the Bogue Islands.
21. We have now reached Port Antonio.
22. That is, Port Morant.

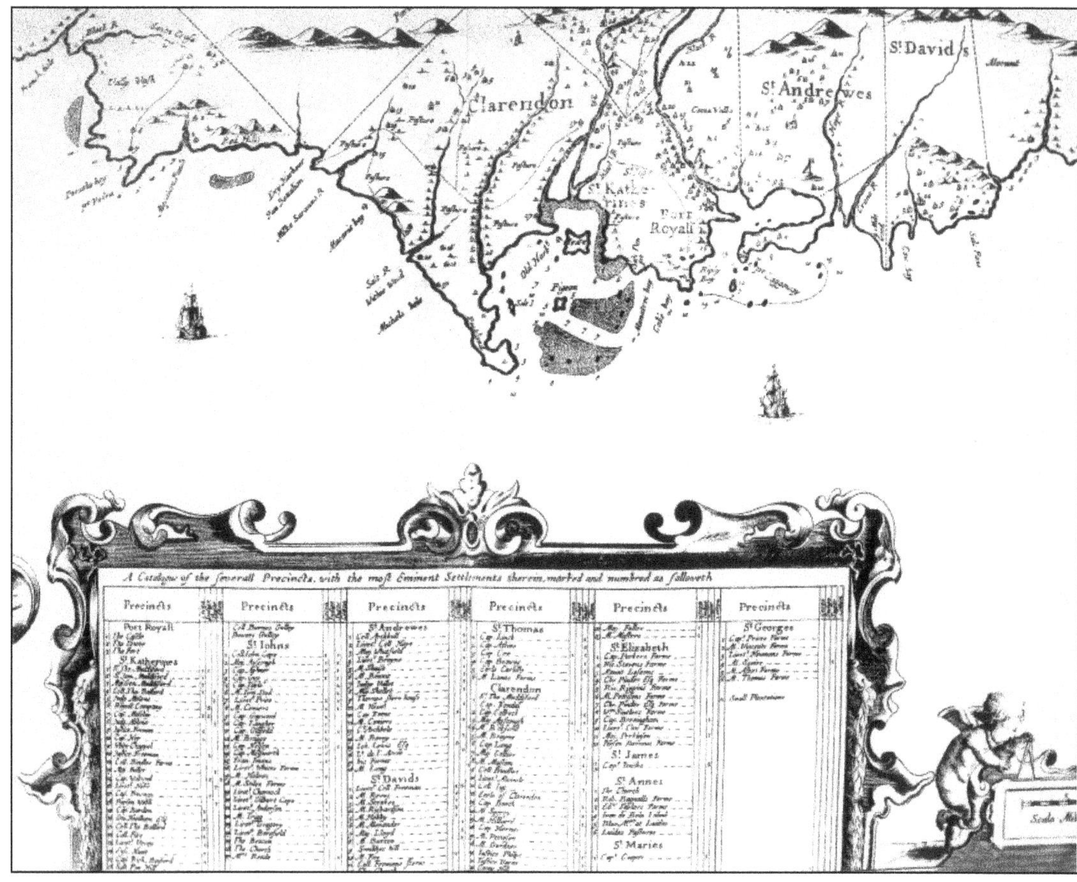

Figure 26 Detail from John Ogilby, *Novissima et Accuratissima Jamaicae Descriptio* (London, 1671) (by courtesy of the Newberry Library, Chicago). This detail shows how the main landholders were listed in each precinct, together with the crops that their settlements grew : "cocoa", "indigo", "sugar" and "cotton".

Collonl Reves, Sir Henry Morgan, Sir Francis Wattson, Hender Molesworth Esquire, Collonl Barrow, Francis Blackmore Esquire, John Sutten Esquire, Collonel Varney, Captain Musgrove, Major Yeoman, Major Peak, Doct. Rose, and Mr. Hales. These are the cheif and principall gentlemen and planters on Jamaica, and have verey large plantations, good sugar works, and live in greate splendor.[23] But if you desier a further catalouge of them and of the plantations and setlements of Jamaica, consult Mr. Bloom's history of His Majestie's dominions in America,[24] Sellars his hydrographicall chart of

23. It is possible to identify almost all these figures by combining information from the *Journals of the House of Assembly* and from James Moxon's *New Mapp of Jamaica* (London, 1677).

24. There is a description of Jamaica in Richard Blome, *The present state of His Majestie's Isles and Territories in America* (London, 1687); it does indeed list the plantations.

Jamaica,[25] and the *Lex Jamaica*,[26] in which you will find a more full account thereof.

In this island of Jamaica are undoubtedly many mines of silver, copper, if not also of gold, but His Majestie of Great Britain will not suffer them as yet to be opened, untill such time as the island is more full of people, and hath gathered further strenght. Suer I am that in the bowels of the earth in Jamaica is inclosed inestimable treasurs of silver and copper, if not of gold itself, for I have often seen at the mouth of several springs (which gush forth at the foot of the hills) aboundance of copper oar lie mix't with the sand, which the watter hath drove out from the secret caverns and bowels of the earth.[27]

(328) Now come we to treat of the inchanted places on Jamaica, for 'tis an undenighable and certaine truth, that the Spaniards, by reason of their hasty flight off Jamaica, had not time to carry with them much treasure. Therefor, the island being then vastly rich, 'tis verey probable and most certain that the Spaniards left much riches buried in caves and the bowels of the earth behind them.

A gentleman of good repute now liveing on Jamaica inform'd me that about twentifive years agoe he sent out allong with a gang of hunters two of his servants to hunt for beves and hoggs, where in their ranging in the woods in the persuite of their game they came up with a cave in the which they saw severall chest, iron-bound, jarrs of earth standing there close stop't and bound over with iron bands. But at the same instant, their doges held at the bay a lust wild bore, about some 50 paces from the cave. Upon which, being unwilling to bank their doges* and lose their game, and not doubting to find the cave again, it being soe very nigh at hand, they theropon left the cave, and made towards their game, and all along as they went they broke off the branches of the trees, quit from the cave untill they came to their doggs. Now haveing shot the bore they returned towards the cave, following their waye thither by direction of the broaken branches of the trees, and came to a rock which they before saw to stand close by the mouth of the cave, but as for the cave 'twas vanished, and not to be found.

Severall others have come up in the wild mountains with such inchanted caves, into the which at (329) ye first sight they have never had power to enter, but 'ave still bin prevented by some instant acident or othere, and at their

25. John Sellers's map of 1671, *Novissimae et accuratissimae insulae Jamaicae descriptio,* has a substantial list of landholders keyed to the map. See figure 26.

26. Taylor is here thinking of Francis Hanson's account appended to *The Laws of Jamaica* (London, 1683).

27. Very little gold has been found in Jamaica, though Edward Long does describe a Spanish gold-washing installation on the Rio Minho. *History of Jamaica* (London, 1774), 2: 241–42.

return with a resolution to enter into ye cave, which they just before plainely saw, the same were totally vanished, and noewhere to be found. At ye west end of Jamaica on the point of land betwixt Rio de Taure and Comoma is a verey larg and an exceeding deep and dark cave, called the Divielshole, into which I could never heare of any that have enter'd, tho' tis supposed there lays treasure there hid.[28]

A gentleman of good worth at Clarlindon[29] on Jamaica gave me this information, that about fifeteen yeares agoe that a couple of younge men (one of which was the first born on the island of Jamaica, the other a privatere) as they were walking betwixt Sainta Jago de la Vega and som of the northern adjacent plantations allong by the woods sides walking together, they espied at a small distance from them a Spaniard standing by the woodside, who becken'd unto them, and soe went into the wood, and they being two resolut blades of fortune followed him towards the wood; the Spaniard (for soe by his garb he seemed to be) retreated backward befor them, still continueing beackening unto them, untill they had sight of a well-built Spanish house, into which the Spaniard enters, and they resolutly followed him into the seming house, where being enter'd they supposed themselves in a large Spanish hall, where at the uper end of a table stood the Spaniard which they had thus follow'd and by him a frier of ye order of St. Francis by his garbb, whoe then was pulling out of a bagg (330) abundance of gold, and there lay a considerable parsell of coin'd gold and silver redy told out on the table before the Spaniard and the supposed frier.

Still these two sparks stood gazeing theron with noe small admiration, and still conceived it to be reall, and one of them being more greed of the booty than the other, rudlie pull'd off his hatt, and with his hand went to swepe off the gold from the table into it, and with an oath swore 'twas not now the custom of the English to take either gold or silver from the Spaniards by account but in the whole, which words were noe sooner uttred, but he grasp't naught else but aire, for both the gold, frier, Spaniard, house, and all vanished, and they found themselves in the wood, inclosed in the midst of a thick fingrigo* bush.

Soe that they were forc't to cut their way out of the same, and now they began to be much afraid, and perceived that they had bin lead into some inchanted place where the Spanish treasure lay hid. And 'tis really believed by many wise and juditious men that had not they used this ruged acction the semeing Franciscan was goeing to bestow that gold on that Englishman

---

28. These names sound imaginary, unless Taylor is thinking of some sinkhole in the karst terrain.

29. Probably Clarendon.

which was the first born on Jamaica after 'twas inhabited by the English. This is creditably reported for a certain truth all over Jamaica, by men of the best ranck and quallytie. 'Tis verey certaine that much treasure hath binn found by the English since they inhabited Jamaica, which was left there hidd by the Spaniards, and 'tis as certain that still there remaines (331) much treasure (inchanted as som will have it) which was hid on Jamaica by the Spaniards when they left the island, which still lies undiscover'd in the sillent caves and secret bowells of the earth.[30]

A gentleman whoe now lives at Saint Jago de la Vega gave me this information, that about ten yeares agoe in the night he chanc't to be verey thirsty, soe he arose and went to look in the watter jarrs for watter, but there was no watter in them. But he being exceeding thirsty took up one of these jarrs, and went to the river (which lies near by his house) for water. Now 'twas about midnight, and the mone shined very bright, soe that as he directed himself towards the river, about midway in the midle of the road, he saw two jarrs lay closed stopt, soe he sat down his jarr from his shoulder and asaid to lift one of the jarrs but could not. He found him to be full of somwhat, which be believed to be dollars by its weight; then he tried to lift the other which he could with ease, and supposed him to be about half full of the same metall by its weight and ratling. These two jarrs were both closed as he suposed with copper covers fast bound on.

But being exceeding thirsty he left those jarrs where they lay, resolveing after he had allay'd his thirst to return and brake them, and soe discover what was therin. But at his return from the river he cold not find them, fore they were vanish't, but he saw the plaine impresion which they had made in the sand where they had laine. Soe he mist of his supposed treasure. Now if he had at first broken the jarrs, 'tis reasonable to thinck he (332) might have broaken the inchantment, and have obtained the treasure, but such are the inducement and wiles of Pluto,[31] that they often deseive the wisest of mortalls as they now did this genteleman.

A gentleman and his servant (whom if required I could name, he being still liveing on Jamaica) were rideing home about midnight towards Spanish Town, haveing binn to vissit a neibouring gentleman. On a sudain they came up with a semeing well-built house haveing candles burning in its lower and upper rooms, and it stood close by the pathside. The gentleman was not a little startled at this sight, well knowing that he never saw any such house (as that sem'd to be) on the whole isle, and was more certain that there was noe house standing there, nor within two miles of the same place. However

30. It is true that over the years many jars of copper coins have been unearthed.
31. Pluto was god of the infernal regions.

he and his man out of curiosity alighted from of their horses, and made severall marks to be known on the bark of severall trees opposit therto on t'other side of the way, and then they mounted and rod home. And the next morning the gentelman with his servant went to view the place, wher they found those trees which they had mark't the night before, but as for the house 'twas vanished, and there was not the least signe thereof.

Those which now inhabit nigh the monastry of S. Maries[32] (which now lays in its ruins) affirm that they frequently towards midnight every night heare verey loud and plainly severall instruments of musick, as organs, lutes, bells etc., and hear the consort of charming voices singing in order of a chorus, or quire* in prossestion in and (333) about the ruins of the convent and church, called by ye Spaniards Nostra Segniora de Maria, the which is now becom soe frequent (besids sometimes the appearance of light, as of large wax candles, or tapers walkeing too and fro among ye ruins), that 'tis not by the inhabitants regarded, neither are they concern'd therat.

In and about the town of Sainta Jago de la Vega, often in the night are seen on the parade, and in the streets, the apparitions of Spanish cavaleirs, riding to and fro on a full carrer, as if they were on the patroule. This is affirm'd by most of the inhabitants of that place for a most certain truth. I could now instance in many othere examples here of the lick nature, to prove inchantments still in force on Jamaica, but I have said enough allredy to incure the censuers and snarles of the vain incredilous of this age, to convince whom that good doctor Glandville, (in his truly learned work intituled *Saducimus Tryumphatus* latly published),[33] hath taken great paines, and used such demonstrations to prove, soe that now none but mosters of men can be soe impudent to denigh soe papable a certainty. Thus we have finished this fouerth chapter of our presant state of Jamaica, the which we have delivered as concise as possible.

---

32. The monasteries at Villa de la Vega were dedicated to Our Lady and to Saint Francis. See Morales Padrón, *Spanish Jamaica*, 206–10.

33. Taylor is thinking here of Joseph Glanvill et al., *Saducimus Triumphatus, or Full and Plain Evidence Concerning Witches and Apparitions* (London, 1681).

Chapter V

(334) Of Jamaica, its products of Beasts, Birds, Fishes, Serpents, Insects, Hearbs,[1] *Trees, Shrubs, Frutes, Roots, Seeds, and Gums.*

Section I: Of Beasts

On this uberous Island are found plenty of variety of beasts fitt for food and pleasure, for first here are found aboundance of well-shap't horses[2] of the Spanish breed, rangeing in the spatious savanas; they are curiously shap't, verey nimble and hardy, easily tamed, and will long be fitt for service. Here they never shoe them, but commonly after they have used them, they turn them out into the savanas without any further care, for here they never use them to the painfull plough or crackling wain, but only to rid on and draw in coaches, for which purpose they have plentie of verey large horses. Besides these horses which are tame (335) in the savanas, there are multitudes which run wild in the woods and mountains; these horses are generally of a light bay and a daple grey. And 'tis a common thing for a planter on Jamaica to have 4 or 500 horses, every man haveing a perticular mark for distinction sake.

Here are also aboundance of moules* and asses of a verey large size, soe that severall gentelmen of Jamaica prefer them befor horses, for their hardiness, and manie times run with six of them in their coaches. For such is the nature of those moules, that they'll live on dry cane-tops, or any other thrash, and be fatt therewith; also they'll travel a whole day together without water, which their horses will not. But as for those asses which are here found, they are verey small and of little estem.

1. This section is actually "Of stones".

2. As Sloane puts it, "The horses here . . . are of the Spanish breed, but very much degenerated, the English taking no care of them, but letting them breed in the savannas". Sir Hans Sloane, *A voyage to the islands Madeira, Barbados . . . and Jamaica* (London, 1707 and 1725), 1: lvii.

Of meat they have here great plenty, not only in the pastures tame, but also wild in the woods and mountains, soe that thousands of bulls and cowes are kil'd here annually only for their hides and tallow, for their flesh is not soe fatt nor solid as our English beef, neither will it be preserved by salt as in Europe, by reason of the heat of the weather. But for present spending it is indeferent. But here they have noe dairies, nor doe they make any considerable profit from the milke, for there is neither cheese nor butter made but only att two or three great plantations in the whole island. For a planter that hath perhapps 6 or 700 head of meat doth not milk above 6 or ten of them, and that only to use in their chocalata, to make custards, chesecakes, and other quelquechoses.[3]

Their cattell are of a verey large size as our Essex breed are, and they are generally spotted, white or red, soe that 'tis a rarity to see a black bullock amongst (336) them. The planters use their oxen to grinde in the sugar mills and hale in their waines. Besides ye tame bullocks in the savanas, there are multitudes of them wild in the woods and mountains, which they hunt with dogs, and either shote them or dart them thro' with their launces, and sometimes they bone their flesh and drie it as we doe herings in Europe,[4] which they call jercking. But they hunt cheifly for ye hids and tallow, which is of considerable profit.

The sheep here found are of a large size, generally of a russet colour, or spoted, haveing a corce wool-like hair; therfore they never sheare 'em in this island. They are here not soe plentiful as other catel, neither are they much estemed, their fleash being not soe swet or fatt as our Europian mutton.

In this island are found aboundance of goates of the African breed, smoth-hair'd and curiously spotted, being very fruitfull, for generally they breed three times in a yeare, sometimes bringing forth fouer young ones at a time and never less than two.[5] Their flesh is most curious food; very gratful to the pallat, and of excelent nutriment. Here are also found multitudes of stout hogs, bouth tame and willd, the flesh of which is of excelent nutriment, and indeed the best food that Jamaica produces, or any other parts of America, far excelling our English hogs' fleash, for here they flea of their skins, and being roasted it eats much like our Europian mutton, but far sweeter; it also maketh excelent broath.[6] They generally kill their tame hogs at six or eight (337)

3. A cheesecake was originally a tart containing cheese. *OED*. The French term *quelquechoses* is used jocularly by Taylor to mean trifles.

4. The dried and smoked herring is still called a kipper.

5. These are the "Guiney goats, *ovis africana*", described by Sloane, *Voyage*, 2: 325.

6. Sloane described how these domesticated swine would forage in the woods during the day, and were then called for feeding by three blasts on a conch shell, whereupon they would hurry to the farmer, seeming "to be as much, if not more, under Command and Discipline, than any Troops I ever saw". Ibid., 1: xvii.

months old, and sometimes barbecue[7] them, or roast them awhole together. Now the fleash of the wild hogs in the woods and mountains eats much more delicate than the tame plantation hogs, for they feed on nothing but excelent frutes as guavers, mammas, etc., of which the woods are full.

And here I think it not amise to give you an account of the manner of the hunting of the wild bore in the woods and mountaines of Jamaica. The best time of hunting the wild hog is in May and October, for then frute being ripe the wild hog is then fattest. And then the hunters begin their march towards the high, craggy and mallancholy mountains, where they find their game in great plenty, both hog and bores, and what else can yeild them either plesure, profitt, or delight (if there be any to be found in such a wild kinde of life).[8] Now those hunters can carry with them some ten or more lusty dogs, and but a small quantity of provition, but sufficient to sustain them untill they are gott to the mountains. But their cheife materials are gunns, launces, and ammunition, soe that commonly each man hath either a musquet, or a launce and a macheate[9] by his side. They also cary with them salt to preserve their meat, and a ketle* to boyle their provitions in. And be sure, whatever they forgett, they never faile to carry with them a good cagg of rumm, to refresh their weary spirits when tier'd by gormodizing on good fatt rosted hog's flesh.

Being thus accutered they sett forward with bag and bagade towards the woody hills, where being arived in a convenient place they build them a hutt, and then they and their dogs (for now they are all haile fellow well met) presently eat up all their provitions that they brought with them (for feare least by long keeping it should grow mouldie), after which they tap (338) their cagg, and forthwith they create a lusty bowle of the Quackers' cold drinck called rum punch, and perhaps, for want of a bowle, they make it in their greassi ketle, but that matters not; they dish it about rumby untill such time that they cannot desern the wood from trees; then they kenell[10] altogether and in their new-bult hutt they sleep soundly all night, being guarded by their watchfull dogs. And the next morning, as sone as Aurora hath chac't away the sable sillent night, these sons of Pallas proceed to hunting of their game.[11]

Now the dogs wherewith they hunt are but small nimble mungrell curs

---

7. This word comes from the Spanish or Haitian *barbacoa.*

8. Sloane notes that "the Indians are very exquisite at this Game". *Voyage,* 1: xvi.

9. This seems to be an early use of this word, deriving perhaps from the archaic English word "matchet", or from the Spanish *machete.*

10. This is an unusual use of the word "kenell" as a verb.

11. Aurora was the Roman goddess of dawn; it is not clear of which classical Pallas Taylor is thinking.

which will never fasten on a bore, but hold him at the bay, and commonly they have a little busking spanell* to rouse their game. These dog will never fasten on a bore but they will allways fasten on a willd sow. Now when these dogs have gott a bore at the baie, the hunter getteth up in a tree and shooteth him down, for the dogs of their own accorde will open to the right and left to give way for the shott, such is the powerfull instinct of nature over 'em. Now if the hunter shotes the bore not down, he furiously presently braketh thro' the dogs and maketh at the hunter, which then must spare another shoot at him. But when their dogs have a sow at ye bay, and are fasten'd in hir, then the hunter steps in and stabs hir with his macheat, without any more adoe.

Now the hunters haveing kil'd their game, saveth only the two sides, giveing the doges the rest. These sides they sindge the hair off from, and then bone them, and after they have slash't them here and there with their knives they put some little salt theron, after which with smoke they dry it on a barbaque (as we doe red herrings in Europe), and afterward pack it up in cabadge leaves, and this they call jerck't hog, which proveth excelent food, will keep long and yeildeth a good price at Port Royall. And of the skine of the hinde leggs of these hoggs, they make shoos (339) withall, without ever sending it either to the tanners or curriers.* Sometimes they kill 20, 30 or more hoggs in a day which they cure as aforesaid, and feed themselves thereon, eating the fleash without bread, and most commonly they have noe other liquor but what the murmuring brook and pleasant springs afford them (for they are lusty topers, and perhaps the first night 'ave emptied their cagg of rum, to prevent leakage). But they are supplied with variety of rare frutes, which the woods of their own naturall groath affords 'em. Thus they live a wild kind of life, marooneing[12] in the wild woods and craggy mountains for about the space of two months, in which time they make considerable profite.

This island produces also another sort of hog of a very small size, and of colour black like the other wild hogs, called a picarie,[13] haveing his claws as sharp as razours and his navell on the ridg of his back, which you must cut out as sone as you have kill'd 'em, else their flesh will stink within two houres. These sort of hog are not soe plenty as the former, and they run wild in the most unfrequented woods and mountaines in great companys. Now if you can at your first shot kill on of 'em, then may ye kill as many of 'em as you thinck fitt, for they'll not leave their dead companion, but stand grunting and

12. Taylor uses this word in the original sense of living in the wild (like a Spanish *cimarrón*, or wild man).

13. This is the "peccary", a word not now used in Jamaica. It comes from the Carib. Richard Allsopp, *Dictionary of Caribbean English Usage* (Kingston, 2003), 434; hereafter cited as Allsopp, *DCE*.

lamenting over 'em, untill such time as they are forc't from thence. Their flesh is of excelent nutriment and of good digestion, and is counted a great rareity.

On this island is also found the raccoon, or Indian cony,* every way resembling our English rabbits, only they have a long smoth taile like a catt (or rather a ratt), and they are generally black, and will run upon trees like our Europian squirills, and there set and stare you in ye face (340).[14] In this island they are not soe plenty as they are on the main of America. They are generally caught in the wild woods and unfrequented mountains; their flesh eats just like our Europian rabitts, and is of good nutriment and digestion, and acounted an excelent rariety.

In the woods and mountains are an aboundance of wilde dogs and catts, which prey on beast and birds, but they are not soe savage as to sett against a man. These are by maney eaten, and accounted excelent food. The tame dogs which they keep here on this island are a small mungrell sort of cur betwixt a mastive* and a greyhound. For here they have noe occations of greyhounds, or draw hounds to hunt the nimble hare or statly hart, nor of the subtill spanile* to hunt ye cackling partridge,* for here is noe such game found on this island. They have also here a small sort of guinea doges, naked and without hair all 'ore their bodys; they are some blak, others white and others spotted. They have noses like foxes; neither can they barke as our Europian dogs.[15] Also in the plantations there are aboundance of ratts, which live on the sugar canes, and are a great detriment to the painfull planter. These are by many eaten, and accounted an excelent dish, and of which they make fricases* and other quelquechoses.

The perigritie, or pigritia, or sloathanie, which is a creature much resembling a catt both in shap and size, but is of a dunn colour, haveing long eares like an ass.[16] This creature is the sloaest of all creaturs on the earth in its motion, far sloaer than a snaile, soe that you can hardly desern 'em to move, for it hath bin observed by severall inhabitants of Jamaica that this creature hath bin climming a trumpet wood tree* (it being not above twenty yards high) (341) for the space of fifteen days, yet in continuall motion all that time, and Mr. Heylin in his geography saieth that this creature will not goe

14. According to Sloane, the raccoons lived in the mountains, and largely subsisted on sugar cane. *Voyage,* 2: 329. It is not clear what this "Indian cony" would now be called; Browne distinguishes between these two animals. Patrick Browne, *The Civil and Natural History of Jamaica* (London, 1756), 454.

15. This "Guinea dog" had disappeared by the time that Browne came to describe the species. Browne, *Civil and Natural History,* 486.

16. This is the sloth, an animal and also a human characteristic, *peregritia* (Latin). Browne observes that "this creature, which is a native of the main continent, is sometimes brought to Jamaica by the curious". Ibid., 489.

soe far in fourteen days, as a mall will at one cast heave ashore,[17] and for my own part I have seen them alive, and in their motion, but I could not preceive them to move, noe more than the hand of clock, or watch. These creatures live by the dues and the leaves of those trumpetwood trees, where they are commonly found, and 'tis thought they breed in the hollow trunck of those trees. On this island of Jamaica there are not many of them, but they are very plentifully found on the main of America apearing as the figure [figure lacking].

The ursagrita, or anntbear is also here found in the woods and mountains. 'Tis a little creature in all respects ressembling a bear, and is of a blewish sandie colour. This creature is about the bigness of a large ratt, and hath a verey long tunge. Now his nature is to lay by the paths which the annt or large American spider make by their passage thro' and fro in the woods, and puting forth his long tung across their path, he suppriseth them, and licketh them into his mouth, and by those stratagem he obtaineth his prey. These ursagritas are not verey plenty on Jamaica, but they are common in ye main of America.[18]

(342) On this island is also found the armadilla, which is a small creature about the bigness of a catt, but is shap't like a hogg; it hath a long spindle taile. This creature is all cover'd over with scales like a rhinoceros, or barbed hors, armed all over with strong scales, which seme to shutt and open. This creature liveth in ye solitary woods, and fedeth on the fruites which there groweth, and maketh a noise when caught like a hare. They are very fatt, and being rosted they are delicat food. They are easily caught for they cannot run verey fast, but when they are assail'd betake themselves to hollow trees for shelter.[19] Thus we have given you a description of all the beast both wild and tame that are found in Jamaica; for here are not found the savage lion, tigger, beare, or wolfe, the subtill fox, weasell, or polecatt, nor the blind talps,[20] which distroy the grass in Europian medows. Neither is here to be found the fearfull hart or timerous hare, tho' they are plenty on the main of America.

---

17. Taylor here refers to Peter Heylyn's *Cosmographie in foure books* (London, 1652). In the fourth book, part 2, page 101, he mentions "the pigritia, a little Beast (not so named for nought) which in fourteen days cannot go so far as a man may easily throw a stone".

18. This anteater, now extinct in Jamaica, belongs to a large family still widespread in the world.

19. The armadillo is not noted by other authors for Jamaica, though it lives on other Caribbean islands. Allsopp, *DCE*, 39. There seems serious doubt about whether Taylor can be correct in asserting that anteaters and armadillos once lived in Jamaica; however, it should be noted that he is always careful to identify those creatures which, he thought, lived only "on the Main".

20. The talpa, or mole.

Section II

Of birds found on Jamaica: as the flamingo, turky, dunghill fowl, Muscovy duck, gose, whistling duck, shovelbill, widgeon, teal, snipes, curlues, pillacan, guinea hen, cloaker, turtle dove, groundove, pidgeons, marcough, parrat, parakatee, vulture, hawk, hooper, bellavia, booby, noddy, longshank, blackbird, American nightingale, yallowbird, and hummingbird.*

In giveing an account of the birds found in Jamaica we shall begin with (343) the flamingo, as being the king of birds in these western parts of the world, both for buty of feather and largeness of body.[21] This bird called a flaming is a bird of verey large size, being when he stands on the ground, his head is six feet high from the earth. His body is full as bigg as a larg Europian turkiecock; his neck is a full yard long and he hath a well-proportioned head and beak. His leggs are blew and full a yard long, being slender like a storck's, and he is foal'd lick a turky, haveing a verey short taile as an ostritch, and hath good proportioned wings of a considerable lenght. Now there are two sorts of them; the one is milk whitte, the other his feathers are all of a curious crimson collour, tho' both sorts are of an equale size, and are potrayed to the life in the above figure [lacking].[22] Now these birds are excelent food, full as good as an Europian turkie or bustard.* Above all, his tung is counted as a great rarity being broyl'd, for it tasteth more delicate than marrow. This bird fedeth on fish, which live in shallow lakes and brooks, for his leges being of a considerable lenght, he wadeth in, and with his long neck hath the conveniency to catch his prey. The flamingo lieth an egg truly globular,[23] and truly the colour of his feathers, for the white bird lays a whit egg, and the other's egg is of a pure crimson collour, and about two inches diameter.

Now (344) in all authors treateing of naturalls, I have never found any to mention an egg truly globular, but I have seen the flamingo's egg, and doe here affirm that they are truly rond and globular, and a lively hieroglyphick* of the world,[24] as the ancient Romans did observe when they performed the

---

21. Of the flamingo, Sloane remarks that "I never saw this bird, . . . but I had an account from several of the Inhabitants, whom I thought very understanding and honest men, that [it] was found on the island". *Voyage,* 2: 321. Browne adds that flamingos "are seldom seen in Jamaica, except when forced over [from Cuba] by stormy weather, or imported by the curious". *Civil and Natural History,* 480.

22. Young flamingos are white, and the pink colour is then acquired from their food, which is small crustaceans (Ivan Goodbody, personal communication; hereafter cited as Goodbody).

23. It is indeed round (Goodbody).

24. As Cicero puts it, "The earth is conglobular by its natural tendency". *The Nature of the Gods,* trans. C.D. Yonge (London, 1907), 2: ch. 39, p. 80.

rites of Ceres, (in their *Pompa Cerealis, vel Ciraencis*) by carying an egg on a pagent aloft, for seeing that under the name of Ceres, they did perform this solemnity to the earth, how could they honour it more than by bearing about the true emblem of the whole world? As if they did intimat thereby that even Heaven itsself were beholding to the earth according to that of Ovid:[25]

> Pecori frondes; alimentaque mitice
> fruges humano generi, quoque thara ministra.

And such an hieroglyphick *bolius rhodiginnus* proved an egg to be, partly from its globelique form, partly from the matter it concisteth off, the hard shell resembling the solid earth, the more speritous part therof aire, the moist and liquid part water, the yeolk the element of fire, He further noteth that as there is *in mundi,* soe *in ovo, vis vitalis,* a certain quickning and enlivening power in both. Now to return, the flamingo bredeth on high rocks nere the sea shore. His liver is a most powerfull medicament against a cathar,* being pulverized and taken in wine. This bird is a considerable space of time before it can raise itsself from of the ground to fly, and liveth to a great age.

(345) This island also produces plenty of a verey large sort of turkeys and dunghill fowles of the Europia breed;[26] also here are great plenty of tame ducks of the Muscovy breed;[27] nere as big are their drakes as our Europian gees. Also there are bred on this island some few geess, but not many, for they do not thrive well here, and those which they bred are of a small size, and verey dear, for commonly a fatt gose is sold at Port Royall for a Spanish pistole* of gold.[28] On this island here are never found any swans, either taime or wild, nor noe peacocks are ther here as ever I could hear off.[29]

In January and June, and soe at other times when the raines happen, on Jamaica are then found aboundance of wild fowle (viz.) shovelers, or shovelbil'd ducks, and whistling ducks, which are much of the size and make of our Europian wild ducks. Also there are found on Jamaica aboundance

---

25. The Ovid quotation is as follows: "quod pecori frondes alimentaque mitia, fruges humano generi, vobis quoque tura ministro", meaning "I provide kindly pastures for the flocks, grain for mankind, incense for the altars of the Gods". Miller, *Metamorphoses,* book 2, line 285.

26. Sloane also notes that the "common dunghill cock and hen" and "the turkey" thrive in the West Indies. *Voyage,* 2: 301.

27. The Muscovy duck was and is a domestic breed.

28. Sloane explains that the tame goose "is common on the Island of Jamaica, but they thrive not, perhaps for lack of water, the Plains of this Country being burnt up for some Months of the year". *Voyage,* 2: 323.

29. Sloane, though, observes that peacocks "are common in the hot Parts of the West Indies". Ibid., 302.

of widgeon, and teal of a verey large size.[30] Also in time of the rains there are plenty of snipes and curlues of a very large size, every way resembling those found in Europe, only the curlues are generally white here on this island and other parts of America.[31]

In this countrey we find the pilican which is a sea bird liveing on fish, and they are of the colour of an Europian hearon,* and much of that size, only they have not such long legs nor neck as the heron hath. Whether or noe that be true which by ye poets is storeyed of him, concerning hir feeding of hir young ones with hir own blood I cannot affirm.[32] 'Tis a bird easily caught, for 'twill sett sleeping on the surface of the watter, soe that you may shoot them with ease. They have a very large craugh* which the Creolians* use for purses and tobacco pouches. The flesh of this bird is verey seldom eaten by any, but by Negros. The pilican is in every respect ressembling the precedent figure thereof, which is drawn by the life [lacking].

On this island is also found plenty of Guinea hens, which is much (346) of the make and coloures of our Europian patridge, but as bigg as a good lusty English capon.* They live in great flocks in the savanas, and will run allmost as fast as a greywin.[33] They will pearch by a dog like a phesant. Their flesh is verey fatt, tender and of excelent nutriment, and are held of great esteme, and are truly potraied in the following figure [lacking].

The cloacher or cloaching hen which is here found, is much about the size of Guinea hen haveing a red head, long legs and taile which with its whole body is blew of the colour of a pidgeon. This bird flieth only by night and towards eavening after the sun is down, setting all the day mute in the silent woods. They make a cloaching noise in the night like a Europian hen when she calleth her chickens together. They breed not on this island, but come hither about September and leav the island towards March. This bird is accounted a rarity being most delicat food and of excelent nutriment, and are in all respects according to the above figure, which is portraied to the original life [lacking].[34]

---

30. The shoveler is now an uncommon migrant, and the widgeon was probably a ruddy duck (Goodbody).

31. The large white curlews were probably ibis (Goodbody).

32. Taylor refers here to the symbol of the Corpus Christi, or body of Christ, exemplified symbolically by the pelican who is said to feed her young from her own breast.

33. Sloane observes that "'tis commonly thought that these birds were brought hither . . . from Africa"; he adds that "they run very swiftly". *Voyage,* 2: 302. They seem now to be extinct in Jamaica. A "greywin" was a greyhound.

34. No doubt the clucking-hen, described in Browne, *Civil and Natural History,* 478. It is similar to the rail and crane. F.G. Cassidy and R.B. Le Page, *Dictionary of Jamaican English,* 109; hereafter cited as Cassidy and Le Page, *DJE.* Although Taylor's description could fit several other birds, it is probably the limpkin (Goodbody).

Here the woods are full of turtle doves of a very large size, and also there are on this island another small sort of doves about the size of a larck,[35] and are lick the turtle dove in feather. These are called groundoves. Both these sort of doves are found (347) here in multitudes innumerable to conceive. They are very fatt, delicat food, and of good nutriment and are here sold at a reasonable rate, for you may bie a dozen of 'em for two royall or one English shilling.

Also ther are on this island abundance of tame house pidgeons of a verey large size, and also innumerable multitudes of large wild pidgeons in the woods and mountains. Pidgons which are soe fatt that being shott, their skin will burst by their falls from off the trees. These, with the doves, make such a noise in the woods and mountains that it seemeth as if the whole island were covered with pidgeon. They are easily shott, for they will hardly move from the trees at the report of a gun, so that in two hours' time a man may kill as many of them as he is able to bare home. About this island are severall small island, or kays as Green Island, Hog Island, Pidgeon Island etc.[36] These island are overgrown with maingrove bushes and the like wherein multitude of pidgeons generally breed, soe that at their cheife breeding time, which is in Aprill and May, peopple resort thither, where they catch thousands of their young ones which are much fatter and better than our European pidgeons, and those islandes are called Pidgeon Islands from the abudance of doves and pidgeons which breed thereon.

Lickwise on this island breedeth multitudes of green parrats of a small size and of two sorts: a whitbil'd parrat, streach't about the head with a faint reed, blew and som yallow, and some part of the feathers on their brest is streach't with a faint red.[37] The other parrat hath a black beak and all his feathers are green. Neither (348) of these two sorts of parrats are at all butiful; the most butiful parrats are found on the Main, some of which are of a very large size as big as an Europian rook.[38] Some are all green, others are butified with yallow, blew, red and white feathers. These parrats speak very loud and plain. Those of Cuba is a large and exceding butiful parrat, and in my fancy the handsomest which I ever saw; they are all green, except ther head, which is adorn'd with curiose snow-white and deep crimson reed feathers, and their beak is of a purer ivory colour.[39] Also, their brest and the ridg of their wings are all covered with curious crimson feathers, and the long feather of their

---

35. If Taylor means the English meadow-lark, this is considerably smaller than any dove.

36. This is Pigeon Island in Old Harbour Bay, the Spanish *cayo de los palominos.*

37. These are the yellow-billed parrot and the black-billed parrot (Goodbody).

38. Their range is indeed confined to Jamaica. See James Bond, *Birds of the West Indies* (London, 1961), 111–12.

39. This may well be the Cuban parrot, though its range does not now include Jamaica. Ibid., 111.

wings are of a curious deep azur colour. These parrats will speak very loud and plain. Next to these are the Portarico parrat, which is a large bird, all green with a whit beak and a curious ring of crimson feathers round the bill or beak.[40] These parrats will spake very well. Lastly, the Affrican or Guinea parrat is a larg statly parrat whose feathers are of the collour of an Europian blew pidgeon. These parrats have a large black strong beak, and hath a large tail whose feathers are of a curious deep scarlet reed. This is a very apt parrat to learn and speaks very plain and loud, in my judgement beter than any other parrat whatsoever. All these parrats are brought to Jamaica and sold at ressonable rates.

Now those parrats which breed on Jamaica will learn to speak anything, but they have a very small and low voice and are here very plentiful, and flie in great flocks together and are excelent food, for they eateth much like a house pidgion, but are much fatter. Also here are found greet plent of green parracetes.[41] They are a small sort of parrat about the biggness of a lark, all (349) green and have a whit beak. These are not soon tamed. They will also speak a little. These sort of birds at time of harvest, when the maiz is ripp, resort from the mountains into the plantation in flocks like cloudes, and their natur is that haveing shoot one of them, you may kill as many of them as you please, for they will not leave their dead companion, but stand chattering over 'em as long as you lett them lie and will not be frightened from thence by the noise of a gun soe that you may shoot as many of them as you please. These with the Jamaican parrats commonly breed in the hollow trunck of cabadge trees up in the mountains soe that they are hard to be come by, and you must fell the tree to come at 'em. They seldome breed above two young ones at a time and that commonly in Aprill and May. You may bie of them dead for two royalls a duzen, but a young one alive out of the nest will cost six royalls at Jamaica.

Here is allso found a most butiful bird called on this island a marcough. This bird is as big as an Europian phesant* cock and of a green colour, haveing his beak white, and of ye same form like a parrat and 's head and brest is adorn'd with butiful azur, crimson and yallow shining feathers, he hath a verey long taile composed of green, purpl azur, yallow and crimson-collour shining feathers and in fine is a most butiful bird, potraied to the life in the above figure [lacking]. (350) This bird will spake much plainer and lowder than any parrat whatsoever,[42] and are held as a great rarity, there being but a

40. This is the Puerto Rican parrot. Ibid., 112.

41. Probably olive-throated parrakeets. Ibid., 113.

42. According to Sloane, the great macaw "spoke very plain, and more Articulate than any Bird I ever heard". *Voyage,* 2: 296. Macaws are not now found in Jamaica (Goodbody).

few of them on this island and those hard to be come at, because they are noewhere to be found but in the woody mountaines. Their flesh is very good but they are seldom eaten, being kept tame as a curiosity. I never saw but one of them in England, which was amongst His Majesty's birds at Saint James's Park.[43]

On this island is found three excelent sort of hawks; first a small hawk of the same size, coloure and make of a merlin. These feed on small fowles, as ground doves, etc. Another sort of hawk, full as big as a faulcon but somewhat longer winged; they are of the same collour. This hawk preys on Guinea hens and other large fowles and would be a bird of good service[44] were they here regarded. A third sort of hawk here found is a fish hawk, everey way resembling a gosehawk,* but only 'tis somewhat bigger and of a larger wing, preying on fish in lakes and shallow brooks, the flesh of which is eaten by many in America.[45] I once eat part of one of them roasted, on Cavalero Bay, and for my part, with it, and a good bowle of punch, I made a suffitient dinner therewith.

On this island are found multitudes of a ravenous sort of small vulturs which the inhabitants call a carrion crow, feeding on nothing but cadavers and doe noe harm.[46] They are about the size (351) of an Europian turkey, are perfectly delineated in the precedent figure [lacking]. This being soe harmless a bird, there is an acct of the countrey made that whoesoever shall kill any of them, or destroy their nests, shall for every offence forfite five pounds, for why, these vulturs devoure the dead carcasses, whose stinck would else infect the aire, and probable produce many contagious destempters.

The hooper or hooping bird, which is here found, is every way of the size, colour and resemblance of our English rookes, only they have a beak lick a parrat and make a hooping noise lick a bittern.[47] These birds are commonly found nigh the sea, for they haunt in boggy morose* ground. Their flesh is very fatt and delitious and of excelent nutriment, being verey much estemed.

Towards the seashore is here found severall sea fowle, as first the belavia, a bird called a man of war. This bird is of the same collour and size of a white

---

43. The diarists John Evelyn and Samuel Pepys both mention visiting the birds in Saint James's Park where waterfowl had been kept since the reign of Queen Elizabeth (1558–1603). But their knowledge dates from the 1660s, and they do not mention the macaw.

44. By "a bird of good service", Taylor means one that could be trained by a falconer.

45. The two larger hawks are the red-tailed hawk or buzzard, and the fish hawk or osprey, the latter now an occasional migrant visitor. The merlin used to be common, but today the kestrel is the common small and resident hawk (Goodbody).

46. Sloane remarks that in 1655 the English at first thought that they were turkeys, and tried eating them, a mistake. *Voyage,* 2: 294. The John Crow was indeed protected by law; see below, p. 295.

47. This "hooping bird" is a mystery.

Figure 27 Taylor's drawing of a belavia, page 351.

seagull and flie verey lofty from which they only differ by a tuff of read feathers which growe on the head of these birds like a hellmit.* They breed on high rock and on unfrequented small kays or islands in the sea.[48] Their flesh is pleasant, of good nutriment and esteme and appears thus: [figure 27].

(352) On this island is also found another sort of sea fowle called a booby, which is a fowle about the size of a pidgeon haveing a head and beak like a stareling,* long wing'd and blackish feather'd and is footed like a duck being a verey simple bird, for at night you may catch 'em how you please with your hands at their rosteing places.[49] I have catch'd 'em verey often at sea, for they'll nest on the yards and riging soe that you may catch 'em with ease. These birds are verey lousy and their flesh is seldom eaten by anie. They commonly breed on small uninhabited island in ye sea and are portraied to the life in the above picture: [figure omitted].

Here is also found another sea foule called a noddy[50] which is a bird of a grey coulour, hath large wings and a short taile and is about the bigness of the sea mew and hath a long neck with a verey great and ill proportion'd head which with its beak is bigger than its whole body. They are footed like a duck. These birds are seldom eaten. They breed as the bobby and appeare as the figure [figure omitted].

(353) Also on this island is found another sort of a watter fowle called a longshanck,[51] by reason of the length of his legs. This bird is of a dark grey colloure, and his body is about the bigness of a pidgeon, haveing a well proportioned head and neck with a long sharp bill or beak like a stareling. His wings are verey short as if natur had designed them for little use, for he seldom flies; but it hath verey slender long legs, and is footed like a duck and will runn at a great rate. This bird preyeth on fish and haunteth nere lakes and morose ground. He breed amongst the maingrove bushes. The flesh of

48. This sounds much like a frigate bird, or man-of-war bird, though it is in fact black (Goodbody).

49. This is probably the Brown Booby, though it, like the other boobies, is much larger than a pigeon. Bond, *Birds*, 25

50. This is the brown noddy. Ibid., 100.

51. This may be the black-winged stilt (Goodbody).

this bird is seldom eaten neither are they here verey plenty. The liver of this fowle pulverized is a most powerful diuretique, and is portraied to the life in the above figure for illustration sake [lacking].

Here are also found three severall sorts of blackbirds, much of the same make and size of our English (354) blackbird.[52] As first a black bird whose feathers legs and beak is all black and his beak is in the form lick the beak of a parrat. These sort are here in inumerable flocks like claudes.* There are a second sort of black birds, whose feathers, leges and beak are all black, every way resembling an English blackbird. These are here verey plenty and they have a third sort of the same size and feather. These have yallow legs and a yallow bill or beak lick a parrats. Neither of these 'ave any notes like our Europian blackbird. Neither are they eaten or regarded because they have here plenty of variety of better fowles.

On this island (as well as on many other parts of America) is found a verey rare nightingale, much bigger than our Euro nightingale, being about the bigness of a larke, and is of a curious assur* colour, shadowed with pale sable and snow-whit spotts.[53] This bird hath all the notes of our Europian nightingales, and many others which are more rare and charming. This bird I have potraied here to the life [image lacking] and here 'twill not be amiss to insert the plesant history of the nightingale out of Plutrach, whoe hearing that little chantress sing hir warbling[54] notes sweetly in the silent woods, desiered one to be kill'd to feed on, not doubting but their flesh would be as gratefull to the pallat as their sweet charming harmony was mellodies to the eare. But when 'twas caught, and strip't out of its fethers, and he saw what a pore little creature 'twas, he stood in great admiration saying "truly they are *vox et preteria nihil,* a meer sound and nothing else".[55] And 'tis observed by all natuaralists that this bird shall chaunt most swetely and sett all hir skill and strenght at werk when she perceives attention, and is soe ambitious (355) that she chuseth rather to die than be outvied by any, of which we have a notable instance from Strada, which is concerning a nightingale and a lutanist* which I have translated thus:[56]

---

52. These three are probably the ani, the grackle and perhaps the white-chinned thrush, or hopping-dick (Goodbody).

53. This is probably the rufous-throated solitaire, still common in forest areas but hard to see (Goodbody).

54. These notes are often to be heard, when other birds are silent.

55. This comes from Plutarch's "Sayings of the Spartans": "A man plucked a nightingale and finding almost no meat said; 'it is all voice ye are, and naught else'." *Moralia,* trans. Frank Cole Babbitt (Cambridge, Mass., 1956), 3: 399.

56. Roughly the same "Translation out of Strada" was published in *The Poetical Works of William Strode (1600–1645),* ed. Bertram Dobell (London, 1907), 16–19.

When the declineing sun did downwards tend
From higher sphears and to the earth did lend
A gentile flame, then near to Tiber's flood
A lutanist allay'd his reeds and stood
In sounding charmes, under a greeny seat
Of shady oak took shelter from the heat.
A nightingale 'ore heard him which did use
To sojourne in the neiboring grove, that muse
That filled the place. This syrene of the wood,
Poor harmless chantress stealling nigh she stood
Close lurking in the woods atentively,
Recording the unwonted mellody.
She con'd it* to hirself, and every straine
His fingers play'd, hir throat resounds againe.
The lutanist perceived an answer sent
From the imitating bird, and was content
To share hir play; more fully than in hast
He tries his lute, and giveing hir a tast
Of the ensueing quarrell, nimbly beats
On all his strings, as nimbly she repeats;
And wildly ranging 'ore a thousand keys
Sounds a shrill warning of her after layes
With rowleing hand the lutanist then plies
The trembling threads, sometimes in scornfull wise
He brushes down the strings, then takes 'em all
With one eaven stroak; now stricks 'em severall,
And culls 'em 'ore againe, his sparkeling joyntes
With buissie discant mimeing on the points.
Flies back againe with nimble stroak, then stays
The bird replies, and art, with art repaies.
(356) Sometimes as one unexpert and in doubt
How she might weild her voice she draweth out
Her tone at large, and doth at first prepair
A solemn straine, not weav'd with winding aire
But with an equall pitch, and equall threat
Makes a cleare passag for hir glideing noat.
Then cross divitions nimblely she plaies
And loudly chaunting on hir quicker laies
Raiseth hir sound, and with hir quavering voice
Falls back again, and wondering how soe choice,
And various harmony could issue out
From such a little throat doth goe about
Some louder lessons, and with wonderous art
Changeing the strings, doth up the treble dart

And down the base doth smite with powerful stroak
He beats, and as the trumpet doth provoak
Sluggards to fight, even soe his wontten skill
With mingled discords, joins the hours with shrill
The bird this also tunes and whilst she cutts
Sharp notes with melting voice, and mingleing putts
Measures of midle sound, then presently,
She thunders deep, and sings it inwardly
With gentile murmur dear and dull she singes
By course as when the martiall morning rings.
Beleive't the minsterall blush't with angery mood
Inflam'd (said he) thou chauntress of the wood.
Either from thee I'll bear the bell away
Or vanquist break my lute without delay;
Unimitable accents now he straines,
His hand flies 'ore the strings, in one he chaines
Far different numbers, chaceing here and there,
And all the strings he labours everywhee
Both flat and sharp he stricks and statly growes
To prouder straines, and backward as hee goes
Like a full quire, a quavering consort plaies
Then pausing stood in expectation.
(357) Of his corrivall, nor durst answer on.
But she when prach'et on hir voice had whett,
Induering not to yield, hir voice did sett,
And all hir spirits strove to work in vain!
For whilst with labour to express again
With nature's simple voice, such diverss keys;
And slender pipes such lofty notes as these
O're matcht with high designes, o're match't with woe,
Just at the last encounter of hir foe,
She faints, she dies, falls on his instrument
That conquer'd hir: this is hir monument.

On this island is found a verey butiful small bird called a yallow bird about the bigness of a chafinch,* and hath a long sharp reed bill and leggs.[57] His feathers are all of a gold colour, except his head which is curiously adorned with azure and green shining feathers, and he is butified with a large taile, the uperpart of which is a curious green and the other of a deep crimson shineing coloure. There are many of these birds found on this island, which with the nightingale continually chaunt forth their warbleing musicke in the silent

57. This yellow bird is probably the oriole, or aunt katie (Goodbody).

Figure 28 Theodor de Bry, image of a Carolinian "sorcerer", *Americae,* part VI (by courtesy of The Newberry Library, Chicago). This image shows the way in which small birds were worn on their heads by some Indian "magicians", or medicine-men.

woods. This bird will not be easyly tamed, nor will they live home to England. This bird I 'ave portraied to the life in the above figure: [lacking].

Here is found another small bird called a humming bird which is the smallest bird upon the earth, and next to the bird of parradize (found on the Molluccoes Islands and noewhere else),[58] is the most butifull creature in the whole creation. The humming (358) bird is about half the bigness of the little wrenn, haveing all parts of a suttile and due proportion. His beake is of a derk bround mixt purple spots, sett like saphiers. His wing are composed of shining gold-couler'd feather, shadowed with a deep crimson and a curiouse azure. His head lookes like a most precious sparkling jewell, appearing of severall colures, as he varys his posture in standing, glitering like the changable rainbow, for 'tis arrayed and adorn'd with currious shineing feathers of all conceiveable butifull colour. His eyes appeare like two sparkling diamond sett in bright gold. His tayle is compossed of crimson, purple and green feathers, shadow'd with white and a pale sable, spotted checquerwise with diversity of colours.

Thus this bird is the butifulst creature that I ever saw, and I beleive the butifults creature in the whole creation, for nature always appearth most glorious in its lesst worker. This bird is by the Indians preserved and dried and worn in their ears and nose as a choice jewell.[59] Indeed 't would make anyone

58. These birds, the *Paradisaeidae,* still inhabit New Guinea and adjacent islands.

59. There is a celebrated illustration in de Bry, *Americae,* part 6, showing an Amerindian of the Carolinas wearing a bird on his head in this way (figure 28).

ravish'd with admiration to see this little butifull creatur in its liveing glory. But when 'tis dead it loseth much of its vivall lusture. These birds make only a homeing noise like a bee from whence it receives its name. It breedeth and haunteth about cotten trees, and I beleive feedeth on small worms. It makes hir nest of silke grass and layeth two small eggs, about the bigness of a pea and of a blewish colour. These birds are found here very plentyfull. There is noe way to make them live to be tame in caiges, for they'll prive themselves to death. This bird I 'ave here portrayed to the life: [lacking].

(359) On this island are found all the yeare round aboundance of swallows and martines, in all respect such as wee have in England. Thus we have given you a full description of all the birds that are found and known on the island of Jamaica.[60]

Section III

Of fishes found on Jamaica[61] *as the manatee, green tortoise, lackerhead-tortois, hawksbill-tortoise, terraphinn,* jewfish, parrat fish, dolphin, baracoda, grooper, albecole, boonera, Spanish-macrell, mullet, rock fish, cavalie, tarpum, grunt, audwife, garfish, stingaree, swordfish, sharck, allagator, conny fish, snapper, sea urchin, remora, flying fish, pillot, whitfish, stonebass, leather coats, smelts, elle, mudfish, crawfish, prawns, sea crabb, land crabb, cuncks, wilkes,* calphia, soldiers, oyster and sea egg.*

As a supplie to this uberous place, the sea and fresh rivers yeild their assistance, being well stored with fish, multituds and variety of 'em. Such rareties, which the Europian parts of the world 'ave not neither for bulk, shape or delicate food. We shall here give you an account of 'em according to their dignity, and first:

In these western parts of the world is found that amphibious creature called a manatee or sea cow. 'Tis a fish of a verey large size and a mighty monster. This creature called a manatee, or seacow, hath a head with teeth every way shap't like a cowe's, only it hath noe ears nor horns (360). It hath two very small eyes. Its skine is black without haire or scale, rough like an nurss [?] skin of an exceeding thickness, at least when full grown of an inch thick by its guiles.* It hath two small finns, or paddles, under which are two large duggs* like a cow when it gives it young one suck. It hath a ridge of high strong fines on its back, and hath a brod round tayle. These creatures are of

60. This description is not of course "full". It leaves out, among others, owls, woodpeckers and herons.

61. Taylor's idea of "fishes" essentially includes "water-creatures", taking in many that we should now call mammals.

a prodigious bigness. I have seen a bull manatee full thirty foot long and he weiged sixteen hundred and thirty pound weight avoir du poire.[62] I have seen a young sucking manate calve which we caught in the Gulph of Samana on Hispaniola which was sixteen foot long and weighed fouer hundred weight. This monster I 'ave here potraied to the life for illustration sake: [figure lacking]

The fleash of this creature is most delicat food, and in my oppinion the best of meat in the whole world.[63] It lookes whiter than veale or mutton and eateth exceeding swett and tender, much like (tho' much better than) a good fatt Europian capoon curiously (361) larded. For you must understand that this is naturally larded with its own fatt, for after you have taken out the paunch and intestins (which in every way resembles that of a bullock, both gutts, cowle,[64] kidneys, hart, liver etc.) and 'ave fleced* of the skine, then you come to the *vela pinguinosa* or laire of fatt, about an inch thick (and is exceding white) which extends itself over the surfface of the whole body.

Below this vela is another vela, which is of flesh whit like veal, about an inch thick, extending itself as the former. Below this is another vela of fatt, about half an inch thick, which extendeth itself as the former bellow that flesh, soe that 'tis naturally larded with a vaile of fatt and lean from the skine quite to the bones. This creature hath strong jaweboons like a cow, and broad ribbs and an exceding strong backboon. But none of its boons are cavious* nor have they any marrow in 'em. The taile of this fish is (all save the bone) a clod of fatt, of which commonly is made montego[65] de manatee. This creatur breed as a cow and in the like manner nourishes hir young one with milk. The female hath the perfect member of a cow which grow nigh the navell and the male hath the members of a bull which nature hath placed within the *Regio Venneris.* They breed but one young one at a time. This creature feedeth on a sort of grass which groweth in the sea, and liveth in shoul'd gulphs, langoons etc. It constantly, both morning and eavening, goes twice a day up to the mouths of fresh watter rivers, and ther drinketh like an oxe; when they are caught, for you must know that those that make it their bussines to catch them goe towards break of day to those rivers (362), in a small dory or canoa, wher they find their game, for the manatte runs as far up into the rivers as he can float himself, and therefore their canoa must draw but little watter.

62. Sloane estimates a large manatee at "fifteen hundred weight". *Voyage,* 2: 330.

63. As Sloane puts it, they are "the best Fish [*sic*] in the World, and appear like beef or veal". Ibid., 329.

64. This is a caul, or membrane.

65. "Montego" is from the Spanish *manteca,* or lard; hence Montego Bay, from which lard was shipped.

Now they aproach to him with all the silence imaginable (for he is exceding quick of hearing, tho' he sees scars* att all) and being nere him they strick him with a harpoon, ore harping iron,* in all respects as they doe whales in the norther countreys. He being struck furiously beats himself, and makes to sea, towing the canoa after him, but he is soon tier'd, soe that they tow him aboard with ease. Now whilst their skin is slack in their diving posture, the harpoons enter them with ease, but when you are at sea they will not, for you 'ad as goods heave the harpoon against a rock, as against them.

After they are caught, if they are not much wounded, they will live on board ten daies and will drinck watter out of a bucket like a hog and are brought in sloops to Jamaica. This is here counted the best of fish and is sold for two royalls a pound. There are not many of 'em about this island; those which are be found on the north side but they are verey plenty on Hispaniola. I have seen great schools of 'em in the Gulph of Samana on Hispaniola, wher I saw two of 'em caught and eat part of 'em with which, and a good bowle of brandy punch for sauce, in my opinion I made the best diner that I did in all my life. Now if you would know the phisicall vertues of this amphibious monster, read Doctor Trapham's *Present State of Health* which will give you satisfaction therein.[66]

Next we shall treat of the green tortoise, or turtle, which are a (363) strange kind of an amphibious creature. This tortoise have a strong covering of thick boony substance on the back called the callapatch,[67] the iner part of which is of a bonnie substance, about an inch thick. In the inside 'tis form'd with ribs growing fast to the same. This calapatch is covered with a thinn horney greenish shell, about the thickness of a lanthorn.[68] Now the belly of this creature is defended with a thick soft yellow shelly substance, called the callape. This creature hath a strong short head and neck with two exceeding quick-sighted eyes, but it hath not in the least measure the sence of hearing.

This creature hath fouer long strong leggs or finns, which serveth him both to swim in the sea and walke with on the sand. The male tortoise hath a long thick taile and the female a short one, and are both deffend with a horney shell. Now that we might make all plaine and obvious, we have here potraied this creature to the life: (364) [lacking] Now this creature is of a prodigious bigness; I have often seen one of 'em to way above two hundredweight. The flesh of this creatur when boyl'd or roasted eats just like our English veal. They are very fatt and their fatt is of a sea-green colour and

66. Of the manatee, Dr Thomas Trapham observes that when she visits us "she brings a feast with her as well as a good medicine for the afflicting Stone". *Discourse of the State of Health,* 64.

67. The carapace ("callapatch") is indeed attached to the ribs (Goodbody).

68. That is, a lantern, or transparent case enclosing a light.

eateth as delitious as marrow. They cutt 'em out in fouer quarters, and the callapee or belly-peice, which rosted is most excelent food, and being baked fare excelleth a venison pastie. Now you must understand that altho the fatt of the quarters etc. of this creature is green yet the *vela pinguinosae intestinorum* or the fatt on the gutts is yallow as gould. These gutts are accounted some of the best in the tortoise and eateth delicat and tender. The flesh which grows on to the bakepeice is sold with the callapatch, of which they make fingrigo and sippets,[69] a dish common at Jamaica.

Now come we to the vitalls. This creature hath a large liver, lungs and gale like a calfe. The liver is most delicat food. This creature is saide* to have three harts, but that is a mistake of the ignorant. Thus it is; it hath one very large hart, one each side of which grows two curious large tunnickels[70] or veals, which nature hath made for a safeguard to the hart. These three looks like three harts and is therfor thro' ignorance soe reported. The malle tortoise hath a very large pissell,* and stones;* the stones are eaten and counted excelent food. These creature engendors for the space of a whole Egyptian years, and continue in their close embraces during the full revolution of a whole moone. Now the female after this cooting time, which is in December, begins to grow very bigg and fatt, and goeth to ye Caymanes[71] and other places to lay hir eggs, which she burieth about a foot deep in the sand, by the heat of which they are hach't and brought to prefection. Now the female tortoise are in season, she being fatt and full of eggs (365); they have in them above half a bushill* of eggs.

I have seen in a turtle's nest in the sand above 700 eggs. A tortoise egg is about the bigness of a hen's egg, but round, and hath a thick soft white skine instead of a shell. They have both yolke and white as the egge of a fowle and eateth full as good when they are taken out of hir belly, but those which are not come to prefection but lookes yallow are the best eggs. Now as soon as they are hach't, the young ones presently crawle into the sea, where they live on the sea grass, butt I beleive scarss one half of 'em geets safe into the watter, but are devouered by the fowles. Now you must know that when the female is in season, the male is not, for he is mauger* and pore, haveing worn out 'em self in his veneriall copullations. Also, his yard every yeare rotteth off and a new one comes like the hart. The female breeds not untill she is three yars old. These, in ther cooting time,* cling soe fastt togeather that haveing struck

69. "Sippet" is an archaic word for a small piece of toasted or fried bread.

70. "Funnicle" means filament.

71. As Sloane puts it, "The Turtle or Tortoises come to Caymanas, two small isles west of Jamaica, once a year to lay their eggs in the sand, to be hatched by the sun." *Voyage,* 1: lxxxviii. See Roger Smith, *The Maritime Heritage of the Cayman Islands* (Gainesville: University of Florida Press, 2000).

the male with a harpone etc, you have caught 'em both, for he will not sepperat from the female untill you cutt off his pizsell with a knife.

Now these tortoises are thus caught; toward February sloops goe from Jamaica to the Kaymanes, the north side of Jamaica etc., but cheifly to Caymanes, wher they geet ashore and watches, and in the eavening the tortoise comes ashore to lay hir eggs. Then they with a leaver turn 'em on their back and let 'em lie (for they can't rise) till such times they have done their tide, and perhaps in an eavening shall turn 50, 60, 100 or more of 'em, som of which they cutt up and salt up the quarters in barrels, and the rest they stow alive in their sloops, for they will live 15 days without meat or watter and her 'tis observable that this season they catch nothing but females, there being not one male to be found amongst 'em. Now when they 'ave loaded (366) their sloops, they bear away to Jamaica, where being arrived they putt their tortoises in penns or crawles* made with piles in the sea in Chocolatahole,[72] at the entrance into Port Royall Harbour, and here they feed 'em with sea grass (on which they will feed and live and agree together) untill such time as they sell 'em to the butcher. A good turtle will yeild five dollars, and their flesh is sold in the market for a groat* a pound, or two pound for a royall. Inded the flesh of this creature is the great and cheife provition on Port Royall, and on most other places on Jamaica.

This creature is an exceeding sencible creature, for when he is layn on 's back, and he preceiveth the butcher coming to cutt his throat, he will sigh, groan and weep like a child that is beaten, or a woman when she wants mony from hir husband. The flesh of this creature is of a strong life, for I have sene the fleash, but the heart especiall, have motion and life in it ten houers after 'twas cutt out. The flesh of this tortoise makes excelent broath; ye finns boyl'd tendor, and then scour'd, eats much like a need's* foot. Now towards June, July etc., the malle tortoise becoms fatt and in season and is caught thus.

They goe from Port Royall in sloops to ye Northside of Jamaica, and soe to other parts wher tortoise-grass grows in the sea, and ther in the eavening toward sunseet, they see 'em putt up their heads above watter and blow, then they are comming nigh the shore to feed. Then the turtler pitches his foile or nett, in the which, when they come to feed, they are caught. Now this neet is made with deepsea line, the meash being about half yard square. He is about 20 yards broad and 100 yards long, the ground line leded and the other boied with corckes. Now they pitch one end fast on the shore and soe runn out the rest of their nett and they ride at the seaward end with their canoa, and (367) as soon as 'ere they fell one strike into the neet, they rowgh and hall him ashore, for else he would bare their netts, he is so prodigious strong. Now

72. These pens are described below, p. 236.

some time they shall in this maner catch 20 or more tortoises in a night by which they make great profitt.

Thus we have fully discribe that amphibious monster called a tortoise or turtle which pretaketh partly of ye nature of a beast, of a fish and of a fowle, for he feeds on grass and breeds on land. Secondly he lives in the watter and swimeth like a fish, and lastly he laieth eggs by which he is produced to life, by which he partaketh of the essence of a fowle. Now if you would know its phisicall vertues, read Dr. Trapham's *Present State of Health,* where you will finde a plaine description therof, by which you may gratifie your curiosity.[73]

About this island is also found and caught plenty of another sort of tortoise called a lackerheat tortois, hiccarie[74] or toad turtle. This turtle is not above half soe bigg as the green tortoise, and he hath a verey great ill-proportioned head but also 'tis every waie made like the former, both external and internall, but is not soe fatt, white or tendor, and is therfore here of little esteem, being seldome eaten by the English, but given to Negros, whoe will feed as hartly thereon, as Saundy the Scott on a sow's baby. These feed on grass,[75] lay eggs and breed as ye former.

The hawksbill-tortoise is caught on the Northside of this island. This tortoise is shap't in all respects as the former, only it is not above two foot long and 1½ foot broad on the callapatch. When at full growth it hath a head like the green tortoise, but it hath a bill or beak like a hawk (from where 'tis named) and very sharp. None of these turtles have teeth, butt a kind of a sharp bill with which they eat their food. This tortoise feedeth on grass[76] and leith eggs. The flesh of this is like the green tortoise, but his fatt is not green but yallow. Their flesh is not estemed nor is seldom (368) eaten by the English.[77]

They are caught only for the shell which is a good commodity. This shell is curiously spotted, and is that which is used in England to make hafts for knives etc.[78] This is about a quarter of an inch thick and grows on the callapatch, and they geet it from thence by warming it against fire, but these tortois is caught cheifly about the small Cativas Island on the cost of Porta Bella, on the main of Peruviana. 'Tis a good comodity worth a dollar a

73. Dr Trapham writes only of "the great vitality of this creature, and consequently the advantage the feeders thereon may well expect from converting it into themselves". *Discourse of the State of Health,* 64.

74. A hicatee (now known in parts of the Caribbean as a "hiccatee" [Alsopp, *DCE,* 291]) is a turtle, from the Spanish *hicotea.* Cassidy and Le Page, *DJE,* 224.

75. This loggerhead turtle is in fact a carnivore (Goodbody).

76. In fact, it is more of a carnivore than herbivore (Goodbody).

77. As Sloane puts it, this turtle is "not so good Victualls" as the green turtle". *Voyage,* 2: 332.

78. It was also used for decorative items such as comb-cases. See Pawson and Buisseret, *Port Royal,* 142–44.

pound; commonly a tortoise yeilds five or six pound of shell.[79] The shell of the green tortois is spotted in the like manner, but is noe thicker than paper, by which means 'tis little worth and used only in lanthorns.

In the fresh rivers, swamps, laks and morros ground are found the terraphin or land tortoise.[80] These are of a small size and are defended by a small callapatch and callape and have leggs with claws, whereas the other have finns. Their head and tailes are somwhat like the green tortoise (only whereas ye one hath a kind of a beak, these hath teath, which they can secure by drawing 'em within their shell and can again putt 'em out at pleasure). The shell of the callapatch is naturally curiously wrought in chequerwise. These live sometimes in the watter, but mostly on the land. Their fleash is fatt, gratefull to the pallat and of hollsom nutriment and a great restoritive in consumptions.* They engendor and lay eggs as the other tortoise. They are a very strong and hardy creature and may with ease be caried home to England, wher they will live (369) in gardens and eat the snailes and other worms, and in winter will make themselves a cave in the earth where they will lie dormant unless in faire sunshine weather. This creature I have here portraied to the life [figure lacking].

The jew fish which are here found in great plenty is a large fish; some of them I have seen ten feet long.[81] His body is inclining to roundness, defended with strong scales and adorn'd with well-proportion'd finns. The head of this fish is of the shape of a salmon, and hath a large mouth and a broad forked taile. This fish is generally caught by strickeing 'em with a harpoon. This is an exceding fatt and delitious fish, and in fine, one of the best fishes in America. They are of a great bigness, some of 'em weighing 150 pounds weight. Of this fish they make a great dish at Port Royall by cutting it into small peices and frieing it very dry in oyle, and then puting it up in a pickle flavour'd with spices, which is of excelent use and proffit to 'em for a regale.* This fish so ordered, they call caveich.[82] See the figure [lacking].

Here is also found in great plenty another sort of an excellent fish called the parrat fish.[83] This fish is full as large as the former, and soe shap't, only

79. See also Sloane: "These are chiefly valued for their scales, called tortoise 'shell'." *Voyage,* 2: 332.

80. Sloane claims that the land tortoise is "common in the woods between Guanaboa [Vale] and Town [Spanish Town] everywhere". Ibid., 331.

81. Taylor makes this fish very long and rather light. A large modern specimen might measure seven feet long and weigh seven hundred pounds (Goodbody). It is now called a June fish. Cassidy and Le Page, *DJE,* 246.

82. "Caveach" or "escovitched" fish derives from the Portuguese/Spanish *escabeche.* Allsopp, *DCE,* 218.

83. As Sloane puts it, "This Fish hath its name from its Mouth, being like that of a Parrot." *Voyage,* 2: 281.

he hath green scales and yallow finns, and mouth shap't like a parrat's bill. This fish is a very fatt (370) and delicat fish, and is caught by stricking as the former, and is here drawn and portraied to the life [figure lacking].

The dorado, or dolphin, found in these western parts, are here in great plenty.[84] 'Tis a very butiful fish in the watter as he swims, appearing there of diveres rare and shineing colours, but when out of the watter and dead, it losseth all its butie. This fish is not att all of that shape as by paintors portrai'd on sines.[85] It is a very swift fish in swimming, and a grat enemy to the flieing fish, and is here portraied to the life [figure lacking]. They are generally about three or fouer foot long. The entrailes of this fish callcined* to powder is good in epilipsies.

The dolphin by naturallists is observed to be a very amicable fish, much delight to gaze on man. I have read a story of a dolphin in Plutarch who frequented a place where some of the Syracusian children used to swim.[86] Amongst these children their was a boy of an extraordinary fair skin and butie, to whom the dolphin took such affection that he would swime side by side and keep 'em companie. This boy was at last soe well used to the dolphin that he could stroak 'em with his hand, and wantonly play with 'em in the warter, and at last the dolphin knew his voice and would com at his call, and the boy would get up on his back and he would carry 'em too and fro on the surges and againe set him safe on land. But one time it chaunced that the boy being on the back of his maritin courser, some of the sharp (371) fines of the dolphin wounded his cods* soe that he died therwith. The pore dolphin seeing the watter stain'd with the boy's blood and hereing him cry, run with him to the shore and after he had dismounted him on the drie sand and saw him dead, such was the love of this creature that he leapt out of the watter and forsook his native element, and ther on the sands was found dead by the side of the Greatian boy; such was its amitie to man that it died for love.

A worthy friend of mine, one Mr. Richard Bowes, formerly a captain in the Royall Company's service trading to Affrica,[87] gave me this information, that he being at Cape Coast att anchor, there were three dolphins used to play about his ship, and he takeing delight, would not suffer none of his men to

84. There is confusion here between the dolphin fish (*coryphaera hippurus*) and the true dolphins, which are small cetaceans (whales) (Goodbody).

85. "The Dolphin" was a favourite name for taverns in England, and so was shown on their signs.

86. Taylor here conflates the story of a dolphin and a boy of Iassus, found in slightly different versions in Aelian, *On the Characteristics of Animals,* tr. A.F. Scholfield, 3 vols. (Cambridge and London: Harvard University Press and Heinemann, 1959), book 6, 15; and in Plutarch's *Moralia,* tr. Harold Cherniss and William Heimbold, 15 vols. (Cambridge and London: Harvard University Press and Heinemann, 1968), 12:984–85.

87. And then master of HMS *Falcon,* on which Taylor sailed. National Archives, Adm 33/132, 108.

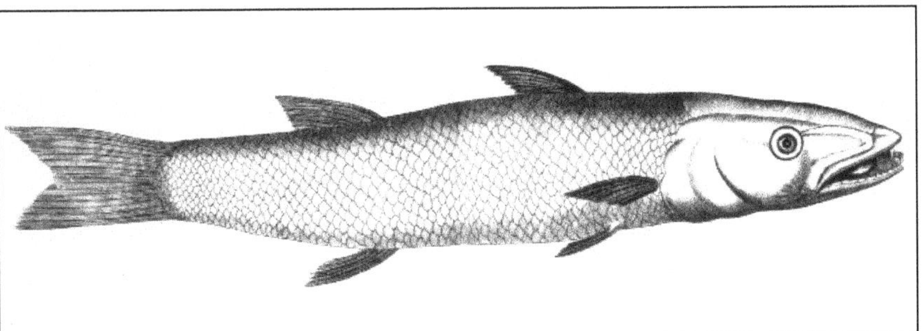

Figure 29 Engraving of a barracuda, from Sir Hans Sloane, *A voyage to the islands Madeira, Barbados . . . and Jamaica,* 2 vols. (London, 1707 and 1725).

hurt 'em, but caused one of his servants to feed 'em with the guts of fowls, etc., and at last this dolphins were soe accquainted with their server that at his call they would come to the surface of the watter, and take anything out of his hand. But on a time it chanc't that as the lad was feeding them, there came up a shark under the ship unseen and caught the lad by the hand, and bitt him soe that the blood fell into the watter. The dolphins seeing their benefactor thus wound'd, fell on that devouring shark and continued fighting with him until he had kill'd and devoured 'em. Thus these pore fishes lost their lifes, in the revenge of the misery done to their benifactor when with ease by their swift swimming they might have saved their lives. This was sene by Mr. Bows and above ten of his men and recorded in his jurnall for a most certain truth, he being a man of known integrity.

The baracod here found is a fish of a verey considerable bigness, weighing somtimes 60 or 100 weight. 'Tis a well made fish, (372) of a roundish body, well fortified with strong shineing scales and hath large finns and a forkeed taile. It hath a head much like a pikefish or jack. This fish is very fatt and good from September to June, but in July and August during the canicular daies, 'tis saied many have been poysoned by 'em.[88] It is a hungrey fish and will take allmost any bait on a hook, but you must use him gentilly, for his jaws are tendor, and often by his strength he breaks lose. There are many of 'em catch't dayly in Port Royall Harbour, with store of other good fish. I 'ave seen some of these fishes six foot and more long, which here we 'ave potraied from the originall to the life [figure lacking].

A grooper is a large fish, much of the bulk and shape of the baracoda, only his scales is blacker on the ridge of the back and he hath somewhat a bigger mouth and head and his sides are spotted with redish spotts. This is also a very excelent fatt fish and are on this place found in great plenty, and is here portraied from the originall to the life [figure lacking].

88. Sloane also notes that this fish is periodically poisonous (*Voyage,* 2: 285); this is presumably *cigautera* poisoning (Goodbody). The canicular or "dog days" are indeed in July and August.

An albecoale is a verey large fish, much of the shape of our Europian fish called a sconcer in England (373).[89] This fish is strongly fortified and deffended with strong shineing scales and adorned with well proportioned fins, which toward the extremeties are of a blackish collour. He hath a thick strong head and a verey large forked taile. These fishes are generally betwixt two and three foot long and come in great scolls onto ye harbour at Porta Royall, and by the fishermen are caught with great facility and are sold at a resonable price. 'Tis a very fatt, solid fish and of good nutriment and is here portraied to the life [figure lacking].

The booneta is a fish in all respects like the former, only they are not full so bigg, nor soe black on the back, neither have they soe forked a taile. These also are caught in great plenty in Port Royall Harbour and are sold at a reasonable rate. Their fleash is verey fatt, solid and of good nutriment. 'Tis a mighty nimble fish in the watter and therfore by some called a skip jack or ship-skipper.[90]

The Spanish macrell are here found in great abundance. 'Tis a fish every way resembling the baracoda, only 'tis somewhatt flatter and nothing nigh soe fatt, yet 'tis an indeferent good fish. There are some of 'em three and fouer foot long. Of this fish they also make caveich.[91]

The mullet is here found verey plentyfull. They are of the same shape as in England, only those here are much larger and fatter and is here of a dere price and much estemed.

The rockfish, of which there are here found great plenty, are (374) much of the shape of our sea carp.[92] 'Tis a short strong thick fish, whose body is fortified with strong close scales of a redish colour and adorn'd with well proportioned finns which are of a yallow coloure, and its taile is forked and of the same collour. It is spotted on ye sides with purple spotts and hath a verey great and ill-proportioned head and mouth and are here portraied to the life [figure lacking]. Some of these fishes I have seen to waiegh 30 and 40 pounds weight. 'Tis a verey fatt good fish, of excellent nutriment and good digestion and are here well esteemed.

The cavalie[93] is a fish plentyfully found in Port Royall Harbour. This fish

89. This cannot be an albecore, which is longer and more oceanic. Perhaps it is the black-finned tuna, no longer found at Port Royal, but periodically common off south-west Jamaica (Goodbody).

90. A skipjack is "any of various fishes which have a habit of leaping out of the water".

91. Of salt mackerel, Sloane remarks that "they have here a great Provision especially for Negroes, who covet them extreamly in pepper-pots etc.". *Voyage,* 1: xviii.

92. The rockfish is a generalized term for groupers. Cassidy and Le Page, *DJE,* 212.

93. This is probably the "yellow-fin" or "jack" (Goodbody). Cassidy and Le Page also report that the "cavally jack" is well known in the waters around Jamaica. *DJE,* 96.

is a thick short fish and broad withall, haveing a covering of strong shineing scales, and is well adorned with large yallow finns and a forked yallow taile. It hath a short thick head and is portraied from the originall to the life [figure lacking]. This fish is a most delicate fatt fish and is here verey much esteemed. In the head of this fish are found two stones oblique like a date stone, which pulverized and taken in wine is a powerful diuretique.* This fish I have seen sometimes to weigh 20 pounds weight (375).

A tarpum is a fish here found in great plenty. 'Tis a large fish which somewhat resembles oure English puliques.[94] This fish is fortified and defend with strong scales and adorn'd with well proportioned yallow finns and taile. It hath a great head and mouth. 'Tis a large strong fish; I have seen some of 'em full five foot longe which weighed 78 pound weight. This fish from September untill May is verey fatt and an excelent good fish, and is well esteemed, after which 'tis pore and mauger and soe little regarded. 'Tis a verey bonny fish and is caught plentifully in Port Royall Harbour. Sometimes 'twill take a hook, but most commonly they are caught by stricking 'em with a harpoon. This fish is here portraied to the life in the above figure [lacking].

A grunt is a fish here also found, tho not soe plentyfull as other fish.[95] This fish when at full groath is about two foot long. 'Tis a thick broad fish shap't in body somewhat like a bream. His head is thick and short which with his body is strongly cover'd with shineing silver-coloured finns and scales. His finns are conect and strongly defended with sharp barbes and is here from the originall potraied to the life [figure lacking]. This is an excellent fatt fish, of good esteem, which when (376) 'tis taken out of the watter maketh a loud grunting noise like a hog from whence it receives its name.

A drumer is a sort of fish found here in great plenty. This fish when full grown is about two foot long. 'Tis every way of the shape of our English grundell fish,[96] only its scales are of a more brighter collour. This is an excelent fatt fish and of good esteme. The nature of this fish is that when it is caught on the hook, and you are drawing it up out of the watter, it maketh a strange loud rumbling noise like a drumm, from whence it takes its name.[97] Some of these shall weigh 15 weight.

An audwife is a fish found here, tho' not soe plentyfull as other fish.[98] This

94. According to the *OED*, a tarpon is a Jew-fish. But Taylor has already mentioned this fish, somewhat in the same terms. "Puliques" are probably pollocks, a cod-like fish.

95. As Cassidy and Le Page put it, a grunt is a "certain fish . . . which makes a grunting noise when caught". *DJE*, 213.

96. "Grundel" is indeed an archaic word for a fish. *OED.*

97. Cassidy and Le Page describe a drummer as "a fish which makes a sound resembling drumming against the underside of boats and elsewhere". *DJE*, 160.

98. This seems to be Sloane's "Old wife or Cunny-fish" (*Voyage*, 2: 280); but there are several fish with this name in Jamaican waters (Cassidy and Le Page, *DJE*, 7).

is a fish without scales, brode, thick and short like a beam, and when at full groathe they are about half a yard long, and a quarter of a yard broad. Now alltho' nature hath denigh'd it scales, yett it hath lent him a thick and strong covering of skine of a dark collour, as thick as a bull hide. This fish hath a head made like a beam, spooted on the skine with purple spotts. It hath a small mouth, at the fore part of which stands out some great snagling* teath, so that its mouth is like the mouth of an ill-favoured old woman (which is an infalible antidote against leachery), from whence it takes its name. Now this fish is adorned with large purple finns and a forked taile of the same colour, and is heare potraied to the life [figure lacking]. When they are dressed the skin must be taken of. It eats just like a good soal fish. Some of them I have seen weight 14h. weight avoirdupoize.*

The garfish is also here found in great plentie, and are in all (377) respects such as we have in England, only they are fatter and are larger, and are here accounted the worst of fish on this island.

The stingaree is a fish here found in great plenty and is a verey uglie monstrous fish, about some fouer foot long and more than a yard broad, and hath a taile some five foot long like the thong of a coach-whip with which 'twill stricke most desperately. This fish is in all othere respects shap't like our Europian scate, or thornback,[99] and hath a skinn as black as inck, and indeed is ye ugliest monster that I ever saw. This fish is of a great bigness; I have seen severall of 'em to weigh above two hundredweight. This fish layeth eggs as the tortoise,[100] and when fatt and full of eggs, which is in May, then are they excelent food. This creature I have here potraied to the life [figure lacking]. Here are also found porpusses in all respects such as we have in Europe.[101]

(378) The swordfish here found is a fish of a great strenght and bulck. This fish hath a body much like a sharke, about thirty foot long, and of a proportional bigness, covered with a thick hard black skinn full an inch thick. It hath a large broad taile, and a ridg of strong finns like a dolphin on the back. It hath a strong great head and mouth, and from his snout on the upper jaw issueth forth his sword which there is about six inches broad, and soe growes taper to the extream part where he is about two inches broad. This sword is made of a strong bonny substance and of a greenish colour, and at the extream point about half an inch thick, and when cut off from the head 'tis hollow with three curious fistulas.* Now out of each side of this sword growes forth two and thirty sharp prongs white as ivory, about two inches

99. Thornback is an alternative name for the common ray or skate.

100. In fact, they are ovoviviparous; the eggs develop inside the female, and the young are born alive (Goodbody).

101. These are bottlenose dolphins (*tursiops truncatus*) (Goodbody).

long at the point, and fouer inches toward the head. These prong are verey strong and sharp and are straight, bending two waies. These prongs grow about two inches distant assunder from one another. This sword is about five foot long, and a most desperat and sharp weapon.

This swordfish is a verey furious fish and hath continuall warr with the whale and grandparse,[102] for this swordfish, with the fish called a thrasher, kills many whales, for the swordfish with his sharp weapon continually pricks, stricks and wounds the whale in the belly and will not suffer him to lie at rest in the deep, but forces them to lie on the surface of the watter where the thrasher continually beat 'em with there taile, and soe beats and persueth 'em night and day untill they have destroyed them.

I have often seen them engaiged on the Ambrogias, when we lay on the Spanish wrack,[103] and the whale swim and blow'd on the surfface of the ocean, and the watter where they swum would be all stain'd with the whale's blood which flowed from his wounds, which was made by the furious swordfish, and the thrasher continued stricking him on the back with such violence that it resounded like the heavy stroak of a maule* driveing (379) of pilles into the ground, and thus they would belabour him as long as he keep't above the watter. Sometimes the whale would get cleare from 'em and keep under the watter for a half houre ore more, then they would rouz him up againe, and soe tormente him againe. Thus have I seen 'em nere the Ambrogias for a whole day together, and I beleive they never left the whale untill they had destroyed him over att Porta Plata on Hispaniola.

We caught two small swordfishes, which were about 15 foot long, by which means I had my full view of 'em and have potraied the swordfish to the life [figure lacking]. This fish is verey fatt and his flesh look like beef, but is seldom or never eaten.[104] The pissell of this fish is a powerfull diueretick, and its sperm hath the same vertues with the *sperma beti*.[105] They have members both male and female, and produce there young by seminall copulation. It hath verey strong bones, and broad ribs lick an axe, and hath sharp strong teath and is every way as you see in the figure [lacking].

(380)The sharck is a verey ravenous and a monstrous large fish, and are here found in great aboundance both at sea and in Port Royall Harbour. This fish will seize on a man or anything swiming in the watter, and such is their strenght that at one gripe they will bight off a man's thigh. This fish every way resembleth an Europian dogfish, but of a farr greater bulck. I have seen one of 'em caught which was twenty-six foot longe and weighed three

102. This is surely a grampus, one of whose early names was a "graundpose".
103. On the Spanish wrecks, see Volume 3 of Taylor's work.
104. Swordfish has become a popular food, perhaps over-popular.
105. "*Sperma beti*" is perhaps spermaceti, used in medicinal preparations.

hundred and eight six pounds weight, the liver of which made fouer gallons of oyle. This fish was such a monster that she was as much as fouer men could hoise into the ship with a teackle, and it proved to be a femall sharck, which when we had opened hir belly, there came out thirty-six young ones, which were about a foot long. These we threw overboard and they semed to be dextrous at swimming for some of 'em followed the ship at least two houers.

For you must understand that this monster breed by seminall copulation, and when hir young ones are come to perfection, nature hath taught 'em to follow hir, and when she hath fedd 'em, for feare that other fishes should devour 'em, she taketh 'em into hir mouth, and soe conveyeth 'em down into a certain rescepticqule which nature hath for that purpose prepared in hir belly, where they are preserved, and when she thincketh fitt she throwes 'em out againe, and they swime after hir.[106] The jawbone of this shark was full five foot wide in circumference, and had in't five rowes of strong teath, one within anothere. It is covered with a strong and thick skine and hath large tinens [?] and by reason that its nose and upper jaw stands without it under, therefore allways when it goes to take its prey, it turnes upon his back. In the head of this fish is two cavities neare the eyes, in which is found two lumps of jelly of a whitish collour, which being taken forth and dried in the sunn, becomes a stone white (381) and hard lick chalck. This is of eminent use being a most powerful diureticque and powerfull to hasten the birth with women in travell.[107] The flesh of this fish is eaten by many and is of hard digestion. This monstrious fish I have here potraied to the life [figure lacking].

Here is also found that fish or rather a monster called an allagator,[108] a great devourer and verey ravenous. This monster liveth not only in the water but also on the land, travelling many miles up the sides of rivers in a short space. This subtill monster will lie sleepeing on the surfface of the water like a logg of rotten wood, where the harmless cattel coming to drinck he seizes 'em, and soe obtaines his preay. But now they doe not soe much mischife to the inhabitants as formerly they did, by reason they are now acquainted with the wiles of this cunning monster. Besides, you may smell 'em above one hundred paces by (382) reason of their muskie smell or strong scent before you come nigh 'em.

And to give you a just description of 'em you must know that this monster is of a prodigious bignese; some of 'em I have seen to be full thirty foot long and bigger about than a Cannarie win-pipe.[109] They have fouer short thick

106. This receptacle is imaginary; once born, the little sharks are on their own (Goodbody).

107. According to Sloane, this substance is "commended very much by all Sufferers in the Stone, and difficult Labour, as a very great Remedy". *Voyage,* 1: 23.

108. This is in fact the American crocodile (*crocodylus acutus*) (Goodbody).

109. A Canary wine-pipe was a large cask, the equivalent of four average barrels; a "pipe" was sometimes identified with a "butt".

strong leggs, with longe sharp tallons. There body is everywhere defended with strong hard brazen scales, everywhere soe closely united that noe sword nore spear will pirce 'em. They have a short neck, with a long head sharper than a greyhound, all fortified with scales of a greenish colour, as strong as brass. In his head it hath verey strong and sharp teeth and four great tusks like a bore, but this monster hath noe lung, nor could I ever hear of any which evere heard this monster to make any sounding noise. His body backward is shap't taperwise and when he runneth on the land he turneth in upwards in a lumilary form. In his neck in each side therof, and in his belly on each side of his navell lieth a bagg of a yallow substance smelling verey strong of musk, and I beleive would prove of good value, had they but found out the arcanum* of its preservation.

The fatt of the allagator is of excelent force and power to discurss tumors, and ease in nodes, and veneriall night pains in the joynts or bones, and is of such a penetrating quallity that noe blader will hold it, neither will it be confin'd in anything save glass, for if you anoint the back of the hand therwith, in less than two minutes of time you shall perceive it to work out thro the palm. The fatt of this monster is refined from it *pinguinosius grossues.* Thus, after they have taken it off from the fleash, and is cutt in small peices, then they putt it in a blader and hang it up in the sun, and soe leting it drop out into a glass vesell by which mean 'tis reduced to a pure cleare thin oyle of a great vertue (383) were it improved.

The blood of this creature is powerfull in convultions, being dried in the sun, and then burnt or calcin'd to powder and given zii in a glass of generous win. This monster is of a prodigious strenght, for being on the water in that subtill posture before mentioned, the inocent beast comming to drinck, not suspecting any danger, the alagator layeth hold of 'em and will hale 'em quit away under water, and there devouer 'em, and not only beast but alsoe many men have binn devouered by 'em. This monster is found on this island in most rivers and moross swampy places, but espetiall in, and neare Black River,[110] where if a musket be but discharg'd, you shall see many putt their heads above watter, and altho' this monster is a generall devouer of all creatures he can catch, yet more espetiallie he loveth dog's fleash above any other, and is a continuall enemy to 'em soe that they devouer them more espetially.[111]

The fleash of the alagator is eaten by many. I myself for curiosity sake eat part of a young one which was about five foot long, the fleash of which when boiled loked very white and eat much like veal, only it hath a muskyfied scent

110. Where it is found to this day.

111. As Sloane puts it, "Alligators love Dogs extreamly". *Voyage,* 1: lxxiii.

and is of a verey strong life in its nervious parts, for I saw the heart of that young monster have life in it above ten houres after 'twas taken out of the body. And that we may the better satisfie the curious with the vivall strenght of the alagator, we shall give you this account, which I had from my worthy frinde Mr. Rich. Bowes, Fellow of Trinity House, one of ye [illegible] Grand Pilots in England, and now Master of his Majestie's Ship *Faulcon,* under ye Command of Captain Thomas Smith.[112]

This Mr. Bowes was master of the *Selby* in the Protector's service at the takeing of Jamaica from the Spaniards, Anno Christi 1655, which when Jamaica was taken, the *Selby* with other ships were left there to guard it, and for their better (384) subsistance severall of the men were imployed in hunting of beves and hogg, and one time this gentleman and about some twenty more of the *Selby* and the *Massamore*'s[113] men went over to Ligourney side to hunt for bevees, and being come there they divided themselves into two companies, and meting with good success they kiled severall bullocks and caught severall alive. And when they came to part their game they had an odd beast, a verey larg and sturdy bull, which they had roap't and fix't to a tree. Now whilst they were in contest which party should have him; the bull broake lose and ran into the watter where he was seized by an alagator, and roar'd out in a most hidious manner, and for all his great strenght, the alagator puled him quit under watter before any could come to rescue him and they never saw sight of him more, only the watter stain'd with his blood. And thus the contest ended, which otherwise might have produced difference and quarells betwixt the contending parties.

And here 'tis necessary to observe that 'tis falcely tho' commonly reported of this monstor that it hath noe joynts, for I have carefully disected one of 'em and doe here declare that they have joynts both in the neck, back and leggs, and they have jawbones and ribbs like a beast, but none of their bone have marrow, or are anywhere cavious or hollow, but firm and solid. This monster layeth an egg round, and of the size of the green tortoise, butt it hath a hard shell like a fowle; they burie their eggs in the sand, wher by it, and the heat of the sun, they are hatch and come to perfection, and such is their nature, that being hatch (385), they presently run into the water and there live and grow to a monstrous bigness. This monster will live home to England,[114] and

112. Richard Bowes was indeed master of HMS *Falcon,* according to National Archives, Adm 33/132, p. 108; this document shows that he and Thomas Smith, captain, signed the muster-rolls at the end of *Falcon*'s voyage. National Archives, Adm 33/132, p. 114.

113. These two ships, *Selby* and *Marston Moor,* seem to have operated together. See Taylor, *The Western Design,* 18.

114. Sloane's alligator, like all his other live creatures, died on the voyage back to England, near the Banks of Newfoundland; *Voyage,* 2: 345.

may be keep with any sort of fresh fleash. Now that we may truly satisfie the curious, we have here potrai'd this monster from the originall to the life [figure lacking].

The conny fish found on this island is a verey strang and ugly monster to look on.[115] 'Tis a fish seldom above a foot long. It is cover'd with a broune hard shell on the back and yallowish on the belly. It hath a short thick head, from whence grows right forward two sharp sphers, or horns. It hath a small mouth with teeth ressembling a cony. It hath two small finns or padles by it guiles, and toward its taile the body growes rounding and it is cover'd with sofft skinney (386) substance, and it hath a small yallow forked taile. 'Tis a verey fatt and good fish and is potraied here to ye life [figure lacking].

The snapper is a fish here found in great aboundance; 'tis a fish exactly shaped like a perch, and when at full growth is about a foot long, and is covered with red scales, and adorn'd with well proportioned yellow fins, and is a verey good frying fish and is here portraied to the life [figure lacking].

The sea urchin is a verey ugly monster, being round as an hedghog, covered in the same manner with sharp spears, [and] hath two small finns, or padles nere his guiles.[116] Out of this round body proceed a head with a verey short neck, and it hath a mouth or beak like a bird; also it hath a small forked taile. This fish is seldom eaten and is here potraied to the life from the originall [figure lacking].

The remora or sucking fish is also here found. 'Tis a small fish not above two foot long. His body is not covered with scales, but with a thick slipry gray skine, veined and spoted (387) with whit spotts. It is a slight round fish, with a sharp head licke an elle, hath well proportion finns, and a broad forked taile and is noe wise a seming strong fish tho' indeed 'tis indued with more than a common strenght, for it hath a certain ruffness on ye back nigh the head, by which they will cling soe fast to anything they lay hold on, that with great strenght they must be pulled from thence. And Plinny reports of this fish that it will stop a ship under saile, the truth of which let everyone judge as they thinck fitt.[117] Indeed for my own part I scarsely beleive it, altho' I am not able to resolve weither or noe nature indued it with that facculty, for indeed she is mighty curious in many of hir products. The flesh of this fish is verey sweet and gratefull to the pallatt, and is here potraied to the life [figure lacking].

In those western seas and parts of world, we find abundance of fish called *piscis volantis,* or flying fish, which is a small fish about the bigness of a

---

115. This is the cowfish (*acanthostracion*), one of the trunkfish family, still quite common among seagrass beds (Goodbody).

116. This is actually a porcupine fish (Goodbody).

117. See *The Natural History of Pliny,* ed. John Bostock and H.T. Riley (London, 1857), 6: 2–3, book 32 on "the power of nature".

herring, and somewhat like a pilchar.* It hath a small short head and a forked taile, the upper side of which is longer than the lower side (388). Their wings are composed of a thinn filmie substance thin as ye webb, but is supported by some small spines extended from the body. Their wings when extended thoroly are about fouer inches long. This pore fish when she is persued by the swift dolphine (which are their greatest enemies) is forced to forsake hir native element of watter, and commit hir body to the soft blast of Eolus,[118] for they will then flie up in whole flock like birds, and flie some 50 or more paces, and then fall into the water or flie thro' the billow of a hollow sea, and wett their wings and then rise and flie again if possible to escape their devouring persuor, the nimble dolphin. For you must understand that they cannot flie any longer but while their wings are wett, and nevertheless [in] their swift flight, the dolphins hunteth 'em soe furiously, so to avoid their enemy, they often flie into ships which are in their waie, where striveing to escape one danger, they fall into another. They are verey fatt, and eat much like a new-caught pilchar and are here potraied to the life from the originall [figure lacking].

(389) The pilot fish is also here found, and this fish 'tis saied hunteth only ye prey for the sharck, as ye jackall doth for the lion, fore be suer wher or when soever you see a pilot fish, you may be assuere a shark to be nigh, and will appear on the surface of the watter in a little time.[119] This fish is about a foot long, and of a well-proportioned bigness, much shap't like our Europian maccrel.* It sides is of a glistning changable silver and copper colour, spotted with dark brown spotts. 'Tis a verey fatt fish and gratefull to ye pallat and is here from the original potraied to the life [figure lacking].

Here in the Jamaican bays, harbours, etc., are found multitudes of small fish, as whit fish, stonbass, jacks, leathercoats, smelts etc.[120] The whit fish is a flat brod fish about half a foot long, fouer inches brod and one thick, [with] shining scales like cloath of silver. 'Tis a good frieing fish (390) and is here potraied to the life [figure lacking].

The stone bass is a short snubbed fish, about fouer inch long and one thick and full as broad as long, and hath a long finn on his back and belly. 'Tis a good frieing fish and is here potraied to the life [figure lacking].

The jack is a fish about a foot long, hath scales as a mullet, and a head like a pike. 'Tis good fatt fish, and is here potraied to the life [figure lacking].

The leathercoat is a fish about the size of a large North Sea hering, whose

118. Aeolus, the wind god of Greek and Roman mythology.

119. This small carangoid fish is "reputed to act as a guide to the shark". *OED*.

120. "Whitefish" refers to small "harengulias", of which there are about five species in Jamaican waters (Goodbody). The "leathercoate" is still known as the leather-coat (jack). Cassidy and Le Page, *DJE*, 271.

body is covered with a thick whit shinning skin like a leather. 'Tis a well proportioned fish, with yallow finns and a forked taile of the same colour. 'Tis a fish of noe great esteem because they are here verey plenty. 'Tis none of ye worst of fish; this fish we have here potraied to the life [figure lacking].

Lastly, the smelt is in all respects such as we have in England, only they are somewhat smaller, and have two bright silvere-couler'd streak on each side. They are full as good as Europiane smelts, and are daily caught in aboundance in Port Royall Harbour, and used by the fishermen as bait.

The rivers and lakes are also plentifully stored with variety of excelent fish of the same sort which live in the sea,[121] as the rock fish, parrat fish, snapper, mudfish, ell, and crawfish, prawns etc. And 'tis to admiration, for on the tops of the mountaines (from whence most of these rivers receives their springs) even there shall you find multitudes of mullets, rockfish, mudfish, etc., which when the rains come, by reason of the violence of the streams running down those rivers, the fish is carry'd down therby, and soe forc't into the sea; yet multitudes of them in their passage remain behind in the holes and deep places of the rivers, which, when the watter is abated, are easelie caught. And now we shall describe those of 'em which we have not yet treated of, and first of the ele.

(391) There are in the rivers found two sorts of elles; the one an ele of all such respects as we have in England, full as big, fatt, and swett, but they are of a more short size.[122] The other is an ele of the same groath and form, having somwhat a bigger head, and his skin is of a seagreen colour everywhere and hath yallow finns and taile. This fish is called a numbed ele, for if any man or beast be wadeing in the watter and this ele chances to twist himself about their legs (as many have don), then is the man or beast soe presently benumbed (as with a strong cramp) that he hath neither power nor strenght to stire, and without help in a little time he hath not strenght to stand but falleth down and perisheth in the watter, for he hath noe power nor strenght anyway to help himself, and indeed by this fish many men have lost their lives. This fish is never eaten but distroyed wherever they are found and are loked on as a diabolical creature. They are some fouer foot long of 'em. They are not here found soe plenty as on the coast of Guine in Africa where they are often found.[123]

In the rivers and lake and pondes are here found aboundance of mudfish, soe called by the inhabitants. This is a fish without scales, haveing a verey large head and a mouth, and his skine is of a verey dark brown colour and

121. The river fish are in fact quite distinct from those that live in the sea (Goodbody).

122. Sloane notes that this eel was "exactly the same" as those of England. *Voyage,* 2: 278. He does not mention the "numbed" or electric eel.

123. They are also numerous in the basins of the Orinoco and Amazon rivers.

sliprey like the elle. It hath finns and a broad taile not forked. 'Tis a fish which lieth nere the ground and in the mudd will bight at a shrimp on a hook but they are esily caught by hand, for wading into ye watter you may fell 'em with your feet in the mudd and soe take 'em up in your hand. This fish is never above two foot long, is roundeish and of a proportionall bigness. 'Tis an excellent sweet (392) fatt and delitious fish, and in my opinion, next to the manatee, the best fish I ever eat of in any part of America.[124] In all rivers and lakes there are plenty of these fish which breed in the springs on the mountaines, which when the raines happen are driven down in great plenty, curiously befor the currant, and are gathered up by people (in great aboundance) who wade into the watter, and catch 'em up either with bassynets* or with their hands in the shallow watter, as the rivers cometh down, for it stuppifeies the fish by their violent driveing before the stream soe that they are caught with ease. Now to make all obvious we have here potraied the mudfish to ye life [figure lacking].

In those seas and rivers on Jamaica are found plenty of a verey large sort of crawfish, everyway such as we have in England. Some of 'em I have seen weigh nine pound weight.[125] They live both in the fresh and salt water.

In the fresh rivers on Jamaica, and in the standing lakes on the mountains are found a sort of a verey large prawns (393) everey way such as we have in England, only they have one great leg on their right side like a lobster's legg, and they are also somewhat bigger than our Europian prawns. These live sometimes in the sea, but they breed and are cheifly found in the fresh rivers, springs and lakes on the mountains, from whence they are driven in time of the violent raines.

The sea crabb here found is a small blue crabe, about the size of a pound crabb in England the biggest, but for ye generally noe bigger than oure Europian green crabbs, but according to their bigness they are verey fatt and good.

The land crabb found here, and in most other parts of America are of two

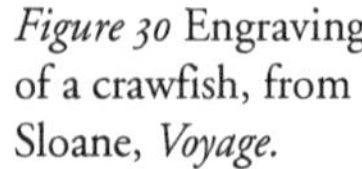

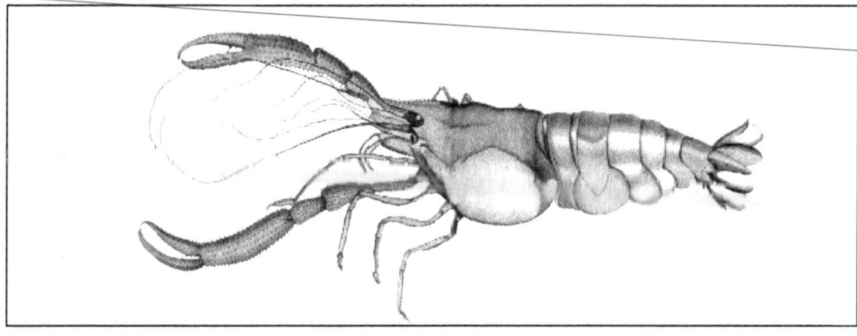

Figure 30 Engraving of a crawfish, from Sloane, *Voyage.*

124. Sloane also notes that it is "accounted one of the most delicious fish". *Voyage,* 2: 286.

sorts, a grey and a black. The grey land crabb is much of the size of the sea crabb, hath the same number of leggs, but they are big and long; his shell at the edge is not sharp but rounding; this crabb is verey fatt and good, but they seldom eat any part of him save his flesh in the clawes, and to it adjacent. The black land crabb is every way of the same shape and size, and his shell is black. This is a mutch better crabb than the grey crabb, being most commonly fatt and full of eggs and is sold comonly at Port Royall both clawes, and its tramales [?] redy dres't. Both these sort of crabbs live on the land in swampy moros ground nere the seaside where they make holes in the earth like moles and there hid 'em selves when they see any danger approaching. These crabbs lay a small egg with a blew shell of much the size of the hedgsparow, which they bury in the sand, where their young ones are hatch and brought to perfection. Now after the raines, these crabbs, thousand in a company, will leve the low land (which then is to wett and cold for 'em) and travel up many miles up into the woods and mountaines (394) in a little time (for they'll run at a great rate when persued, allmost as fast as a man) and in their passage, if they come up with a house, or the like, they wil not break their way to goe round him but will clime up at one side and soe go quitt over him down at the other side.[126]

Now these crabbs are easily caught, for you may find where they are by their holes in the sand, where with ease you may dig 'em out and in two or three houres time geet a horse load of 'em, for they lodg allways thousands of 'em nere one another in a little spott of sand, in moross grounds and swampy places.

The cunck is a shellfish found here in the sea in greatt aboundance. 'Tis a large fish; some of 'em in their shell shall weigh eight or tenn pounds weight. They have a strong thick shell in outside red, and when drie whit, and the inside towards the mouth of a puer cherry flesh colour. This shell is there besett with some great sharp barbs. The shell of this fish callcined to powder is a powerfull suderificque.[127] The flesh is indifferent good food well stewed with shalets* etc. and a great restorative in consumptions. This fish for ye satisfaction of ye curious is here potraied to the life [figure lacking]. Also you must know that of the shell of this fish the Indians of New England, Verginia, Carolina, etc., make their waempeig[128] or the currant passable mony, with which they trade with the English and amongst one another.

---

125. This weight seems high, but Sloane illustrates a large crawfish about a foot long. Ibid., 271 and figure 30.

126. Land-crabs are indeed known for the massive straight-moving streams that they form, at the time of the annual migration.

127. A sudorific, or substance promoting perspiration.

128. Wampum could indeed be made from some of these shells.

The wilck is a shellfish found here in the sea verey plenty.[129] 'Tis everyway resembling our sea snailes or Europian winckles, only they are much bigger and are nigh the size of Getlepin Bowle [?]. 'Tis a most lovely fish and a great restorative in consumptions. 'Tis a great encreaser of seed, and good for barren women.

(395) The calphia is a shellfish also here found.[130] This fish is here about three inches long and the shell formed ovilar like an egg, and in the lower side 'tis open with a slite from one end to the other, where the fish thrust himself out of his shell, one each side of this slitt or passage. The shell is ringed and rowellie.[131] This shell is of a curious whit or sord coloure, spotted with crimson, purple and yallow spotts, and is accounted noe small curiosity for a lady's clossett. The fleash of this fish is a great restorative in consumptions. These shell goes for currant money at Zeiland and other places in the East Indies, and by our merchants and brought from thence, and carryed to Cape Coast, Caramantine, and other places of Guinea, in Africa, to bye Negro slaves and gold oar with all, for 'tis the Negro's currant coine.[132] But these shells are not above an half an inch long, and of a proportionall bignes, all white except at the mouth where they are veined with black, but are every way shap't as the calphia, which I have here potraied to the life in the next page [figure lacking].

The soldier is a shellfish here found.[133] This fish liveth sometimes in the watter, but mostly on the land, for you shall find 'em in great companyes about the spurs and rotes of cotten trees, and other trees some miles up in the wood. This fish hath clawes with a hard red shell, every way like our English gaunces[134] (caught off of the south side of ye Isle of Wight) and they have severall sort of shells, some cuncks, other wilke shells etc., whatever they can geet, for you must understand that when they are grown to big for their shells, they quitt it and goe to the sea, and there the first wilke or other shellfish they find, with their clawes by violence (396) pull him out of his shell and posses it and live theirin themselves, and from this hostillity they receive the name of soldiers. They are verey fatt, but indeed but mean diet, and are seldom eaten by any but by Negros and privaters, to boile with their maize insteed of montego. This fish will when he please quit's shell and travel without it. Now if you take the taile of this fish, (which is all fatt) and put

129. The whelk is a top shell (*cittarium pica*) mostly found on rocky shores, with very tough meat (Goodbody).

130. This is surely the cowrie shell (Goodbody).

131. "Rowellie" is an old word for knobbly. *OED.*

132. It is correct that cowrie shells were once the main currency in many parts of Africa.

133. Taylor refers here to the hermit crab. See Sloane, *Voyage,* 2: 272.

134. This may well be a very local word, from Taylor's birthplace on the Isle of Wight.

it in a glass bottell, and hang it in the son, it will dejest* to a puer thin oyle which is of good force to give ease to rhumatismes, gouts, and veneriall paines to admiration when other medicaments 'ave proved unsucesfull therto.

(397) Here is also found plenty of a small sort of oysters of an oblong form which grow in great clusters in the watter about the roots of the maingrove trees, where you shall find bushells of 'em. They are nothing nigh soe large, fatt or good as our Europian oysters, but however here they serve insteed of better.

The sea egg is also here found on the flatts, amongst the sands and rocks in great abundance.[135] This is a round ball about the size of a man's fistt, armed all over with sharp barbs, of the same colour with, and just like the hedghog, soe verey prickly that you can hardly touch 'em. The shell being open'd 'tis full of a yallow substance like the yeolk of an egg, which is verey delitious, and a great restorative in consumptions. This sea egg hath life, but little or noe motion in itsself. Thus we have given you a full description of all the seafish, freshwater fish and shellfish found on and nere the island of Jamaica and most of the western parts of America, the which for the finall satisfaction of the curious, we have illustriated with the draughts of the most remarkable, which we have potraied from the originall to the life, and now we shall proceed on our discourse in giveing a description of the serpents found on this island, and in most of those western parts of America.

Section IV

(398) Of serpents found on Jamaica, as the whisler, blacksnake, guana, lizard, centapes, scorpion, toad, spider, and red spider.

On this island are not found many sortes of serpents, neither in shape nor quality, like those which are a great annoyance to many part of America as Verginia, Saranam, and other places on the Main.

First here we find the whistler, or whisling snake,[136] whose residence is cheifly in the silent woods. This serpent is about three yardes long, and of a proportionable bigness. Their skin is of a silver colour, curiously spoted with green and yallow spotts, and their fleash is commonly eaten by the Negros, and very often by ye English whoe commend it, and say it eats fatter and sweeter than an ele. This serpent is of noe poisonus quallity but of a prodigious strenght, for if they girt themselves about a man's wast as he lays

135. This is the sea urchin, probably the white one (Goodbody).

136. Does Taylor perhaps mean the hissing snake? (He surely refers to the yellow snake, figure 31.)

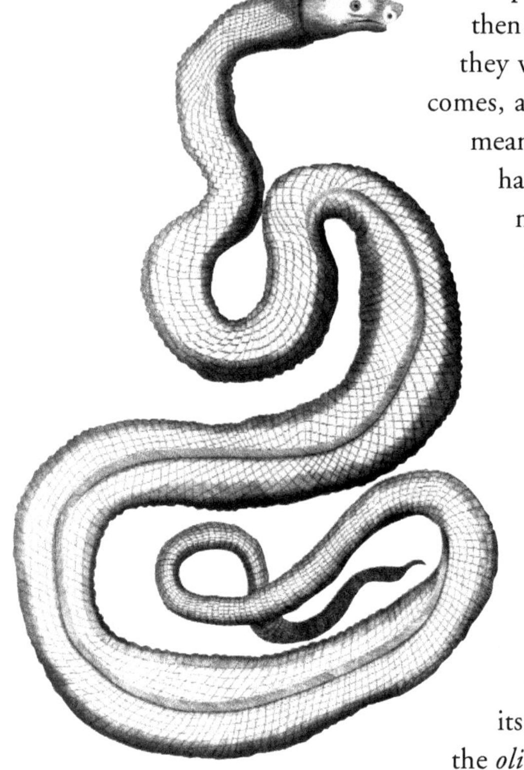

Figure 31 Engraving of a yellow snake, from Sloane, *Voyage*.

sleeping in the woods (for soe they have done to many) then will they twist themselves soe close about him that they will sone strangle him, unless some one or other comes, and with a knife cutts 'em off, for by noe othere means can they be forced to ungirt themselves, neither hath the man power to (399) help himself in the least manner, and indeed many men have bin strangled by 'em.

Nay it hath bin observed that this snake hath twined his taile about the body of a tree, and as a wild bull came to rubb himself against that tree, the snake twisted his head and forepart of his body about the hornes of the bull and for all the great strenght of the bull, yet this snake held him untill he was almost starved, and a huntere coming by chaunce that way, with his mucheat* cutt the snake in two and set the pore beast at liberty. In the woods, this serpent maketh a loud whisling noise in the night from [which] it receives its name. The fatt of this snake reverted into oyle (as the *olium millitis*) is of excellent power to repel tumors and ease gout and veneriall night paines. This snake layeth an egg which she hatcheth in the sand, by which they are produced to perfection.

Here is also found a little black snake,[137] which is a serpent seldom above a foot long, which is a verey venomous and poysonous serpent. These lurk in the savanas. Also here is found a small yellow snake of the same size, spotted on the back, with fiery copper coloured spotts. This snake resides nere houses but is noe ways poysonous. These three severall sorts of snakes are of the same form and shape as those found in Europe and hisheth in the same maner and also jumpeth as Europian snakes.

The guana is a creature here found (which I reckon one of the Jamaican serpents, because it takes up its residence in the sand). These creatures are here found in great plenty towards the seashore among the sand and rocks on the Northside of Jamaica, and on most of the low sandy kays or islands which lie round the island of Jamaica, (400) and there is an island which lies at the east end of Jamaica betwixt that island and Hispaniola called the Navasa, which is a low sandy island, wheron are found thousands of guanas, but noe other liveing creature is ther else to be found. The guana is a creature

137. This sounds like Browne's "small black snake", thought by some people (though not Browne) to be venomous. *Civil and Natural History*, 461.

which hath a short strong head with verey sharp teeth, and is joyn'd to a well proportioned neck. His body is about fourten inches long and about the thicknes of a man's legg. It hath fouer short strong leggs arm'd with sharp tallons, and a long spindleing taile about a foot or sixteen inches long, and is in all respectes here portraied to the life [figure lacking].

The guana is covered with a thick strong skinn. Some of 'em are of a darke brown, and others yallow, curiously spotted with purple and changable spoots, but they are both of a size and shape. They hid themselves in the sand; they will run verey fast and bite despratly. Their flesh is delicat food; being fricassed, they eat better than young rabbits, or well-fedd fowles.[138] (401) The bones of this creature callcined to powder and taken in a glass of genorus wine is a powerful medicament against ye green sickness. The guana breeds by eggs which she hatches in the sand, which by it and the sun are produced.

Here are also found aboundance and various coloured lizards, as green, yallow, spotted, and black. The lizard is made in every respect as the guana, only they are small, never being above eight inches long from head to taile and are of a proportionall biggness. 'Tis a pretty litle creature, very harmless, and much delighted in man's company, and feedeth on flies. They layeth an egg and bredeth like the guana; they will also run verey fast. There are aboundance of 'em among the prickle pare busshes, neare the Pallasadoe* Gate on Port Royall. This creature will live home to England, being kept warm in a box with brann, on which 'twill feed and live. 'Tis storyed of 'em that if a man be sleeping in the woods, and any venomous serpent or hurtfull beast be nigh, then shall ye preety inocent lizard by some means or other awaken him, that soe he may be preserved from the approaching danger. The whole body of this creature being callcin'd to powder is a powerfull medicament against the vertego,* epilipses, megrine* etc.

The centapes is a venomous creature here found and a little yallow serpent about five inches long, haveing many leggs (from whence it receives its name) and is hairy like the Europian worm called the palmer.[139] This is a most venomous creature, and the worst found on this island, for where 'ere it bites or passeth over the flesh, it certainly envenoms with a poysonous tumor, for which there is noe cuer but by anointeing it with oyle made of themselves (402), which will quickly cuer any of their bittes.[140] The oyle is thus made; you must take the centapes as sone as he is kil'd, and put him into a small

138. According to Sloane, iguanas were much eaten by the early Afro-English inhabitants of Jamaica, being "commonly sold for Half a Crown a Piece in the Publick markets". *Voyage,* 2: 333.

139. A term found in the sixteenth century; see "palmer worm", *OED.*

140. Browne also describes the "centapie" as "very venomous", though not life-threatening to a person. *Civil and Natural History,* 426. The centipede is not venomous in temperate countries.

glass viol, which stoop close, and in a few daies being hang'd up in the sun, he will turn and thro'ly disolve into a puer thin oyle.

The scorpion is also here found, but not soe large as in other places. They every way in shap resemble a lobster and are of a light brown colour and seldom above two inches long. This serpent is most poysonous of all others and where 'ere he touches, he bittes, poysons and envenoms, and noe other medicament but *olium scorpionis* will allay the paine, expell the venom, and cuer the bite, and this oyle is made as the former. This serpent and centapes commonly lurck in houses and about rotten woods, and bitts many when they sleep on their couches and on their beeds, which is sone felt by its smart.

In the mountains, in the woods, are here found aboundance of verey large toades, some of which are above a foot broad on the back, and of a proportionall bigness. These toads in the night make a most hiddious loud noise, much like a cry of hound when chaceing the fearfull hare.[141] These toads are not at all poysonous, nore are they ever found in the plantations or lowlands, but here are noe frogg 'ere found on this island of Jamaica.

On this island we find a most prodigious spider enclineing to a greenis colour, spoted with black spots, and is everyway made like our Europian spiders.[142] These spiders have large legs or claws, with a shell like the small claws of the crabb, and I have seen severall of those spiders which 'ave bin broader on the back than the palm of a man's hand, and (403) these the inhabitants say are not half soe bigg as they have often seen. They layeth an egg round, and about the bigness of a sparrow's egg, with a hard blew shell.

Here is also found a small red spider, which is verey poysonous, for where 'ere it biteth it certainly envenoms, and is cuered by annointing the place with *oleum scorpionis.*[143] Thus we have described all the serpents which could evere hear to be found on Jamaica, but on the main of America there is found the rattlesnake and others.

Section V

Of insects found on Jamaica, as the muscata, merrywig, galanipper, botleears, chegar, fierflie, cockroach, timberworm and annt.

Jamaica in most parts is miserabley plauged with stinging and tormenting insects which swarm in great aboundance everywhere, but cheifly near the

141. Jamaican toads are indeed noisy, but not nearly as large as Taylor claims.

142. This is perhaps the "large grey House-Spider" cited by Browne, *Civil and Natural History,* 419.

143. This is surely Browne's "red-arsed spider", whose "nip is said to be very venomous". Ibid. Is it perhaps the black widow?

watterside and uncleared places, soe that the inhabitant in most places are much both by day and night anoyed by 'em, in such sort that those which live nigh the woods att eating time, as at diner etc., allwaie hath a Negro slave with a green bow stand to fann 'ore the table to keep 'em away; otherwise they would not only torment you by stinging, but flie into your mouth and perhaps poyson you. Also as sone as the sun's sett, those planters shut up their windows and make a smoak in all their lodging romes to drive and (404) keep 'em from thence. Now of those stinging tormentors, ther are these five sorts (viz:) the muscata, merrywig, botleears, galanipper and chegar, all which we will discribe.

The muscata is the least of all fleas or insects of the make of the knat, tho' not above half soe bigg, but yet is a great tormentor to man and beast. These are in open places cheifely troblesome in the night times, but in the woods they annoy both day and night.[144] They breed in the watter. The place where this insect bitts (as sometimes when you travell in the woods, you shall be allmost cover'd with 'em, and your flesh stung to a crimson colour) itches most intolerably, but you must not scrach it, which if you doe (such is their venom) 'twill certain turn to a running sore, and leave signe behind it.

The merrywig, or merriwing,[145] that continuall tormentor, is somwhat bigger than a knatt,* and makes a noise like 'em. This singing insect torments both by day and night, and where 'ere it bites it leaves a purple spot behind on the skinn.

The galanipper[146] is a small blew flea, and hath a long spear or hollow trunck which it thrust into the skin, and therby fills itself with man's blood, and the place so stung becomes a troblesom blister, which, if you break, will prove a certain ulcer, and leave a blackish spoot in the skin never to be worn out, and indeed all such which have vissited those western parts have suerly this Jerusalem mark[147] in their leggs or arms, by which they may be known. This insect tormenteth only in the day time, but more espetiall befor and sone after a showers of rain.

The botleears[148] is a long black flea, with a botlears residing chiefly in the woods, and stingeth violently, where it riseth a hard tumor for some time and

---

144. Taylor does not mention the use of mosquito nets, as do Browne (ibid., 427) and Sloane: "Beds are sometimes covered all over with Gauze, to hinder the Mosquitoes" (*Voyage*, 1: xxxvi).

145. For Sloane, the "common Musquito" and the "Merriwing" were the same insect. *Voyage*, 2: 225.

146. This is a now obsolete word for a large mosquito. Cassidy and Le Page, *DJE*, 193.

147. "Jerusalem letters" were tattooed into a pilgrim's skin to mark a visit to Jerusalem. *OED*.

148. Perhaps this is Sloane's "bottle-arse", common near Black River Bridge. *Voyage*, 2: 226.

very painful. The chegar[149] (405) is a small ground flea, far more troblesom than any of the former. This insect getteth into the flesh (most commonly the feet) and there eateth a hole, and in a bag which it there makes, it sone breeds multitudes of young ones, which quickly increaseth, and cruelly torments those in whose fleash they are, soe that all of note which inhabit Jamaica every morning hath a Negro slave to loke their feet and pull 'em from thence, which is as customary as to breakfast or bose the gage[150] in good rum punch.

This is such a divilish insect that many Negros and English inhabitants have lost their feet or toas by 'em for want of timely care, for when they are in, if they be not carefully pulled out, in a litle time they will so encrease and spread in the foot, that ye last remedy to be rid of 'em is cutt of the toas, or perhaps the foot itself. Therfore to prevent this danger, in the first place never imitate the countrey fashon to goe without stockins and shoos, unless thou art driven therto by want and then *necessitas non habet lex.*[151] Therfore be sure as sone as you fell 'em in the fleash, (which you will sone doe by the itching therof) you must with a sharp nedle pull 'em out clean, bagg and all, not breaking the bagg (which if you doe ye young ones will remain in the fleash and ther breed more) and into the hole put tobacco ashes, or a gourd leaf round the same, and 'twill distroy 'em and dry up the sore, which otherwise will prove an ulcer of dangerous consequence and hardly cured.[152]

The fierflea is an harmles insect found here in the woods. This is a flie every way like the cantharda,[153] both in size and shape. In the daytime it hath little lusture and buty, but in the night as they flie to and fro, from their litle bodys proceeds as great and glorious light as from rich diamonds (406) or shineing saphires, which give soe great a light that belated travelers are guided in their right path by their illuminating glory, and such is their light that if one of 'em fly into a dark rome, it will make it soe light that therby you may see a pinn on the floar, and if you take two of 'em and putt 'em under a clear flint glass, by their light you may either write or read, as well as by the light of a good match candell.[154] Some of these creatures carry this glory in their heads and some in their tailes. It appears on each side, when they are in your

149. Now known as a "jigger"; Taylor's account is full and accurate. Cassidy and Le Page, *DJE*, 247.

150. A gage was a quart pot. *OED*.

151. Necessity knows no law.

152. Sloane recommends exactly the same treatment for jiggers, and had himself been cured by "a Negro, famous for her ability in such cases". *Voyage*, 1: cxxiv.

153. Perhaps the cantharides. *OED*.

154. Sloane recounts equally improbable feats achieved by fireflies. *Voyage*, 2: 206–7.

hand, like two shinning gems of a greenish lustour of which Du Bartas saieth:[155] [passage lacking].

The cockroach is an insect found here in aboundance.[156] They are much of the shape of a chaffer (tho' twise as bigg) and hath a red shell and large velom* wings; they renew their shell every year. This is a verey hurtfull insect to books, cloathes etc., and their is scarsly anything but what they damnifie. They flie at night in the aire two and fro' and shrick noisomly.[157]

(407) The timberworm is a verey hurtfull insect which liveth in the water and is of great anoyance to the bottoms of ships etc. by distroying the planck, soe that in those western parts they are forc't often to careen their vessels to distroy this worm, which at first is but small when it getteth into the planck, but there groweth to be as big as a man's finger.[158] 'Tis a blackworm and hath a sharp bill like a garfish where it goeth in. The hole is scarse perceivable, but where it lodges as big as a half-inch auger hole. When it eateth in the night, you may here 'em gnaw in the planck as if a man were at work with an auger, and 'tis observable that this worm always eateth with the grain of the timber, which if it did otherwise 'twould be of a greater detriment than now it is. This insect comming into fresh water is soon distroied and quitteth the ship.

Here are aboundance of annts or pismires[159] of severall sizes, one sort of which is as bigg as a wasp and maketh their nest with earth one the limbs of trees as bigg as a kilderkin,[160] and by their travelling two and fro in the woods makes beaten paths for severall miles together. These annt are a prey to the ursagrita or annt bear; they will sting desperatly. Here is also found a small sort of red and black pismires, such for shape and size as in England.

Here are also found fleas, wasps, catterpillars and yallow butterflies in aboundance (tho' I never saw any of another colour) such as we have in England, which are very distructive to the tendor plants. But here is neither shell snaile[161] nor drie snaile of any sort, neither millepedes nor lumbricores,[162] as we have in the fatt soyles in England. Thus we have given you a large description of all the known insects found on Jamaica.

---

155. Taylor is here thinking of Guillaume de Salluste, sieur Du Bartas, a French author whose work was published in London in translation in 1605 as *Bartas: His devine weekes and works*. I have been unable to find the exact reference.

156. That is, a cockchafer, or maybug.

157. Taylor mentions only one of the two types, and seems wrong in claiming that they "shriek".

158. This is the teredo, famous for its ravages.

159. "Pismire" is an archaic name for an ant.

160. A kilderkin was a cask holding sixteen to eighteen gallons.

161. It is not clear what Taylor means here, for there were many kinds of snails in Jamaica, as he must have known. see Browne, *Civil and Natural History*, 44–403.

162. The lumbricus is an earth-worm.

Section VI: Of Stones

(408) On this island of Jamaica there is not much variety of stones, for their cheife buildings are of brick.[163] Now to proceed in a genuin method, 'twill be necessary here first to discribe the nature of the earth and soile of Jamaica, in regard that all stones are earth before stone, which they are converted into by some spetiall accident or other. As the marle stone, which is an enemy to all weeds (which other ground produces of itself) and giveth a generative vertu to all seeds sown on the ground, it being a certain rich and stiff clay of a consolidating substance, and in quality cold and drie. I say this stone was earth before it became marle, and altho' being a semeing stone, yet is but hard clay, and all chalk stones and limestones whatever, which are subject unto calcination as whit corrall, flint etc., were marle before they came to be stone, and therfore its originall was earth, becaus marle was first earth, and stones made of marle was first earth, and stones made of marle, and only hardened by accident, and soe not possible to be disolved but by fire, and seeing all stones are generated from marle, it hath binn soe estemed by some philosophers that they would make it a fifth element.[164]

But to omitt that curiosotie and to return to ouer discourse, you must know that the soyle (409) is of three kinds; as first in the mountains 'tis stony and rocky, only cover'd with a black earth, which is made by the rotting of leaves, forests and trees, and often by the violent raines wash't down into the low valys, and then the mountains are butt a bare rugged flinty stone, alltho' to admiration all overgrown with wood, whose roots are entormed with these rocks from whence the trees receive nurishment, and grow and flourish, as well as those in the lowlands by the riversid; a thing of noe small wonder, to behold lofty cedars, and the biggest of all trees, namly the cotten tree, to grow out of a perfect rock or craggy flint.

The second sort of soyle is that of the vally and savanas, nigh the foot of the mountaines, which is a light rich and fruitfull fatt sand, for the generallyty of a blackish colour, and continually fatten'd by the rotting of trees and dung driven by the violent rains from off the mountains thither, soe that the plantations are as much improved after the great raines, as our Europian cornfield are by soyling with dung.

The third sort of soyle is the lowlands nere the seashore, which is for the most part moros and swampy, or of a light drie red sand, whereon scarsly

163. Taylor is here thinking of early Port Royal, for later buildings were chiefly remarkable for their use of local limestone. His section "of stones" is marked by what seem to us many misconceptions.

164. After earth, air, fire and water, the traditional four elements.

growveth anything. The morros and swampy low grounds are generall of a blackish sand, in which is a certain flegmeticke* toughness, cold and barrenness, being overgorged with a salt speties which it receives from the sea; and altho' salt in a medium is good, yett excess of saltness is pestilent to the earth, for of *omne nimium,* too much of anything is vitious, as is seen in strong poysons, as mercury, antimony, collinquintida,[165] etc., taken in a medicall nature, are most helthfull (410) and expellers of those superabounding vitious humors which ofend the body, and occation sickness; but if taken in excess, then they (and of their own vitious and poysonous quallitys) shall suddenly distroy all health, and bring on the body inevitable death.

And such is the nature of salt to the body of the earth, for as by a moderat distribution therof, it correcteth all barren quallity, disperseth cold vapours, and yeildeth a fruitefull fattness to ye soyle, but being bestowed on the earth in excess, it becometh surfitted therby, and metamorphosied from all its properties and fruteful vertues, to all maner of mallevolous vitiousness. Its wholsom sharpness is changed to distroying greedyness, its comfortable warmness to a salt, burning quallytie, and its gentle dispersing quallity to, is changed into venomous pollutions. By all which the low swampy lands of Jamaica by the often washings of the sea is made unfitt to receive any seed from the hand of man, or to produce anything of itself, because all its naturall quallities are visiated, and nothing but barrennes (like a serpent) lodgeth therin, and will suffer noe good vegitiable to have society therwith. This is the natuer of the soyle on the lowlands of Jamaica next the sea, for this island is not invirourned with steep high cheaves,[166] like in Great Britain.

A foureth and last sort of soile, is that one the bancks of fresh rivers, which for the most part is a smoth, stiff, red clay of which is made most excelent tilles, bricks, sugar potts and jarrs. Also the Negroes makes tobacco pipes with it.[167] Thus we have discribed the soyle and natuer of the earth of this island, and have proved it to be the generative originall of stones and rocks, the which we now shall here handle and discribe; in order to which know (411) that on this island is found neither marble, freeston, slatsone nor chaulke, but here we find the flint of all sorts both whit, black, grey etc., such as we have in England. Also, the sandstone of both a red, whit, blew and grey coloure.

Also we find here in the sides of some lowe mountains nigh the sea plenty

---

165. This is coloquintida, or colocynth, a herbaceous vine from which a powerful and bitter cathartic may be prepared. *OED.*

166. These "cheaves" may be related to the chines, or narrow valleys leading down to the sea, of the south coast of his native Isle of Wight.

167. On these pipes, see Kenan Paul Heidtke, "Jamaican Red Clay Pipes" (MA thesis, Texas A & M, 1992).

of marle of a red and white, mix't or veined like prophry,[168] soe caused (and changed from its ordinary whiteness) by the differing clime and heat of the sun, and is noewhere found up in the mountains within the land, for marle is allways found in mountanous country nere the sea, lakes and small brooks, and in lowland country in the highest parts therof, as on the tops of small hills or within the cheaves nigh the sea. But of this marle they neither make lime, build, nor have they occation to manure their land therwith, for as yet 'tis rich enough of itself alltho woody, and inclining thereto, soe that it may well be said, *incultae parantur vomere Sylvae.*[169]

On this island they make their lime for building with cunck shells and whit corall rock, which here by ye shoreside and also in the sea is found in most places round ye island, and scarsly a rock of any other sort of stone to be found. Now this corall rock groweth up in the sea in branchs or bowes like trees, and by the heat of the clime 'tis hardned and becoms stone, and is generated from a marly earth or clay, which is found in the deep. At first it groweth up in small twigs, butt in some few yeares it joyns itself and unites itself into a rock of solid stone,[170] interwaving itself as you see in this figure [figure 32] for 'tis of a quick growth as may be with ease demonstrated (412) if you but consider how that in less than 50 years the corall rock on the Ambrosias, on the northeast part of Hispaniola, have grown into huge rocks, above six fadom high, and allmost now even with the surface of the watter, and hath inclosed the stem part of that great Spanish gallone called the *Golden*

Figure 32 Taylor's drawing of "a corrall rock", page 411.

168. This is porphyry, a hard reddish rock.

169. This quotation comes from Horace, in his Epistle II to Lollius Maximus. It translates as "the wild woodlands are tamed beneath our ploughshare". See *The Collected Works of Horace,* trans. Lord Dunsany and Michael Oakley (London/New York, 1961), 232.

170. An interesting theory for the creation of coral.

Lion (lost on that banck in the yeare of redemption 1644, and discovered by Sir Wm. Phipps in August 1687)[171] in a perfect rock, soe that I have seen when I lay there severall corrall rock hall'd up, which being beaten to peices, there have bin severall thousand dollars and other plat found to be intombed within the bowels of this groweing stonny sea tree called the whitcorall. 'Tis a stone harder than marle, white and maketh most excelent lime.

Now before we conclude this section, you must know that on this island is made aboundance of most excelent whit bay salt, made by the froath of the sea, which being cast up on the hott rocks and scalding stones, therby, and with the heat of the sun concerted into a puer whit salt, some of which is in lumps of 10 or 20 pounds weight. Allso there is much made in the same manner of the salenas or standing ponds of salt watter, as at Sir Henry Morgan's salt pond nere Passage Fort, and on divers other places on the island of Jamaica.[172]

Section VII

Of trees found on Jamaica: as the guacum, manchanilla, ironwood, granadilla, cedar, mahogony, brazalleto, elm, buttonwood, cherry tree, yallow wood, whitwood, cotten tree, tamarind, fustick, logwood, launcewood, borewood and the dogwood tree (413). These are the principall timber trees. Now of fruite trees there are these, viz: the pomgranat tree, pomcitteron, figg, orange, lemon, lime, cushsoa, mama, custard apple, tamarind, sowersop, guava, nausberry, coco, piemento, cassia, cherry tree, alagator pare, cocarnutt, paupa, vine, grap tree, mullberry, Spanish plumb, hog plumb, the cabadg tree and the callabash tree, and lastly the sapadilla tree.

This is an island which affords plenty of rare and choice trees, not only most excelent timber, but also most incomparable fruite-bearing trees of many kinds. But first we shall discribe the timber trees found on this island of Jamaica.

The guacum, *vel* [or] *lignum vitae,* is a tree of a most hard, solid and the enduring'st wood on earth,[173] and is found here in great plenty of a verey large

171. In fact, it was the wreck of the *Nuestra Señora de la Concepción* that Captain Phipps found in January 1687 on the reef off Hispaniola, where she had been lost in 1641. See Peter Earle, *The Treasure of the* Concepción (New York, 1980).

172. The most productive ponds were probably those just to the west of what is now Port Henderson Hill, on the coast of the Hellshire Hills. Perhaps Taylor means the ones established by Sir Thomas Modyford. See Carlton R. Williams, "Sir Thomas Modyford" (PhD diss., University of Kentucky, 1978).

173. As Sloane puts it, these trees are "soe hard as to break the Iron Tools used in felling them". *Voyage,* 2: 134.

groath. This wood is employed to many excellent uses; of it is made sheves for blooks, punch bowels, cupps, bowls, and many other curiosities. 'Tis of soe solid a weight that 'twill sinck in the watter lick a stone. It hath many rare phisicall vertues; it dries up wattery tumors and refineth the blod from all acidd and vitious pollutions. A decoction of this wood is good in dropsies,* scurvey, veneriall distempers, gonnoreahs. The cortex* herof and its gum hath many rare vertues which shall be treatted of in their due places. This tree groweth up straite with a thick smooth bark and short branches, covered with a smoth thick lefe, somewhat bigger tho' lick the box[174] leaf. This tree is exceding fatt and full of gum, and as sone as cutt down will burn like a torch or taper (414). And 'tis admirable to observe how that this tree can grow out of perffect flinty rock whereon is noe earth, or any moisture can possibly be dessern'd, and yet all the year round clothed in its fragrant and verdid gallantry, as I have often seen by the Three Rivers in Jamaica.[175] Guacum and other trees of a prodigious bigness grow out of the midst of high dry and craggy rocks. This tree cal'd guacum or *lignum vitae* yeildeth a small seed.

The manchanilla is a tree of great durance and very hard wood, yallow-veined with green and red, and of excelent use not only in building for its strenght, butt also most butifull to make cabannits and othere curiositys.[176] These trees grow straight and large with greet shady limbs, haveing a very thick bark, and yeildeth a gum of a poysonous quallytie, for wher it dropeth on the flesh, 'twill imediatly raise a blister. Its leaves is smoth, thick and gummy, yet sone falls and rotts. It produce an apple of the size, shap and collour of a golden pipen,[177] plesant to the eye and smell, but eaten is verey poysonous and brings on the body inevitable death. Nay soe poysonous is the nature of this wood, that those land crabbes whoe hath there residence in the earth under the roots therof, being eaten unawares, have poysoned many. Neither will any hog or other beast (tho' never soe hungry) eat of its apples, nor will they drinck of the watter which runs or stands below its roots, being instructed by the secrett instinct of nature to shun that which would otherwise distroy them.[178]

The ironwood is a tree of excelent substance and durance of the collour of rustie iron, and the hardest wood yet found in the whole universe. It hath a thick bark and a narrow smooth gummy leafe. (415) It yeildeth a small seed

174. Box is a genus of small evergreen shrubs.

175. Three Rivers lay just to the east of Harbour View, now an eastern suburb of Kingston.

176. Sloane also reports that this wood was "very much coveted by all People". *Voyage,* 2: 4.

177. "Pippen" was a late medieval word for many varieties of apple.

178. Yet, curiously, Sloane notes that goats both ate the fruit, and could then themselves be eaten without harm. *Voyage,* 2: 4.

or berry and this wood will endure to the end of many ages, if not to perpetuity itself.

The granadilla[179] is a tree by some called ebbony and by some mecanicks in England *lignum diaboli.* 'Tis a kind of a serbed tree of noe considerable bigness. It grows up strong and its bark is rugged just like the whitthorn.[180] It hath a little gummy leaf which is allways green. 'Tis a hard wood of a darck brown collour and its sapp is yallow. 'Tis a wood of good use and groweth here in great plentie in most places.

The cedar is a tree here found all over the island in greatt aboundance, growing verey bigg and lofty; some I have seen full fifteen foot in circumference and full 70 foot long. 'Tis a curious wod and of a verey sweet scent. Of it they make their cheif beames used both for building ships, slopes,[181] houses, etc., for 'twill last long not only drie but also in watter.

The mahogony is a tree here also found verey plenty.[182] 'Tis a hard reed wood, good timber, and will last long. They are huge, lofty trees allmost parallel with the cedar. It bears a large thick leafe and hath a thick bark.

The brazalleto is a tree here found in some parts of the island.[183] 'Tis a kind of a bastard brazill, not quit soe red and of noe considerable biggness. 'Tis verey tuff and strong and used to making cabannits and other curiosoties.

The Spanish elmn is here found. 'Tis a tree much like English elmn in groath, bark and leaf, which is only grenner and thicker and its fruite is a small berry. It maketh excelent planck and will last long,[184] and differs from English ellm only in this, namely, 'tis tuffer, and wheras ours will not splitt, this will cleave with great facillity.

The buttonwood tree is a yallow wood and very hard and an excelent tree for shade. Its bark is smoth and its leaf oblong (416) and is verey good timber according to itts groath. The coals of this wood is more hott than the fire made of any other wood found in America, and used by ffounders to melt down their mettall.

---

179. "Granadilla", from the Spanish *granadillo,* is an old term for ebony (Cassidy and Le Page, *DJE,* 204); the term is now used for a climbing vine that yields the pomegranate (*OED*). No doubt the English carpenters called it wood of the devil (*lignum diaboli*) because it destroyed their tools.

180. This is the whitehorn or hawthorn.

181. Perhaps "sloops".

182. Of mahogany, Browne noted that "this tree grew formerly very common in Jamaica" (*Civil and Natural History,* 158); curiously, Sloane does not appear to mention it, unless under the heading *juniperus maxima.*

183. According to Browne, "in every part of Jamaica where the soil is dry and rocky". Ibid., 227.

184. According to Sloane, "this tree was much used by the Spaniards, for it made not only excellent planks, but also wood for cabinet-makers, who called it 'Prince Wood' ". *Voyage,* 2: 63.

The cherry tree is also here found.[185] 'Tis a tree of smooth bark and a broad smoth leafe, much like laurell, but thicker and not quite soe long. It bears a fruite ressembling a cherry both in shape and collour, but twice as bigg, and hath a verey large stone. This is good timber of a reedish collour and a free grain, and is used much for planck in building both for land and sea.

The yallow wood is a tree here found, verey bigg and lofty. It hath a thick gray smoth barck, tho' besset all round with strong sharp spears or barbs soe that they can't be easily climed. It hath a thick round leafe, and yeilds a gum good in combustable compositions. The wood is yallow of a flexible graine, and are cheifly used for staves for casks and shingles to cover buildings withall. Now this sort is called prickle yallow wood, and there is another tree every way like this, only it hath a smoth bark without barbs.[186]

The whittwood tree here is a tree of the same groath in every respect as the prickle yallow wood, growing with the same leaf and prickly cortex. 'Tis a very whit wood and put to the before-mentioned usses, tho' not soe much esteemed.

The cotton tree[187] is the tree of the biggest bulk and largest found anywhere in these western parts (or indeed I beleive in the whole world). This is the tree of which Plinny reports many famallys to inhabite the hollow truncks and spurrs thereof.[188] In the East India these trees are commonly verey straight and without branches, some 70 or 80 foot high, and in circumference at the spurs 50 or 60 foot, and in the solid body full 30 foot. They have a smoth bark, but from (417) the branches downwards midway is all besset with sharp barbs like the prickle yallow wood tree; it spread not untill the verey top. It hath very large roots and spredeth at the spurs with cavities, soe that many men may stand there as behind the arches and great supporting pillars in churches and statly structuers.

Now, this being a tree of such magnificence and bullck, we therefore have, for the finall satisfaction of the curious, potraied it to the life [figure 33]. It is a tree full of leaves which is a thin long leaf. The wood is verey soft and therfore not used in buildings but employed to make large boats called periaquer[189] (418) and canoas, some of which will carry seven or eight tunns

185. The identity of this cherry is not clear, unless it is the "Barbadoes cherry tree" described by Browne, *Civil and Natural History*, 230.

186. This is the tree called by Browne "Prickly Yellow-wood, or yellow Hercules". Ibid., 189.

187. More often known as the "silk cotton-tree".

188. Taylor is probably thinking of the fig-tree, said by Pliny to be "capable of affording shelter to a whole troop of horse". Bostock and Riley, *The Natural History of Pliny*, 2: 129. Sloane also reports that some Guyanese people lived in cotton trees, when the rivers were high. *Voyage*, 2: 74.

189. The "periaquer", also known as the "piragua" or "pirogue", took its name from the Carib word for a canoe. *OED*.

of watter, they being full 8 foot broad and deep and nighe forty foot long. These boats are made of but one cooten tree hollowed out and curiously shap't with a keal, stern and stern-post, cutt out in the same wood. They are flatt-bottomed because they should goe up in the flatt rivers for watter, yett these canoas will both rowe and saile well, and when they comes new off the stocks are sold att Jamaica for noe less than 120 or 160 dollars, which'll last many years if used well and always keept in the water, but if layed drie on the land will soon roat and decay. These canoas are more used in those Western parts of the world than any other boats whatever (boath as watterboats, lightors* etc.) for they will boath rough and saile well. In 'em they use not long oars, but short paddles. Now, this cotton tree beareth a small seed or bery, but doth not yeild cotten, altho' soe called, but is a softy springy wood as whit as cooten, and beareth a leaf like the cooten shrub, and it hath a bark like the sicamore,* and tho' bescattered with barbs, yet I say the bark's smoth, it not being chapp'd like the cortex of the oak or wallnut tree which I count rugged bark.

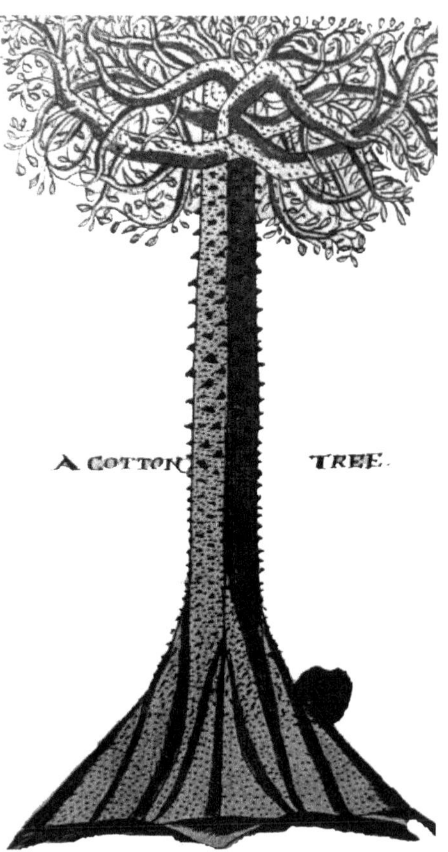

Figure 33 Taylor's drawing of "a cotton tree", page 417.

The tamarind is a tree of a considerable bulck, but not verey lofty.[190] 'Tis a verey spreeding tree of most excellent shade. It beareth a long pale green leaf like the yew tree,* and a flower of a sweet scent ike the camomill* flower, and bareth a most excellent fruitt, whose pulp preserved is good in many distempers (see page the [blank]). The wood of this tree is reed like to cedar, tho' much harder and tuffer. It makes excellent planck and is much estemed both in land and sea building on Jamaica.

The fustick is a tree found here in great plenty and is large lofty tree with a thick bark and a long thick gummy leafe (419), and is a hard yallow wood, full of a gummy sapp. It beareth its seed in a small berry and is a timber used here in their buildings and other works, but this wood is an excellent diewood and is vended home to England and other parts, proveing a good commodity.[191]

The logwood is a tree here found in some swampy places nigh the sea shore, tho' in noe great plenty. 'Tis a cragged nurly* tree of a small growth,

190. Taylor here appears to conflate the qualities of three distinct tamarind trees described by Sloane, *Voyage,* 2: 45 and 54–55.

191. As Sloane puts it, this tree "is felled and cutt into Loggs to be sent for Europe, to be used by the Dyers for a yellow Colour". Ibid., 3.

growing always in the watter. It hath a thick smoth bark and a soft yallow sapp; it bears a broad thinn leafe. The wood is red and of much use in dieing and is an excelent commodity worth about five pounds a tunn, and was within these seven years worth fiveteen pounds a tunn. When 'tis cutt they hew off the sapp and sell the spind* by weight. 'Tis a quick and certain commodity and many ships are loaden from hence with it yearly home to England etc., the greatest part of which is cutt at the Bay of Compechy, and from thence brought to Jamaica and soe vended to England.[192]

The launcwood is a tree here found and soe called because with yonge slendor trees the Spaniards and Indian hunters make theire arrow shafts and launces therwith, for 'tis a tall slendor and an exceeding tuff and strong tree.[193] It hath a thick bark lick the holm* and leaf like the mirtle, and is a yallowish free grain'd wood, strong and hard, and is of good use for raffters, sparrs, small timbers and masts for boats. It yeilds a small seed.

The borewood is a tale slendor tree, and verey tuff-grain'd and excellent for the aforesaid uses. It hath a red thick bark lick ye birchtree, which yeilds a soverangn gumm (see page [blank]) of execellent value. It bears a thick laurell-licke leaf, but more rounder. 'Tis a yallowish strong wood, and receives its name from this occation, for 'tis reported by hunters and other sons of Sylvae, that as soon as the sturdy wild bore is wounded and felleth (420) his woundes smartt, then imediatly he resorts to this tree (being therto directed by the secrett instinct of nature) and with his tuscks launces the bark thereof from whence presently issueth out a milky gumm which he rubbeth into his woundes, and soe thereby his soars are healled in a short space.[194]

The dogwood is a tall slendor tree very strong-grained and employed to the same uses as the launce wood for rafters etc.[195] It hath a bark like the sicamore, a leafe lick the poplar,* and beareth a flower lick perwinckle,* some white, some blew, and some of a yallow colour. 'Tis a hard brown wood and will last long. Its sapp, juice and bark are of a stupifieing nature (see page 485) soe that if a man should drinck or eat therof, he either falleth mad or else for a long time [is] possest with a continuall drowsines, soe that this tree bears a simpathy (and may be compared) with the Aethiopian Fountain of which Ovid thus spakes:

---

192. Sloane confirms that logwood was chiefly derived from Campeche, though he maintains that its dye was blue. Ibid., 183–84. According to Browne, it was purple and black. *Civil and Natural History*, 221.

193. Sloane also calls this "silver-wood", mentioning that it makes good "scouring-rods for Guns". *Voyage*, 2: 78–79.

194. Sloane also recounts this quality in the boar, and gives the tree the alternative name of the "Hog-doctor tree". Ibid., 90. Browne repeats the story of the boar, but calls the tree "the Hog-gum tree". *Civil and Natural History*, 177.

195. Browne remarks that "this tree is a native of Jamaica". Ibid., 297.

Aethiopesque Lacus, quos si quis faucibus hausit.
Aut furit, aut patitur mirum gravitate saporem.[196]

There are many othere trees which are good and excelent timber and here imployed in building, but these are also most excelent fruite-bearing trees and therfor preserved for fruite and not soe frequently used for timber, the which we shall discribe among the ffruite trees, and thus wee have finished the description of all the principall timber trees found on this island and of most use and esteme for that purpose on Jamaica.

Of Fruit Trees

Haveing allredy given you an account of all the principall (421) timber trees found on this island, we shall now give you a full description of the many excellent fruit trees here found on this uberous island, which are those which follow.

First the pomagranat tree is here found in great plenty and are planted in the delicat walks in theire settlements.[197] 'Tis noe huge nore large tree, butt a tree of an excellent shade. It hath a thicke green leafe and a smoth bark, and yeilds its fruite plentiefully twice a yeare, and is every way such as are found in Europe. This tree thriveth verey well here, and is never trobled with the worm or cancker as our trees are in Europe, for you must know that among the many thousands of trees which I have seen in the West Indies, I have never saw any in the least touched therwith, from whence I conclude that noe trees of that sort or kind soever found in these western parts of America are ever tainted with the cancker, because they are not filled with a raw unconcocted humor or sapp, because the country is far hooter than England, for cold or unconcocted sapp is the second cause of that taint as the learned Pliny hath proved.[198]

The pomcitteron tree also groweth here in great plenty, are planted in walkes in the plantations as the former, and here are of good esteem.[199] They

---

196. In the *Metamorphoses.* It translates as " . . . the Aethopian lakes. / Whoever drinks of these waters either goes raving mad or falls into a strange, deep lethargy." Ovid, *Metamorphoses,* William S. Anderson, ed. (Norman, Okla., 1966), book 15, 320–21.

197. Browne confirms Taylor's judgement here: "Both these species [of pomegranate] are cultivated by many people in Jamaica, and thrive very well in most parts of the island." *Civil and Natural History,* 239.

198. In his book 16, "On forest trees", Pliny does indeed have reflections on the qualities of sap, but not quite those that Taylor describes. See *The Natural History of Pliny,* 3: 379–82.

199. "Pomecitron" seems to be an archaic name for the citron, a fruit related to the lemon and lime. *OED.* Sloane confirms that "these trees are frequently to be met with set in Walks". *Voyage,* 2: 177.

yeild plenty of fruit twice a year and are in all respects such as are found in Europe.

The figg tree here found is larger than those found in Europe, but in every other respect like 'em.[200] Here they are continually loaden with green, ripe, and mellow fruite all the yeare round. In the woods is also found a wild figg tree, in leafe and groath like the former, but its fruite is not half soe good nor soe larg, for the othere is a rare large fruit.

The cassia fistula tree is here found.[201] 'Tis a verey large spreding tree, hath a smoath bark and a baylick* leaf. It produceth verey large fruite (422) once a yeare. These trees are not verey plenty here.

Here is also found the China and Sivilla orange trees in great plenty, not only planted in delicat walks in their settlements, but growing in great aboundance wild in the woods and mountaines. 'Tis a tree of noe considrable groath. It hath a thick smoth bark, a smoth brod leafe much like the bay tree, and prickly branches. They yeild most excellent large fruite which shine like the golden apples in the walks of the temple groves in Thessaly, and smell more charming than the fatt jecimons of Sisillia, for they are allways loaden (unless in droughts) with aboundance of flowers, green and ripe fruit, all at one and the same time.

'Tis a most excelent tree both for buty and shade, under whose shady bowes the painfull planter and's faire Creolian ladies withdraw themselves from the schorching heat of Phebus, the troblesome affaires of their plantations when tiered in backbitting their neibours, choack't with their hoot prid and envey, their stommocks cloged with riot, and their brains surfitted with the steme of rum punch. Then doe they preepaire either with their lady, houskeeper (and if they are waiteing a young African Amazone must keep 'em company) to ease their lacivious heat under the shades of these sweet bowers, which by the great Creator wer created for other purposes (and not for such horrid practices), namely to be place of sweet retierments filled with holly meditations, to renue and refresh man's spiritts and to call home his wearied senses to their centor of rest and sweet repose.

The lemon tree is also found here, not only planted as the former in their settlements, but also grow wild in the woods in great aboundance. This tree and all others found here are continually cloathed in their verdid livery all the yeare round. It grows just like the orange (423) here, only their leaf is somwhat longer. It is allways loaded with sweet flower, green lemons and ripe fruite at one and the same time.

200. See Browne: "This tree has long been introduced and cultivated in the low warm lands of Jamaica, where it thrives very luxuriantly . . . It is planted almost in all the gardens about Kingston." *Civil and Natural History,* 109.

201. Also identified so by Browne, ibid., 222.

Figure 34 Taylor's drawing of "a cushoa tree", page 423.

The lime tree or wild lemon tree grows everywhere here in great plenty, and is one of their cheife hedges or fences. 'Tis like ye lemon tree, only more prickly, and yeild its fruite in great plenty all the year round.

The cushoa or cushsoa tree is also here found, and is a tree of great esteme, and with great care planted in their setlements. 'Tis a longe spreading tree of excelent shade, bearing a thick oval broad leaf; it hath smoth bark. 'Tis allways green and produces its fruit twice a yeare,[202] which 'twill yeild in seaven years after planted. In fine 'tis one of the butifulls trees (when laden with fruits) which I ever saw and I have here potraied it to the life [figure 34].

(424) The mama is found here.[203] 'Tis a tree of a tolerable groath, and spreads like the former. It hath a thick smoth ovall leaf and a smoth brown bark, and for its fruitt sake is planted in most settlements. This tree grows also wild in the woods and mountains. They are continually green and yeild plenty of excellent fruitt in their seasons. Their are two sortes of these trees; the one yeilds a fruit with but one stone in't, and this is called the Mama Saporta, and the other hath three stones in its fruite, and this is called the Mama or maneetree?, but they are both every way alike in groath.[204]

202. The cashew yields once a year, in fact (Sidrak).

203. The mamee-apple.

204. These trees are now known as the "Mammee-apple" and the "Mammee-sapote". Allsopp, *DCE*, 366.

The custard apple tree is here found plenty groweing in the plantations, but also wild in the woods and mountains. 'Tis a lofty tree of noe great shade haveing a thick smoth bark and a smoth long leaf, allways cloath in its summer livery, and yeilds its fruit plentyfully twice a yeare in their seasons.[205]

The tamarind tree we have allready discribed among the timber trees (in page 418) and therefore we shall not make a second repitition therof.

The sowersop tree is found here in great plenty, both in the plantations and also wild in the mountains, in all respects like the custard aple tree, only its leafe is somewhat larger. It yeildeth aboundance of fruite in its seasons twice a year.

(425) The guava tree is found on this island in aboundance.[206] 'Tis a high and spreding tree, haveing a smoth bark and a leaf allmost like the lime tree. 'Tis a tree allways green, and yeilds its fruit plentifully, on which the wild hogs feed and becom fatt, for they grow everywhere wild in the woods, and therefore they take not that care to plant 'em, as they doe other fruit trees, although their fruit is large and of good esteme.

The nawsberry here is also found on this place.[207] 'Tis a tree of a large groath and a thick broad leafe, and of barke like the mullberry tree, and is greatly estemed by reason of its most rare fruit, which it produces plentifully twice a year in its seasons. 'Tis a tender tree found in most plantations where the soyle will produce 'em but are seldom found wild in the woods.

At first when Jamaica was taken by the English from the Spaniards, here were many excellent plantations of coco trees,[208] or coco walks, which since are run to much decay, by reason they had not time to look after 'em.[209] This coco tree is a small fruite-tree or shrub, seldom above ten foot high. 'Tis a tree of both bark and leaf like the almond, and yeildeth its fruite plentifull in clusters. 'Tis a very tender plant, and will not endure the winds, nor but little of the heat of the sun, and is therfore planted amongst plantation plantaign* trees, ye which both shade and shelter them.

(426) The piemento tree is also here found. This is a tree growing high, covered with a very thinn smoth bark, and a leaf in all respects like our

205. As Sloane explains, "The pulp is for Colour, Consistence and sweetish Taste like a Custard, whence the name." *Voyage,* 2: 167.

206. The name probably comes from the Taino/Arawak *guaiaua*. Allsopp, *DCE,* 272.

207. The name "nawsberry" (or "naseberry") comes from the Spanish *nespora,* since it was thought to resemble that Eurasian fruit. Ibid., 399. As Sloane notes, it was also called the "sappadilla-tree". *Voyage,* 2: 173.

208. Taylor's "coco tree" is in fact a cacao bush or tree. When he then wishes to describe the coconut palm, he calls it a "coca-nutt tree" (see below). Sloane calls this a "coco-tree". *Voyage,* 2: 8.

209. In fact, it was a blight which "blasted" most of the cacao walks during the 1670s. Ibid., 1: lxxi.

Europian bay tree. Indeed, 'tis every way a tree soe alike, that the difference concisteth only in the thickness of their barks. The pimento tree yeild its fruite verey plentifully in great round clusters, as big as a man's fist, growing togeather like ivey berrys. This pimento berrys, Jamaica pepper, or allspice (for soe 'tis called) is somewhat bigger than East India pepper, which when ripe look reed like blood, but aftere they are dried and cured in the sun becoms of a blackish coloure. 'Tis an excellent spice, and proves a good commodity.[210] 'Tis a tree soon raised and will yeild its fruite six years after planting. Its fruit is ripe in August, butt these three years they had have had but little of it on Jamaica, by reason the trees for the most part were blasted by lightning. The bark and leaf of this tree both tasteth and smelleth like the spice.

This tree is not only planted in severall plantations where the soyle is agreeing, but also in many places in the country. You shall see many hundred of accars of 'em grow together in their own naturall planting,[211] soe that there are many wealthy planters on the north sides whose plantations concist of litle else but these (427) trees, for where they find 'em in such woods they cutt down all the other trees mixst amongst 'em, and soe clare the ground of other trumpery and setle it for a plantation which very plentifully rewards their painfull industry, the spice being a certain and good commodity, and a hundred accers of those trees will be well managed by ten Negro slaves, and in seasonable years produce a thousand-pound profitt. Now their is a duble advantage attends it; first 'tis a more certain and good commodity than sugare, and secondly a plantation or sugare-worke probable to produce ye forementioned profitt shall require 50 Negro slaves to manage, besids the charge of sugar boyling etc., whereas this requires but five men and five women slaves to manag it, which are farr easier purchas'd and maintained than fifty Negro slaves, which noe ordinary planter at their first setling will be able to purchas and employ.

The cherry tree we have allredy discribed amongst the timber trees (see page 416). This is a tree growing wild in the woods, always green, and seldom planted in the plantation becaus its fruite is of noe estem. It produces its fruit plentifully twice a yeare.

The alagator pear tree is here found.[212] This is a tree whose grwoth resembles the sowersop tree, both (428) in leaf and groath. 'Tis allways cloathed in its verdid hue and yeilds its fruite plentifully twice a yeare.

---

210. As Sloane puts it, "having a very fine Relish of many [other spices, it is] from thence called All-Spice". Ibid., 2: 77.

211. The pimento is indigenous to Jamaica. Allsopp, *DCE*, 440.

212. Sloane calls this the "avocado, or alligator pear tree". *Voyage*, 1: 133. This tree was indigenous to Mexico.

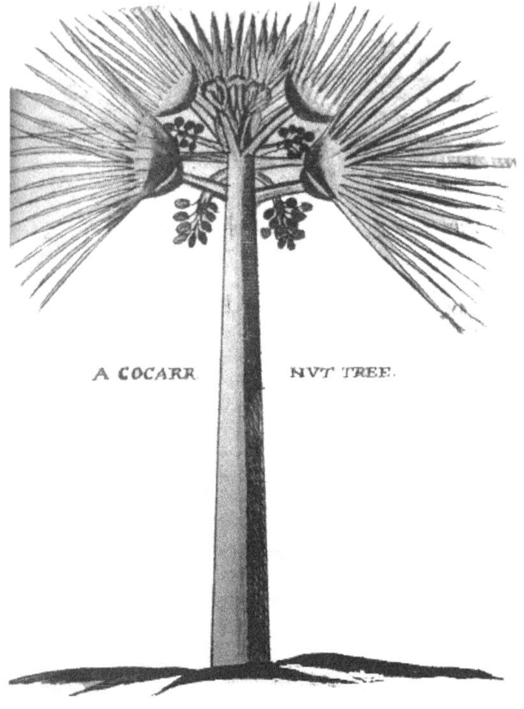

Figure 35 Taylor's drawing of "a cocarr nut tree", page 429.

The cocarnutt tree is a verey butifull tree and a rare tree for shade. It hath a smoth thick bark and is smoth without branches, of a considerable height. The leaves, or rather branches, grow by the stemm like a cabadge leaf and divides itsself into severall long leaves, which are above six foot long, and soe grow from where they beginn to the verry top of the tree, and as the trees grow higher, the under-leaves dropp off and leaves a smoth barke. It bears the nutts in clusters amongst those large leaves ishueing out from the body of the trees, growing tenn ore more nutts in a clustre, there being allways green and ripe fruite thereon at one and the same time, which allways comes ripe in course, one after anothere.

This is a kind of a palm tree and a verey tender plant and on this island are not found very plentifull, tho' on the Main of America they are found in great aboundance. This tree will produce fruite in seaven years after planting for 'tis a plant of a quicke groath. These leaves (as well as the palm, palemeto and cabadge leaves) being drie become exceding white, soe that they make hatts, baskets and matt cloath therewith, which look much whiter than those straw hatts used in England and other parts and are made in great aboundance at Burmodus by the English, and here by Negros, and are much woren by Creolians in the plantation.[213] Now this tree for the finnall satisfaction of the curious I have here potraied [figure 35].

(430) The paupa tree found on this island is of a large groath and a good timber tree.[214] 'Tis covered with a ragged bark and hath a broad great leafe, and yeilds its fruite plentyfully in its season and is found everywhere plentifully in the woods and mountains, allways cloathed in its summer livery.

On this island in the plantations are found some most excelent vines which yeild a fair muscadine* grape far better than ours in England, and these vines thrive well here.

The grape-tree found here wild in the wood is a very spreading tree, hath a smoth bark, and a very broad thick leafe, veined with red phibers. It

213. As Sloane puts it, "The Leaves of this tree, whitened by the Air, is made into Women's Hatts, such as our Straw Hatts, to keep their Beauty and Colour from the Injuries of the Sun." Ibid., 2: 118.

214. The paw-paw is certainly not a good timber-tree (Sidrak).

produces a large fruite like a grape, but verey sharpe and but litle estemed. The wood of this tree is hard, of a flexible grain, and as reed as blood.

The mullberry tree found here is in all respects such as we have in England, allways green and yeilds plenty of fruite.[215]

The sapadilla tree is found here in some places.[216] This is a tree both in leaf and bark every way like the almond tree, but of a greater growth. It yeilds plenty of fruite.

The Spanish plumb tree is a tree of considerable growth, haveing a smooth thick bark and a leafe like the ash in Europe.[217] They grow allmost everywhere without planting and yeilds plenty of fruit which is not much estemed.

The hog plumb tree is in every respect like the former; the difference is only in the fruite. These grow in great aboundance everywhere wild in the woods and mountaines,[218] and yeild such aboundance of fruite that many times with weight therof their bowes are broaken down.

The cabadg tree[219] groweth on this island in most wett grounds both in the lowlands and mountains. 'Tis a tree of about three foot circumference at the ground, and perhaps 120 foot high,[220] exceeding (431) straight and smoth, without either branch or leaf untill within fouer foot of the top, out of which growes the leaves every way such as the cocarnutt tree (before potraied) both for shape and size, and its seed growes out like that, one a large stem, and is a busshy clustre of a small round berry, green and about the bigness of a strawberry, but round, soft and cavious on which the hogs and fowles feed. This tree at the ground is a hard sort of wood, but hollow.

Now, at the very top of this tree grows the cabdage, which to attain you must fell the tree which is a great truth, altho' by many in England accounted to be a most notorious lie. This cabadg is not a round one as our English cabdages are, as some thinck, butt is the upper part of the tree, which yett is fill'd with sapp, soft and tendor, being not as yett wood, for you must understand that about a yard of the very top part of the tree you must cutt off with a knife, for 'tis verey soft, and after you have taken off the bark, and another filmn, the remain part is the cabadge, very white, sweet, and tendor. This would as the tree grew higher, shoot out into leaves, then harden and become wood, for 'tis the top shoot or budd of the tree, for it hath noe branches but shoots upright, and their comes forth new leaves, ye old one

---

215. Sloane and Browne say nothing of the mulberry tree.

216. The sapadilla is in fact the same as the naseberry, mentioned above.

217. This could be the Spanish lime, or genep (Sidrak).

218. The hog-plum "thrives in rough and wild environments". Allsopp, *DCE*, 294.

219. Better known as the cabbage-palm. Ibid., 127.

220. Here Taylor seems more accurate than Sloane, who affirms that the cabbage tree could be two hundred feet high. *Voyage*, 2: 116.

drop off (like Europian colworts)[221] and the barke hardens and becoms smoth. The cabadge raw eats as sweet as almonds and makes a good sallad, which must be eaten carefully for 'twill occation a lask,[222] but when the cabadge is boyled it eats every way like our Europian cabadge, butt sweeter. These trees grow in solide woods of a hundred acres in some places, as on the northwest sid of the Gulph of Samana etc., and are planted in manie (430a) plantations, being of noe detriment for anything may be planted under 'em, and they will be fitt to cutt in fouer or five years time, and will yeild a good cabadge, tho' they are rather planted for curiosity than profitt.

Lastly, on this island is found the calibash tree all o'er the island growing wild in the mountains, woods and savanas. 'Tis a knotty tree, with a rugged barke, allways full of fruit; its leafe is long, thick, and smoth. Thus we have given you a large and true description of all the known timber trees and fruit trees found on Jamaica, and most other of those western parts of America, the which is noewhere else by any other author whatsoever soe largly and truly treated on and described.[223]

But before we conclude this section, we shall give a philosopicall account of the groath, durance and decay of trees, the which we shall handle and plainly demonstrate according to a true ratio of natural philosophy, soe the the proposition is: how long is a tree in its growth, how long in his strenght, and how long before finnally decayed? The ancient sages and readers of the works of nature, with the learned and eagle-eyed philosophers as Plato, Aistortle, Pliny, Virgill and Cicero, tell us that art hath hir first originall from experience, which allways teacheth infalliably and plainly, as drawing hir knowledg out of the course of nature by the sences with the help of the mind, folloing and compareing the works therof, for *Deus et natura nihil fecit frustra.*[224] What's art but an oritor to declare its secretts, and a correctrix to refine its defects? Therefore these ancient philosophers, guided by art and reason (431a), after all their Herculian labours and toile in the study of natur's works, doe all with one unanimous consent affirm that all firm and solid trees, by the course of nature (if not are circumvented by accident) shall remain and abide one earth (from their first sprouting out therof, untill their finall decay) at least nine hundred years, namely 300 in its growth, 300 in its full strenght, and three hundred yeares in its declining station, all which they have learnedly proved. Therfor, let noe man thinck strange, but being

221. A "colewort" was once any plant of the cabbage family. *OED.*

222. A "lask" was diarrhoea; the word is now used by veterinarians.

223. This was true, before the publication of Sloane's first volume in 1707.

224. "God and Nature do nothing in vain", a central idea for Taylor. "Deus et natura nihil facient in frustra" is cited as a "medieval proposition" in the *Oxford Dictionary of Quotations,* ed. Elizabeth Knowles (Oxford, 1991), 33.

endued with reason, let him consider the philosophicall and naturall cause thereof, which wil make all plain and obvious.

I have seen severall thousands of trees in America and have dilligently obsurved the growth of some of 'em, and shall here instance in the cheif of 'em for bulk, namely the cotton tree, one of which I saw whose circumference at the spurrs nigh the earth to be full sixty foot in girth, and his hight exceed 160 foot, which tree I supposed to be at his full growth. This I compared with another cotton tree which was a landmark and hath bin known by a learned and worthy gentleman these 35 years, and in that space of time is supposed to have grown one-third part of its now stature and bulke, soe that according to a reasonable computation of time, this tree must now be 115 years old, according to its late observed growth. Now I say this tree groweth in the like good ground with the former, and yet is not grown to the bulk of the same, by more than two-thirds part therof. Hence I gather that if a tree be one hundred and fifteen years old, and yet wants two-third parts of the growth of other trees of the same kind, then must his growing or increasing (432) space of time be allowed (according to that proportion) to be more than 300 years, which is certainly but the third part of its life or time of continuance.

For consider that every liveing creature bestowes the best part of its age in its growth, and soe must it indeed be with trees. Man comes not to his full growth till thirty, and some slendor and lean bodys not tell forty years; soe long also stands his strenght, and soe long also by course of nature must he be allowed to decay. Now if man whose body is nothing but a tendor rottenness, whose course of life can't by any means be restrain'd within the limitis of modesty neither by councell, restraint of laws, punishment or hopes of praise, profit, or eternall glory, but degenerates totally from its naturall feeding to efeminate richness, surfitting his body with excess of meat and drinck, sleep etc., and to some nothing is soe pleasant as the cause of his own death as idleness, lust etc., I say if such may and doe live to such a proportionable age, then well may a tree of a strong and solid substance (not damnified by heat or cold, feeding naturally, and of its own accord avoideing those things which might annoy him) quadruple the age of man in its growth, which many other creatures far exceed, as the elephant, hart, raven etc., as wittneseth that famous Roterodam out of Hesiodus, and the testimony of that matchles oritor M.T. Cicero in his book *De Senectute* is weighty to this purpose; saith he, *in posteras aetates serere arbores,*[225] which can have noe other force but to prove that trees enduer for many ages.

---

225. Taylor seems here to be thinking of the passage in Cicero's *Cato maior de senectute,* ed. J.G.F. Powell (Cambridge, 1988), 5: "he plants trees for the use of another age".

(433) Now trees in comparison to the earth are but as haires to the body of man, which for the major part enduer to the last with the body of man unless by some fattall accident poyson'd and destroyed. Wherfor I resolve upon good considerations founded on the true ratio of naturall philosophy and experience, that trees may last a thousand years and bear fruit more plentifully large and faire than at first, becaus the viger of his sapp is more proud and strong when his age is many than when it first yeilded fruite, and you may allways observe old trees to put forth their buds and blosoms sonner and in more plenty than younger trees because their sapp is more strong and proud.

Seeing therfore that man and other creatures treble the station of their lives by course of nature as we have allready proved, then 'twold be folly to denigh the like property to those monstrous bodys whos sapp is strong and bitter, whose barke is hard and thick, and their substance solid and stiff; all which are propogators of strenght and long life, for their strenght withstands all forceable winds. Their sapp is of soe prime a quallyty as not subject either to worm or taint, and growing here in the unfrequented woods they seldom receive wounds from the hand of man, which sometimes use trees as they doe themselves, namly unskillfully and carelessly and soe ocation their death, soe that I declare 'tis my opinion that many of those hugh trees which I have seen in America have not bin propigated according to limitation of time before mentioned only, but hath and will acquire the age of many Mathusalas[226] from their first sprout untill their finnall decay off the earth. Thus we have plainly demonstrated the proposition, by the true ratio of naturalle philosophy which (434) is the golden kay of art and knowledg, and the maintainer of all siences. 'Tis ancient, profitable and plesant, and demonstrates the secretts of nature, and is estemed and aproved by the most learned sages and late modern philosophers, justly diserving its atributed honour.

Section VIII

Of shrubbs found on Jamaica as the jecimon palmeto, palmeto royall, lemnia, mahoa, corrato, sabina, Jamaica cocarplumb, maingrove, fingrigo, racoonwithh, pudingwithh, dildo, pineapple, pricklepear, plantann, boonana, cataputia, sage tree, bell pepper, mallagata, bird pepper, sugar cane, and wild cane and the cotton shrubb in our chapter of planting discribed.

On this uberous island is found the fatt jecimon tree, whose flowers and fatt choice gumm perfume the circumambient aire with its plesant smells, and adorn the earth with its gaie flowers. This jecimon tree is a small shrubb, of

226. Methuselah was the biblical patriarch of fabulous age.

no considerable growth, having a tender bark and a large smooth underfleaf, allways arraie'd in summer livery, and adorn with its gay flowers, by which the aire is perfumed with its sweet odure.[227]

The palmeto royall groweth in all respects like the cabadge tree, but is not full soe large in bulk or highth, and it beares a leafe just like the same,[228] and its fruite is a small berry, when ripe (435) of a dark colour, the vertue of which is shown amongst the seeds. The Burmodians make of these leaves hatts, capps, basketts, matts etc., and in great aboundance, which they themselves weve and bring to sell at Jamaica. Also, they make bromes of ye leafs much like a flacc* brome. The palmeto is a tree in every respect like the former, only 'tis not above half soe large, neither in body or leaf, and its body is not of lignumetique substance, but soft and spongy; its fruit is like ye former.

The lemnia or birch tree here found is in all respects both in bark and leaf such as is found in England, only 'tis of a farr greater growth, allways green, and yeilds plenty of gumm, whos vertues are many; see the *Pharmocaphiae Londonensis* wher you will find sattisfaction.[229]

The mohoa is a shrubb found on Jamaica in most swampy places, but more espetially betwixt Carlisle Bay and Portland in the moho gardens nere the seashore. This is a shrubb which groweth up like and ouzier,* seldom biger than the small of a man's legg. It bears a large thin leaf, and it hath a smoth thinn brown barke of excelent use. This barke will stripp like hemp, and worke as fine and strong as flax. It makes excellent roopes, and most incomperable cables for slops, and were it improved 'twold be full as good, if not better than hemp for any of the same purposes, and I belive if managed by artificers* in flaxes, 'twould make incomparable fine cloath.[230]

The corrato is a small shrubb,[231] a kind of a palmeto. It grows of a considerable umbretique* hight, and bears a leaf like ye palmeto, above which sprouts out some single leaves, about six foot long, (436) one foot brod at the tree, and half a foot thick, concave at the upper side, and convex at the

---

227. Probably the jasmine tree (Sloane, *Voyage*, 2: 61–62), or perhaps the frangipani (Sidrak).

228. The royal palm does indeed resemble a smaller version of the cabbage palm. Allsopp, *DCE*, 127.

229. I have not been able to find this in the *Pharmacopeia Londonensis.*

230. This seems to be the "Mahot, or mangrove tree", of which Sloane writes that "'Tis chiefly useful by its Bark, which is pull'd off, and made into Ropes of all sorts, for the use of the Island". *Voyage*, 1: 215. It is called by Browne "The Mohoe, or Bark-Tree". *Civil and Natural History*, 284.

231. Coratoe is *agave Americana*, though Taylor's description is not very accurate. Cassidy and Le Page, *DJE*, 122. He seems to be referring to Sloane's *aloe Americana*, of which Sloane writes that "the leaves are us'd to Scour Rooms, Platts or anything withal, instead of soap". *Voyage*, 1: 246. It seems to have many of the qualities of Sloane's "Sope Apple Tree", *Voyage*, 2: 132.

lower. These leaves are the opening leaves of the budds which makes passage for the growth of the tree, and the sprouting forth of other leaves, which when they come forth, these fall off, and new ones begin to shoot forth to project the next sprout of the tree. Now these leaves are green and full of sapp, and are here useed to wash linnen and scower plate and putter* withall. Thus they cutt this leafe in peices and lay it in sleep with their cloaths in water all night, and in ye morning they wash it out useing it like sope, and it fetches out all stains, spotts, and make the cloath exceading whitt.

This is all they use for their large linnen; and castill soap for their finn linnen, for there is noe other sort of sope bought to Jamaica.[232] Now for scouering they use it thus; they make a lixivium* with it, then they putt their puter or plat therin and rubb it with new cutt peices of the leaves, and it makes it exceeding clean and bright, being far beter than chalke or sand, because it doth neither scrach or wear it out. Lastly, a decoction of this leaf will cleance and heall all foule and rotten veneriall ulcers on any part of the body, alltho they have foul'd or parfirated the bone. It creats fleash and dries up any runing or old sore to admiration.

Sabina Jamaicae;[233] the Jamaica savian or flower tree, is a verey green and butiful shrubb. It hath a longe branching leafe like eive, or savian, and is at all times full of flowers which grow mixt with yallow, blew and red veins and much like an emerin,* haveing within it severall large blades like blades of saffron; these flowers grow in clusters (437) together. It yeilds its fruite in a slendor long codd* like to calavanca[234] which is a small flatt seed. Finally, the barke, leaves, seeds, and flowers of this tree have many rare phisicall vertues which are fully discribed in their due places. This is a shrubb of noe considerable growth, but of exelent shade and butie, being allways green and full of flowers, and is of a quick growth, and is therfore here planted for walks, arbours and banquetting houses, for 'tis a verey butifull shrubb.

The cocar plumbtree is a shrubb found on Jamaica in ye low sandy grounds nigh the seashore, as at the salt ponds by the hill,[235] and without the Palasadas up towards Yallowes etc. This is a low busshy shrubb, somewhat like our Europian hazell,* both in growth, bark and leaf, which is like the same, only thicker and smoth. It produces plenty of fruite growing together in large clusters.[236]

232. In Taylor's day, "Castile soap" had come from Castile in Spain. *OED.*

233. Perhaps the "Indian savin tree". Sloane, *Voyage,* 2: 50.

234. A word probably derived from the Spanish *garbanzo,* see n. 330 below.

235. These salt ponds were probably located in what is now Hellshire Hills.

236. This is the coco-plum, known in the Bahamas as the bay-plum. Allsopp, *DCE,* 162. According to Browne, it "is very common both in St Elizabeth and in Portland". *Civil and Natural History,* 250.

The maingrove is a shrubb growing in swampy places or in the shoal'd water of the sea. This shrubb is about the size of a hazell, and groweth mighty thick. It hath a smoth thick leafe which is allways green. It produces neither fruit nor seed, but increaseth by its slendor twiggs which when grown up to a certain height, turn their heads downward and grow into the earth, take root, and sprout up again, and soe overruns much ground. The bark herof is used by tanners and commonly on the root grow aboundance of oysters.[237]

The fingrigo is a thick bushy shrub growing in the woods.[238] It bears a long smoth leaf, and is allways green. 'Tis sharp and prickly like a thorn and growes in slendor twigs which take root and grow like the maingrove, growing soe thick that a bird can scarsely fly thro' 'em, and yeild a hard fruit called cockstones.[239]

(440) [438, 439 left out of Taylor's pagination] The raccoon withh is a shrubb here found.[240] This groweth up against ye sides of great trees like woodbind,* and soe runeth up to the very top, and then turn its head downwards to the earth, and taketh root and sprouteth up again, and soe continueth increasing until it hath overgrown and covered the tree. It is small and straight, seldom biger than a man's thumb. 'Tis exceeding tuff and used as withy to bind railles, poles, used in thatching etc. It bears a long thinn leaf and its fruit or seed is the raccoon nut.

The pudding withh is a shrubb growing in all respects like the former about the bodys of trees, and is employed and used for the aforesaid purposes.[241] It yeild a long nutt twice as bigg as a hen's egg, soft and spungious, full of seeds like to the nutt or fruit of the calibash.

The dildo is a shrubb which groweth up of a considerable hight in a small time, which hath neither leaves nor branches, but sprouteth up into some strait spraies which are covered with a thinn green bark and besett all round with long sharp slendore prickles.[242] This shrubb is verey soft like a colwort stalk,[243] but at the ground its prickles are fallen off, and it hath a bark like granadilla, and these semeth to be very hard wood. It putteth forth a larg yallow blosom or flower resembling the single lilley, and produceth a fruitt as big as a hen's egg. Now for the finall satisfaction of the curious, I 'ave potraied this shrubb to ye life [figure 36].

---

237. For the bark, see p. 227; on the oysters, see Sloane, *Voyage*, 2: 64–66.

238. The fingrigo was "a prickly climbing shrub". *OED.*

239. A cockstone is now a large variety of kidney-bean. Cassidy and Le Page, *DJE*, 112.

240. This is probably Sloane's "Prickly-With". *Voyage*, 2: 155–56; it may be one of the *cereus* species (Sidrak), and the word is more commonly "with" in English. *OED.*

241. The pudding-with is still common in Jamaica. Cassidy and Le Page, *DJE*, 365.

242. The dildo is in fact a type of cactus. Allsopp, *DCE*, 192.

243. A cabbage stalk.

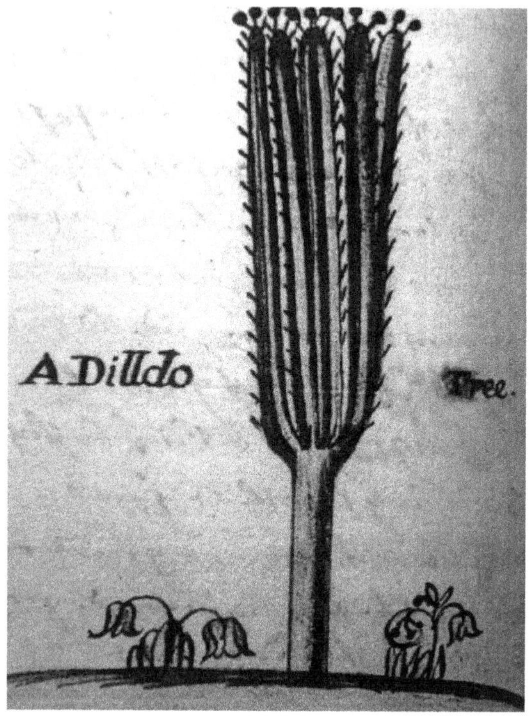

Figure 36 Taylor's drawing of "a dilldo", page 440.

(441) The shrubb wheron the pineapple groweth is a shrubb growing about a yard high from the ground, haveing a stalk like an Europian artichoak,* with long thick leaves, the edges wherof are verey prickley. On this stalke groweth ye pineapple on the top of which apple growes a tuff of leaves like a crown or coronett. They yeild one apple a yeare according to their seasons, for they are planted thus; they prepare ground for 'em, and after the seasonable raines, they pull off the tuff of leaves which grow on the apple and plants 'em, and in nine monthes' time it will produce fruite, which when they gather, they cut off the stalk within two inches of the ground, which will again the next yeare produce fruit, and soe for five or six years according to the goodness of the soyle will it live and bear fruite, and when decayed in their rowes, they plant more and hav of 'em ripe all the year round.[244]

The shrubb on which the prickle pear groweth is a low bushie shrubb groweing cheifly in hott drie sandy ground.[245] It runns out into interwoven branches, bearing a broad square thick leaf all besett with sharp prickles, and produces a yallow flower, from whence proceeds his fruite. These trees grow all most everywhere unreguarded.

The plantann tree is a shrubb of great advantage to the industrious planter, soe that the first thing a new setler plants is a good plantann walk, which in the second yeare will bear fruite. Now the plantann tree growes up commonly some 10 or 12 feet high, with long soft thin leaves (somewhat like the palmeto tree) from the ground and soe formeth this shrub (442) which is sofft and spungious, and in noe waies inclining to lignummetique[246] substance. The pith or inward part of this tree boyled either in wine or watter is of excellent use in phisicks. It bears its fruite in large clusters nigh the top which it hath allways (unless in verey unseasonable years) both green and ripe, great and small, comeing in season one after another. They are planted from younge branches which is slipt off from them.

244. See also Sloane: "The Tuft [is] planted in any hot Soil, and seldom misses to prosper." *Voyage,* 1: 191.

245. The prickly pear is a cactus-like plant. *OED.*

246. This exuberant word for woody (also appearing as "lignumesque") seems peculiar to Taylor.

The boonana tree is a shrubb in all respects like the plantann, only not soe large either in growth or fruite.[247] They are also planted in the same manner, and yeild their fruite. The inward part or pith made into a pectorall* decoction cueres all obstructions of the splene.

The cataputia or phisick nutt tree is a shrubb of a tall slendor growth, growing much like a hazell, and beareth a leaf broad and like the sicamore, and yeild abundance of fruite called by the Latinis *Cataputia majoris;*[248] by the Creolians called phisick nutts, and by us in England the greater spurge seed, which it yeild in its seasons. Of this shrubb they make their cheif hedges and fences about their plantations.

The sage tree is a shrubb seldom above a yard high, with a small green ruff leaf which smells like sage and tastes [like it].[249] It bears clusters of yallow flowers, somwhat like cammomill, smelleth also like sage, and indeed is excellent to discurss hard tumors etc., and it hath all the vertues of our Europian sage, soe that of it the monkish proverbe holds true, which is *tritum cur moritur homo, cum salvia crescit in horto*?[250] This sage tree yeilds a small round seed.

(443) The bell pepper tree is a small shrubb which is planted in hedges in some plantations as wee doe box in England.[251] 'Tis of a soft lignummetique substance, hath a smoth barke with a long thin smoth leaf, and twice a yeare yeilds its fruite in great plenty.

The mallagata tree is a shrubb of groath and leafe like the former. The differences consisteth only in the fruite, which is not of that size, nor shape.[252]

The bird peeper is a shrub of a lesser stalk, but also in growth and leaf like the former, growing everywhere wild in the savanas, woods and mountains, and yeilds plenty of fruit on which the birds feed.

The Jamaica cinnamon tree is a shrub of a midle growth, seldom bigger than the small of a man's legg, haveing a thick bark which is a verey strong cinamon, both in taste and smell, and proves a good commodity in England

---

247. In Taylor's day, it would seem that the plantain was more highly prized than the banana.

248. The medieval term *cataputia* was the lesser spurge (*OED*), but this is not the same as the physic nut (Sidrak). Sloane also describes how this bush is used "for Hedges at all times". *Voyage*, 1: 128–29.

249. This is probably the Caribbean sage-bush. Sloane places great emphasis on its therapeutic qualities. *Voyage*, 2: 81–84.

250. This phrase, in praise of the healing qualities of sage, comes from the medieval *Regimen sanitatis Salerni.*

251. Sloane notes that "it is the most commonly used of any of the Capsicums, and used extremely by Indians and Blacks". *Voyage*, 1: 241.

252. This is probably the malaguetta bush, whose seeds are used in spices and in medicine. *OED.*

for distillers and others. It bears a broad leaf and yeild a small seed. This shrub in three years' time receives its bark againe, and is fitt to stripp for sale.

The sugar cane is a shrubb which groweth with a blade or leaf like a flagg,[253] some six foot high. The cane is softt and solid, growing in short joynts towards the ground, and larger upwards, fill'd with a meleficious* juice, which produceth sugare, but yeilds neither flower, fruite, or seed. This is indeed the most emminent thing of profit on ye whole island. The leaves of this cane serves to feed their cattell, and thatch their cottages or Negro wigwams.[254]

(444) The wild cane is a shrubb which groweth in freash water rivers. The leaves of these are much like the former, but narrower. They are soft and solid and grow high with large joynts. Some of those canes are forty or fifty foot long and on their top runs up a bolt with a brushy top like sedg. These are used instead of laths, and to build the sides of their Negro wigwams, and other hutts withall.[255] Thus we have discribed all the known shrubs, both fruite-bearers and others found on this uberous island of Jamaica.

Section IX

Of hearbs found on Jamaica as Europian hearbs, occara, viva, semper-vivum, agnus-castor, indigo, tobacco, maize, guinea corn, crocus metalorum, collaloa, catapilla, scotgrass, Jamaican cinquefole, and common grass.

This island afords not only many rare excelent hearbes such as we have in Europe, but also many others which those parts of Europe never saw, nor enjoyed, the which hath many rare phisicall vertues appropriated to 'em. For 'tis certain that the great Creator left nothing of his works uncapatiated* to perform his commands, according to the testimony of the heathen sages whoe declare that *Deus et natura nihil fecit frustra.*[256]

(445) On this Island are found plenty of those following English hearbs, (viz.) rosemary, sage, sorrel, rue, thyme, mint, marjoram, hysope, cammomill, wormwood, vervain, wood sorrell, parsly, lentills, spinage, watercreasces, sparagus,* collwarts, cabadg, sampire, and purslain (which growes everywhere in great plenty in the savanas, woods and mountains),

253. Taylor here uses the word "flag" in its archaic sense, to mean the prominent blade of a plant. *OED.*

254. Taylor here uses a word recently derived from the Algonquins of North America. *OED.*

255. Sloane puts it slightly differently: "The Cane-split is made use of for laths, and to make up the walls or sides of Houses with Mortar." *Voyage,* 1: 109.

256. "God and Nature do nothing in vain", a favourite idea of Taylor.

all which hearbs are full as good, if not better than those of the like kind found in England, and are here found in all sesonable times in there plantations.[257] These are all the Europian hearbs which I could ever find on Jamaica, but they enjoy many rare hearbs of their own, such which England never enjoyed, as first:

Occara is an hearb growing up with a long stalk, and in many branches, haveing a thick broad wolly leaf, much like *herba fussilaginis,* and yeilds its seed in a large apple.[258] This in my opinion is the king of hearbs which I ever saw. 'Tis a most excellent sallad, and boyled, 'tis a most powerfull restorer of the decays of nature. It powerfull restores the consumption of the lungs, fortifieth the stomack, cleanseth the blood from all malignant salt and vitious humors, and causeth a due circulation therof. It creates plenty of seed and maketh the barren woman to conceive, and is an herb not to be paralleled for its vertues in the whole universe. Of the tender budds of this hearb the Spaniards in America make a most excellent chocolata of which they'll not by noe means suffer their women to tast, 'tis of such power to propigat strenght and enable 'em to walke in ye nocturnall labours of Venus.

(446) Viva is an hearb here found in some plantations, and carefully preserved as a great curiosity.[259] This is a tendor plant of a small growth haveing a long thick leave, set with barbs, the interior part of which is concave, and the exterior convex. It yeild a small whit flower and a small round seed which hath many wonderfull properties (see page the [blank, but in fact 474]) known to admiration. This hearb is a choice peice of natur's workes, for 'tis soe strangely sencible that being in the least but touched by the hand of man, 'twill shutt up cloce together, and never open untill the toucher is out of sight, and then 'twill open again. Also if

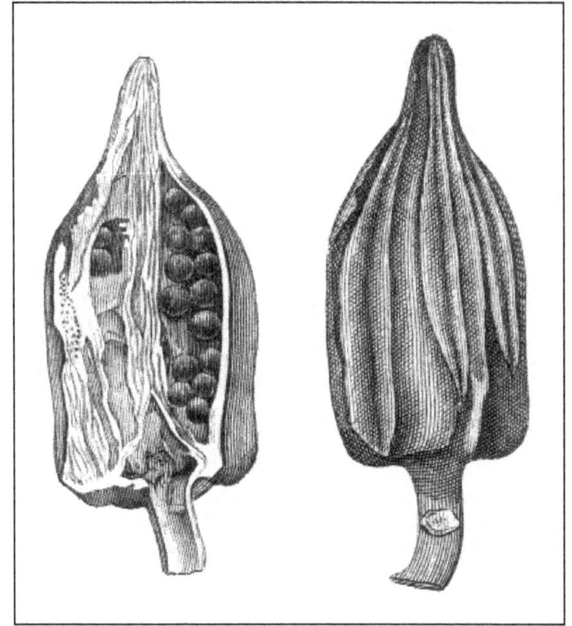

Figure 37 Engraving of an okra pod, from Sloane, *Voyage.*

257. Many of these plants are also enumerated by Sloane as being found in the Liguanea garden of Captain Harrison, "the best furnished of any in the Island with European Garden Plants". *Voyage,* 1: lxxiv. "Samphire" was a shore-growing plant often served as a pickle, and "purslane" is a low succulent herb, used in salads. *OED.*

258. Sloane identifies two types of okra, mentioning that "they are both very carefully planted by Europeans, as well as slaves in their gardens". *Voyage,* 1: 223; see figure 37.

259. Taylor here speaks of the sensitive plants, of which Browne identifies six, belonging to the mimosa family. *Civil and Natural History,* 253–54.

this plant be put into the hands of the sick, and they look merrey, 'tis a certain signe of their recovery; but if they look sadd 'tis an infallible token that their life is allmost at a periode, and that then they'll certainly die. This plant is also found on Peru in America; see our *Thesaurarium Mathematice,* page 177.[260]

Semper-vivum is an hearb of a long thick leaf, smoth and full of sap like houseleek.[261] The leaf is about a foot long, convex in the exterior side and concave in the interior side, and about the edges prickly. This hearb is cold and moist in 3° and full of strong thick oylie sapp, most excellent in burns or scalds to draw forth the inflamation, cold and heal the same. This hearb being taken carefully up out of the earth, and its rote cloce rap't up in a piece of scarlett wollen cloth kept moist with olive oyle may be caryed home to England, and being hanged up in a drie warm room may be preserved for many years, for 'twill sprout forth new leaves to grow and continue in its florishing verdure.

(447) Agnus castor groweth here in great aboundance and is much better than that in Europe.[262] It hath a broad thick leaf full of an oyli juice, [and] hath many rare and choice phisicall vertues. The Creolians boyle out from this hearb much oyle which they burn in their lampps. It beareth a small brown seed whose vertue is shown in page the [blank, but in fact p. 477]

Indigo is an hearb yeilding aboundant profit to the industrious and painfull planter. It growth up about half a yard high on a slender stalk full of branches haveing a small long thick leaf having a dark green colour and bearth a small round seed like corriander seed which is hott in 2 and moist in 3 of which we shall say more when we described the manner of the planting of indigo (see page the 425). There is also a wild sort of indigo not soe large growing in ye fields but is not regarded although tis saied that good indigo hath binn made often therewith.

Tobacco trives here verey well, and proveth a good sorte of tobacco, tho' somewhat hotter and stronger than Verginia tobacco; but because indigo and sugare proves a more profittable and certain commodity, therfore they bestow but litle pains herein, neither doe they plant but enough to serve the island, which they spinn upp in ropes like malch,* and then make it up in rowles of 25 li/weight, and commonly sell it two pounds for a royall or

260. There is nothing to be found in his *Thesaurarium* on this subject.

261. Taylor's "semper-vivum", now known as the sempervive, is a form of aloe (Allsopp, *DCE,* 498), much recommended by Browne for its medicinal uses (*Civil and Natural History,* 199–200). "Houseleek" is a succulent herb, *sempervivum tectorum.*

262. Probably the castor-oil plant. Allsopp, *DCE,* 140. This is also probably Browne's "oil-nut tree", which produced an oil used in lamps. *Civil and Natural History,* 350.

bitt.*[263] This hearb bears a verey small seed. Of the green leaves of tobacco the Creolians make an oyntment by boyling 'em in the oyle of *agnus castor,* wherewith they cure the maung and yaua sores on their Negroe slaves.

(448) Maize grows up with a blade like a flagg, and a stalk some 8 or 10 foot high. It blooms like sedg, and the cod or hose[264] in which the ear is comes forth by the side. Its eare is commonly eight or teen inches long, in which sometimes is 500 grains; and sometimes two or three such ears on a stalk. 'Tis a great increaser. I have heard a planter of good worth affirm that from three busshils of maize which he planted, he received 860 busshills increass at harvest. This maize grows to perfection and yeilds its seed in three months' time in seasonable weather, which standeth the planter in good steed in the maintainance of his Negroa slaves, horses, hogs and fowles, and is the principall food of ye Indians.[265]

Guinea corn[266] is an hearb growing with a long blade like wheat, but much broader and grosser, growing upp some fouer or five foot high, and in three months time produces its seed which is much like hemp seed, haveing a thinn husk and eating like French barly; but 'tis planted cheifly for their stable horses, soe that when 'tis grown up to a considerable hight they feed 'em there with and it will spring again and hold in the ground fouer or five yeares without planting, and distroy all other weeds which growe under it, and is of good profitt.

Crocus mettalorum[267] is and hearb found here of the same groth of that of the like speties found in Europe, tho' farr stronger and better haveing all the vertues of the former tho' in a stronger and fuller measure.

(449) The collaloa is a wild hearb,[268] grows here in most places in great aboundance, haveing a long thinn smoth leafe, and groweth up in branches. This hearb boyled by itself, or with potatoa leaves with salt beef or pork, eateth much better than colworts. 'Tis an excelent pot herb, being hott in 3° and moist in 2° and is a great refinner of the whole mass of blood.

Catapilla or caterpillar[269] is an hearb here found groweing up like maidenhair* in branchs, with red stalk, and a long thin smoth leaf, and yeild

263. Sloane shares Taylor's view that tobacco was not very carefully cultivated, adding that the island had been famous for the crop in the time of the Spaniards. *Voyage,* 1: lxii.

264. This is an archaic term for the sheath containing a kernel of maize. *OED.*

265. It is still called "Indian corn" in England.

266. A small-grained corn sometimes known as millet. Allsopp, *DCE,* 273.

267. This sounds like a reference to *crocus martis,* a red agent used in polishing metals. *OED.*

268. Calalu, with many variant spellings, is the name given to several edible greens. Cassidy and Le Page, *DJE,* 89.

269. Sloane does not distinguish between "culilu" and "caterpillars", both of which, he claims, "eat as Spinage, etc., for the same purposes". *Voyage,* 1: 143.

its seed in a kind of ear like our English plantaine.[270] The young tender top stalk of this hearb being boyled eats full as good, and tast just like sparagus, but being boyled both stalk and leaf together with salmone it proves an excellen pott hearb and a great refiner of ye blood. This hearb, collalo, purslain and potata leaves are the cheife pott herebs used to boyle with salt meats all 'ore this island of Jamaica.

Scotgrass[271] groweth up with a long spiery blade like sedg and is planted cheifly in wett swampy places and will hold in the ground for many years. This they plant cheifly to feed their horsses withall being of considerable profitts, for in the inns, taverns etc, they sell but a small bundle therof for a royall.

In the savanas and woods is a common sort of spierie rough grass nothing soe sweet as our common grass in England. Also there grows aboundance of a fine-leaves hearb or Jamaican cinquefoile,[272] which grows more higher and grosser than our Europian cinquefoile. This is not spotted with milky spotts. This is a bitter grass and the cattell will scarsly eate itt, but feed on the other rough grass which growes in the savanas (450), as also this fine-leaved herb, for after the raines those savanas are cloath herewith in their verdid liverly like our Europian medows wher the cattell feed and becom fatt. Thus we have given you a full account of all the hearbs as yett known on the island of Jamaica.

Section X

Of Jamaican fruites: as the pinnaple, coconutt, Chinna orang, Sivill orang, lemmon, lime, custard-aple, mama-saporta, pomgranat, figgs, pomcitteron, nauesberry, cushoa, plantann, boonana, grappes, water-mellon, musk-mellon, sapadilla, guava, alagator-pear, sower-sopp, tamarin, paupa, cassia-fistulla, mullberrry, prickle pear, cocarnutt, cocarplumb, pompion, cowcumber, wild-cowcumber, gouards, Spanish-plumb, hogplumb, manchanilla-aple, dilldo, callabash, wild grapes, racconenutt, puding-nutt, occaraple, and Jamaican cherries and lastly the cottonaple.[273]

To proceed in order to our discourse, we now come to give an account of the many rare and excelent fruites which this uberous island afordes in great

270. The English plantain was a low herb with broad flat leaves. *OED.*

271. This plant is said to have come from Scotland, in Barbados.

272. The cinquefoil is a plant with compound leaves each of five leaflets. *OED.*

273. This section on fruits overlaps to some extent with the previous ones on trees and on shrubs.

plenty, of their own naturall growth, being such which the lady Europia never enjoyed (451), neither for the delicacie of tast or collor. And these fruites are found here ripe (for the most part) all the year round, to adorn the tables and satisfie the appitite of the curious and are in order thus:

Here we first find the pinnaple which is justlie accounted all 'ore the world to be the king of all fruites yet known.[274] This is a large fruit about the bigness of a man's head, haveing a rugged outward bark growing chequerwis like the fruit of the pinntree in which chequers are sharp pricklers. This fruite is shap't and formed like the hayball,[275] on the top wherof growes a tuff of leaves like a corronet, and this fruite I have here potraied to the life [figure lacking]. Now the outward bark when thro ripe looks yallow, and when pared away, you come to a most delicat sweet fruitt filled with meleficious juce, which taste far more dillitious than sweet wine or any other thing which tast is capable to enjoy. This fruite is hott in 2° and moist in 3°, good in obstructions of the mesentery* etc.,[276] and being rosted and putt (452) into a tankard of good Madera wine makes liquor soe meleficious that ther's none equall to it.

The coconutt[277] is a most rare and choice fruite, in much estem'd by the Spaniards and others, espetiall those which inhabit those western parts of the world. This princley nutt is small and long with a verey thin shell and grow some ten or more in a cluster (as you see in ye figure) [lacking]. The curnall* whereof is of a very fatt and oylie substance tho' when green is of noe plesant tast, but when made into chocolata is of excelent nutriment and estemed and used by the greatest princes in the world. This nut is a rich and certain commodity, worth this present year 1688 fifteen pounds sterling for 100 weight here at Jamaica and vendable to all parts. Also the Creolians useth much thereof themselves, and the residue is transported to other parts.

Now the manner of makeing chocolata is thus; they take the coconut and parch 'em, then strip off the shell and beat the curnall to a thick fatt oyly past in a marble mortar (for 'tis soe fatt that by long beating 'twill all turn to oyle) and then rowle it up in balls and drie it in the sun. Then when drie, they grate it verey fine and with sugar, cinnamon, cloves and mace[278] they mix it and wett it with rume and make it up in cakes (453) or roules which they sell at a dollar a pound at Jamaica, and also at London the best chocolata is solcd at a crown a pound. Now 100 weight of the nutt will make 160 pound

---

274. Sloane does not fall in with Taylor's enthusiasm, writing that pineapples "are too sower, setting the Teeth on edge very speedily". *Voyage*, 1: 91.

275. Perhaps Taylor means a "haycock", with its conical shape.

276. The mesentery is the intestine.

277. This is the cocoa pod.

278. Mace is a spice consisting of the dried outer coating of the nutmeg.

of chocolata, the manner of whose ordering into liquor is soe commonly known that it needs not any discription. This chocolata is of excelent nutriment, and a powerfull restorative in consumptions, and is every morning drunck by the laborious planter and letcherous Creoliann Amazons. In the taverns on Port Royall you shall have about half a pint therof for a royall.

The Chinna and Sivill oranges grow here verey large and in great plenty, haveing a curious thinn cortex and are in all respect such from Spain and Portugall to England.[279] They are very cheap here.

Lemons of a verey large size both sweet and sower are found here att all times very plentyfully, and are every way such as are daily sold in England.[280]

The lime is a small hedg lemmon found everywher here in multitudes, the woods and hedges being loaden with 'em all the yeare. They are only estemed for their juice which serves 'em to help make punch withall. This juice is a good commodity, soe that many tuns therof is transported from hence yearly home to England. 'Tis worth here about a royall of plate a gallon, to try the goodness of which you must take 3/4 part of a wine glass therof and into it put as much sand as will fill up ye glass. Now if it be true juice, 'twill presently boyle and clen purge forth the sand (454) out of the glass and not leave the least mole* therof therin, which if it doe, you may be suer 'tis the puer juice of the lime, but if in the least it be adultarized with water, then will the sand stick to the bottom, and there remaine. This is a choice arcanum known but to a few tho 'tis indeed an infallible way of triall.

The custard aple which is by some called the sugarsopp[281] is a large fruite, groweing with a rugged bark, in the outside of a greenish yallow and in the inside of a purple collour, and being rip is a verey swett and delitious fruite, composed of a soft substance which eats much like a curious-made custard (from whence it receives its name) and is a fruite much estemed. 'Tis cold in two degrees, and drie in one, good in fevers and obstructions of the lunges, and is in all respects such as you see here in the figure therof [lacking].

The mama saporta[282] is a larg fruit haveing a brownish barke, and consisteth of a most excellent melefitious soft substance of great estem in America both by the Spaniards and English, being a great restorative in consumptions and the defect of the liver. It hath in't a large smoth brown

279. Sloane mentions that some oranges came from the province of Canton in China. *Voyage,* 2: 181. Taylor curiously uses the modern term for "Seville (sour) oranges".

280. Sloane mentions, apparently precociously, the use of lemons and limes in preventing scurvy. Ibid., 178–79.

281. Sloane distinguishes between the custard-apple tree and the "sweet-sop-tree". Ibid., 167–68.

282. Sloane confirms this distinction between the mammee-apple and the mamme-sapota. Ibid., 123–24.

stone, full as bigg as a pidgeon's egg, which pulveriz'd (455) is a most powerful diuretique, see the figure of this fruite [lacking].

The mama or mamme is a fruit of the same groweth, shape, coloure, size and tast with the mama saportta. The difference is only that wheras the saporta hath one stone, this fruit hath three stones of the shape and collour of the former, but of a far lesser size, tho' their vertues are the same.

The pomgranatt is here found plentyfully in some plantations, tho' 'tis not soe common a fruit as the others before mentioned. This fruit groweth here of a verey large size, being full as good as any which growe in a dry part of East India, Italy, Spain, Portugall or France, and are such in shape and growth which are daily soald in England, tho' much more delitious. They have all the vertues of 'em also, and are here much estemed. See the figure therof [lacking].

The figgs which grow here are a verey larg, choice, and delitious fruite, fare larger and better than any which grow either in Spain, France or England. They have all ye vertues of the Europian figg. Here is also found a willd figg in the woods of the same shape, small and blew, but nothing comparable to the former, nor are they estemed.[283]

The pomcitteron is here found in most plantations, of a very large growth, every way such which are sold in England.

(456) The nausberry is a most rare and excellent fruite and are of the choicest found in the West Indies. This fruit is of a considerable growth, full as bigg as a man's fist, and shap't like a rasberry, being of a crimson or purpleish collour, verey full of a meleficious juice, and a most rare flavoured fruit of good esteme. This fruit is most excelent in fevers, and to allaie the heat of the liver, or palpatation of the hart. This fruitt I have hereon the sprigg potraied to ye life [figure lacking].

The cushoa is an excellent fruite in growth resembling a katharin pear, covered with a thinn cleare skinn, on the one side red, and on the other of a bright sky collour. This is a verey juci fruite of much esteme, and not without true desert, on the top of which growes its seed, which is as big as a bean and in the forme of a kidney, haveing a thick oylie blewish husk, and a curnall verey sweet and good.[284] This fruit is a great antisorbutique[285] and (457) refinner of the blood from all salt and vitious humorrs. As for the vertues of the seed, or stone, see page the 4 [in fact, p. 476].

The plantann is a sort of an excellent fruite, growing twenty or more in a cluster. They are about a foot long, and as bigg as a man's wrist, and are three-

283. Sloane also mentions these two types of fig. Ibid., 138–40.

284. A good description of the cashew nut.

285. It is curious that Taylor notes the anti-scurvy properties of the cashew nut, but not of the citrus fruits.

square somwhat enclineing to roundness, and are curved, and when ripe they looke yallow. 'Tis a sweet drie fruite and are often boyled with salt meats, but they are badd in the wind, collick being very windy. This fruite I have potraied from the originall [figure lacking].

The boonania is a sort of a rare fruite, and groweth in clusturs like the plantann, and is of the same shape and culler in the outside when ripe, but this fruit when mellow is of a redish collure,[286] full of juce, soft and of a most plesant tast. Of this fruit is made a better marmalad or concerve than of quinces. Also of the juce of this fruit is made an excellent wine, very plesant and good for presant drinckeing, being good to ally heat and cold the liver. This fruit growes not above half soe long as the plantann.

The grapes here found is an excellent larg red muscadin grape which would thrive well here, and if improved would make plenty of excellent wine.

(458) The wattermellon is a royall fruite found here in great plenty,[287] of both sorts of the redd and white, fare better than those found either in Spain or Italy, and are here to be had rip all the year rounde. This is one of the gourd, growing on a midle growth'd running shrubb or ground vine like our Europian musk mellons. This fruite when ripe looks verey green in the outsid, and are covered with a soft thinn bark, and the inside is compos'd of a white melleficious juice substance, and the juce of ye whit wattermellon is cleare like watter and sweet like wine, and the red watermellon is fill'd with melleficious redish juce like clarret wine. Both these sorts of watter mellons are full of a small black seed. They are used in phisick, and are one of the foure greater colding seeds used in fevers, emultions etc. These mellons are thro'out solid and not in the least cavious in the inside as muskmellons or pompions are.[288] They are of a large size, seldom less than a man's head, and are commonly sold at Port Royall for a royall apeice, and are a fruite generally served up at dinner which wee have here potraied to the life [figure lacking].

(459) The musk-mellon is a fruit found here in great plenty and are in all respects such which are found in England, only they are much better and sweeter and quadruple as large, being as bigg as our English pompions. There seeds are good in cold emultions, being one of the greater colding seeds.

The capadilla is here found tho' not verey plenty. This is a fruite about the bigness of a hen's egg, every waie shap't like a date, and being ripe lokes of a gold collour, is covered with a thinn skin. Ye fruit concisteth of a soft

286. The fruit of the banana is indeed sometimes reddish.

287. Browne concurs that this fruit "is frequently cultivated in the gardens of Jamaica". *Civil and Natural History*, 354.

288. The term "pompion" was used in the seventeenth century for a kind of pumpkin.

mellefitious substance, verey gratefull to the pallat, and in't it hath a longe stone like the date. This fruit is a verey excellent fruitt of great esteem, and hath all the vertues of the date with many more. This fruite on the sprigg we have here potraie to the life for ye satisfaction of ye curious [figure lacking].

The guava is a fruit found here everywhere in ye plantations, woods and mountains in great aboundance. This fruit when they are young and green are shap't like a fig, but very hard, but when they are ripe, they are of a gold collour, covered with a thick cortex which being pared off, the fruit appears of a fleashy reed, is a very good swett fruit, being filled with small stones like ye pomgranat (460). This fruit is hott and drie in 3°, a great restringent,* and the green fruitt eaten will stopp fluxes, when all other means prove uneffetuall.[289] This fruit on the sprigg, we have here potraied from the originall to the life [figure lacking].

The alagator pear is of a large growth of a dark colour, haveing in't a large stone like the mama saporta. 'Tis a jucie fruite, firme and solid, about the bigness of a penny loaf, and is counted an excellent frute, a great restorative in consumptions, and increaser of seed and lust, soe that the Spaniards will not suffer their wives to eat thereof, least it should propigat their lust beyound their satisfaction. 'Tis hott and moist in 3° and is eaten by the English with salt, peper and ye juice of a lemmon.[290] This fruite on the sprigg we have here potraied to the life from the originally fruite itself [figure lacking].

The sowersopp is a large and excellent fruite, of a green rugged bark when ripe, and is of whit soft substance (461), and is of a currious sharp tast, being cold in 3° and moist in 2°, and is an excellent colder in feavers, good in ptisicks, obstructions of the liver and spleen. This fruite we have here on the sprig potraied to the life [figure lacking].

The tamarind is here also found very plentyfully which is a fruitt of great esteem and use in phisick. This fruite is a small, green, flat fruite, in which is a large stone. These grow many together in a cluster; of the pulp of this fruitt is made many sort of excellent concerves good to allay heat in fevers etc.[291] This fruit on ye sprigg we have here potraied [figure lacking].

The paupa is a large fruit, about the size of a large English cowcumber, not round but on squares, covered with a smoth green thinn skinn, and in the inside cavious and full of seeds. This fruite is seldom eaten raw, but is commonly boyled with salt beef or porke and eates excellent sweet and good, being of holsome nutriment, and a generall refinner of the whole mass of

289. As Sloane puts it, "They have only this Inconvenience, that being very adstringent, they stop up the Belly if eaten in great quantity." *Voyage,* 2: 161.

290. This "alagator pear" is the now widely eaten avocado pear.

291. Sloane also mentions this use. *Voyage,* 2: 45–46.

blood.[292] This fruit on the sprigg we have potraied on the next page [figure lacking].

(462) The cassia-fistulla is a fruitt also here found, growing verey good, and is here more fulle of pulp and longer than that brought from East India to England and hath all the same vertues.[293] This fruite growes ten or more canes in a clustur, and it being a thing soe well known by all drugist and apothecaries, I shall here say no more therof. This fruit is not here as yet much regarded, neither is it made a vendable commodity, alltho' if 'twere planted and look't after 'twould turn to good profitt and prove as good as that brought from East India. This fruit on ye sprigg we have potraied from ye originall [figure lacking].

The mulberry found on this island is alltogether such as we have in England, both for tast and collour, only somwhat larger. It hath the same vertues but more powerfull.

(463) The pricklepear is a wild fruite found here, and tho' good yett (because of its commones*) of little esteme, as our brambleberrys* are in England. This is a fruit when ripe 'tis covered with a cleared thinn red skin, but when green 'tis all prickly. This fruite is of the make and size of the katharin pear fil'd with a plesant thick juice of a deep crimson collour, and the fruit consist of a soft substance of the same coulour, intermixt with small stones. This fruit is a great restringent, and were it improved by art, 'twould be of excellent use in phisick, for 'tis s hott in 2°, and drie in 3°. Of the pulp of this fruit might be made an excellent ellectuary,[294] and of the juce maybe made a most powerfull astringent syrup, good in all fluxes of the belly. This fruit on the sprigg we have here potraied [figure lacking] and you must also be carefull that you eat not many of 'em, for they'll bind up the body, and makes yor urinn as reed as blood.

(464) The cocarnutt is a verey large nutt, growing in clusturs (as you see in page the 429th) [figure 35]. This is the biggest nutt found in anie part of America, for the shell therof will hold a quart or more. It hath a very thick sheall or husk about itt of a hemppy substance, of which is made ropes, etc. This husk when the nutt's ripe openeth like the wallnut, and then the nutt appears with a thick hardish black shell, on the top of which is three soft pitts or eyes thro' which the blade sprouts. This nutt contains within it a curnall about half an inch thick, all round within ye shell; cavious, as the whit of the egg involves* the yolke.

292. Sloane also treats the paw-paw as a vegetable, used before it is ripe, boiled like turnips or baked like apples. He adds that it can be eaten ripe, "'tho in my opinion it is not a very pleasant Fruit". Ibid., 164–65.

293. Sloane indeed calls it "The ordinary Purging Cassia". Ibid., 42–43.

294. An electuary was a medicine consisting of a powder mixed with some syrup. *OED.*

This curnall is sweett as the almond, but bad in phisick. Being candied 'tis a good drie sweet meat. Now, within the cavitie of this curnall, the whole nut is fill'd with a wheayish-colloured* liquor, a verey sweet and plesant drinck, tasting like sweet clarified whey, and is an excellent cold drinck either simplely, or mixt with good Madera wine, and is a powerfull duretuque to cleans the adines and blader. Of these nutts' shells are made in England and elsewhere curious bowles and drincking cupps of much esteem.[295]

The cocar plumb is a verey delitious juicie fruit, about the bigness of an egg and shap't like our Europian violet plumbs. They are of two sorts, some reed, and others white, but both of one growth and size, haveing in 'em a verey large stone.[296] They are hott in two, or drie in three degrees, a powerfull restringent in fluxes, and are here on the sprige potraied from the originall in the next follio [figure lacking].

(465) The pompion growes here every way such as is found in England, only these are farr larger and sweeter. They are not soe yallow butt of a redish colloure, and knoblie. They are planted in the plantations, and stands the planter in good steed in the maintenance of his Negroa slaves etc. Also beside those planted, there are a greatt many which grow of themselves wild in the woods, and by the sides of some rivers on Jamaica.

Figure 38 A sixteenth-century loving-cup (by courtesy of the Master and Fellows, Corpus Christi College, Cambridge, England). In early modern Europe, coconut shells were often used to make cups, sometimes supported by precious metals, as in this case.

Here we also finde in great aboundance the garden cowcumber,[297] every way such as is found in England, butt larger and better being not of soe cold a quallity. They are here to be had ripe all the year round.

On this island in the woods and elsewhere are found aboundance of a small wild cowcumber[298] of a poysonous nature by being cold in the highest degree. These grow like ye former, only they are rough and prickley.

The gouards is a fruit common in most of the southern parts of Europe,

295. Including the loving-cup shown as figure 38.

296. Browne also notes that some fruit were white and others red. *Civil and Natural History*, 250.

297. Writing of the cucumber, the *OED* observes that it was sometimes known as a "cowcumber" in illiterate speech.

298. Browne notes the presence of these two types of cucumber. *Civil and Natural History*, 353.

and is also found here growing verey large with a thick smothe brown shell, some of which will hold six or eight gallons, and are much used by the Negros and native Indians as vessell for their rumm, perinno,[299] mobby, rapp etc. Their seed is one of the four greated seeds used in emultions etc. The leaves with hog's lard made into a cataplasm* will supporat and break hard tumores in an easie and speedy manner.

The Spanish plumb is a fruit found here in great aboundance, being as bigg as a English horsplumb, and of a gold collour, being allmost all stone, haveing but a slight substance (466) over it. 'Tis a sweetish plumb, tho' not gratfull to the pallat and is good in fluxs.[300] Here the Creolians have a way to boyle 'em befor they are fully ripe, and then they eat like codlings* made of our small English apples. This fruit with the cocarplumb we here on the sprige potraied to the life from the originall fruite itself [figure lacking].

The hog-plumb is a fruite every way like the former, soe that there is noe difference betwixt 'em,[301] only that this is more sowere, sonner ripe, less regarded and groweth wild in the woods, on which the wild hogs feed and become fatt.

The manchanilla apple is a poysonous fruite, of ye make and size of our small English golden pippen, looks curious yallow, and smelleth well, but is a verey strong poyson, for being eaten it bringeth imediatly on the body inevitable death itself and 'tis observed that noe beast will eat 'em, be they never soe hungrey, as being by the verey instinct of nature instructed to avoide soe eminent a danger which would be incur'd thereby.[302]

The dilldo is a long fruit about the biggness of a hen's (467) egg, haveing a ruff barke. This fruit in the inside concisteth of a white soft substance, swett, and full of small black seeds, and is seldom eaten. This fruite is good in cathars.[303]

The calabash nut found here everywhere both in the savanas, woods and mountains, are of two sorts,[304] (viz.) the sweet calabash and the sower calabash. The sweet calabash is a verey large nutt. Some are round and others ovillar,* haveing a thick smoth shell, some of which will hold three or four

299. Perinno was made from cassava root, and mobby and rapp from potatoes.

300. This fruit is also described by Browne, *Civil and Natural History*, 229.

301. Browne also found it difficult to distinguish between the Spanish plum and the hog-plum. Ibid., 228.

302. This tree contains "a highly poisonous, skin-blistering latex". Allsopp, *DCE*, 367.

303. Sloane distinguished between the greater and lesser dildo-trees, both growing near the sea in sandy places. *Voyage*, 2: 157–58.

304. Browne, too, distinguishes between the large and small "gourds". *Civil and Natural History*, 354.

gallons, and are used by the Negros and Indians as vessels to keep their liquors in. These nuts are full of small seeds, a soft substance and swett juice which made into a catoplasm with hogs' lard discusseth* tumors, and easeth gal pains to admiration. The sower calabash is a nutt of a smaller size, some round and others ovilar, haveing a smoth thin shell, which will seldom hold above a quartt: the nuts are fill'd with a soft substance, small seeds, and a sower juice, the which with oyl of olives made into a cataplasm, doth wonderfully repell and ease rumaticque and veneriall night paines. Of these nut-shells are made (by the Negros and Indians) botles, cups, dishes, spoons and many othere convenient utinsalls, for this nutt will work smoth and pollish as clean as marble. This fruite on the sprig we have here potraied from the originall fruite itsself [figure lacking].

(468) The wild grape is a fruite found here in great plenty allmost everywhere in the wood. This fruite is about the bigness of a pidgeon's egg, reed and cleare with a thin skinn, and shap't like a grape. These grow not in clusturs like other grapes, but singlely upon a long stem. This fruite is a verey sower fruit, and but of litle estem. They will make good vinagre, and because there is none of this sort of fruit found in England, wee have therfore here on the sprigg potraied it to the life from the originall fruite itself [figure lacking].

The raccoon-nutt is a fruite also found here, being a nutt in the forme of a kidney bean, haveing a brown, smoth, strong shell, about two inches long, and every way proportionally shap't. Of these shells are made fine snuth* boxes and other curiosities. Now within this shell is found a solid hard bitter curnell, which is a strong water purge, a good hydroptick and anti-scorbutique. This fruit we have on the sprigg here portraied to the life [figure lacking].

The pudding nutt is a fruite found here and is in all respects of the shape and size of the ovillar fruit of the sower callibash and is fill'd with seed like the gourd. Thee seeds are good in the collick.

The occar-apple is a small green fruite, about the size of a egg (469), convex on squares on the outside, and inwardly cavious, and full of seeds of a curious smell. This apple if boyled in broth when they are green are good for those which are weakned by long sickness, a great restorer of nature, and plenifier of the spermaticque vessels; likewise they will wonderfull increass milk in women, when all other things in those parts faile. They are here used in broaths, boyled with salt meats, and greately estemed by the English. This fruit on the branch we have here potraied [figure lacking].

The Jamaican cherry is a fruit every way like our Europian cherries, both for shape and collour, only they are farr bigger, being as bigg as a hen's egg, and have in 'em a verey large stone, allmost as big as a mama stone.[305] In fine 'tis a fruite of litle esteme on this island. This is a great restringent. This fruite on the sprigg we have also here potraied to the life [figure lacking].

Lastly here we find the cotton aple.[306] This is a fruit about the bigness of a hen's egg, but of twice the lenght, ovillar and covered with a soft thick brown shell, which when ripe bursts open, and the snow whit cotton appears, for this shell yeilds the cotton woole being fill'd therewith, and intermixt therewith, it yeilds its seed (470) which is a small flatt black seed, like the gourd seed, and is goot from out the cotton-woll by an enginn which they call screwing.[307] These nutts hang verey thick on the cotton shrubb, and commonly ten nutts yeilds a pound of cotton-woole verey white and good, which proves a good commodity home to England.[308] Now wee forgott in our sections of shrubs to discribe this shrub. Therefore know that the cotton shrub is a small tree seldome above six foot high, verey branchy, haveing a brown bark like the hazell, and a leaf like our English currant trees, and yeilds plenty of fruite in their season. They will grow in any ground and are nott here much planted. They are green and flourish all the yeare as I have seen att Madam Greg's cotton plantation nigh the rock at Yallows persinct on Jamaica. Now for the finall satisfaction of the curious, we have potraied the cotton nut on the sprig (in the aforegoing page) from ye originall to the life.[309] Thus we have given you an account of all the fruites found on this island that are yet known with all their phisicall vertues, and shall now proceed to discribe the growth, nature and vertues of the principall roots found on this uberous island of Jamaica.

Section XI

Of roots found on Jamaica: as Europian roots, potatas, the yam, cassavia, ginger, chinnaroot and wild lilly root.

This island aforedeth some of English roots, of the same growthe; (471) they have in a more powerfull measure the same vertues as those in England. Now

305. This description of the fruit of various cherries does not seem accurate. Perhaps Taylor was thinking of some type of plum.

306. "Apple" does not seem a term widely used.

307. It is not clear what this "engine" is, but evident that its name comes from its function of "extorting by pressure". *OED.*

308. Cotton is not normally cited among the extensive exports of seventeenth-century Jamaica.

309. Browne, writing in 1789, gives a full description of this shrub, explaining how its fruit has become the staple of the industry centred on Manchester, England, and employing 120,000 people there. *Civil and Natural History,* 283. Mrs Gregg's plantation had in March 1682 been the scene of a revolt by the slaves. Bridenbaugh and Bridenbaugh, *No Peace beyond the Line,* 362–63.

the Europian root which are here found are these: (viz.) onnions, garlick, shallots, leeks, radish, horse-radish, turnipps and carrats. These two later grow here very small and are sold verey dare at Port Royall market, soe that you shall have but one small bunch of 'em for a royall or an English sixpence. Also here growes aboundance of excellent liquorish, much stronger and better than that in England; also it groweth much larger.[310]

Here are also found in every plantations aboundance of a most delicat sort of potatas, such which the lady Europa never enjoyed in hir garden, and they are of two sorts, a red and a white.[311] These rotts grow in sundry shapes; some are long, otheres ovillar, but the major part of 'em irregular and knobbly. This roots are verey drie and sweet, of most excellent nutriment, and of great profitt to the painfull planter, for with them he feedeth his servants in his famally, and his Negroas slaves, but allso with this root they make an excellent sort of cold drinck, called rapp and mobby, which is a plesant cold liquor. Both these sorts of potatos are both of one nature and tast, and are here commonly roasted and eaten insteed of bread. They eat drie and as sweet as honny, and are sold at Port Royall market some ten or twelve pouinds for a royall or an English sixpence.

The yam is a large root, black and knobby in the outside, but when boyled and that black skinn strip't off, it appears a whit root, veined with purpple. This root is much drier than a potata, but not soe sweet. This root is here eaten by many instead of bread.[312] 'Tis of like profitt to the planter as the former and sold in the marckett at the same rate.

(472) The casavia, or cassadar is a large root as bigg as the thick of a man's thigh, and commonly two or three foot long, whit, and resembling a parsnipp.* It bears a bough knobly like a calibash, being perfect wood, and a broad smoth leaf. Of ye root is made a verey white bread (eaten not only here by most of the inhabitants, but also in most other parts of America, by the Spaniards, English, Dutch, French and the native Indians), altho' the juice of this root is a verey strong poyson. Yet of this root is not only made bread, but also an excellent cold drinck called perinno. Now they make bread with this root in this following manner. They take the roote, and scrape it, and press out all the juice, then they drie it in the sun 'till it becoms white and loke like finn flower, then on a broad smoth stone (which they have for that purpose) they spreed this flower, in broad round thin cackes, and on this

310. Liquorice was much prized for its medicinal properties. See *Culpeper's Compleat Herbal* (London, 1652; reprint New York, 1950), 106.

311. Sloane also describes these "Spanish patatas", of the red and white varieties. *Voyage*, 1: 50–51.

312. See also Sloane: "Yams are likewise used here in lieu of Bread." Ibid., xix.

stone by the heat of ye sun 'tis baked and looks white and becomes a pretty sort of bread, but I believe but litle nutriment is found theirin.

Now the perino is made thus by ye English at Jamaica; they take this casava or casadar breed, and steep it in stale rapp, and then press it out, and put it up in a jarr, and 'twill foment like ale, and become a delicat cold strong drinck, and will keep good for 8 or 10 days and prove good liquor. This is the most estemed cold drinck found on Jamaica.[313] Now the Indians make their perinno thus; they cause their old women which are past their labour to chew the cassadar root in their mouths, and spitt it out into a vessle of water, that soe the poyson of their teeth which have bin tainted with a thousand poxes may maccarate* (473) the poyson of ye root. After it hath purged itself in the watter from its one naturall poyson and thren off the invenomed poyson which it receved of the stincking mouths of the old pocky-yauie Indian women, they strain it forth drie, and put ye root into rapp, and then work it upp as aforesaid. This is the way used by the Caribi-Indians, and the native Indians of Florida, Saranam, Coraso and most other parts of America.[314]

Ginger is a root found here in most plantations, verey good and strong, and proves a certain commodity home to England. It grows verey thick in the ground and bears a large green leaf.

The chinna root is found here in some parts of this island very large and good but is not here much regarded, becaus they have not the way to cuer it as those doe in East India, for lett 'em be never soe carefull, the worms will here sone distroy it.[315] The vertues belonging hereto are undoubtedly the same with the East Indian roote, and had they the arcanum of its cure, 'twoud certainly prove a good commodity.

Lastly here in the woods we find a verey large whit lilly, haveing a flower and leave every way such as our English whit lilley, only the flower is twice as large. This yeild a very large root, whose vertues are the same with our English lilly (vide *Pharmacophaeae Londinensis*) tho' farr more strong and powerfull.[316]

Thus we have described the properties and vertues of all the estemed roots which this island affordeth, tho' there are others as yet unreguarded. Alltho

313. Sloane also explains how to make perinno, "a Drink much used here". Ibid., [illegible]

314. Coraso is probably Curaçao. A similar way of making perinno by the Indians is described by Richard Ligon in *A True and Exact History of the Island of Barbadoes* (London, 1673), 32.

315. According to Browne, "this plant is frequent in the more cool inland parts of Jamaica". *Civil and Natural History*, 359.

316. Of the white lilly's many qualities, Culpeper observes that "they are under the dominion of the Moon, and by antipathy of Mars expel poison". *Culpeper's Compleat Herbal*, 106.

'tis certain that nothing in the whole creation remains without a noble vertue, for God and nature created nothing in vain, but indued everything with a propertie to glorifie its Creator, and to sound forth the glory of his omnipotent majestie, that soe man might be drawn by his glorious workes to love, honour and fear him.

Section XII

(474) Of seeds found on Jamaica,[317] *Europian seeds, viva, occarseed, sabinna, salvia, cataputia, cushoa stones, piemento, cockstones, palmeto, agnus castor, gouards, indigo, maize, guineacorn, blackeyed peas, rouncavilla, calvanca, boonavis, redpeas, Spanish beans, and tobaco seed.*

On this island are found plenty of some of our English seeds, namely mustard seed, cabadge seed, sorrell, marjorum, rue, thyme, hisope, wormwood, parsly, purslain,[318] spinage, lentills, oniouns, leeks, turnipps, carrats, and radish seeds, none of which are inferiour or less vertuous than our English seeds of the like speties; besides which we finde here many other seeds of this island's own naturall product, in which are inshrin'd many rare vertues and admirable properties, as first:

Here we find the viva, or liveing seed, which is one of natur's peices of curiousity. This is a small round seed, about the size of ye hemp seed. 'Tis cavious, and grows on ye herab viva (see page the 446). Now this seed is noe less rare and wonderfull than the hearb itself, for if you (475) lay two of these seeds one a table, the one at one end, and the other end, at five or more yards distance assunder, these two seed shall of themselve move and jump towards one another, untill they mett, and then lie close together, without any manner of motion. This I have often seen with noe small admiration, and doe here afirm it for a certain truth. This seed containes many other rare vertus and many other admirable properties, as witnesseth the learned Doct Trapham in his *Present State of Health.*[319]

The occaraseed is a small seed, flatt and hairie, and much like carratt seed. It smells of verey strong curious musky scent, and is a dellicat perfume to lay amongst linnen.[320] This seed is and excellent cordiall seed, good in fainting and a great comfortor of the hartt.

317. As before, this section on seeds overlaps with previous sections.

318. Purslain was once a well-known salad herb.

319. For these tall stories, see Trapham, *Discourse of the State of Health,* 30.

320. See also Browne: "The seeds of this plant, when grown to full maturity, have a strong and perfect smell of musk, a few grains being sufficient to perfume a whole room". *Civil and Natural History,* 285.

The sabinna, or flower seed, is a small flatt seed like a ciddney bean,* growing in a long codd like 'em. This seed infused in Rineish wine it provocketh the terms,* distroyeth conception, purgeth the reines, and cuereth gonorreas, and all running of the vessells.

Salvia or sage seed is a round small seed, and hath all the vertues of sage tree (see page 442) and all the vertues of our Europian sage, tho' more strong and powerfull.

Cattaputia majores, or the greater spurge seed,[321] grow on the phisick nutt shrubb. 'Tis a small black seed or rather a nutt, growing fouer together in a round yallow fruite like an apricott, which when the seed is ripe, opens, and letts the seeds drop forth. These seeds are a good emeticque and cathartick and purger of choller.

The cushoa seed, or stone, is about the size of a broad English bean, convex and form'd like a kidney, haveing a thick blewish (476) shell full of a brown oylie substance. Within this shell is a verey good sweet curnall, a great restringent in the blody flux, etc. Now the oyle of this shell is an excellent visicitor,* for if you wett finne lint with it, and aplie it to the fleash, it shall safly (in less than half the time which cantharades[322] requier) raise a blister. Now if you callcine the nut both shell and curnall together, the powder thereof shall cleanse teeth to admiration, leaveing them as white as snow and cleanse and strenghten the gumms.

The piemento, Jamaica peper, or allspice, for soe by some 'tis called, is a seed or small berry much resembling East Indian black pepper, being cavious. 'Tis a spice of the flavour of a clove, but more stronger being badd for the head, as all other spices are. It growes in clusturs like ivey berries, proveing a good commodity, and is transported home to England and other parts.[323] This fruit puts out like the iveyberry, being at first green and when ripe blood reed, and being gathered and dried in the sun it becomes hard and black.

The cockstone is a hard stonny yallow nutt, about the bigness of a hazell nut, haveing a strong shell, almost as hard as a stone. The curnall is a good purger, of excellent use and powerfull in the cuer of gonorehaes and veneriall boiles, and running of the vessels, for 'tis a strong safe purger.

Palmeto seed of all sorts, as the cabadge palmeto, palmeto royall, etc. is a round berry one seed bigger than pepper, soft and black, much like juniper, being good in the colick and gripes. 'Tis hott and moist in three degrees.

Agnus-castor seed is a small seed long and black. 'Tis a vereie fatt oylie

321. As we have seen, physic nut is not the same as the spurge.

322. Cantharides is a vessicant made of the dried beetle cantharides.

323. In Sloane's words, "the cured Fruit [is] sent in great Quantities yearly to Europe". *Voyage,* 2: 76.

seed, being hot and moist in two degrees, being good (477) in emulgent clustors,[324] for it cleanseth and healleth all fistulas or ulcers of the collon, and abateth all heat or tumors in the intestines, with safty and great facillitie.

The guorde's seeds are these, viz.: the watermellon, muskmellon, pompion, guoard, garden cowcumber, wild cowcumber and the cotton seeds, all which seeds are cold and moist in three degrees, used in cold emultions, being of excellent power to cold the heat of the liver, to purge and cold the veines when scallded with the hott drops of veneriall spots.

Indigo seed is much as hemp seed, only small.[325] 'Tis not cavious but solid, being hott in 2° and moist in 3°, powerfull in cataplasmns to discuss and mundifie* hard tumors in any outwards part of the body. This is a verey deare seed, being this present yeare 1688, sold to plant at Jamaica for 10 dollars a bushill, and at that price thought cheape.

Maize or Indian corn groweth here in ears about one foot long and as bigg as a man's wrist having some 500 graines in one eare and sometimes three eares on one stalck. This corne they pound to flower and boyle it for their Negro slaves which soe order'd they call it hommone after the Indian name.[326] Also this corn stands 'em in great steed in ye maintenance of their horsses, hoggs, and fowles; and also of this maize is here made with molloses an excelent plesant strong liqor, which they here call corn drinck, and the Indians call cawwough.[327]

Guinea corn is a small grain, round and of the dementions of indigo seed, being filled with a curious whit flower and hath a very thinn husk. This corn when blanch't and boyled eat full as good as rice or French barly [and] have the same good properties. This corn is a graine of great increase (478) and maketh fatt sonner than any other corn, yet nevertheless there is not much thereof saved, by reason they cutt up the green corn to feed their cattell withall; whilst in the blade this corn is excellent in cold pectorall decoctions.

The blackey'd pea[328] growes on a stalk and in a codd like a French bean, both in shape and size. 'Tis an excellent swett peas and a great encreaser, for one bushill will commonly produce one hundred bushills, and are of great supply to the plantors to feed the Negro slaves and other servants in his famyly.

---

324. "Emulgent clusters" are draining clysters.

325. The plants of the indigo family were indigenous to both the Old World (India, Egypt, Greece) and to the New World (Central and South America).

326. Now written "hominy", as in the Jamaican "hominy-corn". Allsopp, *DCE,* 296.

327. This surely must be the strong black medicinal drink of various Indian groups, but the word does not seem to be found elsewhere.

328. Sloane mentions a great many different peas, among which is one "with a black eye". *Voyage,* 1: 84.

The rouncavilla[329] growes on a vine in all respects like ye former. This pea is almost twice as bigg, an excellent swett pulse, and produceth the like increase. This is a blewish white pea not spotted nor blackeyed.

The calavanca[330] growes also on a running vine like the formmer; is much larger, being white and spotted. 'Tis a firm sweet pea, and produceth a great increass, if it prove good seasonable wether, otherwise distroyed by ye caterpiller.

The boonavis[331] is a small pea, some red, and others white, about the size of an English fitch,[332] being the greatest encreasor of all seeds. This they plant all along by hedges or woods' sides about six foot assunder, and they spring up and runn all o're it like a hopp, or vine, and have a leafe much like a hopp, and a larger stallk which will be covered with codds to admiration, yeilding more than thrice a thousand-foald, and these will hold in the ground for many years, and twice a yeare spring up and yeild its fruite in the like aboundance. This is not soe good as other pulss,* yett they are indefferent swett, and of good nutriment.

The red pea growes on a runing vine and codd like calavanca, being (479) but a small pea, yet the best and swettest of all pulss found on ye island and is of great increass and profitt to the planter, which moved one of their late preists, preaching 'ore a lusty bowle of rumm punch, to fall out into this extasie, protesting to his then congrogation that rumm punch and redpeas was the stafe* of the land. This is evere since a common proverbe at Jamaica. In some plantations at Lighorne,[333] they have some few English peas, but they are very rare, for they do not thrive here. Neither doth our English beans of any sort; yet with great care they produce some few, which are accounted a great rareity.

The Spanish bean[334] is a sort of a pulss found on this island, full as broad as our English beans, but not soe thick. They are spotted and shap't like a kidney bean, growing three or foure in a long codd, like French beans, and they grow on the like running vine. This is a sweet bean and of good nutriment, yet are they not much planted by reason they produce but litle incress and yeilds nothing considerable to the profitt of any of ye other pulss.

---

329. The rouncival pea was cited in the sixteenth century (*OED*); the name survives now only in Barbados. Allsopp, *DCE*, 477.

330. The calavanca was a pea known in the seventeenth century, apparently named after the Spanish *garbanzo,* according to the *OED*.

331. Now known as the "bonavist", among other names in different Caribbean islands. The name comes from Bona Vista, the Cape Verde island "from which the beans were imported into the New World". Allsopp, *DCE*, 110.

332. Fitch is an archaic form of the word "vetch", meaning a bean-like fruit. *OED*.

333. That is, Liguanea.

334. The "Spanish bean" is now a variety of broad bean. *OED*.

Lastly here we shall discribe the tobaco seed, which groweth in a small codd, of a greyish colour, round and indeed is the least of all seeds, for 'tis soe small that being in a vessell you can scarsely distinguish the seeds assunder. 'Tis a powerfull phisick seed; see the *Pharmocophaeae Londinensis* which will enform you therein.[335] Thus we have given you a just account of the growth, shape, magnitude, vertues and usses of all the seeds of note on this uberous island, which I have carefully collected.

Section XIII

(480) Of Jamaican flowers: as the jecamon, orange, lemon, sabina, salvia, tammarind, lilly, dilldo, dogwood-flower and the cammomill flower.

What is their in the whole universe capable to please the curious sences of man more than the infinit variety of swett-smelling flowers? When butie bespangles and decks ye green mantle of ye earth, with sundry rare and shinning collours, soe that we view the universall mother of us all, soe butified and adorn'd therby, that all the creation can't parallel it in any other thing, by which means our sence are rapt up in a labarinth of delight, and raised to a holy admiration of ye infinit wisdom and power of our Creater, seen in these his curious workes which not only butifie the earth with ye shining glory, but also prefums the aire, and revives man's spirits with their plesant smell, and yeild such benifitt to all mankind, that the wise philosopher, O matchless orator, M.T. Cicero prescribed nothing more fitt to mitigate the (481) burden of old age, then the plesant refreshment of a flowery garden, ye shaddy bowers of green walkes, and the swett murmur of christial strems.[336]

But this island of Jamaica is deniged those currious butifiers, for here we find her green mantle voide of flowers, for Europe is the lady Flora's garden, which she hath array'd in her own liverey, and these western parts she hath withhold hir favours from, for here is not to be found the rose, violot, carnation, juliflowers, pinck, tulip, nor any other sort of our rare Europian flowers, for here they will not thrive nore grow.[337] Soe that this island is none of the lady Flora's favourit, for here we only find those few flowers, as we shall now describe according to their order, and dignity:

---

335. It does not seem possible to find this reference.

336. In his work *On Old Age and on Friendship,* Cicero did indeed give this advice. See the translation by Frank O. Copley (Ann Arbor, 1967), 29.

337. "Juliflower" is a version of the gillyflower (*OED*); Taylor speaks of the tulip as an English flower, but it had been introduced from Turkey during the sixteenth century (*OED*).

First here we find the fatt jecamon,[338] in all respects such which are found in Itally, being a flower of fragrant gallantry and strong prefume, being useed in both liquid and drie prefumes. This flower is hott and moist in two degrees.

The orange flowers is a small white flower, growing in clustures, being prefumed with a most plesant smell. These flowers distilled in good Gasconian wine becoms an excellent cordiall, of a curious flavour. This water comforteth the spirites, restores naturall heat, and causeth a due circulation of the blood.

The lemon and lime flowers grow in all respects like the former, and smells curiously. These flowers being distill'd in vinagare takes away all yallowness, morphen,[339] and freckles out of the face, leaveing ye skinn smoth and white.

The sabina flowers growes in clusters on a slender stalke composed in leaves like a primerose, redish and veined, and spotted with azure, purple and yallow veines and spotts, and out of the (482) midle of this flower sproutts fouer blades like the blades of saffron. These flowers hath a sabinique smell. This flower provocketh the terms in women and distroys conception. In men it purgeth and cuereth the running of the reines, cuereth gonorrehaes and all fluxes of the vessells, and being disgested in wine it killeth worms in chilldren, and fortifieth the stomack, and createth an appatite. The blades dried like saffron hath many rare and choice phisicall vertues, not fitt here to be mention, as being choice arcanums which ought to be conceal'd.

The salvia or sage flower is a yallow flower, veined and spotted with red and white, smelling verey strong and odourifius and are good to prevent contagious distempers and infections, being disgested in wine. They are hott and drie in two degrees.

The tamarind flower is of the growth and make of a cammomill flower, being of a gould collour and hath a pleasant scent, being good in consumptions and obstructions of the stomack, and is hot in two, and moist in three degrees. It also makes a good snush* for the head.

The whit lilley is here found growing wild in the woods and savanas, and is in every respect such as we have in England, only 'tis twice as large. This flower hath the same vertues with our lilleys but more strong and powerfull.

The dildo flower is a large single flower, growing in the form of a bell, some of 'em are yallow and others snow-white. This flowers are good in palsies, rumatismns and gout pains, being colld and drie in three degrees.

The dogwood flower is a single flower, like a periwinckle. Some are yallow,

338. This is probably jessamine, a variant spelling of jasmine, or perhaps the frangipani (Sidrak).

339. It seems impossible to know what Taylor meant by this word.

others blew, and others white, yet are they all (483) of one nature, being hott and drie in the highest degree. An essence made from these flowers and mixt with past, made in little pillets and thrown into watter in rivers or lakes where fish haunt, shall presently make 'em drunck, soe that they will swim on the surffacce of the water, and you may take 'em up with your hand. But such is its nature, that in some two howers' time the fish recovereth himself again, the strenght of the essence being spent, for it stupifieth him but for a time, until its stupifieing faccultie is decayed.[340]

The cammomill flowers found here ar both the same in growth and vertues as those found in England, being hott in two and drie in one degree. Thus we have here given you an account of the flowers which this island afordes, with their nature, properties, and phisicall vertues.

Section XIV

Of phisicall barks found on Jamaica; as the guacum, Jamaica cinnamon, piemento, lime, sabina, dogwood, bark of prickle yallowwood, manchanilla, and the barke of mainegrove.[341]

On this island are found many choice and rich barks, for those rare vertues and faculties which they conteyne, both usefull to man in the preservation of his health and strenghtening of his body; of all which barks we intend here to treat.

(484) First here we find the *cortex guaci,* or pretious bark of the wood of life, which is a smoth thick gummy bark, good against all veneriall deseases, as gonorehaas, pains, nodes, tumors, shanckers* etc.; also 'tis a powerfull antiscorbuticke,* and hydropticque.* It thinns, cleanses and swettens the whole mass of blood, tho' never soe much polluted with viscious humors, causeing therin a due circulation, soe that to give it its due praise where altogether above the spheare of my slendor cappasitie.[342]

The Jamaica cinnamon is a thick red barck, verey strong in scents and tast. It hath the same vertues with the East India bark, but is more ruff, and cheifly used by distillors in their waters and spiritts. This bark is good in hott baths and fomentations, for 'tis a great externall strenghtenor and comfortor of

---

340. Taylor further explains under "barks" the use of dogwood to stun fish. It is possible that this name comes from the use of a decoction of the bark to cure mange in dogs. Allsopp, *DCE,* 198.

341. It is curious that Taylor does not mention Jesuit bark, or cinchona, the quinine remedy much used in his doctoring by Hans Sloane.

342. Browne also lists many of these pharmaceutical uses of lignum vitae bark, adding that it is also useful in "other disorders arising from the fizzyness of the juices". *Civil and Natural History,* 226.

the loines, and easeth old aches and gout paines to admiration. This bark is transported home to England and proves a good commodotie.

The piemento bark is a verey smoth thinn bark, haveing the same smell and tast with the spice, but not quite soe full and hott. It hath the vertues of the spice, and is good in hott baths and fomentations, being hott and moist in two degrees, and in fine 'tis an excellent bark.

The barke of the lime tree roots is hott in one and drie in three degrees, and not cold as some suppose. A decoction made of this bark, and drunck in a medicall cours, is an infallible cueror of shanckers, fluxes of the vessels and gonorrohaas when all other means have proved unsuccessfull. It also sweetens and purgeth the blood from all thick and vitious humors, and causeth due circulation.

The bark of the sabina or flower tree hath the like vertues with (485) the flowers (see page 481). Also 'tis excellent in fomentations to discuss hard tumors and callices in cavious parts and vessels, and also being made into a tincture, it cleanseth old stricking ulceres and incarnats new fleash to admiration.

The dogwood bark is of a strong poysonous or stupifieing nature, soe that if a mane should eat hereof, or drinck of the juice, he would either fall madd, or else for a long time would be posest with a continuall drowsiness, for this bark bears a simpathy with that fountain in ye province of Xoa in Ethiopia of which Ovid thus speaks:[343]

> Aethiopesque Lacus; quos si quis faucibus hausit
> Aut furit, aut patitur, mirum gravitate saporem.

This bark is use cheifly for fishing in the hole in freash rivers after the raines, and in standing lakes, for if you take this bark green from the tree, and bruise it with a maule,[344] and putt it into the holes of water or standing pools wher fishes haunt, and then stire the watter with poles, then shall all the fish that is therin, both small and great, presently become drunck and lay as dead on the surfface of the watter, soe that you may take 'em out at plesure. Now if pressently you put those fish into other clean freash watter, they will sone revive and live; otherwise they are noe better than dead.[345] This have bin still practiced at Jamaica till of late, for now there is an acct made against such poysoning of rivers, soe that whosoever shall be found to practice the same lies under the penalty to pay five pound for every such offence, and receive one month's imprisonment also for the same offence.[346]

343. This is the passage already quoted, concerning the Aethiopian lakes (p. 187).
344. A hammer, from the Latin *malleus. OED.*
345. This process is described in Browne, *Civil and Natural History,* 297.
346. For this act, see p. 295.

The bark of the root of prickle yallow wood is hott and moist in two degrees. This (486) bark ussed in fomentations will abate all veneriall night pains, soften and disperss nodes, easeth all manner of gout paines in the nerves and joyntes, and discusseth all manner either of hard or soft tumors in what part of the body soevere. Also it disperseth blood coagalated in contused parts to admiration. An unguent made of this bark will also preform the licke sooner, and with more faccillity, and will also draw forth ye venomous poyson of ye bitteing of serpents, or madd dogs.

The bark of manchanilla is a strong poyson both internally and externally, for wherevere its sapp falls it raiseth a blister on the fleash, and causeth an inflamation and sore, and if this juice, or the powder of the drie bark, should in the least quantity fall into the eyes, it destroyeth the sight, and causeth a continuall blindness; therefore be carefull hereof.

Lastly the maingrove bark is here used by all tanners,[347] and by itt leather is here tan'd and in one quarter of the timme that 'tis in England, proveing also much better, for it leaves the leather verey hard and of a deep brown or redish collour. Thus we give you an account of all the Jamaican barks whose worth and vertues are as yet known; many other undoubtedly there are, if some ingenious person (who hath time and abillity to maintaine himself in the studie and sirch thereof) would examine and prove ye same, which would be of excellent worth and beniffitt, not only to the inhabitants themselves, but also to the whole race of mankind and would add great satisfaction to the ingenious enquieror. I wish I were blest with time and ability to follow the same vertuous enquery. I would not delay, but alas! 'Tis my fate to be born to study to live, and not to live, to study.

Section XV

(487) Of Jamaican gumms and naturall ballsoms, as gumm guaci, yallowwood, plumbtree, cherry, manchanilla, balsamum vitae and balsamum aurariu Jamaeicae.

Nature hath blest these western parts of the world with all things which are rich and pretious, not only provideing in great abundence for the inhabitants' foods and cloathing, which even the verey earth itself proffers before demanded, but also it yeilds many rare presarvatives of health, and vanquishers of malladies are here found flowing plentifully from the verey

347. Sloane is more specific: "The Bark tans leather well for Shoe Soals, not for Upper Leathers, it thus tan'd burning the Skin." *Voyage,* 2: 64–66.

hearbs and trees which weep forth drops of rich balms from their clefty barks to comfort and heal the sick and fainting inhabitants; nay to cuer even the wounds of bruite beast, whome nature hath taught where to seek for cure from the here growing plants, trees, and shrubs. But to spake of the gumms and natural balsams found on this island, we shall now in order discribe those of 'em which as yet are known, but there are some others found in wild places (488) not as yett taken notice of. Now first,

The gum of guacum is here found verey plentifull, being a grenish solid gum, rich and pretious, and ought to be more estemed than gold. It hath all the vertues of the wood and bark, but more strong and powerfull in its efeccts.

The yallowood gum is a thick substanciall yallow gum, issueing from the trees in great aboundance. This is an excellent cleansor and cueror of foule stincking ulcers (if made into a tincture with *spiritum vini*) tho' foul at the boane. It eateth off nodes and all carnatious excressences. Besides this 'tis most excellent in combustible compositions, being fare better than gum benjamin[348] or any other combustabile gumm.

The Spanish plumb tree also yeilds aboundance of a soft gold-colloured gumm, which is hott and moist in two degrees, being good to discuss cold hard tumors. It also heals cutts or puncturs to admiration in a verey short time.

The cherry gum here issueth out from the tree verey plentiefully, being verey cleare, solid and white and for any use undoubtedly as good as the Arabian gumm.

The manchanilla gum is a strong hard gumm like sandrick,[349] of a poysonous quallity, but of great force in fierworks, for 'twill burn underwater, and will be extinguished by nothing untill it hath consumed itself in burnning. This gumm if applied to combustible compositions would perform wonderfull effects and prove verey serviceable both by see and land, adding praise to both the artt and ye enginere.* Now of naturall balsams found on this island:

First here we finde ye *balsamum vitae*, by some called bore gum. This balsam proceeds from the bark of the borewood tree, being a thinn whitish balmn, of most powerfull vertue to cuer any externall wound, as cutts, punctuers etc., only by dropping (489) it into the wound, and it will sone preform its dessier'd effect and perfect the cure. This balsam taken inwardly in wine heals the lunges, and removes all obstructions and restores the vitalls

348. From the North American Benjamin-bush. *OED.*
349. Sandarac was a resin from an African bush, used in the preparation of spirit varnish.
350. Sloane offers a different set of qualities for this balsam, called "hoggum". *Voyage,* 2: 91.

when consumeing, and is of great value.[350] You must take ten drops of this balm in a glass of generous wine every morning, and 'tis the only remedy in consumptions, it being a most pretious balm, not only yeilding help to man, but also to ye bruit beast, for the sturdy wild bore, when wounded by the hunter, imediatly resorts to this tree, and with his enraged tusks launceth the bark and letteth this balm drop into his bleeding wounds which pressently stops ye efflux of blood and cuereth the wound, which otherwise would prove deadly.[351] This balm smells like that of Peru, and in time growes thick and hard, but may with ease be disolved, and will retaine its vertues for many yeares. It is also observed of this balm that noe annoying insectt will come nigh a wound that this hath binn applied to, for its odourifius smell distroyeth 'em. In fine this is a verey pretious balasam, haveing many other rare vertues which are yett undiscovered.

Balsamum aurarium jamaicae, or the golden balsam of Jamaica, proceeds from the Jamaican lemnia tree. This is a thinn liquid balm like puer oyle and of a shineing gold collour, smelling like the balsam of Peru, and hath all the vertues therof. Externally it cueres all manner of fresh woundes, cleanses and healeth ulceres, removes paines in ye joyntes, easeth veneriall night paines in the joyntes and bones, and giveth imediat ease in the gout by anoynting ye place afflicted therwith. Internally, this pretious golden balm or balsam, (ten drops thereof taken in a glass of generous wine) healeth all maner of ulcers in the lunges, (490) cuereth the ptisick, removes all obstructions of the mesentery and spleen, restores naturall heat, comforteth and fortifieth ye stomack, prevents contagious infections, sweetenes the whole mass of blood, and is of excellent worth and vertue in many cronick distempers. Thus we have faithfully given you an impartiall account and true description of the many rare and curious products of this uberous island, the which we have collected with noe small care, study, labour, weary travell and expence, and doe here freely impart it to the publicque, for the uneversall benifitt of all inteligible mortalls, which haveing preformed, we here conclud this fifth chapter of our present state of Jamaica, as now under the government of His Grace Christopher Duke of Albemarle.

351. See the similar account above, p. 186.

Chapter VI

(491) Of Port Royall;[1] *its situation, extent, buildings, forts, the manner of the inhabitants' liveing, as to their eateing, drincking, lodging and recreations. Also the manner of their tradeing, with an account of their vendable goods and commodoties.*

Port Royall, the metropolitan* place of trade on the island of Jamaica, lies betwixt the equinoctiall and tropick of cancer in the torid zone, being in the latitude of 17° 50',[2] and in the longitude of 304° 50' north. This town is built on an ithsmush of land on the extrem wester point therof, called by the Spaniards Punta Cagada,[3] it being a place by 'em unregarded, for when this island was taken by the English, they found only two old timber store-houses standing thereon. But now on this sandy neck of land is built by the English a formadable city, well-built, strongly fortified, and populated by a valiant inhabitant. This town is called Port Royall, haveing a good and comodious harbour (492), wherin may safly ride five hunder saile of ships safly and securely, there being noewhere less than nine fadom water therin, all cleare and safe ground.

Now you must understand that this town of Port Royall was began in the government of Collonel Minns[4] anno 1661, and is built on a drie sand peninsula, not above a quarter of a mile broad, but extends itself at least twelve miles before 'tis joyned to the continent of ye island. In this town are now at least 600 well-built brick houses, and as many more built with timber. Ye houses are built fouer story high, cellar'd, covered with tiles and glazed with sash windows, haveing large shops and comodious store-houses

1. This section on Port Royal has often been used by historians, architects and archeologists. See the bibliography under Bridenbaugh and Bridenbaugh, Dunn, Mayes, and Pawson.

2. Taylor had previously (p. 110) given this figure as 17° 44'; the actual latitude is 17° 56'.

3. In fact, the Spaniards called it "cayo de carena", careening cay; the Spanish "Caguaya" applied to Kingston Harbour as a whole. See Taylor, *The Western Design,* 30–131.

4. As in volume 2, chapter 2, section 2, Taylor speaks of "Minns" when he actually refers to Lord Windsor.

belonging to 'em, but here they need not feare paeing hearth mony,[5] for they build noe chimneys, but only in their cookrooms, which stand at some distance from their houses. These houses yeild as good rents as those in Cheapeside[6] in London, seldom less than 80 or 60 yearly rent, and lodgings are here verey cleane, soe that you must give six dollars a month for one chamber reasonably furnished.

Now the cheif buildings of Port Royall are these, viz., St. Paul's church, the Audiencia, the King's House, the Governor House, the Marshallsea, Bridwell, the Sea Fort, Morgan's Line, Charles Fort, James's Fort, Carlisle Fort, and ye markett places; see the mapp [figure 39]. First St. Paule's church is a small, well-built brick structure, bulte crosswise, haveing a dore to the north and anothere to ye south etc. This church is bulte high with batlements* of stone, being paved with marble, well adorn'd with cedar pines and good marbele steps, and curious carved work. At the north side of this church is a paved walk, built for an exchange for merchants to meet on (493). Over this exchange or walk is built a good stonen gallerey, supported with large cedar pillars of ye dorick* order. This gallery is railed around with curious twisted balisters.* The tower of this church is raised square about twenty foot at the base, and sixty foot high, built on ye topp with batlements of stone. In this tower as yet is but one small bell, but they are in preparation to have a seet of good sizeable bells. The minister of Port Royall is an ancient man named Dr. More.[7]

The Audiencia is the courthouse of Port Royall, where they hold their courts of judicature. The King's House is the place where the governore holds his courts of chancery. This is an old timberwork house, alltho' called the King's House. The house which I calle the Governour's House is the best-built house on Port Royall, bult by one Tho. Martin esquire and is now the residence of His Grace Christopher Duke of Albemarle etc. when he visites this place.[8]

The Marshallsea is the prison house standing nigh the Palasado Gate, kept now by William Peat deputie marshall, under the worshipfull Smith Kelley esquire, now provost marshall of Jamaica. Bridwell is a brick structure

5. This refers to a tax of two shillings a year on every fire-hearth in England and Wales. Imposed in 1663, it was for a time repealed shortly after Taylor wrote this passage.

6. Cheapside was the marketplace of medieval London, just to the east of St Paul's Cathedral.

7. In general, the excavations of Philip Mayes (1969–70) confirmed this account of Taylor, whose information here is unique. See Jamaica National Trust Commission, *Port Royal Jamaica: Excavations 1969–70* (Kingston, 1972), 55–67. It is not possible to identify Dr More.

8. Thomas Martyn's house lay on land "recovered out of the sea" on the north side of Port Royal. See the Spanish Town Archives, platt no. 420 of 21 December 1678.

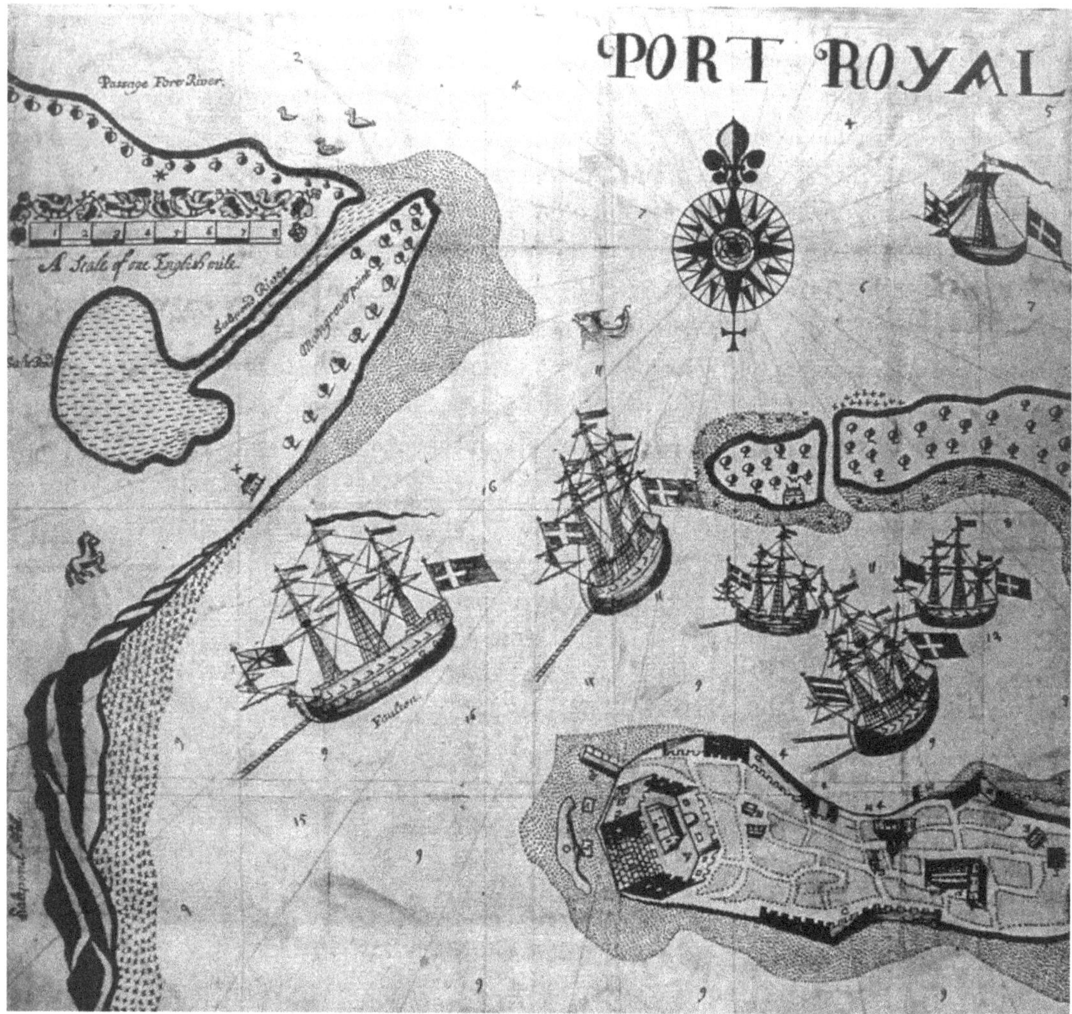

Figure 39 Taylor's plan of Port Royal and its harbour, page 509.

finished this summer, for a house of correction for lazie strumpet of which here are plenty, and these are the principall buildings of Port Royall; as for its fortifications, we shall treat thereof hereafter in the following paragraphs.

Now you must understand that this point (called Port Royall) lieth verey low, being a firm rock covered over with a hott lose burning sand and therefor the streets are not verey regullar; however the maine street is above a mile in lenght.[9] In (494) this town are three marketts keept every daie, the one an herb and fruitt markett held in the hart of the high street, where stands the stocks and markett bell; to this markett is brought plenty of herbs, fruitts and

9. A considerable exaggeration; High Street was a little less than half a mile long.

fowles fresh every morning, unless on the Sabath day. The second market is for fleash and turtle; this market is keept att the wester end of the high street, nigh Chocalata Hole. Over this markett there are overseers as Judge White, etc. and clarke and beadle* who rings the market bell at times appoynted. The now clerke of the market is Mr. Char. Whitle. This market is plentifully stored with beef, mutton, hog, veal, lamb, kid and tortoise, and the cheif times of market is in the cold of ye morning and eavenings. The third market held here is for fish, which is keept on the wharf nigh the Wherry Bridg, where is every morning plenty and variety of excellen fish, verey cheap, soe that for a royall you may have enough well to satisfie fouer reasonable men's appitites.

The town of Port Royall is strongly fortified, soe farr as the situation of the place will admitt. First at the enterance into the harbour at ye easter end of the town is built a strong blockhouse, called the Sea Fort, wherein is 20 peice of ordnance mounted; this blockhouse commandeth any ship passing allong the chanele betwixt it and the kays (as you see in the mapp [figure 39]), soe that none can pass within it but with great danger of being sunck. Now about 100 paces further on ye exteriour line of the fort is built a brestwork with a battery of sixteen guns, [which] flanck inward and outward all ye passage in towards the harbour. This brestwork is called Morgan's Line, being built by Sir Henry Morgan in ye time of his lieutenance.

(495) Now come we to the mouth or enterance into the harbour, the which we find securly defended by a strong fort called Charles Fort (in honour to our late soveraigne of ever blessed memory Charles the second). This fort was built by Collonel Minns in time of his lieutenancy. This is a low strong-built fort; according to its dementions 'tis an octogon polygon, each side being flancked, but it hath noe bastions;* in this fort are mounted thirtie-eight peices of ordinance and a mortar peice. This fort commands the whole channell, and flancks the entrey or mouth of the harbour both inward and outward, soe that noe ship can pass either in or out. In this fort is built lodgments for the gunners, and a fine small house for the captain of the fort, whoe resides therein; the commander therof att present is Collonel Walker,[10] and the late commander was my worthy friend Collonel Beckford, which at the arrivall of His Grace was discharged, and went home for England, comeing off with much honour, haveing discharged himself right worthylie in the point of trust commited to his charge.

Now come we to ye northwest point of Port Royall, distant from Charles Fort about two hundred paces. Here is built a brestworke called James Fort

10. Who a little after this would construct the fortification by Fort Charles long known as Walker's Fort. Pawson and Buisseret, *Port Royal,* 52–53.

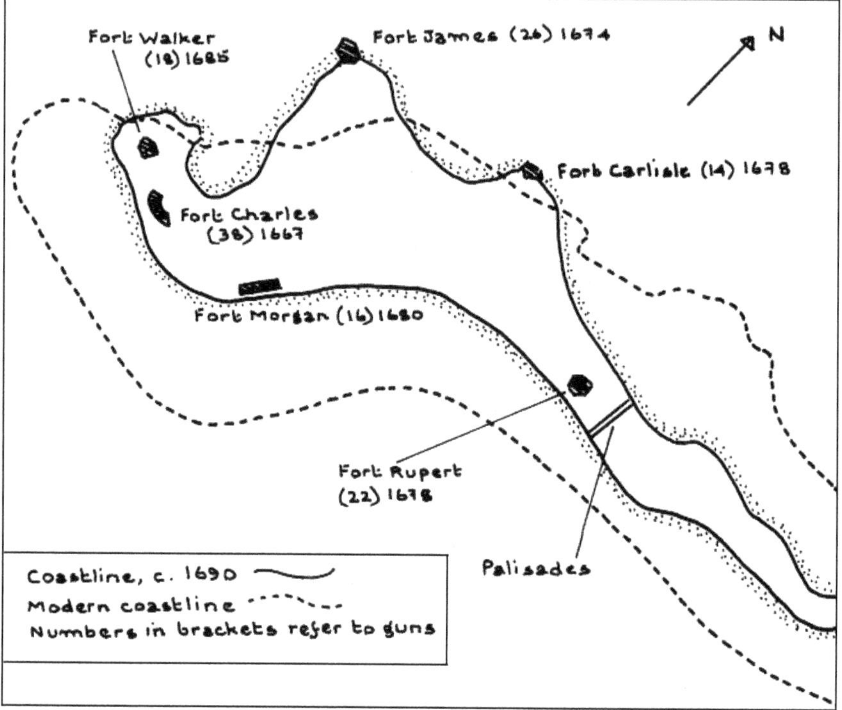

Figure 40 Plan of the fortifications of Port Royal about 1690, from David Buisseret, *The Fortifications of Kingston, 1660–1900* (Kingston, 1971).

(in honour to our late soveraigne James the second of worthie memory). This fort was built by Sir James Mudiford in time of his lieutenancie; this brestwork is formed with a bastion, with flancks and faces, haveing towards Charles Fort and from the other flanck two lines extended which are the segments of curtaines.* In this fort are planted eighteen peices of ordinance, which to the southward commands the entry into the harbour, and on the otherside it flancks all along the harbour, soe that it seems difficult in my oppinion for any (496) ship to enter in or pass out by these three fortes without being sunck and distroyed.

Now we pass along by the wharfside untill we come up to ye Marshalsea, where we find another strong brestwork, called Carlisle Fort, built by the earle of Carlisle in time of his government. This is distant from James Fort about 400 paces, and according to ye termes of millitary architecture 'tis the segment of an irregular bastion, formed with one face towards ye sea, and of one irregullar flanck (the wharf being supposed the curtaine), and at the exteriour point of the face their runns away a line on an obtuse angle, about 5 paces, which is the segment of another face. In this platform (for soe 'tis most proper to call it) are planted eighteen peices of ordnance, which commands the shipping all alonge the harbour, and allso flancks the uper part therof towards the Palasads Gate. To all these forts there belongs gunners suffitient to play the ordinance, which have a yearly sallary allowed them.

Thus have we given you a full account of ye fortication of Port Royall, and now we come to give an account of their mellitia and standing guards.

To this city bellong one regiment of infantrey consisting of 2500 men, well armed and good disciplin'd soldiers; these men are divided into ten companies under valiant officers. These companies are not of equall numbers, for some have three hundred, others 250 etc.; the collonell of this ridgment is Collonel Walker, Major Yoeman, Captain Musgrove, Captain Ward, Captain Wilson, etc; this regiment (497) are all armed with ffuzee and catouchbox and sword, for they have noe bandolliers,* nor picks. These for the most part have scarlet coats lined with blew. This ridgment commonly perform their duty at arms on the parrade paved with brick nigh the Palasada Gate, where is sufficient room for 3,000 men to perform their exersise.

Now this ridgment keep continuall gaurd on Port Royall night and day at the forts, one company being on dutie att a time, standing from six at night until six the next night, when they are releived, soe that every man once in ten nights performs his dutie on the gaurd. These gaurds marches all round the town twice a night on the pataroule, and all drunck sparkes, and common strumpetts which they then find in the streets, they commite to the gauard and to the cage by the turtle market, for an example to others. Now further the order of ye melitia is such all 'ore the island, as well as att this point; that is that if they espie at any part of the island five saile of ships together, bearing down upone it, they pressently raise allarm and ride with all speed to all quarters, to give notice therof. But if the allaram should be first raised at this port, they fier off two cannons loaden with hollow balls from Charles Port over Saltpond Hill,[11] which by their great report and the thundering echos of the mountains, all the whole island both horse and foot are forthwith in arms at their respective places of rendevoze, waiting for the governour's orders whither to march. Thus we have given you an account of ye mellitia and guards of (498) this town of Port Royall, and also the government of ye meletia in their giveing the allaram all 'ore the island of Jamaica.

Now let us cast our eyes on ye easter or upper end of Port Royall which they calle Palasados, where the point is verey narrow, and here is a drei mote* one the counterscarp defend with strong palasados, a gate, and bridge; without this is the buriall place,[12] at ye upper end of which this peninsulla runns out with an arm to the northwestward, which form the inward part of the harbour; this point is all overgrown with green maingrove bushes. At ye verey wester point of this is there cutt a pass river thro' it, soe that the extrem

11. From the signal station on Saltpond Hill (above what is now Port Henderson) there was visual communication with the beacon on the hill above Spanish Town.

12. Presumably where the Port Royal cemetery is still to be found.

point is now made an island, wheron is a fine house and garden built by one Mr. Swettman; this is called "Swettman's island". Thro' this cutt river boats pass up to ye Rock and cross to Ligourney.

Now on ye north side of this port or town, by the watterside next the harbours, is built a verey strong wharff as at Bellen's Gate, soe that ships of 500 tuns and more may hall close to it, or there crean if there be occation, for the water is six fadom deep close too. This wharff lies all allong betwixt James Fort and the Wherey Bridg, betwixt which and Carlisle Fort there is noe warf but sholl'd watter and a smoth beach, soe that ye watter canoas etc. unload and load there, and the watermen which plie from this port to Ligourney and Passage Fort hale to ye Wherey Bridg. Now this warff beforementioned is of considerable profitt to those whose land it is, for ships comming in daily from England, Ireland, New England etc. keeps the wharff full, paying dear wharffage, and as soon as they are unloaden they hall off to anchor in the harbour as you see in the mapp.

(499) To this port bellongs allway about one hundred stout sloops or shaloops, which trade about the island and with the Spaniards and Indians in those parts.[13] Those sloops when at this portt commonly ride in Chocallat Hole, nere Charles Fort, in which place are also their crawles or tortoise pens, where they are keept for the slaughter. Now His Majestie of Great Britain, for the safty of this new-setled island, is pleased to send hither two of his frigeets to attend the same, cruse about the island, and attend the supressing of piratts. The ffrigots remain here for one year, and then are releve from England, and soe return home. These frigats when at Jamaica ride at the mouth of the harbour, towards Saltpond Hill as you see in the mapp [figure 39]. Those frigots that were there the last yeare 1688, was His Majestie's Ship *Faulcon,* commanded then by Captain Tho. Smith, and the *Drake* commanded by Captain Spragg. But when His Grace Christopher duke of Albemarle came into his government, they were releifeed by the *Assistance* comanded by Captain Wright, and the *Elizabeth* yatch, commanded by Captain Monk, whom we have there now both in safetie. Thus we have given you a just account of this town as to its situation, extent, buildings, fortifications, mellitia forces, and the dalie gaurds to secure its saffty, both by sea and land; wheron we finde one hundred and five gunns mounted, and many more redy to mount if their were occation.

Now come we to treat of the inhabitants, in order to which you must understand that this port is verey populess, there being above 5,000 inhabitants besides as many Negro and Indian slaves. These inhabitants are for the most part English; the rest are Scotts and Irish. Also here are many

13. On this trade, see the articles by Nuala Zahediah cited in the bibliography.

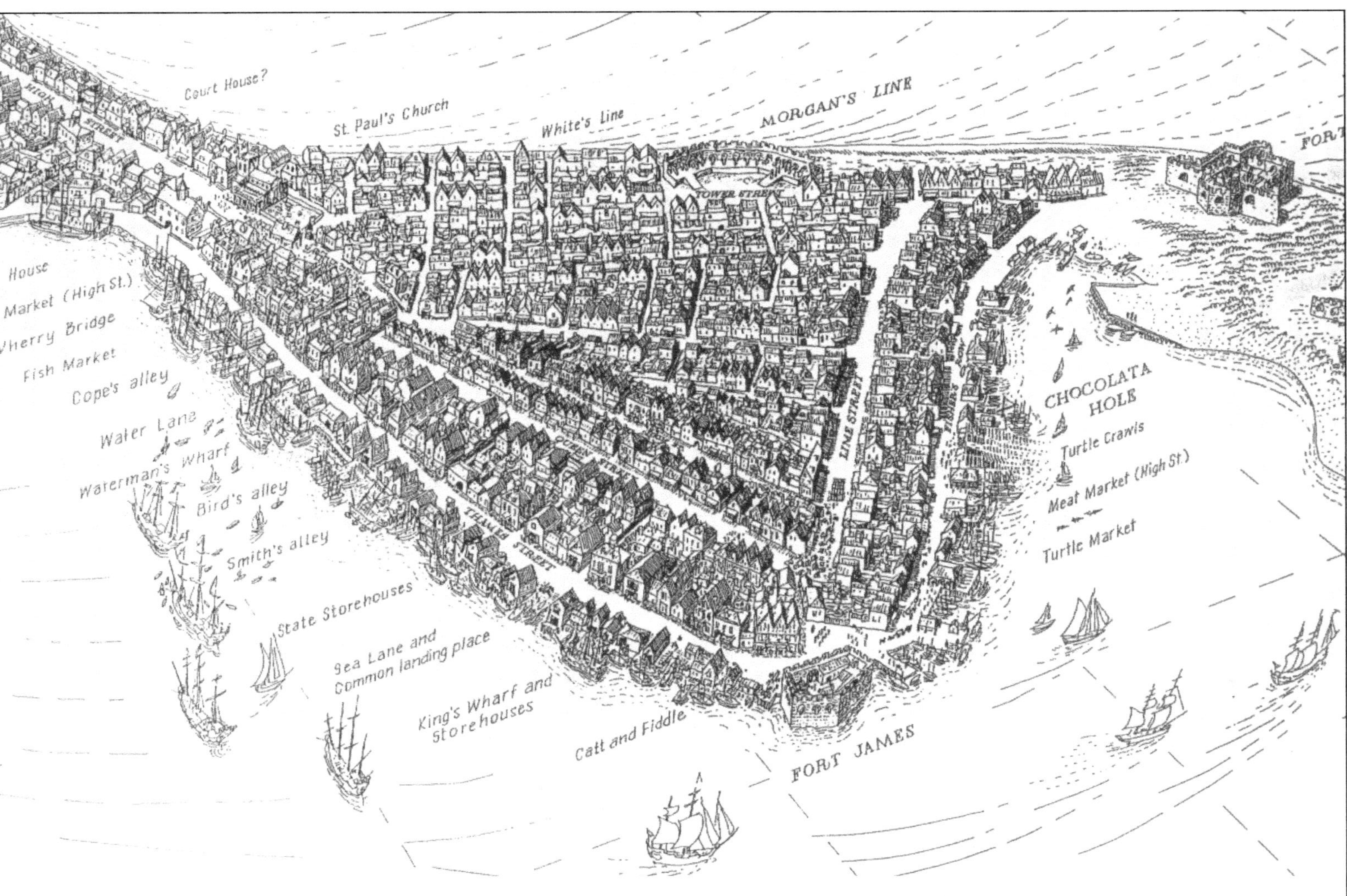

Figure 41 Imaginary bird's-eye view of Port Royal about 1690 (by kind permission of Oliver Cox).

Jewes, verey wealthy merchants haveing free commerce with our English factory. At (500) this port also resideth the Spanish factor, named Seignior San Jago, whoe is a verey wealthy merchant, and hath free commers with the factors of the Royall African Company for Negroa slaves, which he transports to Porta Bella and other places amongst the Spaniards, which bring great riches yearly to this port.

The merchants and gentrey live here to the hights of splendor, in full ease and plenty, being sumptuously arrayed and attended on and served by their Negroa slaves, which allways waite on 'em in liverys, or otherwise as they pleas to cloath 'em. These inhabitants are plentifully supplie with good and holsom meates, as beef, mutton, veal, lamb, kid and more cheifly hog's flesh, both wild and tame, which is indeed the best of meats found on this island. Also they are here daily supplied with manatte and good tortoise, the calapee of which is a prickly* dish. Neither is here any want of fowles, for every day in the markett is plenty of turkies, ducks, cappons, widgern, teell, pidgeon, doves, and parratts at a resonable rate; also they are daily supply with much variety of excellent fish and choice fruits to ardorn their tables, furnish their lady closets with sweetmeats and banquetts with the plenty of curiosoties. As for salt meatts as beef, pork, cod, salmon, butter, cheese, fllower, etc. they are plentyfully supplied with from England (501) and elsewhere, and also with sowers, as oyle, anchoves, currants, olives, caperes, manggoes, and the lick; neither are they wanting as to sutable quelquechoses for regallas,* as cheesecacks, custards, tarts, etc., which are here made as curious as those sold by our pastrie cooks in London.

Indeed the only thing wanting here is good soft bread, such as we in England plentyfully (thro' merceis*) still injoy, for here they have none such; they have here plentyfully brought from England puer white sea bisketts, and also here they make new bread every day with English flower, but what for want of yeast, and by reason of the staleness of the flower, 'tis not comparable to our English bread; and yett they sell but two small rowles therof for a royall. Also here they have plenty of ye casavia bread, sold daily in the market, with fresh roots and hearbs, for here they have plenty of sallading all round the year. Thus they live with full feed tables, not wanting anything requisit to satisfie, delight, and please their curious appitites.

Now as they have plenty of excellent food, soe allso are they stored with strong and delitious vecind [?] brought hither from Madera and England by our English merchant, which here trade. Here they have plenty of good Madera wine, both reed and whit, sold (502) at a reasonable rate, for here you may bie itt in the taverens for one English shilling or two royalls a quart, and at the storehouses for one English sixpence, or one royall a quart; they have also brought hither from England plenty of canary, whitwin, renish, clarrat, brandy, spirits, and good English bear and mum.* Here they sell canary at a dollar a botle, whit, rheinish, and clarrat wine, with brandy and spiritt for half a dollar a bottle, mum at two royalls a quart, and English beer for one royall. The cheif drinck amongst the gentrey and merchants is Madera wine, brandy, punch, beer, perinno, and Adam's ale;* and amongst others rum punch, killdivile,* rapp, mobby and watter, which are the cheife liquour used by the planters in the countrey, and they are soe generous that their tables are seldom free from the servitude of a lusti bowle of the Quacker's cold drinck called rumm punch, to accommodate their friends and visitors.

Now for the accomodation of young merchants, and others which have noe famallies, here are severall ordinary keept, where any may make a plentifull dinner with variety of good fleash, fish, and fruitts, wine and bear, for three royalls a-peice, and at night may spend a royall on a pint of wine, and have their supper free cost. Besides these ordinaries, here are many taverens, and aboundance of punch houses, or rather may be fittly called brothel houses. Here is also a coffe house.[14]

The merchants here commonly at twelve a'clock shut up their shops, and after dinner they devert themselves, either at ye taverens, or else on their couches, or hammocks; about three a'clock the brezes begin to fan the earth strongly, and then they open their shops, and attend their buissines for here 'tis common to sleep in the heat of the day. Att night the take their rest on beads, and cotts, but for the most part in swinging hammock made of cotton, or netts of silkgrass (503), which is most used by the planters in the country both for themselve and English servants.

Att this port is not much variety of recreation for the gentrey, for here they can't hunt the nimble hart, nor fearefull hare, nor flie their hawks in the feilds at ye cackling patridge, for these games are not here to be found, soe that on this island there only recreation is by rideing out in their chariots* in the cold of the mornings and evenings into ye spatious savanas, where they feed their eyes on the plesant prospects of the green woods in their continuall sommer verdure, and refresh themselves with the cold swett breezes, and those which delight in fowleing may here find a plesant recreation, and plenty of game.

Now on this port the inhabitants are denighed all those sweet pleasurs which the country gentrey enjoy; for here they have noe other recreattion, butt by enjoying their friend att the taveren, 'ore a good glass of wine, a sangaree,* or a joly bowle of good punch; on this port is keept a bull and a

14. Originating in Asia Minor, coffee-houses began to appear in western Europe around the middle of the seventeenth century.

bear, for sport at ye bear garden, and billiards, cockfitting, shotting at the targett, etc. is here their cheife recreations. For being pent up on this hott sandy point, they commonly walk in the eavening out at the Palasado gate to Barre's tavern, where they feast with silabubus,* creamtarts, and other quelquechoses; and this is the cheif pleasure of ambulation which is here aforded them.

Also in the eavenings many young sparks and the common sort resort to musick houses to devert themselves, for the port indeed is verey lose in itself, and by reson of privateres and debauched wild blades which come hither (for all the strick restraint of the law), 'tis now more rude and anticque than 'ere was Sodom, fill'd with all maner of debauchery. For notwithstanding the strickt orders of ye governour, and the due execution thereof by the majestrats daily, yett 'tis infected with such a crue of vile strumpets (504) and common prostratures, that 'tis allmost impossible to civillize it since they are only its walkeing plauge, against which neither the cage, whipe, nor ducking stole would prevaile. But now they have prepared that antidote called Bridwell, whose effects perhapps may somewhat abate the mallignity of that walking pest, and allay the furie of those hott Amazons.

Those English children which are here born they calle Crebolians* (becaus born on one of the Crebe islands); they grow generally tall and slendor, of a spare thin body, and pale complection, haveing all light flaxen haire, being at the full growth and prime strenght att fiften years old, and seldome live to be above five and thirty years, for as sone as they are twenty they begin to decline. And here the rude and common sort of people seldom marie acording to the ceremony of ye church, but are soe full of faith as to take one another's words, and soe live together, and begett children, and if they fall out or disaagree, they part friendly by consent. The common people here go generally arrayed in good linen, butt many of them bare-footed, without either shoos or stockinns, soe that you shall see a common woman only in her smock ore linnen peticote, barefooted, without shoo or stockins, with a strawn hatt and a red tobacco pipe in their mouths, and thus they trampouse about their streets in this their warlike posture, and thus arrayed they will booze a cupp of punch rumby with anyone.

On this port, and also in all othere parts of the island, they allow of a free toleration of all sects and releigons, for here on this port we find a Protestant church govern'd according to ye doctrin of the Church of England, also a Presbeterian metting house, a Romish chappell, a Quackers' meeting house and a Jewe's sinagog; all which sects live quietly and peaceably one among another, faithfully serving together in arms for the defence of the island. Neither will ye Quackers here refuse to pledg ye King's helth, nor ye quacks to take a fee.

(505) Now come we to treat of ye manner of trading at this port, and on this island of Jamaica; in order to which you must know that here at this port they bie and sell by the hundredweight, of five score to ye hundred, and that ye cheif mony passable here is Spanish mony, both gold and silver; a Spanish pistole passeth here currant for twenty shillings, and a dollar for five shillings. The least mony found here is ye Spanish royalls, here commonly called a bitt (becaus nothing less can be bought than this will purchas); here our English guineas passes for £1–5s–5d; and English crown, for 6s–3d, an English shilling for 1s–3d and an English sixpence for seavenpence halfpenny. Thus we have given you the account of the weight and exchange of mony passable and customary att this port and all 'ore the island.

To this port merchants daily resort from England, bringing with them considerable cargoes of English commoditys, as wine, cloath, linnen-stuff, silks, fruit, ironwork, pitch, tarr, ropes and other things which they make good returns of here to ye planters and sloop-masters, which trade amongst the Spaniards, and in exchange therof take sugar, indigo, coco, etc. which they send home to their correspondents in England. To this port merchants also daily resort from Dublin and other ports of Ireland, bringing with 'em great cargoes of Irish provition, as beef, pork, salmon, chees, butter, flower, beer, etc.; and those merchant trade here for the like commoditys.

Also to this port resorts many vessels from New England, New York etc. which bring hither provitions as beef, pork, sturgeon, macerell, chees, butter, flower, and peass, with deall boards, speares [?], steaves and hoops for cask, with other the like commodities; these cheifly trade here for sugar, rum, and die-wood. By this quick and free trade, the island begins to gather wealth and strenght amaine. Likewise here the Royall Company of Merchants and African Company have settled a factory here, and bring aboundance of Negroa (506) slaves hither daily, which they sell to the planters for ye sugar, indigo, coco, etc., and give them six months' creditt to pay the same, by which means the island is much enrich't and plantations are improved to admiration.

There are now setled here on this port all sort of mechanicks* and tradsmen,[15] as smiths, carpenters, brick-layers, joyners, turners, cabinett-makers, tanners, curriors, shoemakers, taylors, hatters, upholsters, rope-makers, glasiers, painters, carvers, armourors, and combmakers,* and watermen etc.; all which live here verey well, earning thrice the wages given in England, by which means they are enabled to maintain their famallies much better than in England, by which tradesmen 'tis much advance both in

15. See the extensive list of craftsmen and tradesmen in Pawson and Buisseret, *Port Royal,* 223–31.

strenght and wealth, still becoming more formidable, and will undoubtedly the next age be a most plesant, rich, and uberous habitation.

Now the commodotys which are vended from hence to England and other parts are these, viz. sugar, indigo, coco, cotton, ginger, dogwood, fustick, rumm, hides, and tallow, which is from hence vended home to England and Ireland yearly in great plenty, soe that here are loaden from hence yearly with those commodity above a hundred shipps[16] besides small vessels for England, Ireland, New England, etc., which increas still as the plantations comes to maturatie; these commoditys are ship't off from this port, which is the cheif call of trade and place of resort on this island of Jamaica.

This port begineth now to be much more healthyer than formerly, and people att their first comeing are not now soe subject to the country fevers, etc. as they were wont, tho' many men are cast away for want of a skillfull phisition, for here are creept in a parcell of pittyfull quacks, empericks,* and illiterat pretendors, which have formerly distroy'd many a stout man, which otherwise might have long enjoyed this transatory station. But now it hath pleased God to bestow on this place some few honest chirurgeons, (507) as Mr. Spere, Mr. Robinson, Mr. Smith, etc., which are learn'd, skillfull and men of known integrity; also here is an honest apothecary and drugist one Mr. Mathews.[17] The cheif malladies and destempers common here are aigues, fevers, plurisies, callentuers,* pox, fluxes, yawes* and the *illiaco passio* (here called ye dri-belyach) which deprives many of there strenght and use of limbs for many years, and some forever. Thus we have given you an impartiall account of all noteable occurances, in reference to a genuine discription of this port, in which is layed up the cheife riches of the island; which haveing declared we here conclude this sixth chapter of our present state of His Majestie's island of Jamaica in America.

---

16. A hundred ships was a figure only attained in 1686. Ibid., 91.

17. The surgeons are hard to identify, unless Mr. Spere is Francis Sperry. But the druggist is surely William Mathews. Pawson and Buisseret, *Port Royal*, p. 225.

Chapter VII

(508) Of the situation of Sainta Jago de la Vega, Ligournea, Passagfort, Old Harbour, and Carlisle Town, with the manner of liveing there and att the other setlements on Jamaica. Also an account of the manner of planting and makeing sugar, indigo, coco, rum, cotton and ginger. Likewise a description of the planters' useage towards their Whit servants, Indians and Negroa slaves, with an account of the antique behavioure of those Negroa slaves, and of their late insurrections and rebelions committed on Jamaica.*

Section I

Of the situation of Sainta Jago de la Vega,[1] *Ligournea, Passagfort, Old Harbour, and Carlisle Town, with the manner of liveing there and att the othere settlements on Jamaica.*

The metropholis of Jamaica is that ancientt citie of Sainta Jago de la Vega (or St. James's of ye Plain), which in its first erection by the Spaniards was a verey large and spatious city lieing in a quandrangle as ye ruins (509) make appeare, to then be full six miles in compass. This city is built in a spatious plain, an Indian cornfeild, by the east part of which runns an excelent cleare river of sweet water, seldom or never failling in the greatest droughts. This city now consisteth of about 1,300 houses, most of them Spanish houses, but some few well-built brick houses, for above three-quarters of this city is now thrown down and distroy'd. For when they tooke it from the Spaniards there were then standing in this city above 5,000 houses, many of which were pul'd down, ruin'd, and distroyed by the soldiers and the gauards in a little time. These Spanish houses are low timber-work houses thatch't with palmeta leaves, being but one story high, paved with

1. The Spaniards had named it first Villa de la Vega and then Santiago de la Vega, in honour of St James of Compostela, the patron saint of Spain. The English at first called it St Jago de la Vega, and then Spanish Town.

tilles, haveing letice windows* and great dores opening with two leaves, soe that three horsemen may ride in abrest, for 'tis ye custom of ye proud Spaniards in America allways to ride in to their halls and their allight. But those brick buildings[2] here erected by the English are as lofty and butiful as our buildings in London, and glazed with glass windows.

To this city belong a small church standing towards the south part therof, built by the Spaniards called St. Paul's, which now is much more butified and adorn'd by the English. Here is also the ruins of a spatious church and monastry, called by the Spaniards Nostra Segniora de Rosaria; here His Grace Christopher Duke of Albermarle resides, in a large well-built brick house haveing fouer peices of ordinance mounted befor the gate therof. Here is an audiencia, which is a large house, in which is held the councill of assembly and grand court of judicature; also here is still remaining the Spanish governour's house, fortified with stockadoas after ye Spanish mode. About the midle of this citty is a large perrad,* wheron 5,000 men may perform their exercise at arms; here are the gaurds drawn up, and keep their cheife corps du garde in this (510) part of the city of Sainta Jago de la Vega or Spanish Town.[3]

This town is well inhabited, for here resides the governour and all other the cheife ministers of state, and many welthy gentlemen whose plantations are adjacent. Likewise here are most meckanicks and shops of trade or on Port Royall, and it still daily increases in more inhabitants and well-built houses, for the old Spanish house resembles noe other than our barns or stables in England. In this town are many ordinaries, taverns, and punch houses, as on Port Royall. Now 'twill not be unessesary [*sic*] to understand that those which travels from Port Royall hither commonly goo by water in wherey boats to Passagfort (from whence this city lies northwest, distant six miles), where they may hire either a coach, a chariot, or a hackney horse, to convey them to this city, towards which you have a smoth broad sandy road, in the midle of which stand a tavern (and a large tree of a curious shade before itt) called the halfway house,[4] where you may refresh yourself with wine, or what else you please. Then from hence you have but three miles farther to ye citty, which is all along a smoth sandy drie road in fair wether, but verey deep and mierey after raines. The hier of the coach is fouer dollars, and of a hackney hors six royalls or three English shillings

2. Of these lofty brick buildings, Sloane observed that "they are neither cool nor able to resist the shock of earthquakes". *Voyage,* 1: xlvii.

3. On early Spanish Town, see James Robertson, *Gone is the Ancient Glory: Spanish Town, Jamaica, 1534–2000* (Kingston, 2005)

4. The site of this halfway house seems to have been lost.

At this city the inhabitants live here very plentyfull as att Port Royall, provitions here being allwaies much cheaper than at the port, unless at court time; but here they are not soe well served with tortoise and fish as at the port, by reason they live within land. Here the aire is verey sound and helthfull, and soe are the inhabitants for the most part; neither are they here soe much tormented with those gnawing insects as other parts are, but Port Royall is not at all opprest with 'em, which besides noe other parts of this island is freed from.

Here the gentry in the cold of ye morning and eavenings ride forth in their coaches (511) to recreat themselves in the green and flowery savanas, which pleaseth the eye with it butifull verdure, and revives the speritts with its sweet perfumes, and add noe small delight to man to behold those statly heards of cattel mutually sporting in their uberous pasture. From these aire refreshments they goe to some neiboring plantation (as to Spring Garden,[5] etc.), where they have a regalla of cream tarts, fruites, or what else they thinck fitt, but above all be sure they won't faill of a good glass of wine, and a jolly bowle of punche. Thus the inhabitants of this citty spend their time in ease and pleasure, haveing English servants to manage their cheife affaire and supervise their Negroa slaves, which not only waite on them, butt also doe their work both in their houses and plantations, bringing great proffit to the planters.

Now this city receives its trad cheifly from masters of ships and others, which ressort from Port Royall hither to doe their negoations with the governour; and also it hath great trade in time of the sessions of the grand court of judicature, which is held in this city four times a yeare, holding six daies together, at which the inhabitants of this island resort hither from all parts to dispatch their suites in common pleas, as they doe resort from all parts of England at the terms to the King's Bench bar at Westminster, by which means there is a great concourse of people, and 'tis as a faire duering the session of this grand court of judicature, in which times provition is here excessive deare. Also on the first Thursday in every month is held here a Court of Chancery before the governour (who represent the Lord Chancellor), in which all causes theron deppending are forthwith desided, here being noe delays used therein.

The melitia of this city is about one thousand foot and 250 horse, which are to be redy at arms on all ocations, and every Sunday there is 250 foot and 60 horse in arms to guard His (512) Grace to and from the church, and centinalls are kept att his dore both night and day.[6] Thus the inhabitants of

5. This is a common name for Jamaican estates, but here probably refers to the one a few miles north of Gutters, on the Old Harbour road.

6. In 1680 the militia at Spanish Town numbered 592 infantry and a troop of horse. National Archives, CO 1/45, fo. 59.

this city live in pleasure and plenty, under dilligent majestrates and a godlie minister one Dr. Bennet,[7] whoe takes much paines for their soules, and ye seasoned Dr. Rose[8] great cear of their body's health; for here the air is fine and healthfull, by which means ye inhabitants are not soe much affected with agues, fevers, *illiaco passio* etc. as in other parts of Jamaica, the people looking here much freasher and healthyer than the inhabitants of Port Royall.

Of Ligournea

Ligournea, the garden of Jamaica, lies distant from Port Royall six miles north across the harbour and river, to which you pass by wherry boats which continually plie betwixt that and the port. This place was best estemed and planted by the Spaniards, and by them soe named in remmembrence of their ancient and plesant city of Ligourn.[9] This is noe formadable town, here being by the watterside only a new church, some twenty shops and houses, and two or three taverns; but however this is the plesants place on all the island, being continually plantable, green and flourishing for severall miles together, the plantations lieing like another Eden, whose trees are allways loaden with ripe and delitious fruites, the earth filled with choice hearbs and roots, and the circumambient aire filled with odourous perfumes and the warbling musike of ravishing voices, echoing from the slendor pipes of ye ambitious nitingale.

This compared with the other parts of the island is like Cisillia,* which is said to be soe full of swett flowers that the sweet smells therof reveribat the scent, soe that ye doges can't there hunt. Soe this place is soe truly (513) plesant, that the muses themselves never enjoyed such shady, sweet and delightfull bowers, the verey hedges being full of golden oranges, lemons and sweet-smelling jecamons continually, soe that here is also found most of our choice Europian products, as well as the variety of American vegitables; soe that noe part in all America can outvie it, for it not only sustains itself with all things plesant, but also sends dayly to Port Royall plenty of fleash, fowels, fish, herbs, roots, and fruites with milk, and other quelquechoses.[10]

On this place the inhabitants live extreamly happy by the enjoyment of each other's company, for the plantations all joyn to one another, by which

7. In 1682 Mr Bennett was listed as the parson for St David's parish. *Calendar of State Papers, America and West Indies, 1682–85*, 79.

8. This is surely Fulke Rose (died 1693), brother of Francis Rose; both were assemblymen and members of the Council of Jamaica. Michael Craton and James Walvin, *A Jamaican Plantation* (London/New York, 1970), 40–41.

9. Or Leghorn. It seems much more likely that this name came from the Arawak, perhaps deriving from "Iguana". See Olive Senior, *The A–Z of Jamaican Heritage* (Kingston, 1985), 94.

10. See Claypole, "The Settlement of the Liguanea Plain", 7–16.

means they live the more securelie from the incursions and outrages of their runaway vassals and Negroas. Also here they have liberty and variety of recreations (which the Port is denighed), as fowling, hunting of the sturdy wild bull and furious bore, shooting of the targett, pitching of the barr,[11] and stiffly bowseing a jolly bowle of the quacker cold drinck called rum paunch. In fine the welthy planter lives here in full enjoyment of ease and plenty, haveing whatever his hart can either desier or wish to enjoy, save a scilent wife and a future happyness. In the meantime not considering his pore slaves, whom the sun and tormenting insects in the feild are like to devour, for by the paines of their vassals they becom rich, and live in plenty, ease and luxurie not minding the misery of the slaves.

The melitia of this setlement, and precinct belonging thereto, is 3,000 foot and 600 horse, well armed and disciplin'd, and to be redy on all occations.[12] Here is a new well-built church, and a truly godly minister one Dr. Seller, with a great congrogation.[13] Here is also a Quackers' meeting house and quaacks and Quackers plentie (514). Thus have we given you a full and true description of Ligournea, which is the place to which the gentry and merchants of the Port repaire to take their pleasure, as those of London doe to Isslington, Hackney and the Spring Gardens.

Of Passage Fort

This place called Passag Fort lies at the uper end of the wester end of Port Royall river, northwest from ye port, and distant about six miles. 'Tis the place wheron the English first landed when they took this island from the Spaniards, here being then built a small timberwork fort, with six peices of ordnance to defend that pass, which was by them called La Forta de la Passage.[14] This plase lies in a low valy betwixt two hills being a morros wett sand; here are built about thirty houses, ten taverns, and as many storehouses, where the adjacent planters lay up their commodoties to be conveyed to Port Royall. This lies in St. Katharin's precinct, and is well populated and

11. "Pitching of the barr" is perhaps something like pitching horseshoes.

12. In 1680 the infantry of the St Andrew's precinct had numbered 665, and the cavalry 46. National Archives, CO 1/45, fo. 59.

13. In 1682 the minister for St Andrew at Half-Way Tree Church was James Zeller, who had come from Zürich in 1664. He became a considerable sugar-planter and wrote a description of Jamaica, *Neue Beschreibung der Insul Jamaica in America* (Zürich, 1677–78). Richard S. Dunn, *Sugar and Slaves: The Rise of the Planter Class in the English West Indies* (Chapel Hill, 1972), 267.

14. This name seems to be one of Taylor's inventions. But Passage Fort was around 1680 regarded as "the fair hopeful beginning of a larger Town". Trapham, *Discourse of the State of Health*, 23.

indeferent healthfull. Here are severall hackney coaches* and horses which keep their daily stage betwixt this and the city Sainta Jago de la Vega. This town receives its trade chiefly by those which resort from the Port to Spanish Town and from thence to the Port. The melitia forces of this town and parts adjacent are about 100 horse and 400 foot; here they have plenty of fleash, fish, fowles, herbs and fruites, and are both by day and night miserably torment with stinging insects.

Of Old Harbour

Old Harbour is a port which was called by the Spaniards Porto Dogua,[15] and was their cheife port and place of trade. This port lies west-north-west from Port Royall, and is distant by sea about (515) sixteen miles, and from Sainta Jago de la Vega about twelve miles by land. This is a town concisting of about a hundred houses, shops and storehouses, with a kind of a chappell and minister.[16] This place have few well-built houses thereon, neither is it verey well populated, nor hath it any considerable trade. In this town are some taverns, and you need not question paunch houses, tho' nothin else; here are also setled some few mechanicks and shoopkeepers. This port is situated in good low firm ground, most of it planted, plantable and savanas, and the aire there is indeferent healthfull. This port receives its small trade cheifly from the planters, whoe bring down their commoditys to their store-house in order to its transportation to Port Royall, and from the masters of shalloops, which come hither for the planters' commodities. This was the cheif port of the Spaniards, but now is of noe esteem, becaus here resides noe merchants nor gentrey, neither doe any ships now resort hither.

Twice a yeare doe the horsmen of this port runn with the horsemen of Carlisle for a peice of plate, which this last year was twice wonn by the Carlisle cavaliers, they being estemed to have the best horses found on Jamaica.

This place aforeds plenty of all Jamaican products as beast, fowles, fish, herbs, fruits, roots, sugar, rumm etc., soe the inhabitants lives plentifully, working in their plantations, and looking after their crawles of cattel etc. This lies in ye precinct of St. Dorrothie's, and its melitia forces and parts adjacent is about 150 horse and 700 foot, which are well armed, and allways to be redy in arms on occation. Thus we have given you a plaine and true description of Old Harbour.

15. Taylor refers here to what is now Old Harbour Bay, which he insists on calling Porta Dogua (see p. 77n14).

16. There had perhaps been a minister at Old Harbour in the earliest days of the English occupation, but he had in later years been based at Alley.

Of Carlisle Town

Carlisle Town[17] lies from Port Royall west by south, distant by water about 35 miles, and from Saint Jago, according to the road, forty miles (516). This place was called by the Spaniards Porta Emyas, and by the English at their first setling called Withywood, because 'twas then soe wody and overgrown with withs that 'twas scarsly passible, and is now called Carlisle Town, soe named by the earle of Carlisle, in time of his lieutenancy. This place is situated an a spott of moross low ground, by the bay side; this is a good cleare sandy bay, wherein may safly ride one hundred saile of shipps, and was formerly a place of great rendesvouze both for English and French privateres.

Figure 42 Detail from Philip Lea's map of Jamaica (London, 1696). This detail shows the former site of "Carlisle", in Vere parish. Only the name "Carlisle Bay" now survives.

17. The town of Carlisle lay just to the east of the mouth of the Rio Minho, where Carlisle Bay now is. Were the races perhaps run at Race Course, a little way to the north?

Now this town concisteth of about one hundred houses and a small well-buillt chappel, and is verey populous and well inhabited; to this port belonges about forty shalloops which comes a-tradeing hither from Port Royall and the northside, with Irish provitions, maize, etc. At this port resides many wealthy Jewes merchants, and here are held two faires everey yeare. Here the neiboring planters lay upp their commodoties in store-houses which they transport from hence to Port Royall; here are many taverns and punch-houses with quacks and Quackers plenty.[18]

This place is next to Ligournea, both for plenty and plesantness, for nere adjacent therto are many good and large plantations in which resides many good and wealthy gentlemen. These plantations are verey fertill in sugar, indigo, and corn, and they are also plentyfully stored with cattel and fowles, fish, and all manner of choice American herbs, fruites, and roots, and they keep in their houses Indian slaves, which furnish them with plenty wild hog, fish and fowles, by which they find suffitient provition for the whole famallies, which game they shoot with their arrows and darts, for here after the raines are aboundance of wild fowles in the savanas, as ducks, widgeon, teal, etc., and plenty of variety of excelent fish in the salenas, lakes, and ponds.

The inhabitants are witty, sharp and stout (517) soldiers, for they daily practice shooting at the targett. This part of the island is composed into one redgment of hors and two of foot, soe that the melita here concist of 1,000 horse and 3,000 foot, well trained and disciplin'd soldiers.[19] The inhabitants of this part are verey generous and flattering, liveing verey high, for the most part (as all one this south side of the island) keeping the coaches, neither will they here refuse to bowse a lusty bowle of rum paunch stifly; here they generally lodge in cotton swinging hamock or on cotts.

The people at this town on the bay are not verey healthfull, by reason 'tis a low wett moross ground and not well cleared, soe that therwith and the densitie and stincks of the aire, it is not att all healthfull, altho further up in the country where it is better cleared and the aire more fitin it is verey healthfull. And yet they are here most misserably tormented with gnawing and stinging fleas. Here is a verey worthy Mr. one Dr. More,[20] who by his sound doctrine and examplarie liveing hath much alltered the manners of the people, altho' they are yett verey lose and lude.

---

18. Taylor's account of Carlisle Town seems rather exaggerated. But he had lived nearby for some time, and had actually sailed from there, when he left Clarendon.

19. The militia of these parts, with slaves from the adjacent plantations, played a large part in repelling the French in 1694. See Buisseret, "The French Invasion", 31–33.

20. Presumably this is the "ancient man named Dr. More". See p. 231n7.

In this town of Carlisle is held fouer times a yeare a court for desideing of petti causes for the precincts of Clarindon and Vere. This court is held by Major Peck,[21] judge therof, and the bench of His Majesties' justices of the peace for those persincts. Here is also a goale keept by Mr. Aldred, Duputie Marshall for the precinct of Vere, and in the precinct of Clarendon nigh Ketle Savana is kept another goale by Mr. Arnold Ladore, Deputi Marshall for the precinct of Clarindon. In which precinct is also a chapell, and another minister one Mr. More rector therof;[22] nevertheless, amongst the youth and lesser sort of inhabitants they are verey lewd, and the sabath day is the cheif day for their drincking and pastime. Thus we have given you a true account of Carlisle Town or Withywood with a description of the precincts of Clarendon and Vere on Jamaica.

(518) There are many other large and wealthy plantations betwixt this and Punta Negrilla, but noe towns nor churches, wherfore we omit a description therof; the melitia forces is about 4,000. Now let us cast our eyes on the windward or easter part of Jamaica, that we may also here give a true description therof. And first we shall spake of Morrant setlement, which is a verey plesant and fertill place, wherein are some twenty large and rich plantations, which yeild plenty of provitions and fruits. This is verey healthful but much tormented with stinging insects. This setlement belonges to the rectory of Yallows.[23] This Yallowes is a setlement on the southside of Jamaica, to the eastward of Port Royall; about twentie miles here are about twenty large and rich plantations, fertill in sugar, indigo, etc., yeilding plenty of provitions and fruites; this place is healthfull, but much anoyed with ye stinging plauges which gnawgh and bitt cruelly. Here is a chapel of which one Doctor Goodwin is minister. The melitia forces of these two setlements is about three hundred hors and two thousand foot.

On the northside of this His Majestie's island of Jamaica in America the plantations are not many, [and] those small and scattering, soe that it is nedless to discribe 'em; however knowe that they are more fertile than those on the southside, answering with profitt the cultivator's labour and expence.[24] These inhabitants are armed and composed into a formidable melitia, but their number is not known. Now before we conclude this section, you must know that this present yeare 1688 the whole melitia of this island amounted

21. This may well be John Peeke, member of the House of Assembly for Clarendon in the 1680s.

22. "Mr. More" seems to be Taylor's default minister, so to speak.

23. The rectory at Yallahs was the ecclesiastical centre for the parish of St David's; "Doctor Goodwin" is not to be identified.

24. Taylor here foreshadows the eighteenth-century development of the parishes of St James and Trelawny.

to 21,680 men all armed and well disciplin'd, (viz.) 15,800 foot and 5,830 horse compleatly armed.[25] Thus we have finished this first section of our seventh chapter of the state of Jamaica.

Section II

(519) *Of the planting and boyling, curering and compleating of sugar, indigo, rum, coco, cotton, and ginger; with the manner of planting maize, guineacorn, peas, scottgrass, potatas, yams and the cassavia root.*

Now we come to treat of the manner of planting and makeing sugar, indigo, rum, coco, cotton and ginger, and that we may proceed in a cleare, genuine, inteligible method we will handle each severally, that we may make all plain and obvious: in order to the procecution wherof, we will here first give a description of the manner of the growth and planting of the sugar cane, and the true art of makeing good muscavada sugar from the cane.

Sugar is the juice of a cane, brought by extrordinary boyling to a strong consistance and drie graine, of noe small profitt to the painfull planter, and as much usefull and beneficatiall to others.[26] This sugare is produced from a shrub which is called a cane, growing about the bigness of a man's wrist, and some four, five, or six foot high, haveing joynts at the ground not above two inches long encreasing in length till towards the top, where they are about five or six inches long. This cane bears a long leaf like a flagg, which as the cane shoots up falls off and rots. This cane is smoth, soft and solid, full of a swett juice, and is three years before it comes to its full growth, and then (520) 'tis fitt to make sugar of, and begins to decay.

Now this shrub or cane is planted thus: after the ground is cleansed from woods and weeds, and is howed fine, and moisten'd with the seasoning raines, then they take of the top joynts of this cane about five foot long, which they plant in this ground in rowes about two foot assunder every plant, leting but one joynt of their plant be above the earth; after they have finished their planting, the overseer causeth the Negroes to hill up every plant, as we doe our hops* in England. These canes thus planted will sprout up, and stock some two, three or more canes from every plant, according to the richness of the soile and seasonableness of the weather.

25. These figures are about three times as large as those given in the militia list for 1680. National Archives, CO 1/45, fo. 59. No doubt the population had grown during the 1680s, but not to that extent.

26. For an interesting summary of the way in which Jamaican planters and their slaves learned how to grow sugar, see Bridenbaugh and Bridenbaugh, *No Peace beyond the Line,* 86–97. Taylor's three-year growth cycle seems too long.

Figure 43 Engraving of a sugar-works, from Pierre Pomet, *Histoire générale des drogues* (Paris, 1694) (by courtesy of the Chicago Botanic Garden). This image shows the cane being crushed at the top left; a gutter then carries the juice downhill into the cistern that supplies the boiling vats.

About six months after planting these canes are weeded, and cleansed from their dead leaves, which allways fall off as the cane shoots upp; and thus they weed 'em, and cleanse 'em from their old leaves and drie thrash as often as their is occation, and keep some Negroa slaves to catch the ratts with their clavers* which they find about 'em, which otherwise would doe much mischife by knawghing* those canes, which would sone cause them to rott and consume. Thus they look carefull after their canepeices till they are come to maturity, which is in three years after planting, and they plant them every year to come in course fitt to work up twice a yeare.

Soe that as in there plantations you shall find severall accars of canes redy to be cutt, soe shall you find other spotts not fitt to be cutt in six months, others in a year, others in one year and a half, others in two years, others in two years and a half, and other new sprouting cane-peices not fitt to be cutt untill three years be expired; and thus they keep their canepeices in their plantations to come allways in season every six months one after another, and those canes thus planted will hold in the ground nine years, and be fitt to be cutt three times, and then they will decay and new one must be planted in their rowes. Thus we have given you a full account of the manner of planting and propogating the sugar cane, and now come to shew the manner of makeing good muscavade[27] sugar from this cane or shrubb.

Now the canes being come to maturity, and their stovecoals being furnish with wood, the planter begins to prepare for sugar boyling. Soe the overseer (520[repeated]) setts his Negroas to cutting of canes, which they doe thus; they have a verey sharp hook or bill, made for that purpose, with which they cuts the cane off upward within three inches of the ground. Then they cutt off about fouer foot of the lower part of the cane for sugar, which they make up in bundells and carry to the sugar mill. Then they take the other part of the cane and cutt of the top joynt and leaves, and then bind these up in bundles and carry to the mill to grined upp for rum, of which we shall speake hereafter. Now whilst some of the slaves are imployed in cutting up canes, others are imployed in grinding and boyling, and the rest in carrying away the cane topps, clearing the ground, and hilling up the stocks. For this they doe presently after cutting, and feed their cattle with the tops and burn the drie trash.

Now the canes being cutt and carried to the mill, they are there ground or all their juice prest out in the mill, which is formed thus: this mill is composed of three large iron rowlers, which turn one against another, the two outermost of which move round against the midlemost, which is fix't; these rowlers move close to one another, and are turn'd round by twelve oxen, in the same manner as our horse-mills are in England.[28] Now the canes are putt in (by those which tend the mills) betwixt these rowlers, which by their motions hals them quite thro', presses out their juice, and leaves the trash part of the cane on 'tother side the mill, which is caryed away and laine in heapes for dunge. Now the juice of the cane runs down from the mill in spoutes into a cistern placed in the boyling house for that purpose. Thus we have acquainted you with the maner of planting, cuting, and grindeing the sugare cane, and now we come to shew you the manner of boyling and makeing of good muscavade shugar therewith.

Now the juice being prest out they begin to boyle it, which they doe thus. You must understand that in their boyling house they have fouer large copper furnasse, standing by the side of one another. Now they fill the first furnace with the juice, and the Negro slaves in the outside of the house atends the

27. This term comes from the Portuguese "Mascovado", referring to the molasses-rich sugar which clung to the sides of the sugar cones.

28. From an early period there were also mills worked by wind and water power.

fire, and the overseer or sugar boyler (522 [521 was omitted]) attends the motion of his coppers within the house, scuming off the scum as often as it arise, puting it into a cistern (in the boyling house) for to make rum with all, as we shall shew hereafter. Having boyle his juice here as long as any scum will arise, he emptyeth it forth with ladles into the next copper, whose bottom is thicker, and will induer more heating; here he boyles it as long as any scum will arise, which he takes clean off, and saves as before. Now the juice begins to grow thick and ropey, and if at any time his coppers rise high and are redy to boyle over, he squeazes in some few drops of the juice of a freash lemmon or lime, which will presently cause it to sinck, stopp its furie, and keep it quiet.

Haveing boyl'd it in this second copper as long as 'twill yeild scum and the furnace will induer heating, the boyler laves* it forth into the third copper, whose bottom is thicker, and will enduer further heating; here they boyle it as long as any scumm will arise, which they save as before. By this time the juice is become verey roppy and thick like gelly, and of a light brown collour. Being boyled to this hight the sugarr boyler removes it into the fouerth copper, which is called the tatch;[29] the bottom of this furnas is about half a foot thick, and will enduer much heat; here they boyle it till it becomes verey stiff and glewey, which they often trie by droping it on a plate etc., which when they find it boyled to a concistency highe enough to beare graine, then they put into the tatch a convenient quantitie of puere fine wood ashes to take away its ropy quallyty, and bring it to a due graine, which it sone efects. Now if these ashes prove uneffectuall, then they take a convenient quantity of the fine mould or earth where the canes grew, and applie it in the same manner, and it sone performes the desier'd effect.

Now the juice being boyled in the tatch to a true consistencie and a due graine, the sugar boyler empties it out into the sugar potts made for that purpose, and letts it stand in the colding house to cold and harden, and thus they keep boyling night and day, Sunday and else, untill they have finished all those canes workable at that season. Thus we have (523) shewed you the true way and method of sugar boyling, and now come to shew the true way of its cureing and compleating, till 'tis become good and perfect muscavada sugare.

In the former paragraph we told you how that the sugar was emptied from out the tatch into potts, the which 'twill be necessary here to describe; therfore know that they are made thus. The sugar pott are made either of earth or wood. Those of earth are made round, broad at the top and narrow

29. This is the "tach" of Ligon, who gives an exceptionally full account of how sugar was made. *A True and Exact History*, 90–91.

at the bottom, being the segment of a cone: in the bottoms of this pott is a center hole, like a tap hole, which is stoped with a longe pott stick, which stands all allong up in the pott, and high, being to be pul'd out to lett the molosas from the sugar, as shall be shewed annon.

These earthen poot are the beste estemed, and will hold about half one hundredweight of sugar, besides the drosie* bottom part, and molosas. The sugar potts which are made with wood are fouer square, being the segment of a pyramid, brode at tope, and narrow at bottom; to these belonges a hole and a pot stick as to the former. These are made to hold nigh the same quantytie of sugar also.

Now the sugare being emptied into these potts, and haveing stood there in a collding place some two daies and nightes, the operator[30] pull out the pott stick, and lets the molosas away from the sugar. This molosas is put some up in jarrs for the use of the plantation, and the rest putt in the steep cistern amongst the scummings in order to be destilled for rum, of which we shall spake hereafter. Now the sugar being drined from the molasas, the potts are removed into a very close drie house called the cuereing house; here they are sett in rows, and a gentle fiere made in the midle of the house for about a daie and a night, by which means the sugare is cuered, dried and becomes perfect sugare of a bright collour and a good grain, for here is noe whit sugare, nor powder sugar, clayed or otherwise made but at two plantations on this island, which is at Sir Frann. Wattson's,[31] and Mr. Waterhouse's plantation, where is made a small quantity of white loaf and clai'd sugare to serve themselves and neibouring planters. For the shugar here made is a bright sugare, verey fatt (524) and swetening, richer than at Barbados, and is properly here called muscavade sugar, which was sold here to the English merchants (this present yeare 1688) for 11s the worst, and 15s the best, which was acounted cheape; and here at the shops they sell three pound weight thereof for a royall, or one English sixpence.

Now to draw to a conclution you must understand that after the sugar is thus cured, they emptieth itt out of the potts into large hoggsheads,* and soe heads it up fast, transportes it to Port Royall, and their either sell it to the merchants ore else send it home to their correspondents in London etc., which makes them good returns. Now att the bottom of these potts there will be a lump of hard drosie sugar, of some two pound weight, not fitt for sale; this they keep for their own use in their plantatione. Thus we have given a full

30. "Operator", oddly modern to our ears, dates, in fact, to the late sixteenth century.

31. It is, curiously, hard to tell the location of the plantation of Sir Francis Watson, who came from Clarendon; that of Rainiford Waterhouse was in St Andrews, somewhere under Red Hills. See the map by John Seller, *Novissima et accuratissima insulae Jamaicae descriptio* (London, 1671).

and plaine description of the planting and propogating the sugare cane, with the true manner of makeing good muscavade sugare from the said shrubb or cane according to the custom of Jamaica.

Of Rumm

Rumm is a fatt strong spirit, distil'd from the juice of the sugare cane, being in itsself much hotter and stronger than brandy, and is here a considerable commodoty and the originall generatrice of the chief drinck of this island, called rumm paunch. And this spirit is made after this manner: they take the top part of the sugar cane (as we mentioned before in page the 520) and grind it in the sugar mills, and putt the juice therof into the steep cistern, with the molosas, and scumming of the sugar (as we mentioned befor), where they lett it stand for many daies of stirring it untill 'tis purged; for by standing 'twill become full of live worms, and perhaps the overseer will empt his camberpot into it, to keep the Negroas from drincking it.

Now after 'tis become cleare and sower like vinegar, then they distill it in a still with a copper head and a worm*, and it produces a strong (525) fatt spirit, haveing a sweet burnish tast, and this spiritt is called here rumm and at Barbados killdivile,[32] being farr more safe and holsom for the body of man (either simpley or in punch) than brandy, for wheras that is hott and drie, a great enemy to the liver, vitalls and fountain of blood, this is hott, moist and fatt, a great reviver of the spirrits and nurisher of the body of man in those parts, as I have experimented it by the liver of a beast, and compared it with brandy, and finde it to bee of two different naturs. For this turns the liver to a jelly and therfor must be a great help to disjestion etc.; and brandy I found to drie and hardon the liver, and parfarett it full of spungy hole, from whence I gather that 'tis distructive to man and a great enemy to health, although a small dram therof in a cold morning, or here in the heat of the day will doe noe great harme.

This spirit or rum is here a good and certaine commodoty at the port, seldom worth less than two royalls a gallon; besides it stands the planter in great steed at home in makeing of paunch etc. for himself, friends and servantts. Some here on this island for the use of their own famally distill this spirit overe again, by which means it becomes exceading strong, and loseth its sweet burnish tast, and is farr better than brandy, and lookes full as cleare and fine. Thus wee have given you a full description of the true way of makeing and distilling that Jamaican spirit called rum.

---

32. See the anonymous Barbadian quoted in Bridenbaugh and Bridenbaugh: "the chief fudling they make in the island is rumbullion, alias killdivill, and this is made of sugar cones distilled; a hott, hellish and terrible liquor". *No Peace beyond the Line,* 92.

Of Indigo

Indigo[33] is a blew fatt oylie gumm made from the juice of a Jamican hearb of noe considerable growth, seldom groweing above half a yard high, on a slendor stalk, full of branches, covered with a smoth long thick leafe, of a deep green colour, and yeild a small round seed, like coriander. Now that we may proceed in a genuine method, we will here now first discribe (526) the true way of planting and propigating this plant, and then show how 'tis improved, in produceing that certain and rich commodoty called by us indigo.

Now that we may proceed clearly you must know that haveing fitted and prepar'd their ground for planting, imediatly after the seasoning showers they begin to plant their indigo, which they doe thus: they plant the seed thick in strait rows which stand about one foot assunder, and now haveing planted fouer or five rowes of indigo, they plant one row of maize or Indian corn, and soe doe thro'out all their indigo peice five rowes of indigo and one of maize, five rowes of indigo and one of maize etc.; this maize they plant to defend the indigo from the heat of the sun and scorching winds, for 'tis a tendor plant. Now when 'tis sprung up they take care to keep it clean from weed; this plant in seasonable weather will be fitt to cutt in 3 months' time, and afterwards in two months soe that you shall have fouer crops a year. This herb is fitt to cutt when 'tis at its full growth, and begineth to put forth its buds to blome, and with good cutting and care will hold in the ground for three or fouer years.

Thus haveing shewed how to plant we leave itt growing and come to discribe an indigo work, in order to which you must know that an indigo work is built thus: in the side of some small hill or rizeing ground in their plantation they build a square cistern of brick, closely layed with tiles and paved cloce in the bottom, soe that 'twill hold watter without leaking. This cistern they build about sixteen foot square and five foot deep, with a brazen cock in the desending side nigh the bottom, and this cistern soe finish is called the steip* cistern. Now joyning to this and below itt they build another cistern with brick in the same manner haveing the same dementions, both in lenght and breadth, but is but three foot deep, whose brim is even with the former's bottom, soe that the (527) cock emptieth itself into this cistern, which hath also on the side of descent a brassen cock like the former, and this

33. Indigo was an important crop in the 1670s and 1680s, and Taylor's account of its production is unusually detailed; it would have been abundant around the area of Clarendon where he worked. Very few indigo works have survived, though one may still be seen at the western end of the Hellshire Hills.

Figure 44 Engraving of an indigo works, from Denis Diderot, *Encyclopédie,* 17 vols. (Paris, 1751–65), "planches" for the section on "économie rustique" (by courtesy of the Newberry Library, Chicago). Here we see the stages in indigo production, from the fields "N" to the cistern of clear water "A", down to the canvas bags in which the finished indigo is draining and drying "G".

cistern thus finished is called the draught cistern. Lastly, joyning to this and below it is built a third cistern with brick as the former, haveing the same dementions both to lenght and breadth, but is not above two foot deep, on the lower side of which nigh the bottom is a cock to empty this also on ocation, and this cock throws forth the watter on the ground. This cistern thus finished is called the water cistern; thus we have given you a full description of an indigo work, and now we come to show the use therof.

Now whilst we have bin building our indigo work, the plant is grown to maturity and fully ripe for cutting, which as sone as they perceive they cutt it up cloce to the ground with sharp hooks which they have for that purpose, and carry it forthwith to the work, and fill the stupe* cistern or vatee [?] therewith; then with rammers of guacum the Negroas beat it, poun it and drive it cloce together, lain after laine until the cistern is 3/4 full therwith. Then they fill the residue of the cistern with water and soe lett it stand in stupe for that day and night and untill the next day noon; then they tread it with their feet and take out the hearb, wringing it drie betwixt their hands and afterwards throw it to the dunghill, haveing take ye hearb clean out of the watter both stalks, leaves etc.; they stir all their water togeather with poles, and soe opens the cock and lets it run into the drain cistern, it lokeing now of a blewish green collour, and soe they fills up their stupe cistern with fresh hearb, in preparation to worke another vate.

Now it being in the drain cistern they beat the water with flat poles (made for that purpose) untill it changeth its colloure and lookes cleare like brandy, then to know when 'tis of a due hight, they tast it, which when it tast strong and fiery on the tunge 'tis beat enough, and then they lett it stand for the indigo to settle all night (528). Now on the morrow when the indigo is setled to the botom like blew mudd, and the watter of the cistern looks cleare like water, then they open the cock of the drain cistern, and lett it runn clean out gently into the water cistern, where 'tis keep for some time to save the second setling of the indigo, if there remains any behind.

This being done they take all the mud out of ye draine cistern, and spred it in broad thin cakes in boxes which they have for that pourpose, and soe drie itt in the sun, and soe it becomes a pure shineing blew hard gummy substance, called indigo, and thus they work it vatte after vate until they have finished their hearb. This is a rich and good commodoty, being now worth at the port (this present year 1688) noe less than £9–00sh.–0p. sterling, that is about 3s. 9p. a pound, which was accounted cheap. In fine 'tis ever a certaine quick and good commodity, farr excelling sugar or any commodoty else vendable from this island. Thus we have given you a true and plain description of the maner of planting and propigateing this plant, with the true manner of improveing the same by makeing indigo therwith.

Of Coco

Coco[34] is a small nutt, filled with a fatt nutrificious curnall, of which is made a most excellent liquor called chocalata, highly estem'd by the greatest princes of the earth. This princely fruit is one of the richest and certainst commodotys that those western parts of the world affordeth. Now that we may in this paragraph proceed in a cleare and genuine method, we will first give you a description of this tree and its fruitte, then show you the maner of its planting, progating, gathering of the fruit and cuereing, and lastly we shall discribe the true way of makeing chocalata and of the worth of this commodity. Now let us proceed in order, first:

(529) The island of Jamaica when 'twas taken by the English from the Spaniards then aforded many excellent plantations of coco trees, which since are runn to much decay, by reason that then they had not time to looke after

34. For a bibliography concerning the growing of cocoa, see Bridenbaugh and Bridenbaugh, *No Peace beyond the Line,* 286n31.

'em; however there are yett on this island some excelent coco walks which produce a verey considerable profitt. This coco tree is a small tree or shrub, seldom above ten foot high, and of a slender bulk, haveing both bark and leaf like the almond tree, and is a verey tender plant, sone distroyed unless by other trees sheltered from the wind and sun. Now this tree yeilds plenty of a small nutt of a verey thinn sheall, growing some ten or more in a clustur; the curnall of this nutt is verey fatt and nutrificious, tho' in itself of noe plesant taste, and is one of the richest commoditys of America, vendable to all parts. Thus we have given you a description of the tree and its fruite; we now come to shew you the manner of its planting, propogateing and cuering.

The coco tree is planted with aboundance of care, for after they have prepared a peice of ground of the richest soyle which their plantation affordeth, then upon the out limits therof all round they plant one row of plantann, or boonana trees (which is planted from a young sacarr or slipp), then within it they plant two rowes of coco trees, or nutts, then they plant another row of plantan trees, and then two rowes more of coco trees, or nutts, soe that in a coco wall you shall finde fouer rowes of coco trees and three rowes of plantanns, namely one row at ye two outsides and one row in the midle, as we have said before; these plantann trees are planted to defeend the coco trees from the scorching of ye sun, and blasting of ye winds, for 'tis indeed a verey tender plant and will not endure the winds, nor but litle of ye heat of ye sun.

The coco tree thus planted soon sprouts up, and being carfull looked after [and] cleansed from weed, according its natur, in fouer years time begins to yeild fruite, which it aforeds sometimes once, and (530) sometimes twice a yeare, according to the goodness of the weather etc.; this nut is commonly ripe in three months time, which when 'tis fitt for gathering it lookes of a yallowish brown like an acroon. Now they must be gathered with all the care imaginable, that soe the tree be not hurt therby. Now the fruit being gathered all the stems and leaves must be taken clear away, then must the [word omitted by Taylor] be laid in the sun to drie, allways being carefull that noe dues or any other moisture fall on 'em.

Now in six or ten dayes time they will be suffitiently cuered, which you shall perceive for then will they feele drie and hard, and look of red-brown collour, which when they doe then are they throly cuered, and are fitt to be putt up in bagg, and carefully keept drie for sale. This nutt is a quick and rich comodity being worth at the Port this present year 1688 noe less than £15–12s.-6p., or by the single pound they were sold there for six royalls. Thus we have given a full account of the true planting and propigating of the coco tree, with the manner of cuering the nut to make it fitt for sale at ye Port; now as for the true manner of improveing this nut, in the making of chocalata therwith, we have allredy fully declared in page 452, where you may receive full satisfaction therein, which for brevity sake we have here omitted repetition therof.

Of Cotton

Cotton is a Jamaican commodity, being in itsself a whit soft woley substance, naturall proceeding from the fruite of a shrubb called the cotton tree, which is a lowe shrub, like a hazell, seldom above six foot high, haveing a leafe like our English corrants in every respect, being allways green. This shrubb is not here much planted, by reason cotton is att this Port a commodity of noe considerable advantage, but sugare and indigo yeilds farr greater profitt. However here are some cotton plantatlons on this island, as at Madam Grege's nere ye Rock etc.;[35] and (531) therefore we shell here shew the manner of planting and producing the same, in order to which know:

That after they have planted the seed of this cotton tree, and have plants about a foot high, then they chuse out a parsle* of wett land, ye worst in their plantation, and in it plant those cotton plants about six or eight foot asunder in equall rowes, which they keep allways clean from weeds. Now this plant will come to perfection in six years time, and yeild plenty of cotton which it produces in an ovillar nutt or apple about the bigness of a hen's egg and twice as long, covered with a thin brown shell, which being ripe burst open, and is full of snow-white cotton woll. This nutt being thus ripe is taken from the tree, and laied to drie some three or fouer days in the sun, then the shell is taken off, and the cotton woll is cleansed from the seeds by an engine which they call screwing, which being don the cotton is compleated, pac't up in baggs and cary'd to the Port wher 'twas sold this present year anno 1688 for five dollars for one hundred weight therof.[36]

This cotton tree yeilds its wool once a year in great plenty; cotton is of a verey attractive* vertue and therfore unhollsome to lie on in weet countrey, for if you take a bagg of this cotton wool, and lay it over a cask of watter at some two foot distance from the water, and from the bag lett a thred of cotton woll touch the watter, then by its attractive vertue shall it soon draw all the watter from out the cask into the bagg of cotton woole, which I have experimented to be true, with noe small admiration. Thus we have fully discribe the true way of planting the cotton shrub with the true worth, profitt, and nature of cottonwole.

35. This would have been by the present site of Rockfort; wild cotton bushes may still be found on the Palisadoes peninsula.

36. The early culture of cotton is described in Bridenbaugh and Bridenbaugh, *No Peace beyond the Line,* 55–61, 281–84.

Of Ginger

Ginger is a Jamaican commodity, being a hard yallowish rotte of a strong speicefick substance, whose use and vertues with itself are soe commonly known in England that it needs noe further explanation. Now this root is here planted thus: after they have prepared ground they take some of these roots and plant them (532) all allong their ground in rowes about three foot asunder; now you must understand that this root runeth and increaseth in the ground like knott grass,* soe that in two years' time all this planted ground, both rowes and the spaces betwixt 'em will be filled therewith.

The root being thus come to maturity and full growth (which they know by the yallowness of ye leaf) is then all diged or pull'd up, cutt of from the blade and wash't clean in warm watter, which being done is dried in the sun untill it becomes throly cured, being hard, white, and perfect ginger. Being thus cured 'tis pack't up in baggs and caried to the Port where 'twas sold this present yeare 1688 att the rate of six dollars by ye hundredweight.[37] Thus we have given you a full description of the cheife commodities and products of Jamaica, with the manner of their planting, propigating, and compleating according to the custom of that place.

And now we shall also give an account of the manner of planting and propigating the other plantation products of this island, namely maize, guinea corn, peas, scotgrass, potatas, yams, and the casavia root. All which we shall now describe according to their dignity; first:

Maize, or Indian corn, is a graine of greatt profitt to the planter in the maintainance of his Negroa slaves etc.; this graine we have allredy described in page 477, and therfore a repetition would be needless. This graine growes on a shrube cane or stalk about the bigness of a man's wrist, and some six or eight foot high, bearing a leaf like a flagg, and yeilds two or three ears of corn, and is planted thus: after the seasoning raines they prepare their ground, and in it plant this corn in rowes some two foot asunder, and commonly putt two or three grains in a hole, and in the rowes make these holes about one foot asunder. Now after the grains is sprung up about a foot high they weed it, and hill it up as we doe hops in England; now this will stock some to 'ore three blades out of a stock and yeild each two or three ears, producing great increass. It yeild its corn up commonly in foure months after planting, which when ripe they cutt down and plant the ground anew, and thus for maize.

(533) Guinea corn is a grain here found of great profitt, planted in all respects as maize, growing on a long blade like wheat, but broad and gross like a flagg (see page 448) about fouer foot high, yeilding its seed in ears like

37. Bridenbaugh and Bridenbaugh explain the importance of this crop. Ibid., 284.

hemp in three months' time after planting, which when ripe is cutt down eaven with the ground, and 'twill sprout up and yeild more seed plentifully, and with care and good looking after will hold in the ground fouer or five years without planting, and distroye other weeds which grow under it. This is an excelent graine (see page 477) of great profitt to the planter in his plantation.

Scotgrass is of much use in plantations in hard times, standing the planter in good steed to feed his stable horses and draught oxen withall, and is therfore planted in most plantations thus: they chuse out such swampy wett places in their plantations which will not be fitt to plant with sugare, indigo, etc., and here they plant their scottgrass thus: they cutt out the grass in joynts about a foot long, and the Negroas with the hoes make holes in the ground and plant these plants in rowes about two foot asunder, which thus planted will soon flourish, stock and hold in the ground for many years, growing up with a llong spierry* blade in joynts like sedg, and will be fitt to cut for cattell once a month on which they'll feed and become fatt, for 'tis (while young) a verey swett grass, yeilding considerable profitt, for in the inns they sell butt a small bundle therof for a royall, it being their cheife horse meat, and used insteed of hay.

This island of Jamaica plentifully affords variety of excelent pulse or peas, namely the blackeyed pea, rouncavilla, callavanca, boonavise and read peas, all which are planted after one manner. Thus after they have cleared their ground from wood etc., the Negroas work ye mould fine, then after the seasoning raines they plant these in rowes some one foot asunder as we doe in England, and they spring up and runn all 'ore the ground like a vine (see page 478) yeilding great increase, and are of excellent use in the plantations towards the maintainance of the famaly and (534) the Negroa slaves, for indeed 'tis their cheife food allowed by their master for their maintainance, both green and drie. The pulse yeild their increass in great aboundance, which is ripe in three months after planting; then they are cutt up, and the Negroas sheall out the peas, burn the straw and plant more as soone as the seasoning raines happen.

Now it may be expected that we should here have also given a description of the manner of planting and propigating that plant called tobacco, (which thrives here verey well, see page 447) as well as those product we have allredy discribed, but we have fully omitted it as being superfluous, because all England are nott unacquainted therewith, seeing 'tis a plant allways found in our phisick gardens in London,[38] which moved me to ommit it because I allways love things concise and brevious.*

Now let us give a description of the true way of planting the cheife Jamaica rotts, namely the pottata, the yam, and the casavia which are planted thus:

first the pottata and yam are both planted after one manner, as follows: after the ground is prepared for planting, the Negroas make holes therein about one foot asunder, in ranck etc., then they slip off the leaves of potatas, and plant them in these holes (as our English gardiners doe artichocks) then when they are sprouted up, they cleanse 'em from weeds, and hill 'em up as we doe hops, and soe carefully look after 'em untill they have filled ye ground with large melleficious roots (see page 471) which will be fitt to spend in one year after planting, for then they are att their full growth, and will sone begin to decay.

The casavia or casadar is a large root ressembling a parsnipp, and is the root of a knotty shrubb, bearing a broad leaf like the calabash tree (see page 472) and is planted thus: after their ground is prepared for planting they take of these sticks, about three foot long and plant 'em all 'ore the ground in rowes about two foot asunder, and then hill 'em up and keep 'em clean of weeds, and in three year (535) time they will produce a root grown to maturity and fitt for bread (see page 472) which then they draw up out of the ground, work up, and plant more. Thus we have given a full description of the ways used on this island in their artt [of] planting and propigating the sugar cane, indigo, coco, cotton, ginger, maize, guinea corn, scottgrass, peas, potatas, yams and the cassader root; also we have fully describe the true way of makeing sugar, rum, indigo, etc., and shall now draw to a conclusion after we have shewn their manner of clearing their ground in order to make it fitt to plant.

Now we come to shew the accustomed maner used here in clearing of their ground in order to make it fitt to plant, in order to which know that haveing taken up as many accars as the planter thincks fitt, and haveing layed out the bound lines of his land and received his plat* and patten therof from the governour, and being provided with Negroa slaves, and axes, houghs etc. he begins to work. He causes them to cutt down all the wood both small and great, in as much of it as he is then in ability to plant.

Now they cutt of the wood about knee hight from the ground, haveing fell'd as much ground as is fitt, and the wood being somewhat drie they seet it on fier and burn it on the ground, which being don after the next raines the Negroas hough up the ground and first plant it to pease, which being planted they begin to prepare more ground to plant in the same manner. Now the pease being ripe they plant more and soe doe in all their new-clear'd grounds for the first year, it being not fitt for canes till the stumps are rotten and gone and the roots of ye wood cleans out of ye earth.

---

38. Tobacco was widely planted in England from the middle of the seventeenth century onwards.

Now in the second year in new-clear'd ground they plant potatas and yams, which being come to perfection in the third year, they clear the ground of the stumps and roots of ye woods (which are now rotten) and soe the ground is fitt to be planted with canes, indigo, or what else they please. Thus we have finished oure discourse of planting and with it this section of the present state of Jamaica.

Section III

(536) Of the planter's useage towards his English servants, Indians, and Negroa slaves on Jamaica, with an account of the strang carriage and anticque behaviour of those slaves, and of their many late insurections and rebellions.

The wealthy planter lives here in full enjoyment of ease and plenty, haveing what 'ere his heart can wish to enjoy; he nevertheless is verey severe to his English servants, for alltho' they are not putt to worke att the hough as the Negroa slaves are, yett they are keept verey hard to their labour att felling of timber, hewing staves for casks, sugar boyling and other labours, soe that they are little better than slaves. For whilst there masters live at ease at full feed tables, their servants are att hard labour in the open feild, allmost burnt up with the sun, and stung to death by tormenting insects; feeding only on old salt Irish beef, porke, old stincking salt fish, and casava breed, there cheife drinck being old rapp, mobby or Adam's ale, haveing little othere refreshment. And this provitions they are all owed out by weight everey Monday morning for a whole week's allowance, and on Saturday nights their masters allow 'em some (537) rum and sugar, to make 'em a bowle of punch withall.

Thus they commonly feed, which is not soe hard, but their lodgings is as mean, for when their day's labour is don, and their wery'd bodys requier rest, then their only lodging is hard boards, cotts, or scanty hammocks, from whence they rise with acking boanes; now thus as their diet and lodging is mean, soe is their cloathing as pore, for their masters only give 'em cloathing of blew linnen, or osenburge[39] cloath, att the best, and of that noe more then the lawes of the island forces 'em to, which is to every man-servant fouer hatts, or capps, fouer blew shirts and draweres, and fouer paire of osenburge stockins and twelve pair of shoos yearly.

Now to every woman servant is allowed fouer smocks, fouer pettycoates, fouer capps, fouer paire of stockins and six pair of shoos yearly. This is their

39. "Osnaburg" was a coarse linen originally made in Osnabrück, Germany; it was imported into England from the mid-sixteenth century onwards, and often re-exported to the West Indies.

best allowance tho' seldom given 'em; those women servant which are kept in the planter's famally are keep somewhat better than the plantation servants, being employ to make and mend their clothes for 'em, and if she be but handsome and kind, to be sure hir master cloathes her well and hir mistris bestows many curses on hir and blowes to the bargain. When their English servants are sick, their is not half that car taken of 'em as over their Negros, and when dead noe more ceremony at their funurale than if they were to berey a dogg.

Thus the English servants labouriously weare out their fouer years' servitude, or rather slavarey, haveing sufficient cause to repent their rash adventures in comming from England, to be slaves in America, where many servants are never free; for by their master hard usage (which some doe on purpose) they sometimes run away for a day, weke, month, etc., [by] which means their time of servitude is increased (see page [number lacking]), and many never become free men (by that stratagem) all their days.

(538) Now come we to treat of the planter's usage and government of his Negroa and Indian slaves, in order to which we shall first spake of the Indian slaves. The Indians are of diverse nations brought hither as of Suranam, Florida, New England, etc., and are sold here for slaves, but nott many are here found because they are subtill and by some means or other geet of the island or else murther themselves, for they will not work; they are generally tall, of a well-limbed body, tawny, and have straight long blacke haire. They are very acctive, nimble and good archers in generall.[40]

These Indian slaves have the same allowances of meatt etc. as the English servants, and are employed in fishing and to hunt wild hogs, and kill fowles as doves, pidgeons etc., all which they will shote in abundance with their arrows, soe that two Indian slaves shall maintain their master's famally (if it consist of twenty people) plentifully with fish, wild hog and fowles every day in great aboundance, soe that one faithfull Indian slave is as good as three Negro slaves. This those slaves will doe willingly as long as they are kindly ussed and have now and then some rumm allowed 'em, which will much encourage 'em therein, but they will not work in the plantation, and if you should use blowes to bring 'em therto, they would either runn away or murther themselves. Thus we have given you a true description of the nature, use and profitt of the Indian slaves, and now come to treat of the Ethiopian or Negroa slaves.

After a planter hath purchased some twenty, thirty or more Negroa slaves, he first gives to each man a wife, without which they will not be contented, or worke. Then he gives to each man and his wife one half accre of land for them

---

40. On the nature of Indian slavery, see Dunn, *Sugar and Slaves*, 74.

Figure 45 Amerindian getting ready to blow tobacco-smoke onto a sick person, from Girolamo Benzoni, *Historia del Mondo Nuovo* (Venice, 1563). As this woodcut shows, tobacco was sometimes used as a medicine, like so many of the other substances that Taylor describes.

to cleare for themselves, and to plant maize, potatas, yamms etc., which land they cleare (539) (in their lesure houers) and build them a wigwam[41] on it, and then plant it as fast as they can. Then he gives them a sowpig and a cock and hen to breed on; by this means and some small supplies of saltfish etc. in hard times, without any further charge to theire master they maintain themselves. Also when a bulock or the like dies in the plantation, the carrion carkass therof is given them, on which they will feed as hertyly as a plowman on baccon. As towards their cloathing, they allow 'em neither coate, hatt, shirt, stockins or shoos, only they allow to every man a linnen arsclout* or a paire of breaches, and to the women only an arsclout or linen peticoat, for they deserve noe better, since they differ only from bruite beast only by their shape and speach.

These slaves are commonly strong and healthy, only they are naturally afflicted with the French pox in a more higher degree than evere any Europian bodys were, and this they here call the yaws, and they are also subject to the dropsie in a verey high manner, to cuer which distempers and to keep them fitt to labour, they have a hott house in most plantations, and keep a chirurgeon to cuer them, and loke after 'em, whom they allow a good sollary for his paines.

41. This was correctly a cabin of the type built by the Ojibwa people; Taylor's usage is precocious, in extending the term to any roughly similar structure.

Now these slaves are committed to the government of the overseer, who hath other whit servants under him, as drivers to keep them to their labour, soe that one whit servant commands some twenty of 'em, under the overseers. These slaves thus disciplin'd are called to their work about fouer a'clock in the morning, at which time the overseer sound his horn or shell, and thenn all hands turn outt to labour both men and women together, where they all work at the hough etc., and are followed on by their drivers, which if they loiter sone quickens their pace with his whipp, and soe keeps (540) 'em to their work till eleven a'clock before noon; then the overseer sounds his shell, and they all leave work and repaire to their wigwams to diner and to rest untill two a'clock, at which time the overseer sounds his shell, and they all turn out to work and continues all their labours as long as light will permitt.

Then those pore slaves leave off work and repaire to their houses, where they gett their suppers, make a great fier, and with a kitt (made of a gourd or calabash with one twine string) play, sing and daunce according to their own countrey fashon, makeing themselves all mirth, men and women together in a confused manner; after they have thus sported as long as they thinck fitt, they lay themselves naked on the ground all round their fier, the whole family together in a confused manner to sleep; for tho' the country is soe hott, yett they can't sleep without a fier, and thus these ignorant pore souls spend away their time.[42]

On Staturday at noon they leave off work (unless at sugar-boyling time) and their master gives to each Negro man and his famally a quart of rum and mollosas to make merry witball; this part of the day they spend in their own plantations, and on the Sundays these slaves gather together in great companys, goeing to vissit their countrymen in other plantations, where according to their own countrey fashon they feast, dance, and sing (or rather howle like beast) in a anticque manner, as if they were all madd; and thus these miserable creature spend away their time, liveing without the least knowledg of a true God, many of which are of a pregnant witt, and were paines taken divine knowledge might be infused into 'em, but that labour is spared here, for all their masters' care is to have 'em work, which if they have their bellys full they will doe willingly; otherwise they will not work.

(541) Now if at any time those slaves have comitted robery, prove sullen, refuse to work or the like, then the overseer causeth such to be bound fast to a whiping-post (which they have in all plantations) hand and foot, and

42. The slaves' music is described by Richard Cullen Rath, "African Music in Seventeenth-Century Jamaica: Cultural Transit and Transition", *William and Mary Quarterly* 50 (1993): 700–26. Amerindians are often depicted sleeping on hammocks above a fire, to discourage mosquitoes and other insects.

their he whipes 'em with rods or switches till their back are covered with blood; then he rubbs them with salt brine, and soe forces 'em to their work againe, or if their fault be great, after he hath whip't 'em he rubbs them all over with molasses and soe letts 'em stand for some time for the wasps, merrywings and other insectts to torment. This dealing may be counted hard, but without it they would never be [word illegible], for if you should be kinder to 'em they would soner cutt your throat than obay you, for they are soe stuburn that with all this whiping, misserey, or torment, they shall seldom be seen to shead a tear, but rather at first laugh, and then afterwards stand scilent.

Now if the Negroas are appt to run away from their masters, as soone as they are apprehended they are punished as aforesaid, and an iron yoak with an iron collar fix't fast with revitts* to their neck, which yoack is called the pothock; this yoak stand off with three hoks from the collar each about two foot long, which in the wood hinders 'em from runing, by hanging in the bowes of the trees.

Now if this will not reclaime 'em, they either sell them to the Spaniards, or else cutts off their feet about half from their toes and causes them to eat itt; this commonly reclaimes 'em, which if not they either putts iron feeters* on their leggs, and soe forces 'em to work, which if they refuse to doe they hange 'em up out of ye way and burnd their dead carcass before the Negroas for an example. Thus we have given a full account of the planter's usage towards his English servant, Indian and Negro slaves with their ordering and government.

(542) Now come we to treat of the strange carraige and anticque behaveior of these Negroa slaves, whoe at first when they are sold hither seem in much to grive and lamment the lost of their country feedom, and their now captivity, which they sing or bellow forth in their own language in a mournfull manner. But being sett to work they willingly submitt, and sone understands their buisiness, the master giveing to every Negroa man a wife, which proves very kind and honest to her husband, which one the least afront will desert hir and gett him another wife in his master's or some other neibouring plantation.

These slaves are allowed their rest on the Sabath daies, on the Christmass holy day and at Easter and Whitsuntid, which they call "picanini Christmass" or "litle Christmass", at which times they meet those of one and the same countrey, and feast, sing, and dannce in a confused manner, seeming all mixth men and women together; thus they howle instead of singing, and play on a kitt whilst others drum, or beatt against a hollow tree, or board, and the rest nimbly dance in a strange anticque manner after this their musick, in such sort that they seem all madd.

The Negroas take verey little care of their children (or picaninnies as they call 'em) for the women are delivered without paine, or the assistance of a mid-wife, and commonly the next day goe to work in the feilds with their children naked at their backs; these children are at first when born verey white and faire all 'ore their bodys (except their codds and secrett parts which is black), but they soon change yallow, and in one month's time become cole black; 'tis observed that the whitter they are when born, the more black and butifull they will be when grown to be men.

These Negroa women are very kind and tendor over their children, giveing them often suck (543) 'ore their shoulders as they hang at thire backs, for you must understand that their breast are not round like our English women, but are long lick a bagg hanging down to their navels, by which means they have the conveniency to suckle their picaninnies as they hang at their backs. When they are born the overseer names them, which is all the adoe keep at their groanings. These children commonly goe at fouer months old, and will eat plantains or any other thing, and are of little troble to their mothers. When they are three years old they are imployed in the plantations to loke after the fowles and doe what else they are able, and when grown old and past their labour, which is att fifty years of age or therabout, their haire becomes as whit as snow, their skin yallow, their fleash lean, and theire whole body feble; then are they employed to keep sheep, goats, etc., and doe other light workes and soe suffered to live till nature puts a finall period to their misserable life.

These pore soules live without the sence of a true God, yett doe they bleive the souls's immortallytie, and a future *ubi* for its reception after death, which they saie is beyound the plesant mountains of their own countrey, where after death such which live and die well shall goe to and there in the full enjoyment of all things be eternally happy. These deluded wretches worshippe the divile, which commonly in thear own country appears amongst 'em often distroying many of 'em, carrying away their children, and useing their bodys in a misserable manner if in the least they offend him. This tormentor they worship and feare by the name of *tointa* or *taionta,* which signifies "terible" in their language.

But here none ever saw the divile appear visible among 'em, nor 'twas never known that any of 'em were caryed away from hence by him, altho' 'tis really beleived that once a yeare the divill appears visible amongst them, for about March they are for some two days as it were all madd, some singing, danceing etc., and others weeping, howling, and looking frightfully, as if in great terror, and will by noe means be forc't to their work, at which time 'tis really thought he appears amongst them (544), but noe means will they conffess the same, alltho' they have bin offten whip't and tormented to make 'em confess it; yet still they denigh it, and say they can't tell the reason of their extasie. After this they fall to their work as soberly as formally.

These Negroas have a great veneration for the earth, by which they sweare and bind themselves to punctuall obedience and performance, for if you are dubious of what they saie and they protest it, and thereupon kis the earth, you may be suere 'tis true, and if you bind 'em to secresie by cising of ye earth, then all the tortures that can be inflicted upon them shall never make them confess or discover it, which is the reason they allways die soe obstinat in their rebellion, without tears or conffesing their dissignes or confederats, for if they ciss the earth 'tis to them a solem and certaine oath by which they swear.

When those slaves die they make a great adoe at their burials, for haveing caryed them to the grave in a verey mournfull manner, all both men and women which accompany the corpse sing and howle in a sorrowfull manner in their own language, 'till being come to the grave, into which they gently put the corpes, and with it casadar bread, rosted fowles, sugar, rum, tobacco, and pipes with fier to light his pipe withall, and this they doe (as they say and follishly imagine) in order to sustaine him in his journey beyound those plesant hills in their own countrey, whither they say he is now goeing to live at rest. After this they fill up the grave, and eat and drinck theron, singing in their own language verey dolefully, desiering the dead corpse (by ciseing the grave) to acquaint their father, mother, husband and other relations of their present condition and slavary, as he passeth thro' their countrey towards the plesant mountains, which message they bellow out to the dead corps in a dolefull tone, and soe kise the grave and depart, for they are soe fully possest with this strange oppinion that being (545) dead they shall certainly return into their own countrey, and from thence pass to those plesant mountaines, that verey often many of them haveing binn afronted, have either starved themselves to death or else have cutt their own throats, that soe being free from their servitude, they might return to their own contrey and their enjoy rest, and they are soe naturally rotted in this oppinion that by noe means they will be convinced therof. For I have discoursed with many old Negroas, of witt and sence, and have asked them whither they thought the heavy dead body could pass into soe farr a country. They said noe, not the body, for that rotted in the earth, but said they our *camaix* (which signifies in their language shape and understanding) soon after death passeth into our own countrey, and ther lives for ever, which may be seen in watter or a glass our *camaix* or shape which 'arter death takes its flight to those plesant hills in our native countrey. And in this oppinion they are soe strongly rooted that all the argument in the world cannot move them to disbelieve it, soe naturall is the knowledg of the soule's immortallyty and some *ubi* for its future reception, that we find some tract of it amongst this barbarous and ignorant people.

A wealthy gentleman now liveing at Barbadose, which had in his plantation about three or fouer hundred Negroas, of all countreys, was on a time of late misserably trobled with these his slaves, by reason of this conceived oppinion, for most of them were soe obstinate that neither the threats or blowes of their overseers would make them work, for they obstinatly refused it, and would say to the overseers when correcting them, "Why doe you beat us? Take your knife, and cutt our throats; for then shall we goe to rest in our own countrey, for we will not work, therfor kill us". Thus beating did noe good, neither would they work. The gentleman being enformed (546) thereof was much trobled therat, not knowing what to doe to reclaime them, but at last he resolved upon the following stratagem; he orders his servants to attend them armed and force them to their worke, and he himself went in to a plantann walk hard by where his slaves were to work.

Now their overseer commanded them to work but they said they would not, then they beat 'em all, but all in vaine, saying "Kill us for we will not work, but goe into our own countrey", upon which the gentleman their master stepps forth out of the plantann walk, and demands of them which would not work but would goe into his own countrey, upon which one of 'em boldly sayed to him, "Good master kille me, I noe work, but goe to my countrye". Upon which the gentleman drew forth his simeter,[43] and cutt off his head, and caused his servants before the face of the rest to cutt him in peices, and place it here and there in the plantation on poles, and there forthwith to make a fier and burn his entrails also before them, which the Negroas beholding seemed to be much terrified therat.

Then saies their master, "Come who of you won't work, come and you shall also goe to your own country"; they all stood amazed and said they would not goe soe in their own countrye; what be cutt in peices, burnt and hang on trees, noe, that was nott the way to their countrey. Therfore they betook themselves to their work againe, and by this means were reclaimed, which otherwise would have binn the utter undoeing of that worthy gentleman. By this is plainly seen how these misserable creatures are blinded and deluded by that subtill and lieing disevers.

Those Negroas brought hither are of different countrey, and under severall kings which have continuall warr at home one against another, and such prisoners which they take in the warrs they sell for slaves to our English merchants, which sells them at Barbados and here, and those Negroas speak diverse languages, according to their nation, for here are Capecoast Negroas, Caramintine, Gambo, Angola, Paupauine, Madagascar Negroas, etc.; (547)

---

43. A scimitar was a short, curved, single-sided sword, commonly used in Asia Minor; it is curious to find Taylor using this word.

all these spake each a severall language, which the other dost not understand, and as they have warrs at home, soe here they hate one another and agree together only for feare, for in all plantations these Negroas are mix't one with another, and all sone learn to spake broaken English, by which means they are cappable to understand their work, and yet they allways have a deedly hatred one against another, by which means they are not soe subject to raise in rebellion, as otherwise (were they all of one countrey) they would be, since nott understanding one another's language they have not the benefitt of private consulltation together, and by being at difference, they are each afraid to trust one another with their intention least he should betraie it to their master, or else himself after such an expedition become masters over them. By which means, namely their disagreeing humour and language, they are not soe subject to reble which otherwise they would undoubtedly agitate.

As for all their children born here, they learn not only their mother tung, but to spake English also; by which generall understanding, and a forgetting of old anamosities betwixt their fathers, 'tis to be doubted in the next age the Crebolian Negroas will be propigated to a generall insurrection and rebellion, for they are verey strong, their being six Negroas to one Englishman (or *bacarara,* as they call 'em) thro'out the whole island, and since 'tis common for all men to strive for freedom, 'tis therfore to be feared those slave if ever they have oppertunity will raise in open rebellion, which God in mercey prevent. Thus wee have given a full account of the anticque carriage and strange oppinion of those miserable Negroa slaves, and now come to give a description of their many late insurrections, outrages and rebellions.

(548) These Negro slaves which we have binn now treating of have of late severall times revolted from theire masters, rize in open rebellion, and done much mischeife, betakeing themselves to the woods and mountaines, and att all advantages have done much mischeife, haveing barbarously murther'd whole famalys, cutting off men, women, and children. The first insurection and rebellion commited by those vassalls was in March 1682,[44] at which time Madam Greg's Negroas slaves, being in number one hundred and five, rose in the night and murther'd fifteen Christian soules, all that belonged to the plantation[45] but two, as the overseer which was then at the Port about his mistrise's neogtiations, and Madam Greg herself whom a Negro woman, (a house slave privie to ye rebellion) hid amongst old Negro cloaths when as the Negroas were breaking open the house, whoe by that means escaped their

44. In fact, the first was in 1672. See the various lists provided by Bridenbaugh and Bridenbaugh, *No Peace beyond the Line;* Craton, *Testing the Chains;* and Dunn, *Sugar and Slaves.*

45. Which was, as we have seen, near present-day Rockfort.

furie. For the adjacent plantations, being allaramed (att the noise of two muskeets which soom of ye English servants fiered att those slaves before they were murdered) comeing down to ye assistance, then those slaves fled to the woods with what arms and plunder they could gett, and murther'd this Negroa woman, because she would not tell where she was hid; by this you may see how faithfull they are to their promises, for she rather chused to die than to betraie her mistris.

These Negroas betooke themselves to the wood, distroying many people, and cutting off many whole famally on ye northside, at advantages, and then retreated to their lurcking places; which all that yeare putt the island to great troble and expence in keeping three hundred men out in parties after them, by whose vigalancy severall of 'em were (549) slain, others taken prisoners, and the rest scatter'd and routed. Those which were taken were brought, some to Sainta Jago de la Vega, others to the Port, and others were carry'd to the deserted plantation where they were all putt to death; some were burnt, some roasted, others torn to peices with doggs and others cutt in peice alive, and their head and quarters plac't on poles to be a terror to others; nevertheless for all this torture, they remained soe obstinate that whilst they were burning, rosting, etc. they continued singing and laughing, not one of 'em once been seen to shed a teare, or desier mercey.

The second rebellion contrived by these vassall sons of darkness was about the midle of June anno 1683, att which time the slaves belonging to Collonel Ivey, at his plantation in the precinct of Vere, nigh Withywood, being in number 180, most of 'em Carrammantine Negroas, had all conspiered with one consent to rebell, cut off their master, and murther his whole famally, and then to proceed in the lick manner against the other neibouring plantations. In order to this wicked designe they had combined themselves by oath, had chosen them a king and a queen and a cheife captain, to whome they were to render all due obedience. Haveing thus proceed in their wicked disigne with all the secresie imaginable, and the time being come within three days that they were to putt this damnable disigne in practice, it pleased God to stir up one of 'em to revell it to his master, who in the eavening wentt privatly to his master, and accquainted him with the whole disigne, beseching him to secure him, and help himself with all expedition.

Upon which the collonel order'd him to return about his buisiness, and keep all privat and he would give him his freedom and well reward him. Now the gentleman being much amused hereat, forthwith consulted (550) with his friends what to doe, and in the end resolved on this expedition; on the morrow he got about forty of his neibours and servants into his house privatly and arm'd, and then he cause the overseer to bring all the Negroas up in his hall as if he intended to give them drams of rums, as is customary.

The Negroas willingly went into their master's hall, not suspecting anything, and all satt down upon the floare according to their acoustomed manner; being thus came in, the collonel caused the dores to be secured and gauarded, which being done their master tooke the book of ye laws of Jamaica, and from it read (as they thought) their whole conspiracy and disigne, upon which they began to look frightfully on one another, and were in a great feare; then haveing read a crime to the discoverer, he said that is the divile's book, he hath always spoke truth till now of me, which is not true (and evere since this book is hated by those slaves, and they still say 'tis the divile's book).

Now the collonal caused all his slaves to be bound and fetter'd with irons (except the discoverer, whom he gave his freedom), and then caused them to be severly whip't, caused some to be roasted alive, and others to be torn to peices with dogs, others he cutt off their ears, feet, and codds, and caused them to eat 'em; then he putt them all in iron feters, and soe with severe whiping every day forced them to work, and soe in time they became obedient and quiet, and have never since offer'd to rebell. Thus did God bring to nothing their damnable disigne, and prevent the horrid rebellion and murther they intended.[46]

The third rebellion contrived by these Negroa slaves was about the later end of December anno 1684,[47] att which time (551) the Negroa slaves belonging to Captain Duck, being in number about one hundred, made an insurection, for they rose unanamously in the night, murther'd him and about twenty more of his famally, and sadly abused and wounded his wife whom they left for dead as they thought in the plantation, but she with great care revived and lived. These Negroas after they had gott all the arms and amunition and riffled the house of what they thought fitt betooke themselves to the woods and mountaines on the northside of the island, where they soon joyn'd with other runaway Negroas, and ever since have often done much mischeife in St. Mary's and St. Ann's precinct by cutting of many famallys and have murther'd neare one hundred Christian souls, men, women and children, att all advantages.

By this rebellion the island hath bin ever since putt to much troble and extraordinary charge by keeping out parties of men still after them, which are paied and releived with fresh supplys every month, both foot and horse, which have had often desperat engagements with them, haveing many kil'd

46. This revolt is mentioned only by Taylor, but he probably knew what he was writing about, since he worked nearby only three years later.

47. Taylor surely misdates this well-known rebellion, which took place in 1678, according to Craton, *Testing the Chains,* 76, and Dunn, *Sugar and Slaves,* 260–61. He might have seen the monument to Mrs Duck, still found in Spanish Town Cathedral.

by 'em, but they have putt 'em still to rout, and drove 'em to their lurcking places; they have kill'd many of these Negroas, and have taken many prisoners, which have binn executed as the former. The residue are still out in rebellion doeing all the mischeife they possiblely can, for they have secret places of retreat, plantations, and settlements in some of the unknown woody mountains, which places the English soldiers, hunters nor Negroa spies can't discover, altho' they are dayly employ'd therein.[48]

The fouerth and last rebellion contrived by these Negroa slaves was about the latter end of December anno 1685, at which time all the Negroes on Port Royall had combined themselves together to make a generall insurrection, which they with all the secresie imaginable had cunningly contrived thus; they had apointed a night when to rize, and silently in diverse (552) places to fiere to town in the night, and then whilst ye inhabitants had bin employed in extinguishing the flames, every Negroa to have seized his master's arms, and soe have made a violent onset.[49]

This contrivance was caryed on for a long time with all the secresie imaginable, till within few days before its intended execution, att which time it pleased God to deliver the inhabitants out of the intended distruction of their cruell and barbarous slaves, for their was one Negroa man which had an intier love and respect for his master, to whom privatly be discovered the whole disigne (for which good service he had his freedom with his wife, and had land and one hundred pounds given him by the Port). The disigne being discovered the Port was forthwith all in arms, which apprehend all the Negroa men forthwith and putt them in irons and close prison, and set a stron guard 'ore 'em, and then the cheife of 'em concern'd in this disigne were forthwith executed; some were burnt, others roasted alive, others torn to peices with doges, and others hanged and their heads and quarters seet everywhere here and there on pole, all around and about the Point.

This being done all the residue were severly whip't, and their legs fetter'd with irons, and soe forc't to their labour. This put the Port to excessive troble and charge in securing their Negroa slaves, in daily doubling and strenghtening their gaurdes, and in seending out parties after those which were runn to the woods and mountaines, when they found themselves discovered and like to be apprehended. These Negroa slaves died as obstinatly as any of the former, not semeing in the least concern'd therat, for when they were burnning, or rather roasting at the stake, (for the fier was made at some

48. This was indeed the time at which the two great bands – the Leeward and Windward – were consolidating their power. See Craton, *Testing the Chains,* 67–80.

49. Here again the conspiracy is mentioned only by Taylor, but he was again present at the locality shortly afterwards.

distance from the stake to which they were chained and all round soe that they roasted or burnt by degrees) they would sing (553) and laugh and by noe tortur would they ever confes ye designe, or who was concern'd therein. And soe their torment seem'd in vaine.

And here 'tis worth observation to consider their undaunted resolutions, which I observed by a lusty Negro man executed at the Port while I was there, whoe being chained to ye stake, and the fier kindled about him, and seeing his master standing bie he said to him thus: "Master why doe you burn me? Did I ever refuse to work? Or doe what you order'd me to doe? Or did I ever steall anything from you in all my life? Why therfore am I thus cruelly burnt?"

His master answered him thus: "Samboo (for that was his name), I have done all I can to save thy life, and would now give a hundred pounds to save thee, but thou hast bin in the rebellion and therfore must die, for I cannot in noe ways save thy life."

"Well then (said hee), I thanck you good master, God for ever bless you, and now I will die."

Upon which he threw himself on his face into the midst of the fier, and never stir'd nor groan'd, but died patiently with the greates resolution imaginable.

And alltho' they have used to these rebellious slaves most excessive torturs, as you have heard, by cuting off their ears and members and makeing of 'em eat them, by cutting out their tungs and cutting off their feet etc., yett still Negroas revolt and dayly run away from theire masters into the woods and mountaines, where they lurck together in parties, stealling at night from plantations, and doeing much mischife towards Saint Ann's and the Northside, for many of those vassals have gott arms as fuzzes, swords, etc., the which they run away with, and which they have taken from those places where they have barbarously (554) cutt off whole famalies. Indeed 'tis a great troble and expence to this island to keep continuall parties out after 'em, which from all quarters they are forc't by turn to send for thier own security, but this present year 1688 the island hath binn indeferent at quiet, those vassals haveing don but litle mischeife, only cutting of one famaly of about 8 people in St. Mary precinct; a party being sent out after them, they were sone putt to the rout and they fleed to their lurcking places, which is hard to be found.

These rebellions Negroas have a captain;[50] an old runaway Negroa of Captain Duck's, and 'tis thought there are not above 300 of 'em besides

50. This is perhaps Cudjoe, who may be the father of the Cudjoe who concluded the treaty of 1739 with Colonel Guthrie. See Craton, *Testing the Chains*, 77.

women and children. Many of these Negroas have arms, and are old subtill slaves, and well know the use of them; the rest are armed with bowes and launces according to their own countrey fashion. Now for the incouragement of such which shall goe out after these rebells, they are allowed five pounds a head for every Negroa they shall apprehend, which at the deliverey of the head is paid 'em by the governour. Thus we have fully lay'd down the full matter of the proposed contents of this chapter, which we have deliver'd as plain and concise as possible; which being finished we here conclude this seaventh chapter of our present state of Jamaica.

Chapter VIII

(555) Of the lawes and customes of Jamaica, with an account of the reception of His Grace Christopher, Duke of Albemarle, when he enter'd into his lieutenancy; also some particular directions and advice to newcommers, which is added by way of conclution.

Since in the former chapters of this treatise we have given a full discription of all noteworthy occurrancies and products of this uberous island, soe that thereby the true state thereof may bee seene as plainly as by veiwing the place itself, and that as we have began and proceeded, so we may draw to a conclution according to a true and genuine method, we shall now give an account of the principall accts, laws and customs of the countrey, made and enacted by the body politicke of the state, called the councill of assembly.

In order to a due prosecution of which you must understand that His Majesty of Great Britain, Charles the Second, our late soveraigne of ever blessed memorie, whose eys and herat were allways open to doe good to all his subjects; the disorder and maladministration of justice in his colloneys in America, but more espetially at his late-setled (556) island of Jamaica crieing loudly for his princly aid to rectifie its enormities and setle it in a quiet government, established by just and holsome lawes, in order to which His Majesty forewith sent their his trusty lieutenant, the Right Worshipful Sir Thomas Minns,[1] Knight, with full commition, power and authority from His Majesty under the broad seall of England to govern the same, and forthwith to suppress such enormities, and to put the island into a due *lex methodica,* which he had power to ordaine good and holsome acct[s] fit for the quiet government of the said island, which were to be as farr consonat and agreeing to the fundamentall laws of the crown of England as possible they could.[2]

1. As usual, Taylor speaks of "Minns" instead of Thomas, Lord Windsor.

2. Of course, the increasing number of slaves meant that the laws conformed less and less to those of England.

Figure 46 The Jamaican coat of arms. In this original version of the arms, the supporting Tainos are dressed rather like Brazilian Tupinamba.

Further, His Majesty gave to this his lieutenant a broad seall, particullarly ordain'd for the use of that island, whereon was the true coat of arms which His Majesty in honour was pleased to bestow on the island, by which he was impowered to sign pattens, accts, commitions and the like.

This worthy knight sone after his entrance into his government performed His Majesty's command and pleasur, for forthwith he putt the island into a *lex methodicus*; thus he first constituted a councill of assembly of twelve men of the best ranck and creditt, which were at all times to sett in council with him on all spetiall consulltations, himself being their head, and represented lord chancellor, and they the twelve judges, the chief of which he ordained chief justice, and committed the broad seall into his custody. Having thus proceed, the next thing he did was this, he ordained a court of grand judicature to be held fower times yearly at Saint Jago de la Vega, over which he ordain'd all such officers as we have in our courts in England, as attorney, clerke of the Crown, cleark of ye court, provost marshall etc.

The next proceeding was this, he ordained a court of chancery to be held befor him on the first Thursday of every month, in which all causes depending on chancery were to be dispatch without any delay. His next proceeding was to divide this island into several percincts, as St. Dorothy's, Katharine's, Clarendon etc., and in each ordain'd petit (557) courts of judicature to be held fower times yearly, as our quarter sessions are in England, wherein all petit causes were to be discided by the respective judges, justices of ye peace and juriours for that percinct.

His next proceeding was to authorize judges and justices of ye peace, the which he constituted in every percinct, which were impowered to acct as afforesaid. Thus this worthy and prudent governour soone putt the island into a due *lex methodice.* Thus, that ye governour should acct as lord chancellour, and represent the king's person in parliment, as being supreem in power above the councill; secondly, that the councill of assembly should acct as ye twelve judges, and here in councill represent the house of lords in parlement, and thirdly that all His Majesty's justices of the peace belonging to each respective percinct, being from all the island assembled together in councill at the Audiencia of Sainta Jago de la Vega, should then represent the house of commons assembled in parliment, and where impowered to acct accordingly, and all were to assemble at ye governour's will. The island being putt into this order, the governour forthwith summond the grand councill and assembly forthwith to meet at the Audiencia of Saint Jago de la Vega in order to establish good and holsome lawes for the sure peace and quiett government of the island.

The grand councill and assembly being thus mett togeather, they proceed in a due politicke method, according to the true institution of parlement, and in such sort they created laws and whollsom accts of government, proper for the saffety and quiet government of the same, which said accts were confirmed, authorized and ordained with a joynt councill under the broad seall of the island, and are as followeth:[3]

Section I: Of the Laws

Bee it enaccted by the grand counsell and assembley of His Majesty's island of Jamaica

In primis that all ye persons whatsoever of His Majesty's subjects shall forthwith at their arivall on this island repair to the (558) collonel and president of Port Royall, residing at Charles Fort, and their enter their names according to their dignity, whether planters, servants, merchants, factors etc., and for non-performance thereof to be deemed as spies and enemys, and be imprisoned during the governour's pleasure.

I item, that all men whatsoever comming hither to settle and inhabit shall within six months after their arivall provide themselves with fuzze, sword and ammunition, and list themselves under some one commander or other of the mellitia of this place, and on all occation appear arm'd in the field, and for default hereof to be deemed an enemy, and findd according to the pleasure of the court, and endure one month's imprisonment.[4]

II item, that all persons whatsoever which come to inhabit on this island shall be allowed what land they will take up, in order to setle and plant thereon, and shall be allowed fifty accars apiece to everyone in his famally, and more as his famally shall increase, either in children or servants if it be required.[5]

3. It is not easy to know what laws were current in Jamaica in Taylor's day; the complications of this subject are explained by Dunn, *Sugar and Slaves,* 238. See Vicki Crow Via, "A Comparison of the Colonial Laws of Jamaica under Governor Thomas Lynch, 1681–1864, with Those Enumerated in the John Taylor Manuscript of 1688", *Journal of Caribbean History* 39, no. 2 (2005): 236–48.

4. For a map and an explanation of this system, see David Buisseret with Jack Tyndale-Biscoe, *Historic Jamaica from the Air* (Kingston, 1996), 54–55.

5. According to Dunn, Governor Sir Thomas Modyford allowed thirty acres to planters and to family members. *Sugar and Slaves,* 154.

III item, that all persons which come hither to inhabitt, after they have found out a parcell of land to their lickeing, shall then repaire to the surveyor-generall of this island, whoe shall run out, bound and measure the same, and give them a draught thereof, and shall be payed for the same one halfpenny for every accar soe taken up, besides five pounds for the draught thereof, and then shall such repaire to the secretary of the island, who shall to the plat annex them a patten under the broad seall of the island, by which the land shall be confirm'd to them and their heirs for ever, paying the king's annual Crown rent.

IV item, that all persons whatsoever that hath taken up and enjoy land on this island shall annually pay to our soveraing lord the King of England for every accar thereof one halfpenny year to the King's receiver-generall, and all such which hath taken up land and built on the port shall pay as much for every foot of land taken up, and for nonperformance to be proceeded against by the (559) king's Attorney-generall according to the custom and laws of the Crown of England.

V item, that all persons which have taken up land on this island shall forthwith build a house thereon, and cleare as much ground and plant it with sugar canes etc., as when planted shall be worth ten pounds yearly rent, that soe he may be accounted a possessor, and that all such which have taken up land, and let it lie unregarded without building and planting thereon for and within the limits of three years, shall for the default thereof forfeit the said land to our soveraing lord ye king, to be purchased by some other of his subjects.

VI item, that all the melitia forces of this island, both horse and foot, must at all times be compleatly armed, and have sufficient store of ammunition by them in redyness, and must muster once a month at their respective places of rendezvouze.[6]

VII item, that if att any time five saile of ships togeather (of what nation whatsoever) being espied att sea, bearing down towards this island, those that first espie them shall raise an allaram, and forthwith carry nottice to the gouvernour thereof, and also ride with all expedition to all quarters thereof, and the allaram being thus raised all the melitia forces both horse and foot shall forthwith meet armed with ammunition at their respective places of rendezvouze, and there to remain in arms untill they have orders from the governour whither to march or to return home.

---

6. Lists were frequently made of available powder and shot. See, for instance, the detailed list in the transcripts of Council minutes, National Library of Jamaica, MST 60, p. 245.

But if the allaram should be first raised at the Portt, then shall the governour of Charles Fort fier two cannons loaden with hollow balls over Salt Pond Hill, which by their report and echo of the mountains shall be the signe of an allaram, and soe each quarter to give notice to one another; further that all merchant ships or others then in the harbor shall put to sea to engage the enemy, and the rest shall be hall'd close to the wharffside and their guns run out in order of batarie.

VIII (560) item, that the melitia forces of the port shall keep continuall guard at the forts day and night, one company being on dutie att a time, which shall be relieved everey evening, and that those guards shall be doubled, or strenghtened, as their shall be occasation, and that this gauard march on the patroule every three hower, to see good order keept, and to take up all strumpetts or other lude suspitious persons as in the night they shall find in the streets or punch houses etc. at unreasonable houres, and those strumpets soe apprehended to commit to the cage,[7] and such others as shall be taken to be secured in the guard till they have orders of releasement from ye president of ye port.

IX item, that all such persons which come to settle and inhabitt on any part of the island, by being subjects to our soverraing lord the King of England, shall be admited a free toleration of religion in the worship of God, and that whoosoever shall mollest, affront or disturb them therein shall be punished according as the governour shall thinck fitt.[8]

X item, that noe pople or nation whatsoever, unless subjects to our soveraign lord the king, shall have any free trade or commerce att any port of this island for any Jamaican commodyty whatsoever, and neither shall they trade hither with their commodities, which if they should hereafter presume to doe, their shipp and cargoe shall be seized for the use of the King of England etc.[9]

XI item, that notwithstanding the forementioned acct of council, wee doe allow the Spanish factors a free and peaceable trade at our port with the factors of the Royal Affrican Company for their Negroa slaves, which haveing here purchased we give them a full and peaceable power to transport such salves from hince, whither they please.[10]

---

7. That is, the barred cage at Port Royal.

8. Port Royal was unique in its day for the variety of religious establishments that it sheltered. Pawson and Buisseret, *Port Royal,* 159–60.

9. The Navigation Act of 1660 aimed to enforce a monopoly of trade for the English crown.

10. In 1684 the agent for the *asiento* was James Castillo. Pawson and Buisseret, *Port Royal,* 158.

XII item, be it ennaccted that all merchants and others on any part of this island shall buy and sell by ye standar measure of the ancient citty of Winchester, and that the hundred-weight here be but five score, or (561) 100 pounds avoirdupoiz.

XIII item, be it enaccted that all Spanish mony pass currant here in all faccotries* and all over this island, namely that one Mexico dollar pass here for five shilling, one half-dollar for two shillings and six pence, one quarter dollar for one shilling and three pence, and one royall for seven pence half-penny. Further that one Spanish pistole of gould pass here for twentie shillings, one English guinea for one pound, five shillings and six pence, one English crown for six shillings and three pence, half crown for three shillings one peney half-penney, one shilling for one shilling and three pence, and one English sixpence for seavenpence half-penny, and that noe other money than what is here mentioned shall here be accounted current.

XIV item, be it enacted that as soone as any vessell whatsooever trading at the port shall come to anchor within the harbour of Port Royall, that forthwith the deputy marshall shall goe on board, to know from whence she came etc., and noe person whatsomever else shall presume to goe on board before him, under the penalty of paying eight dollars to our soveraigne lord the king for the said offence.

XV item, be itt enacted that all masters and captains of shipps tradeing to this port shall immediatly after their comeing too anchor repaire with the marshall to Charles Fort, and their satisifie the president of the port in all things he shall be impowered to require and demand concerning passingers etc.

XVI item, be it enaccted that all masters and captaines of shipps which trade at this port imediately after they have dispach't their buisiness with the president shall forthwith without delay repaire to the governour at Sainta Jago de la Vega, and carry with them suffitien sureties (merchants at the port) to be bound with him for his time tradeing at ye port, according to ye custom of Jamaica.[11]

XVII item, that all masters of shipps trading hither from Affrica with Negroa slaves, or from England, Ireland, etc. with English servants, be they (562) convicts, indenture* servants or others, shall not expose them to sale till after ten day are expired after his arrivall at the Port, that soe the countrey planters may have notice to supplye themselves with such Negroa slaves or Christian

11. It will be remembered that the captain of Taylor's vessel, the *Saint George*, had followed this procedure upon arrival.

servants as they have occation of, that if any captain or master of ships shall presume to seell any of his servants within the said ten daies, he shall for every servant soold forfeite forty dollars to our soveraigne lord the king. Now the ten daies being expired, the said captain or master shall hoist up his ensign, and fire one gun, and then 'tis free for any person whatsoever to goe an board and bie whatever servants they thinck fitt.

XVIII item, that all Christian servants sold here, which are servants lawfull[y] bound by indenture, be they of the age of twenty-one years, either men or women, they shall here be sould for noe longer than four year's servitude, and if they are girls or ladds, under age, and if they want more than four years to be of age, they shall nevertheless be sold as servants until they are arrived to twenty-one years old. But if they are within three years of being one and twenty years old, then shall all such be sold for noe more than four years of lawful servitude.

XIX item, that all Christian servants sold here, which are lawfull servants by indentur, shall here on the day of sale be allowed to refuse the two first masters which would purchase them, but noe further liberty in such case to refuse the third.

XX item, that all convicts and criminalls transported hither from England, Scotland or Ireland shall here be sold for servants for seaven year's servitude, and allowed noe benefitt of ye aforementioned acts to refuse those first two masters which proffess to bie them.

XXI item, that all Christian servants sold at this port shall be caryed after sale on shore, and their assigned over by indenture (before one of His Majesty's justices of the peace belonging to the port) from their late owner to their new master. Otherwise the servant is not lawfully bound, but may leave his master att his pleasure.

XXII item, that all gentlemen, merchants, planters and other inhabitants of His Majesty's island of Jamaica shall keep, have and (563) maintaine one English servant in his house or plantation for every nine Negroa slaves which he hath, that soe the island may be strenghtened thereby, soe that if a planter hath nine Negroa slaves then shall he also have one English servant, if eighteen slaves two English servants, if ninty slaves, then shall he have, keep and maintaine ten English servants in his house or plantation, and in default herein to forfeit one hundred dollars to ye king.[12]

---

12. Bridenbaugh and Bridenbaugh cite an act of 1682 stipulating that every master of five black slaves must keep one white servant. *No Peace beyond the Line,* 224. Taylor's law evidently catered to a changing reality.

XXIII item, that all such Negroa or Indian slaves which are bought and sold hither from Africa, or any part of Assia or America, shall never have the benefitt of freedom all their days, but be slaves to their master or his assignees, they and their chilldren, and soe to succseeding ages for ever, to be sold att his pleasure as free goods to any man, or else set att liberty by their master's pleaysure.

XXIV item, that all such Indian or Negroa slaves which are lawfully baptized by a Christian minister and thereby received into the Christian church shall be servants to none after they are one and twenty years of age, but att that time be made free denizens of the country and subjects to our sovereign lord the king, and shall be allowed all Christian benefitt in the law, shall be received as lawfull evidence by oath, and shall be received into the congregation of ye Christian church.[13]

Further that all such Indian or Negroa slaves which are lawfullly baptized by a Christian minister, after they are grown to manhood and past age, shall then from the time of their baptism and reception into the Christian church faithfull serve their masters as slaves for the space of seven years and noe longer, which being expired they shall be made free denizeen of the island, and enjoy all Christian liberty as is aforementioned.

XXV item, that all gentlemen, merchants and planters whatsoever which are inhabitants on His Majesty's island of Jamaica shall allow unto all their English and other Christian soldiers [*sic*] suffitient meet and drinck, both of English bread, beff, porke, flower, fish, oyle and other plantation provisions suffitient for their maintainance, which shall be allowed them every Monday morning by weight according to the custome of the island, and upon complaint, and also proof of their nonperformance hereof, made by complaint of the servant or (564) servants before on His Majesty's justice of the peace of the island of Jamaica, the offender for his first offence shall forfeit forty dollars to our sovereing lord the king of England, and twenty of those dollars to be given to the complaintant for his endured wrong, and for the second offence after admonition (being lawfull proved) ye offender shall deliver up to the servant or servants his or their indenture, and soe they shall then become free denizeens of this island. Also the offender shall give to each servant what cloathes and money is allowed them at freedom, according to the laws of this island.

XXVI item, that all gentlemen, merchants and planters or tradesmen whatsoever which are subjects to our sovereing lord the king and inhabitants

13. On this question of the relationship between baptism and consequent emancipation, see ibid., 355–56.

on this island shall allowe to all their English or other Christian servants suffitient and convenien cloathing according to the custome of this island, that is to say to every man servant shall be allowed fouer hatts or Monmouth[14] capps, fouer linnen ozenburg shirts,[15] either white or blew, four paire of breeches of the same cloath, fouer paires of ozenburg or cotton stockins, fouer neckcloths, and one woolend freez* coate, and twelve paire of English shoes yearly, and quarterly be allowed him every year during the time of his servitude.

And all women servants shall be allowed fouer calicut* hoods, fouer coives,* fouer ozenburg linnen smocks, either whit or blew, fouer linnen petticoats of ye same cloath, fouer paires of ozenburg, or cotton stockins, six paires of English shoes and one coarse cloth Wolton gound[16] or westcoate, to be quarterly allowed them every year during their servitude.

And if any such master or masters whatsoever shall denigh or not allow to all his servants this their allowance in the due appointed time, then shall the offender, after the lawfull proof thereof made by the offended before one of His Majesty's justices of this island, for the first offence forfeit forty dollars to our sovereign lord ye king, twenty of which is to be for the ofended complaintant for his endured wrong, and for the second offence proved as aforesaid the offender shall deliver up to such a servant or servants his or theire indentures, which shall then become free (565) denizeens of this island, being quit from their master's service, also their master shall give them as much new cloaths and money as is allowed at their freedom, according to the custom of this island.

XXVII item, that all gentlemen, merchants, planters and mechanicks whatsoever being subjects to our sovereigne lord the king, and inhabitants on this island, shall allow to all their English or other Christian servants, be they either men or women, att the time of expiration of their fouer years' servitude, or term of lawfull servitude, bee it more or less, two such two sutes of new apparell, that is to say to the men-servants shall be given two hatts or Mounmouth capps, one woollen freez coate, two ozenburg linen shirts, either whit or blew, two paire of breeches of the same cloath, two paire of cotton or ozenburg stockins, two paire of shoes. Also he shall give him in redy money eight Mexico dollars, current passible on this island, and soe he shall be free from his servitude and become a free denizeen of this island.

Further, to every woman servant in such case shall be given two white calicut hoods, two coives, two ozenburg linnen smocks, either white or blew,

14. This was a flat round cap formerly worn by soldiers and sailors. *OED.*
15. Osnaburg was a kind of coarse linen, originally made in Osnabrück, Germany.
16. This "Wolton gound" must be a particular kind of gown.

two linnen petticoats of the same cloath, two paire of ozenburg or cotton stockins, two paire of English shoos and one coarse woolen cloath gown, or wastcoat. Also hir master shall then give hir in redy money eight Mexico dollars currant passable on this island, and soe she shall be free from hir servitude, and become a free denizeen of this island.

Now in case hereafter any such masters of servants whatsoever should refuse to give to their servants such lawfull allowance as is here mentioned, then shall such masters be by warrant brought before on of His Majesty's justices of the peace of this island, and their according to lawe be compelled to make good the same allowance, and further for his offence and troblesome breach of the acct shall forfeit twenty dollars to our sovereigne lord the king.

XXVIII item, be it ennacted that all such Christian subjects to our sovereigne lord, be they either of England, Scotland, France,[17] Ireland or any other of His Majestie's domminions, which shall (566) at any time hereafter be transported hither as servants, or shall soe voluntary come of their owne accord, then after their fouer years or time of lawfull servitude is expired, they shall repaire to His Majesty's surveyor-generall of this island, who shall give them out fifty accars of land, where they find it to their own liking, with a draught of the same, and for his labour shall be paid by the king. Then shall such servants repaire to the secretary of this island, whoe shall to the plat annex a patten under the broad seall of Jamaica, by which the land shall be confirm'd to them and their heires for ever, paying the king's annual Crown rent to His Majestie's receiver-generall.

XXIX item, that all English and other Christian servants on His Majestie's island of Jamaica shall at noe time hereafter during their full time of servitude absent themselves from their master's house, plantation or service, which if they doe then shall they increase their time of servitude after this manner: for every day and night which any such servant shall absent himself from his master, he shall encrease his time of servitude by the space of one week more, and for every week's absence he shall encrease his servitude one month, and for every month's absence such shall encrease their servitude by the span of one year, and for one year's absence from their master's service such offenders shall increase their time of servitude by the following space of three whole years before such servants shall become free denzeens of this His Majestie's island of Jamaica.

XXX item, be it enaccted that noe inhabitant of His Majestie's subject [*sic*] on

17. France is included in this list because the English Crown had never formally acknowledged the loss of Calais to the French in the mid-sixteenth century.

this island whatsoever shall at any time hereafter presume to hid, conceall or imploy any English or other Christian servant whatsoever which hath unlawfully absented his master's service, and in case any should presume soe to do, then shall such offenders and abusers of the law (567) pay unto the master of such servants five pounds currantt money of this island for every day that they shall have either hid, concealled or imployed such servants, contrary to the tenor and meaning of this acct.

XXXI item, that all English or Christian servants whatsoever which inhabit on His Majesty's island of Jamaica, if in case att any time during the space of their lawfull servitude, such servant should either by negligence lose any goods belonging to their master committed to charge or trust, or should unlawfully sell the same, game or squandor it away, soe that his master sustains the damage or the lost of his goods therebye, and lawfull proof hereof be given by the owner of the said goods before one of H.M. Justices of the Peace of this island, then shall the lost goods be aprised to it reall worth, and the servant shall be then bound over to serve his master (above his fouer years' servitude etc.) as many daies, weekes, months etc. as shall satisfie him for the lost of his goods, estemen the labour of the servant to be worth twenty shillings a month, according to the custom of this island, at which rate the debt shall be paid and the sustained lost made good by the offender to ye offended.

XXXII item, having taken into mature consideration the late abuses and cruell usage which many English and other Christian servants of this island have sustained from their masters, overseers etc. by being miserably beaten, their flesh contused and their skin inhumanly cutt by the cruell shock of that thong or whipe made of the hide of ye seacow, here called a manatee strapp, therefore now be it ennacted that what master, overseer etc. whatsoever on this island, which shall hereafter at any time presume to strick or cause to be struck any Christian servant whatsoever with the said whipe called a manatee strap, shall for the first time forfitt five pounds (568) to the said servant soe whip't or struck, and for the second blow which such servant shall be stricken therewith he shall receive his freedom and be quit from his master's service, and shall be allowed such cloaths and money as servants when free ought to receive from their masters according to the custom and laws of this island, and then shall become a free denizeen of Jamaica.

XXXIII item, that all English and Christian servants of this island, being free from their master service, shall here employ themselves as they thinck fitt, either to labour for themselves or serve as hired servants by the month, under whom they please according to their cappacities, and at their quiting any man's service they must take a certificat from their said master concerning their good behaviour, and that they have fully served him during the time of agreement, and soe are free to serve any one else, without which certificate whomsoever shall entertain or imploy such are liable to fall under the penalty of the thirtyeth acct of the laws of His Majestie's island of Jamaica.

XXXIV item, that noe vintner, innkeeper or victualler whatsoever on the port, or living in any other part of this island shall for any time to come give creditt or trust to any seamen trading to this island above the value of one dollar, which shall be liable to be paid by the parties engage[d] before they depart from ye port, but if such are credited further, then shall there be noe compulsion by law used to constrain ye debtor to pay the same, but the creditor is liable to lose his debt.

XXXV item, that noe inhabitant of this island nor trader at the port, or any other part of the same shall att any time from henceforth be arrested by His Majesty's writt of arrest if this debt be under forty shillings, but shall be summoned before one of His Majesty's justices of the peace of this island by warrant, and there to give a full answer and satisfaction for the same.

XXXVI (569) item, be it enaccted that all gentlemen, merchants, planters, tradesmen, servants or others of His Majesty's subjects which came hither to setle and inhabitt from any part of His Majesty's dominions shall here be permitted a quiet habitation and shall be protected by this acct of speticall goodness from all writts, arrest, executions, molestations and troble in the law which are now in sute against the said new inhabitants by writ of King's Bench bar at Westminster; therefore in such case that this newcom inhabitant is indebted to any person whatsoever, and in what sum soever in any other part of His Majesty's dominions, save on this island, yett notwithstanding on this island shall no prosecution in law, writ or otherwise be admitted against him for the time and space of three years after his first arrivall hither, in which time if he hath not satisfied his creditor and the prosecution of the laws against him, then shall he lay open to his creditors, to be proceed against according to ye laws of the Crown of England and custom of this His Majesty's island of Jamaica.

XXXVII item, be it ennacted that noe freeholder and lawfull possessor of land on His Majesty's Island of Jamaica shall at any time hereafter be arrested and imprisoned for debt, but shall by word by writ of appearance to appear at the grand court of judicature held at Sainta Jago de la Vega, and there to answer ye law according to the plaintiff's proceedings.

XXXVIII item, after such freeholders of land have answered the writ of appearance, and yet notwithstanding not satisfied ye debt due to ye plaintiff, he shall not be as yet arrested, butt shall be seized with a writ of *vendisionis,*[18] by which any Negroes, cattel etc. belonging to ye deffendant shall be seized in the king's name by the marshall, in way of execution to satisfie the plaintiff, which goods soe seized shall be sold by outcrie at the next grand court of judicature.

XXXIX (570) item, that all Negroes, catell and other goods seiz by way of execution by writt of *venditionis* shall not be carried from off the defendant possestion untill ten days before the court of judicature in that precinct, which goods shall then by the marshall be seized and carried to the court, and there sold by publick outcrie, and the plaintiff satisfied therewith, and all cost and charges of the court paid, after which if there be any overplus remaining, it shall be returned by the marshall into the hand of the deffendant, and proclamation shall be made in open court that ye plaintiff is paid, the law satisfied and the defendant clearly and absolutely released.

XL item, that if in case the defendant having all his goods seized and sold, and the same will not amount to satisfie the debt of the deffendant, then shall the deffendant be imprisoned by way of execution of a confest judgement, pleading *non sum informatus,* and shall soe be imprisoned for nine months and noe longer, and then shall the defendant be brought to the grand court of judicatur helld at Sainta Jago de la Vega, and there be sold at public outcry as a servant, for soe much wages by month, the which his master (the bierr) shall every month pay to the provost marshall, who shall proportionally divid it amongst his creditors, whoe being satisfied the defendant shall be free from his servitude and master, and become again a free denizeen of Jamaica.

XLI item, that all gentlemen, merchants or others which are inhabitants on His Majesty's island of Jamaica, but noe freeholders and possessors of land on the said island, being indebted to any man on the said island above the sum of forty shillings, shall and doe lie open at all times to ye law of the Crown of England and of this island, that is to say they may be arrest by His Majesty's writt, then imprisoned unless they find suffitient baile; then to be proceed against according to ye customs of judgement and execution (571); then imprisoned for nine months but noe longer, for then shall they have the benefitt of the fortieth act of the laws of this island, and be sold at publique outcry at the grand court of judicature held at Sainta Jago de la Vega as servants for wages by the month, and in such servitude shall remain untill their debts are paid, according to the tenour and true meaning of that acct.

18. This is a writ of vendition, allowing certain goods to be sold.

XLII item, that all prisoners whatsoever, committed to prison in any goal of this land, shall every day be allowed watter and one royal or English sixpence to maintaine them, which they shall dayly receave from the marshall as their allowance from His Majesty's gratious bounty.

XLIII item, that all causes depending on Chancery shall be heard and judged before the Right Honourable governor of this island (who represents Lord Chancellor) att the Audientia on the first Thursday in every month at Sainta Jago de la Vega, the chief city of Jamaica.

XLIV item, be it enacted that whosoever shall from any time henceforward begett any woman with child on this island of Jamaica, if she be a free woman and noe servant then shall they be bound with sureties to maintaine the said child, or else to enduer one year's imprisonment, according to the laws of England. But if she be a servant and noe free woman, then shall those which have soe gott her with child be bound with sureties to maintaine the said child, and further shall pay twenty pounds current money of this island to the master of the said servant, and soe she shall become free, and his servant, during the remaining part of the time which she had now by indenture to serve. But if her master will not have hir in these terms then shall the man be free of the penaltie of this acct. But if the man which gott this woman with child be a servant of the master of the said woman soe begotten with child, then shall that servant paie his master twenty (572) pounds currant mony of ye island by increasing the time of his servitude after the rate of twenty shillings per month, and the woman servant soe begott with child shall goe free.

XLV item, that all such persons inhabiting on this island which shall take and apprehend any missing Negroa slaves which have deserted theire master's plantation shall forthwith carrie them to the next plantation, and theire cause him to be soundly whip't, and from there convey them either to the next goale or to their master (for they may be known to whom they doe belong by their mark burnt either on their shoulder or on thir brest, as we mark our catel in England), and for their paines in soe doeing the apprehender shall demand one dollar for the first mile, and eight pence for every mile thereafter, betwixt the place where taken and the place of delivery, which they are hereby empowered to demand, and forthwith receive at the delivery of the Negroa, either from the master or from the marshall to whom they thus deliver the said apprehended runaway Negroa.

XLVI item, that all such persons which inhabitt on this island of Jamaica, which shall att any time apprehend and take any runaway rebellious Negroas, which are known to have bin out in rebellion, then shall all such have for their paines att the delivery of the head of the said apprehended Negroa to the Right Honorable the governor of this island the full sum of five pounds for every Negroa soe apprehended and delivered to ye governour.

XLVII item, be itt enacted that noe Negroa slave whatsoever belonging to any man on this island shall att any time be soe boald as to lift up his hand to strick any of His Majesty's subjects, which if any from henceforth should presume to doe, then shall that Negro be apprehended and commited to prison, there to remaine untill the next sesions of the grand court (573) of judicature held at Sainta Jago de la Vega, and there in presence of the whole assembly shall his right hand be cutt off from his body by the hand of the common hangman; afterward shall he be whip't, and soe returned to his master.

XLVIII item, that if att any time hereafter should by accident be slain any Negroa slave by the hand of any of His Majesty's subject belonging to this island, that such shall not be demed murther, nor the party he apprehended nor imprisoned as a murther, butt he that soe kill'd the Negroa slave shall forthwith pay unto the owner thereof for the lost of his slave the full sum of twenty pounds current mony of this island, and for default thereof to be proceed against in law in cause of debt.

Butt if he that kil'd the Negroa slave did itt wilfully and out of spight to the owner thereof, then shall the offender or offenders not only paie twenty pound as aforesaid, but shall also for breach and contempt of the lawe suffer one whole month's close imprisonment.

XLIX item, that all common strumpetts and vile prostratures which shall att any time hereafter be found on this island, and soe proved to be, then shall all such strumpetts be apprehended and forthwith conveyed to the cage, where they shall stand publicquly six houres for example to others. From thence they shall be caried to the ducking stole, and their six times be duck quite under water; from hence shall they be commited to Bridwell on the port, and there shall remain for one whole year unless they can find sufitient suretie for their good behaviour and sivill demenior for ye future.

L item, that noe Jew whatsoever shall att any time be sufferd to run out or take up land on this island, nor to plant nor build thereon, but only to have a free trade at the port, and all 'ore the island with this factory, which free trade is allowed them by us in compliance to ye will and pleasure of our sovereing lord the King of England.

LI item (574), that whosoever of His Majesty's subjects on this island shall for any time hereafter shelter or releife any pirate or privateer, of what nation soever they bee, or shall sell them any manner of provition, or trade with them, shall for the said offence be account[edl adherors with 'em, and therefore deemed as traytors and rebells to our soverain lord the King of England, and shall be proceded against accordingly, and shall suffer death for the said offence.

LII item, that whosoever of His Majesty's subjects on this island of Jamaica shall for any time hereafter presume to dig or open any mines of mettal on this island, contrarie to ye order of our soveraigne lord the king, shall for every such offence forfeitt one hundred pounds to our soveraigne lord the king, and also be imprisoned during the governour's pleasure therein.

LIII item, that whoesoever of His Majesty's subjects on this island of Jamaica for any time hereafter presume to poyson any river, or part thereof, any lakes, springs, or fish ponds on any part of this island, either with the barck of ye dogwood tree, tobacco or any other thinge, by which means the waters are robb'd of fish which are hereby taken, and the owner of the waters much enjured, and many men and beast have bin poysoned by such evil practices; therefore whoesoever shall presume to practice the same, contrary to this acct, shall for every such offence forfeitt five pounds to our soveraigne lord the king, half whereof shall be given to the enformer, and shall enduer three months close imprisonment.

LIV item, that whosoever of His Majesty's subjects in this island of Jamaica shall for any time hereafter presume to kill any of those harmless bird called carrion crows or Jamaican vultures, which are soe usefull in devouring carrion carcasses, which otherwise (575) by their stinck and noisom smell would infect the air and so breed foul and contagious distempers, or shall distroy their young ones or their nest in breed times, shall for every such offence forfeit five pounds to our soveraigne lord the king, halfe of which shall be given to the informer, and the forfeture shall be levied on their body or goods, at the governour's will and pleasure.

Figure 47 Engraving of a carrion crow, from Sloane, *Voyage*. This is the bird whose activity in consuming otherwise dangerous carcasses was protected by law.

LV item, be it enacted that all the judges of each respective percinct of, or belonging to this island, with all the respective justices of the peace in each percinct, do from this time forwards att all times in their quarters and setlements take a speciall care and notice of the poor that are not able to help themselves either by sickness, lamness or blindness, and of all poor distressed widows and orphans, and provid for them houses, mett and drinck sufficient for their necessity and maintenance, allowing to every such poor people [*sic*] one dollar a week till further care be taken over them.

Which mony is to be levied according to a proportionall fee on all freeholders and estates throughout the whole percinct by overseers for the poor, to be henceforward yearly elected for that purpose, and in default therein, and complaint made to the governour thereof, the percinct for such neglect and offence shall forfeit one hundred pounds to our soveraigne lord ye king, to be levied on all freeholders and others throughout the said percinct, which have contem'd this acct.

LVI item, be it enacted that from henceforth in every precinct there be yearly elected and ordain'd two sufficient freeholders of the said precinct to act as way-wardens, which at all times shall see the roads repair'd on all occasions and make new roads through the woods if required thereto by the governour's spetiall order, and that all planters whatever shall on all occasions send their Negroas, servants and waines to work in the roads as directed and commanded by the said (576) supervisors of ye roads or waywardens, and that whosoever shall contend there command herein, and refuse to send their servants, slaves, waines etc. to work on the king's road in order to repair them or to cutt new roads, when lawfully enjoined thereto by the said supervisors, then shall all such offenders and contemnors of this acct for every such offence forfeit ten pounds to our sovereign lord the king, and endure one whole month's imprisonment.

LVII item, that noe manner of person whatsoever shall at any time hereafter presume to goe off or depart from this island without the governour's licence of permition, but shall first putt up his name in the publicque office on the port, for that purpose now errected, and his name soe putt up shall remaine for one and twenty days, that soe all persons may have notice of his intentions of departure, and if any of his creditors be not satisfied, they may underwrite him and proceed against him in law accordingly.

But if after his name be putt up in the said office for the space of one and twenty days, and none accuse him of debt nor underwrites him, then shall the clerk of the office grant him a licence of permition, and soe he shall have lawfull liberty to depart att his pleasure, and all captaines of shipps and other masters of vessels may with safety carry such persons off this island, this licence of permition being their discharge.

LVIII item, that noe captaines of shipps or masters of vessels whatsoever, tradeing to Port Royall or any othere port of this island shall at any time hereafter presume to shelter on board or carry off any inhabitant or servant from off His Majesty's island of Jamaica without the governour's spetiall licence or leter of permition in order thereto. But in case any such captains of ships or masters of vessels shall at any time hereafter presume to do contrary to this acct, that is to say (577) to carry off any from this island without the governour's spetiall licence, then shall all such captains of ships and masters of vessels, for every such offence forfeit one thousand pounds to our sovereign lord the king of England, with the whole shipp and goodes to be seized by His Majesty's Naval Officer for the use of the king, and his body to be held in close imprisonment for the said offence the full space of one yeare, and then never thereafter to be admitted to trade in any part of this island.

LIX item, be it enacted that all persons whatsoever of His Majesty's subjects of Jamaica which shall at any time hereafter be found guilty of felony, treason, murther, burglary, petit larceny or any other the like crime shall be apprehend, imprisoned and brought to tryall according to the fundamental laws of the Crown of England in such cases made and provided, and receive sentence and be executed, and the offender or offenders shall suffer death accordingly, being found guilty according to the fundamental laws of the Crown of England.

LX item, be itt ennacted that all persons whatsoever inhabiting on the island of Jamaica, of what nation whatsoever, shall from henceforth prove loyall and faithfull subjects to the septer* of Great Britain, paying all faithfull duties and obedience to our sovereign lord Charles the Second, by the grace of God King of England, Scotland, France and Ireland, and Supreme Lord of Jamaica, and shall be subject to him, his heirs and successors for ever.

Thus we have given a full account of the good and wholesome laws, accts and customs of Jamaica, created, constituted, ordained and confirmed by His Majesty's trusty lieutenant, Sir Thomas Minns, Knight, governour of Jamaica and ye Right Honourable the Grand Council of the said island for ye quiet government of ye same.

Section II

(578) Of the reception of His Grace Christopher, Duke of Albemarle, Governour of Jamaica and Lord Lieutenannt-Generall of all His Majesty's dominions in America, when he received the government of this island.

In order to a genuine discription of His Grace's reception at Jamaica when he receaved ye government of that island, 'twill be necessary first to understand that our soveraing lord James the Second, after the death of our late souveraigne and his royall brother, of ever blessed memory, was pleased to take into his princely consideration the then stat of His Majesty's island of Jamaica, which was at that time without a governour sutible to such a royall island.[19]

His Majesty therefore thought fitt for the suer peace, honour and good government of his said island, and for the honour and safty of his worthy subjects which inhabited the same, to send thither as his trusty lieutenant some eminent person of spetiall worth and honour, and in order therto His Majesty forthwith created his royal cousin and councellor, Christopher, Duke of Albemarle etc. the governour of the said island of Jamaica, and Lord Lieutenant-Generall of all other His Majesty's dominions in America, commanding him to govern the same (579) as his viceroy, granting him full power and commition to make warr with the Spaniards or any other nation inhabiting in America if there were ocation at any time during his whole government, allso to grant out commitions to all whomsomever he should think fitt, either by sea or land, to fight against such enemys to His Majesty of Great Britain, his Lieutenant-Generall in America.

Also he gave him power to coine either gold or silver on Jamaica, according to what coine or effiges he should thinck fitt, and also to open all mines of metall which he should find on the island of Jamaica. All which he gave him full power and lawful commition to doe during the whole time of his lieutenancy, which was to be for three years' space from the time of His Grace's arrivall at Jamaica, unless His Majesty should thinck fitt to call him home sonner.

His Grace now being prepair'd for his voige into America forthwith tooke leave of His Majesty, and with his illustrious dutchess and his retinue took shiping at Portsmouth on the fouerth day of September, 1687, in order to his voige to Jamaica. His Grace and ye illustrious dutches, were with the chiefe of their retinue, ship't on bord H.M.S. the *Assistance,* commanded by Captain Wright, and their servants and goods was ship't aboard two merchant ships which His Grace had employ'd therein, viz. the *William and Thomas* commanded by Captain Slue and the *Salsbury* commanded by Captain Saunders.[20] His Grace was also attended on by his own yatch called the *Elizabeth,* commanded by Captain Monk.

This fleet was to attend His Grace and be allways in company of ye *Assistance,* which wore an union flag at hir mainton top, in token of supremacy in the American seas. The ships being (580) thus redy weighed

19. It was a particularly "royal" island, though acquired under the Commonwealth, because its foundation was not based on a trading concession, as many colonies were.

20. Taylor's account may be compared against the "Journal of Captain Lawrence Wright on H.M.S. *Assistance*", National Library of Jamaica, National Archives, Captains' Journals, 68.

from Spitthead on the 10th day of September 1687, and made the best of their way for Barbados, where metting with good weather and favourable winds they arived on the 15th day of November following.

His Grace being arived at Barbados went ashore and was received and entertain'd with all the joy and tryhump imaginable due to his honour, all the island being in arms att his reception. His most seren grace haveing here received the broad seall and meas of ye island, and invest their supream lieutenant and governour, and haveing setled all nedful affaires of the said island, and setled his deputy as their governour to command and govern the island of Barbados under him, forthwith dispatch'd away a sloop to Jamaica to give timely notice of his approach, and soe on the last of November His Grace and the fleet wayed from Barbados and bore away for Antego and the other of His Majesty's Windward Islands.

And soe he safely arived at each of them, touching at Neives, Antego, Saint Christopher's, Mountserat etc., and at every one of these island was received with all the honour and joy imaginable, and received the dignytie and honour due to their supream governour and His Majesty's lieutenant. Now after His Grace had left on each island his trusty deputies to govern those island under him, and forthwith had setled all nedfull affaires depending on the good government of all the said islands, His Grace with the fleet wayed from Saint Christopher's on the tenth day of December 1687, and bore down for Jamaica.

Now the sloop which was sent by His Grace to Jamaica to accquaint the deputy governor, ye Right Honourable Hender Molesworth Esq. of His Grace's approach arived at the island on the 8th day of December 1687, and acquainted the governour therewith, who imediatly orderd all the melitia both horse and foot how and where to acct, and to be allways in redyness on one hour's warning to be in arms, accordingly to (561) attend His Grace att his reception into his government. Also then he sent forth the frigate H.M.S. *Faulcon* comanded by Captain Thomas Smith to cruse att the east end of Jamaica in order to meet and attend His Grace, with orders not to return in (unless some urgent occation happen'd) until they had sight of the flagg and knew His Grace's pleasure, and that then should make the best of their way into Port Royall, and that being come within sight of the port they should fier fouer pieces of ordnance and let flie their main and fore topgallant sailes, to give notice to the port to arm themselves, for that His Grace was nigh att hand.

H.M.S. *Faulcon* having these orders putt to sea, and on Sunday the eighteen of December 1687, about two a'clock in the afternoon, being about twenty miles off from the east end of Jamaica espied the flage and three saile more in company, and at fouer in the afternoon came up with them and gave His Grace three huzas,* and then saluts His Grace with one and twenty guns, and soe went under his stern.[21] Then His Grace salutes the *Faulcon* with thirteen guns, the *Elizabeth* yacht with due sevean guns, Captain Slue with eleven guns and Captain Saunders with fiveteen guns. Then the *Faulcon* returns nineteen guns for a generall thanks; by this shooting at sea the windward part of the island of Jamaica was allaramed, and soe the curious of Morrant with all expedition gave the allarm to Yallows, and Yallows to the Port, and geet all their beckons* on fire in sign of allarum, soe that by four a'clock on Monday morning, being the nineteenth of December 1687, the Port was all in arms at their respective posts, and they fired two shott from Charles Fort over the Salt Pond Hill to give notice to arm. After which the forts hung out their flages of union, and also hung out four very large stremors or pendants on the fouer pinacles of the tower of the church, ye more lively to express their joy thereby.

(582) Then two hundred men (of the melitia of the port) were drawn up in arms at each fort, with gunnes etc. suffitient to play the artillery, and two hundred men were drawn up in the court of the King's House in order for a gaurd for His Grace's person. The rest of the reidgment, which was about 1,300 men, were drawne up in arms on the Parade,[22] to be comande whither the collonel should see expedient. Thus the melitia forces were drawn up, and all other things on the Port put in rediness to serve His Grace att his reception. Allso all the ships and other vesles in the harbour display'd their collours, run outt their gunns, and prepar'd to spake forth their true joy from the mouths of their cannons.

Captain Smith, as you have heard before, having mett His Grace forthwith went on board the *Assistance,* and was wellcomly received by His Grace, from whome he had immediat orders to make the best of his way into Port Royal, and accquaint them with his approach, that soe they might be redy for his reception, upon which Captain Smith forthwith made the best of his way in, and about nine a'clock on Monday morning, being the ninetenth of December 1687, he being then within sight of the port fired four cannons, and gave the signe of approach as he had orders to doe, and soe about ten a'clock following the *Faulcon* came to anchor in Port Royall harbour, and was by all the forts and shiping saluted, according to the accustomed order.

The Duke being thus approaching, some of the cheife gentry of ye port and chief ministers of state went out in whereys to meet His Grace, namly Sir

21. In general, Taylor's account of this meeting agrees closely with that of the log of HMS *Falcon,* National Archives, Adm 51/345. Thomas Smith, formerly lieutenant, had replaced Charles Talbot when the latter died in October 1688.

22. The "Parade" was probably the wide section of High Street near Fort Rupert, at the eastern end of the town.

Figure 48 Aerial photograph of the signal tower at Yallahs Bay (photograph by Jack Tyndale-Biscoe). The little round tower at the bottom left was one of a line of such signal stations, designed to permit communication between the eastern part of the island and the capital at Spanish Town.

Francis Watson, Sir Richard Dereing, Sir Charles Mudiford, the Chief Justice, Major Reves, secretary of state, Captain Musgrove, the King's Attorney-Generall, Smith Kelly, Esq., the Provost Marshall, Coll. Beckford, president of the port and others, who (583) were received on board the *Assistance* by His Grace with all ye kindness and respect imaginable.

Meanwhile the gentry from all parts of the island ressort from Passage Fort and Ligournea to the port, soe that the harbour seemed to be covered with wattermen plying to and fro, and all the shor around the port was lin'd with spectators, joyfully to congratulat His Grace's hapy arivall, the which they had soe long wish't for, soe that there was never seen such a concourse of people as was this day gather'd together on the port, since this island hath binn inhabited by ye English nation.

Now comes the joyfull tryhump of His Grace's reception, for about one a'clock this afternoon His Grace safly came to anchor in Port Royall harbour, with his illustrious dutches on bord the *Assistance,* which then had three union flags flying, the one at his foretopmasthead, the other at his maintopmasthedd, and the other at his misontopmasthead, with hir jack* and ensigne and twenty-one pendants or stremours flieing at hir yard-arms and other useuall places.

Now as His Grace passed by each fort in towards the harbour, he was received thus; first ye fort salutes him gradually with three severall shouts of huzas for joy, and then all rim'd with a peall of their great artillary. After that the infantry all around the port (beginning at Charles Fort) graduall salutes him with five voleys with their musquetts. Then the *Faulcon* and all other shiping in the harbour makes three shouts, and then salutes him with all their cannon gradually. Then the yatch, Captain Slue and Captain Saunders gradually salutes the fort with thirty-nine gunns, then His Grace (being now come to anchor) answers all by way of a generall thancks with thirteen gunns.

Then all the shipping (by way of gratullation) fiers again gradually, some with seaven and others with five gunns, and then the forts, port and shipping (584) gave His Grace three shouts and the drums and trumpets joyfully sounded their marshall blasts, and then the Right Honourable Hender Molesworth, Esquire, Deputy Governour of the said island, with the rest of the ministers of state, went on board the *Assistance* to perform the ceriomony of delivery to His Grace, presenting to him the mase and seall of the island, which with them were honourably received by him, and soe the port and whole island remained in arms all night, making boonfiers and other signalls of joy.

On the morrow, being Tewesday the 20th of December 1687, about ten a'clock in the morning His Grace's flagg was taken down and placed in the stern of his barge, in which His Grace attended with the cheif gentry of the

island was then rowed ashore by ten wattermen array in whight as His Grace's badg of honour, and was attend with the *Faulcon*'s barge and other ships' pinaces to the Wherry Brige. As soon as His Grace was putt off from the ship side, the *Assistance* fir'd twenty-one guns, then all the other shiping in the harbour discharg'd all their artillary gradually, speaking forth that joy which was now received by the happy presence of His Grace. Then the forts also fier'd, and soe continued fiering for about one half hower, [so] that the loud echoes of the mountaines loudly thunder'd with the noise thereof; then the infantry gave all a volie and a loud shout gradually at His Grace's landing.

His Grace being landed at the Wherry Bridg on the port was attended on by the ministers of state and gentrey of the island, all in their respective order, and all the street from the bridg to the King's House was cover'd with green cloath, and two hundred soldiers drawn up from the bridg to the door, one each side to make a passage for His Grace. Those without the court to the brige gave a volley att his entrance into the court of the King's House (585), and those within the court gave a volly as soon as he was enter'd the King's House and three shouts, Hender Molesworth Esquire going on his right hand and the Provost Marsharall carrying the sword before him, and the secretary, Major Reves Esq. bearing the mase, and seall befor him, and Mr. Wm. Peat marshall going before all with the marsharall's staf.

In this order His Grace entered the King's House, where after some small stay and some complements passed, as is usuall on such occations, His Grace in the same manner attended went from the King's House to the church, all the way being covered with green cloth and gauards as before. In this order they entered the cloyster or exchange on the norther side of Saint Paul's Church, at the east end of which cloyster was placed a chaire of state, cover'd with azur velvet, richly bost, fringed and embroider'd with gold in curious work, with nine steps of assent, with golden lions like Solomon's throne all covered with rich embroderies. Over this chair of state hung a canopy of blew sattin, embos, fringed and embroideried with silk, gold and curious work, with a cushion of the like for his feet, in which was said to be 2,000 pistolls of gold, which with this chair of state was presented to His Grace by the Spanish factor, Seigniora San Jago and Senior Alverious a Jew, merchant on Port Royall. Over this chair of state was curiously portrai'd the king's arms of England and the arms of this island.

This chair of state etc. His Grace seemed to slight, neither would he sett therein.[23] Ass sone as prayers was ended in the church then their in publicke

23. The Duke of Albemarle was notoriously venal; perhaps he regarded this present as insufficient? On the other hand, perhaps he was maintaining the formal protocol of the Court of James II, where the chair of state would remain empty. See H.M. Baillie, "State Apartments in Baroque Palaces", *Archaeologia* 101 (1967).

audience the secretary of the island read His Grace's commition from His Majesty of Great Britain, in which he was honorably intituled Christopher, Duke of (586) Albemarle, the Supream Governour of His Majesty's island of Jamaica and Lord Lieutenant Generall of all His Majesty's Dominions in America. Which being read, and the cerimony of reception finished, His Grace returns from the church to the King's House, haveing the Right Honourable Hender Molesworth Esquire on his left hand, and the other ministers of state marching in the same order as before, where His Grace was entertain't with whatevere rareties the island would afford, the drums and trumpets joyfull sounding forth their marshall blast, the Marshall waiting on him att dinner, and the chife ministers of state and gentrey of the island were admitted to sett att the table with him; His Grace had now a gaurd of two hundred men with their drawn swords to attend him.

His Grace being thus satt down to dinner, the forts fire all their ordnance gradually, beging at Carlisle Fort; then the infantry which guarded the forts and were drawn up on the parade gave each gradually a volly with their musketts. Then the *Assistance* fired twenty-one peices of ordnance, the *Faulcon* twenty-one, the *Elizabeth* yatch eleven, then all the other shipping in the harbour fier'd all round gradually, one after another.

Now His Grace haveing dined, about two a'clock all the ridgment of the infantry on the port were drawn up in batalia in the court of the King's House before His Grace, the drum beating severall points of warr, and the infantry dischard severall volyes before him and then march't off, each to hir respective post, only those of His Grace's gaurd, which still remain'd in their orders at the King's House.

About fouer a'clock in the afternoon, His Grace with his attendance in his barge went off from the port, and soe went on (587) board the *Assistance,* and as sone as His Grace was put off the shore the forts discharg'd all their artillery gradually, beginning at Carlisle Fort. Then the *Assistance* fired twenty-one gunns, the *Faulcon* twenty-one, the *Elizabeth* yatch eleaven, and all the other shipping continued fireing gradually all round, giving three shouts or huzzas.

Soe the melitia of the port were discharg'd from their arms, save those of the dayly guards. All this night the drums continued beatting and the trumpetts joyfully sounding on shore, with other musick, with bonfiers and all other posible signalls of joy, which was fully demonstrated by the great concourse of gentry and others from all parts of the island gather'd together now at the port, soe that the like was never seen since this island was inhabited by the English. Also about eight a'clock at night Captain Thomas Smith, commander of H.M.S. *Faulcon,* lighted up about on thousand candles, which were plac't att the yardarms, trucks, topmast heads, in the shrouds, riging, all along on the gunnell* bulkheads and other convenient places about the ship, soe that it gave a strange and mighty light, and continued burning for the space of one houre, in order to congratulate His Grace's happy reception.

Thus we have now given a full account of the reception of His Grace Christopher, Duke of Albemarle etc., Supreame Governour of His Majesties island of Jamaica and Lord Lieutenant-Generall of all His Majesty's dommmion in America att the time of the entrance into his government, in the which may be seen the great joy and tryhump that was on the port att the reception of soe honourable a governour, the which they had long expected, and thus we leave them now triumphing in the enjoyment of so noble a governour.

Section III

(588) Some particular directions, councill and advice to all such which intend to settle and inhabitt on His Majesty's island of Jamaica, which is here added by way of concultion to this treatice.

Quintilian the famous orator and eagle-eyed philosopher saieth that friendly advice and prudent councill is of more force and strenght to deffend from mischeivious fate than the forces of army to defend a contry, for by the one man is forwarn'd to shun destruction, whereas the other is only a resolute deffence which may be demolish't by the conquering sword. Now as every man is to be innocently harmless, soe hee ought to be truly prudent, which is the grand defence of innocency. For we must unite the wisdom of the serpent with the innocency of the dove, haveing innocency with our wisdom, which else would be but craftyness, and wisdom with our innocence, which otherwise would be weakness.[24]

Therefore as by innocency we should not wrong others, soe we should be prudent that others may not wrong nor circumvent us. By which we shall posses that peace which exercises coertion and restraint o'er all the inferior facculltys, under the empire and conduct of reason, which without prudence will be subject to disorder, and often hurried (589) from its reasonable accting.

Since in the former part of this history we have given a full description in all things whatsoever of His Majesty's island of Jamaica, now we come to

24. Taylor is thinking here of the gospel of St Matthew, 10:16, "Be ye therefore wise as serpents, and harmless as doves."

draw to a conclution, the which we shall wind up with advice and councill to those which shall hereafter goe thither to settle, in order to which let such know: that the inhabitants of this island for the most part (tho' now rich) were formerly rude and of mean birth, men of their witts, which have here advanct their fortune by mere industry of the mind, with the help of the Spaniards' purse, and therefor they are very sharp, witty and flattering when they find advantages by that means, but on the other hand they are disceitfull, cruile and unkind where they take against [blank] ffor first (omitting the worthys of the island, whose goodness may be seen by their own light):

When newcomers are att the portt, if he be a merchant then all those of his function shall sone by their flattering insinuations enter into his accquaintance, under pretence of mere generosity or trading with him; then they will privatly learn from him (as it were by the bie) what cargoe he hath and of what nature, then the responce of his corrispondant, and soe by degrees the depth of his purse, still protesting they were never yett soe happy as in the new enjoyment of his noble company.

Haveing thus learn'd his estate, they will make it their buissiness in all taverns and publick company behind his back to defame and blast his credit by a way of pitty, saying: "I am harty sorry for such a man. He will sone ruin himself; his cargo's of litle worth, and he hath less [illegible] to manage itt". Thus they by degrees blow it all over the port that he is either a knave or a foll or boath, and soe the other merchants slight him, and this honest gentleman is defamed (590) and perhaps further by them wronged, for they having learned his correspondant and the manner of his cargo send home a friendly letter to his correspondant, that out of all possible kindness they thought fitt to acquaint him of ye extravagancy of his factor etc., by which misinformation his correspondent is enragedd and will send him noe more goods. By which means this honest gentellman is utterly ruined, and perhaps imprisoned, which else would have lived happy, being more honest than those silent cutt-throats.

Now these haveing attained their ends by ruining this gentleman and furthering their trades, begins everywhere in publique saying: "I pity such a gentleman's fatte, att the which I am really sorry etc.", when God knows 'tis the greatest joy they have, and that which themselves wickedly caused.

Now lett any artist, chirurgeons, limners* or the like come to setle on the port, then shall all those of his function strive to ruin him in the same manner, by defaming him and blasting his skill all 'ore the Point, and still protest to his face they are really hapy in his company, when perhaps att the same time they will conspier his overthrow, but if in case they find his purse toasty, then they will if possible inlure him to some extravigancy or other, and if possible by that means ruinin him. Butt if this proves ineffectuall, then by some treat of kindness they'll either surffeite him or drinck him to death, and then after his death they blast him with extravigancy and brand him with the name of a sott, and thus many are ruined.

A third snare they lay for newcomers is this; after they have sounded the depth of his cappacities and purse by their flattering insinuations, then they praise him and use all the flatterys immaginable till they have brought him either indebted to themselves, or some other of their like, still (591) acting under the vizard* of frindeship. Then they sone imprison them, ruin them, and soe bring them in as servantts, and thus and many other ensnaring flattering ways they use the newcommer, not as yett accquainted with their crafty knavishness.

Thus we have shown the treachary and perfidious deallings practice by some at this island, although I doe here solemnly declare that there are some really honorably and just, altho' the major part is thus and farr worse than I am cappable to discribe. Now let us come to give our councill by way of pure advice to all such which shall hereafter goe to setle on this island, and that we may in the same proceed in a genuine method, we will reduce all to three heads: first, advice to merchants, secondly to privat gentlemen and artificers, and thirdly to servants, and soe conclude all with a generall advice towards the preservation of health.

First, let all merchants att their arrivall att the port be sure to keep their concerns close to themselves, and carry themselves statly and reserved, giving noe such flatterers (which I have here lively portraied) opportunity to undermine their buisiness. In the next place let them assotiate themself with those of the best ranck and quality by birth, for such will sooner advance them than others; they being rich enough will not desire to engross their trade, but will be well pleas't to see any industriously thrive, and being well born and educated they will scorn to practice mischife against them, and now by being assosiated with them the other Asmodeus's will be affraid to attempt any such thing.

Now in the next place lett him be sure to be bould, and answer quick and sharply, and never betake himself to the tavern, which will not only ruin his purse butt also cause all those which before were his friends to dispise and slight him. Lastly lett him make quick returns to his correspondent, by all which he may soon become (592) a wealthy merchant.

Secondly, my advice to private gentlemen is this: only to take care of these lewd company, which under the disguise of grandeur and fashion swarm here, and lett him take care that he besorr himself not to to [*sic,* with fresh ink] the tavern, which if he doe will not only exhaust his estate and prejudice his health, butt will also eclipse his worth and render him contemptible in the eys of all men, for alttho' they are here in general boon companions and very loose, yett nevertheless they abhor sotishness in others. Also let such be sure to associat themselves with those of the best degree, which will add honour to their worth, whereas the society of those upstarts of mean birth, tho' rich, will render them mean, and on all occation strive to undermine their reipute and exhaust their estate. Therefore lett such privat gentlemen offten vissit the country, where I am suer they will find entertainment sutable to their quallity.

My advice next is to artificers and tradesmen which come hither to setle, of what proffestion soever they bee. Lett them first be suer to keep all their concerns close to themselves, and if it be possible conceale their profestion for some time. Then let them observe the fashions of the place and then proceed boldly, wisely and ingeniously in their profestion, that soe those envious deceivers may neither out-hector 'em, outwitt 'em or outwork their ingenuity.

Butt let them be sure to be plausable and diligent, and keep themselfe within the bounds of modesty and reason, not besotting themselves to the taverns, which will here (as at home) render them contemptible and caus them to be generally slighted. But by observing these rules, lett them walk narrowly and (593) to be sure he may here live very happly, maintain his famaly gentely, and in some reasonable time geett a competent estate, for here those that are sufficient workemen in what profestion soever will never want employ, but will here geet thrice the day-wages that they could in England, which will not only well maintaine them but also give them good encouragment.

Our last advice is to servant in generall, which when they are weary of Old England and are minded to try the advanctment of their fortune in Jamaica, let such first lawfully bind themselves as servants by indenture to some honest responsable captain of a ship tradeing thither, and to noe other of the ship's company, which if they doe they must not expect such good usage as they wold receive were they the captain's servants. In the next place let all such servants behave themselves diligently and honnestly on shipboard in their transportation* thither, by which they will gaine a good report when they come to be sold. Now when they come to be sold, lett them have the captain's recommendation, and lett them be suer to take that master which proffers most money for them, for he that profers most for them, likes them best, and he that will give most for them is most probable to be able to maintain them best in time of their servitude.[25]

My next advice to such is to advise them to be diligent and humble and faithfull in their trust, which being they will live with [illegible], pleasure and

25. It will be remembered that according to Taylor's act XIX, indentured servants had some choice in the matter of whom they would serve.

comfort than in England. Our last advice is that they serve out their full time and not give their minds to running away, by which means they'll only (594) increase their time of servitude and perhaps never became free. Now all such as will observe these rules may here live happy, and in prosses of time advance their fortune, for those manservants which come hither come commonly (if of a cappacity) employed in shops and to be supervisors of storehouses and in plantations, and women servant are keapt to work at their nedle and the lick, and if honest live here comfortable in their four years' servitude.

Now we come to give a general advise to all for the preservation of their health, in order to which lett all in the first place live moderat in their diet and nott give themselves to too much drincking, neither of wine, punch or perinno, which will soon vitiate the blood. Then let them take a spetiall care to keep their brest warm and drie from the dues, by which they may well here enjoy their health and avoide dangerous sickness.

Thus thro' the blessed assistance of the Divine Omnipotent power we have finished this treatis of the present state of His Majesty's island of Jamaica in America, as 'tis now under the government of His Grace Christopher, Duke of Albemarle etc., whom God grant a happy life, an honourable and quiet government, with a safe returne to his native contrey.[26]

26. In fact, after a governorship filled with quarrels, Albemarle died in October 1688. His body, preserved in pitch, went back to England with his ever more eccentric duchess, who then lived until 1734.

Glossary

Adam's ale: a jocular term for water
Amain: at full speed
Antique: antic, or grotesque
Antiscorbuticke: of use against the malady of scurvy
Arcanum: a profound secret
Arsclout: a pair of trousers
Artichoak: a thistle-like plant found in Europe
Artificers: craftsmen
Assur: azure, meaning blue
Attractive: absorptive, or attracting water
Audiencia: Spanish term for a court and for its court-house
Avoirdupoiz/avoirdupoize: weight
Balisters: balusters, short upright posts
Bandolliers: shoulder-belts for cartridges
Bank their doges: to hold their dogs in check
Bassynets: wickerwork baskets
Bastion: the projecting part of a fortification
Batalia: in order of battle
Batlement: battlement, an indented parapet at the top of a wall
Baylick: bay-like
Beadle: a parish officer
Beckons: signal-beacons
Belensgate/Bellens-Gate: Billingsgate, the fish market in London
Beves: "beeves", an archaic word for oxen
Bitt: bit, a small silver coin
Boatswain: an officer on a ship, in charge of the sails and rigging
Brambleberry: an old word for a blackberry
Bries: "breeze", a fairly recent word for wind, in Taylor's day
Broile: disturbance
Bushill: bushel, a measure of capacity
Busking spanell: a hunting spaniel

Bustard: a genus of large birds
Calicut: calico, cloth originally from Calicut in India
Callcined: reduced by fire
Callentuers: calentures, a delirium-like disease common among sailors
Camomill: a creeping herb whose leaves have medicinal qualities
Capon: a castrated cock
Caraigous: probably "courageous"
Cataplasm: a poultice
Catches: "ketches", smallish two-masted vessels
Cathar: catarrh
Cavious: hollow
Chafinch: a small bird, once common in England
Chariot: a light four-wheeled carriage
Chirurgeon: a doctor
Ciddney bean: kidney bean
Cisillia: Sicily
Claudes: clouds
Claver: probably cleaver, or chopper
Cleave: a narrow valley
Codd: a rare word, meaning the inner curve of a bay
Codling: a variety of apple
Cods: scrotum
Coives: a coif was a close-fitting hat
Combmakers: those who fashioned combs from turtle-shell
Commones: commonness
Con'd it: studied it
Consumptions/consumption: a pulmonary wasting disease
Cony: an old word for a rabbit, still used in heraldry
Cortex: husk or, here, skin
Coteing time: among tortoises, to coot is to copulate
Coud: pod
Coule: cowl or hood
Craugh: craw, or crop of a bird
Crawle: the enclosure where turtles were kept in captivity
Crean/creane: careen, meaning to haul a ship down in order to work on her hull
Crebolian/Creolian/Creoliann: Taylor's jocular term for West Indians
Curnall: kernel
Curriers: dress leather after it has been tanned
Curtaines: walls forming part of a bastionned trace
Dejest: digest, or render down

Deragate: probably "derogate", meaning here "divert"
Discues/discuss: disperse
Distemper: an illness, now applied only to a disease of animals
Diureticque/diuretique: an encouragement to urination
Dorick: the Doric order formed part of the classical architectural ordinances
Draught: a plan
Dropsie: dropsy, a condition involving excessive retention of water
Drosie: probably "drossy", or dreg-like
Dues: dews
Duggs: a dug was a breast or udder
Emerin: a flower, but which one?
Empericks: "empiric", one who practised medicine without scientific knowledge
Enginere: an engineer, in this case a fire-master
Ensigne: a flag, probably with the union device in its corner
Equinoctiall: the equator
Expiated: extirpated
Faccotries: factory, in the old sense of a place of trade
Fallowed ground: newly ploughed but unplanted ground
Feeters: fetters
Ffuzee and cartouchbox: a light musket and ammunition
Fingrigo: prickly climbing shrub found in Jamaica
Fistulas: tubes
Flacc: flax
Flea'd: probably flayed
Fleced: this word seems akin to "flench," meaning to skin
Flegmeticke: abounding in phlegm, or moistness and coldness
Flux: often, dysentery
Flyboat: a fast-sailing, flat-bottomed Dutch boat
Forrena luna: an astronomical term, referring to the waning moon
Freez: frieze, a kind of coarse woollen cloth
Fricassed/fricases: fried or stewed/stews
Fustick: a yellow dye-wood
Gosehawk: the goshawk is a large, short-winged hawk
Groat: a denomination of coin, no longer issued after 1662
Guiles: gills
Guinea hen: perhaps a Guinea-fowl
Gunnell: gunwale, a timber extending round the top of a ship's hull
Hackney coach: a hired coach, the word probably coming from Hackney, in England

Hale: haul
Harping iron: an old word for a boat-hook or barbed spear
Havena: harbour
Hawse: a hawser, or cable, anchoring the ship
Hazell: hazel, a bush or small tree
Head, the: toilet in the bow of the ship
Hearon: heron
Hellmit: helmet
Hieroglyphick: a figurative symbol
Hoggsheads: large casks, often used for sugar or for liquor
Hollow sea: a sea with steep waves and troughs
Holm: holm-oak, an evergreen tree
Holsom/holsome: wholesome
Hops: the hop-plant, used for giving a bitter flavour to fermented liquors
Hundredweight: roughly 100 pounds
Huzas: hurrahs
Hydropticque: substance taken for epilepsy
Indenture: a contract, particularly one binding a servant to a master
Indiferent/indeferent: neither good nor bad
Intrinsique: inmost, and so hard to apprehend
Involves: surrounds
Irons: iron shackles
Jack: a small ship's flag, often indicating nationality
Jecimon: jasmine, sometimes known as "jessamine"
Katch: a ketch, see also "catches"
Ketle: a cooking-pot, not necessarily with a spout
Killdivile: West Indian name for rum
Knatt: gnat
Knawghing: gnawing
Latharone: pirate
Laves: ladles
Letice windows: lattice, or slatted, windows
Levet: a trumpet-call, generally given in the morning
***Lex methodica*:** a systematic legal system
Lightors: lighters, boats used for unloading ships
Limners: artists
Lixivium: a lye
Lutanist: a player of the lute, a stringed instrument
Maccarate: macerate, or steep
Maccrel: mackerel
Magazine: chief stronghold

Maidenhair: a fern, once much used in medicine
Main, the: mainland America
Maine: a mainsail
Malch: perhaps mulch
Mastive: presumably a mastiff
Mauger: a Jamaican (but not English) word meaning thin, from the French *maigre*
Maule: a heavy hammer
Mechanicks: craftsmen
Megrine: megrim or migraine, a form of severe headache
Meleficious: probably mellifluous, or sweet
Merceis: mercies
Mesentery: the intestine
Metropolitan: central
Mier: mire
Mizonpeek: the stern of a vessel
Mole: a spot
Morose: a word usually applied to people, meaning gloomy.
Mote: moat, or ditch
Moules: mules
Mucheat: a broad and heavy knife or cutlass, from the Spanish *machete*
Mum: a kind of beer, originally brewed in Brunswick
Mundifie: an archaic word meaning to cleanse or purify
Muscadine: muscadin grapes had the flavour of musk
Neat: oxen, cattle
Need: probably a neat
Newgat: Newgate, a celebrated London prison
Norths: northers
Nott grass: knott grass
Nurly: knarled
Ordinary: an eating-house providing customary fare
Ouzier: an osier, or species of willow
Ovillar: oval
Pallasadoe: a palisade, or fence of stout stakes
Parsle: parcel
Parsnipp: a plant with a pale yellow root used in cooking
Partridge: a game bird much hunted
Patten: letters patent conferring ownership
Pectorall: pertaining to the chest
Periaguer: a piragua or periagua, a long narrow canoe
Perrad: parade

Perwinckle: periwinkle, a shrub
Petit: small
Phesant: a game bird.
Picarie: a word for a hog, from the Carib *pakira*
Pieces of ordnance: guns
Pigg: a billet of metal, as in pig-iron
Pilchar: pilchard, a small sea fish like a herring
Pinck/pinke: a small sailing-vessel, from a Dutch word
Pinnace: a light sailing-vessel, often employed as a tender
Pionners: pioneers, foot-soldiers prepared to clear the way for an army
Pissell: an archaic word for a penis
Pistol/pistole/pistoll: a Spanish gold coin
Plantaign: plantain
Plat: survey establishing the boundaries of land
Plaza major: the central square in a Spanish city
Plurasie: pleurisy, inflammation of the lung
Poplar: a tall tree
Port: a port-hole
Prepetuous: impetuous
Preposterous: meaning extreme, or absurd
Previous: here, meaning prompt or prior
Prickly: one of Taylor's far-fetched words, meaning delicious
Pulss: pulse, the seeds of leguminous plants
Pursser: on a ship, this is the officer in charge of financial matters
Putter: pewter
Quarter deck: a small elevated deck, used by the ship's officers
Quire: choir
Regale/regalla: feast
Restringent: having binding properties, for instance for the bowels
Revitts: rivets
Royall: a coin
Saine: seine-net, for fishing
Salenas: salt-ponds
Sampier: samphire, a plant that grows on rocks by the sea
Sangaree: a drink consisting of wine and fruit juice (Sp. *sangria*)
Scars/scarss: scarcely
Semeter: a short, curved, single-edged sword
Septer: sceptre, an ornamental rod symbolizing authority
Shalets: shallots, small flavourful onions
Shanckers: probably cankers, or ulcers
Shrouds: a set of ropes sustaining the mast of a ship

Sicamore: the sycamore, a species of fig-tree or maple
Silabubus: syllabub, a drink or dish made of milk or cream
Sloop: a small one-masted vessel
Snagling: probably snagged, or jagged
Snush/snuth: snuff
Sold by outcry: sold at auction
Spanile: spaniel
Sparagus: asparagus
Spierry: spirey, spire-like
Spind: perhaps meaning the trunk of the tree
Splindeling: tapering
Stafe: staff, in the sense "staff of life"
Stareling: starling, a bird found on both sides of the Atlantic Ocean
Stearage: steerage; in a frigate this would have been the second cabin
Steip/stupe: variants of steep
Stone: testicle
Streame cable: cable of the stream, or medium, anchor
Terms: menstrual periods
Terraphin/terraphinn: terrapin, a word of Algonquian origin
Terrena luna: literally, the earthly moon
Tibourn: Tyburn, a place of public execution in London
Transportation: in Taylor's day, this was coming to mean deportation
Trumpet wood tree: a tree with a hollow stem, parts of which could be used for music
Tunns: large barrels
Tutch: touched at
Tyros: a novice
Uberous: an archaic word meaning fertile
Ubi: a place, from the Latin *ubi,* or where
Umbretique: shady, perhaps an invention of Taylor
Uncapatiated: incapable
Velom: vellum, meaning parchment-like
Vertego: vertigo, or dizziness
Viand: article of food, not necessarily meat
Victualls/victuals: articles of food
Visicitor: a poultice
Vizard: an archaic word for mask
Wain/waine: this was a large, open, four-wheeled vehicle
Wakes: wax
Warping: hauling a boat on a "warp"
Wayed: variously spelled, this word means to weigh [anchor]

Wheayish-colloured: the colour of whey, the watery part of milk
Wherry: a light rowing-boat, often used as a ferry
Wilke: whelk
Woodbind: also woodbine, an ancient word for a variety of climbing plants
Worm: a long spiral tube, connected with the head of a still
Yard: a spar for sustaining a sail
Yawes/yaws: an ulcerating disease once common in Jamaica
Yew tree: a tree associated with churchyards and the manufacture of longbows

Bibliography

Acts of Assembly passed in the island of Jamaica from the year 1681 to the year 1754 inclusive. Saint Jago de la Vega [Spanish Town], 1769.

Allsopp, Richard. *Dictionary of Caribbean English Usage.* Kingston, 2003.

Anderson, W.W., ed. *An account of America (1671).* Kingston, 1851. (Includes a chapter by John Ogilby on Jamaica.)

Andrade, Jacob. *A Record of the Jews in Jamaica.* Kingston, 1941.

Anon. *Interesting tracts relating to the island of Jamaica.* Spanish Town, 1800.

Battick, John F., ed. "Richard Rooth's Sea Journal of the Western Design". *Jamaica Journal* 4 (1971): 3–22.

Blome, Richard. *A description of the island of Jamaica.* London, 1672.

Bond, James. *Birds of the West Indies.* London, 1961.

Bridenbaugh, Carl, and Roberta Bridenbaugh. *No Peace beyond the Line: The English in the Caribbean 1624–1690.* New York, 1972.

Browne, Patrick. *The Civil and Natural History of Jamaica.* London, 1756.

Buisseret, David. "The French Invasion of Jamaica, 1694". *Jamaica Journal* 16, no. 3 (1983): 31–33.

———. "John Taylor's Ideas about Seventeenth-Century Jamaican Slavery". *Jamaican Historical Review* 21 (2001): 1–7.

Buisseret, David, with Jack Tyndale-Biscoe. *Historic Jamaica from the Air.* Kingston, 1996.

Calendar of State Papers, America and West Indies. 27 vols. London, 1860–1926.

Calendar of State Papers, Domestic Series, Reign of Charles II. 17 vols. London, 1860–1947.

Cassidy, F.G., and R.B. Le Page. *Dictionary of Jamaican English.* Cambridge, 1967.

Claypole, William. "The Settlement of the Liguanea Plain between 1655 and 1673". *Jamaican Historical Review* 10 (1973): 13–14.

Claypole, William, and David Buisseret. "Trade Patterns in early English Jamaica". *Journal of Caribbean History* 5 (1972): 5–20.

Craton, Michael. *Testing the Chains: Resistance to Slavery in the British West Indies.* Ithaca/London, 1982.

Craton, Michael, and James Walvin. *A Jamaican Plantation.* London/New York, 1970.

Culpeper's Compleat Herbal. London, 1652, reprint New York, 1950.

Cundall, Frank. *Historic Jamaica.* London, 1915.

———. "Tortoiseshell Carving in Jamaica". *The Connoisseur* 72 (1925): 154–63.

———. *Governors of Jamaica in the Seventeenth Century.* London, 1936.

Cundall, Frank, and Joseph Pietersz. *Jamaica under the Spaniards.* Kingston, 1919.
Davies, K.G. *The Royal Africa Company.* London, 1957.
de Bry, Theodor. *Americae.* Frankfurt, 1596.
Dunn, Richard S., *Sugar and Slaves: The Rise of the Planter Class in the English West Indies, 1624–1713.* Chapel Hill, 1972.
Earle, Peter. *The Treasure of the* Concepción. New York, 1980.
Esquemeling, John. *The Buccaneers of America.* Edited by W.S. Stallybrass. New York, 1987.
Firth, C.H., ed. *The Narrative of General Venables.* London, 1900.
Glanvill, Joseph et al. *Saducimus triumphatus.* London, 1681.
Hanson, Francis. *The laws of Jamaica.* Spanish Town, 1683.
Haring, C.H., *The Buccaneers in the West Indies in the 17th Century.* London, 1910.
Heidtke, Kenan Paul. "Jamaican Red Clay Pipes". MA thesis, Texas A & M, 1992.
Heylyn, Peter. *Cosmographie in foure books.* London, 1652.
Howse, Derek, and Norman Thrower, eds. *A Buccaneer's Atlas: Basil Ringrose's South Sea Waggoner.* Berkeley, 1992.
Ingram, Kenneth. *Manuscripts Relating to Commonwealth Caribbean Countries in United States and Canadian Repositories.* Barbados, 1975.
———. *Sources of Jamaican History 1655–1838.* 2 vols. Zug, 1976.
———. *Manuscript Sources for the History of the West Indies.* Kingston, 2000.
Jamaica National Trust Commission. *Port Royal Jamaica: Excavations 1969–70.* Kingston, 1972.
Journals of the House of Assembly of Jamaica. 14 vols. Kingston 1811–29.
Ligon, Richard. *A True and Exact History of the Island of Barbadoes.* 1657; reprint, London, 1976.
Long, Edward. *A History of Jamaica.* 3 vols. London, 1774.
Marley, David. *The Sack of Veracruz: The Great Pirate Raid of 1683.* Ontario, 1993.
McCusker, John J. *Money and Exchange in Europe and America, 1600–1715: A Handbook.* Chapel Hill, 1978.
McDonald, Roderick, ed. *West Indies Accounts: Essays on the History of the British Caribbean and the Atlantic Economy in Honour of Richard Sheridan.* Kingston, 1996.
Morales Padrón, Francisco. *Spanish Jamaica.* Translated by Patrick Bryan, Michael Gronow and Felix Oviedo Moral. Kingston, 2003.
Pawson, Michael, and David Buisseret. *Port Royal, Jamaica.* Oxford, 1975; revised edition, Kingston, 2000.
Petrovich, Sandra M. *Henry Morgan's Raid on Panama: Geopolitics and Colonial Ramifications, 1669–1674.* New York, 2001.
Roberts, W. Adolphe. *Sir Henry Morgan, Buccaneer and Governor.* New York, 1933.
Robertson, James. "Rewriting the English Conquest of Jamaica in the Late Seventeenth Century". *English Historical Review* 117, no. 473 (2002): 813–39.
———. *Gone is the Ancient Glory.* Kingston, 2005.
Senior, Olive. *The A–Z of Jamaican Heritage.* Kingston, 1985.
Sloane, Sir Hans, *A voyage to the islands Madeira, Barbados . . . and Jamaica.* 2 vols. London, 1707 and 1725.
Smith, Roger. *The Maritime Heritage of the Cayman Islands.* Gainesville, 2000.

Taylor, S.A.G. *The Western Design.* Kingston, 1965.

Taylor, S.A.G., and David Buisseret. "Juan de Bolas and His Pelinco". *Caribbean Quarterly* 24, nos. 1–2 (1978): 1–7.

Thornton, A.P. *West-India Policy under the Restoration.* Oxford, 1956.

Trapham, Thomas. *A Discourse of the State of Health in the Island of Jamaica.* London, 1679.

Ward, Estelle. *Christopher Monck, Duke of Albemarle.* London, 1915.

Williams, Carlton R. "Sir Thomas Modyford". PhD diss., University of Kentucky, 1978.

Wright, Philip. *Monumental Inscriptions of Jamaica.* London, 1966.

Zahediah, Nuala. "The Merchants of Port Royal, Jamaica, and the Spanish Contraband Trade, 1655–1692". *William and Mary Quarterly* 43 (1986): 570–93.

———. "Trade, Plunder and Economic Development in Early English Jamaica, 1655–1689". *Economic History Review* 39 (1986): 205–22.

Zeller, James, *Neue Beschreibung der Insul Jamaica in America.* Zürich, 1677–78.

Index

Note: When Taylor's word is alphabetically close to the modern spelling, it is given thus: Caramantine/Coromantine. But when the words are far apart, it is more formally referenced: Caveich. *See* escovitch.

Printed in the USA
CPSIA information can be obtained
at www.ICGtesting.com
LVHW050250290923
759609LV00008B/717